THIS BOOK BELONGS TO :-

PATRICK WOODS
  5 Albany Avenue
    Springboig
      GLASGOW G32 0HJ

The Making of Hibernian
3
1914–1946

The Romantic Years

This book is dedicated to
my much loved and remembered
late mother and father
Fay and George
who never won to Jeffrey Street

Also to my dear brother Roy

THE MAKING OF HIBERNIAN
3
1914–1946
The Romantic Years

Alan Lugton

JOHN DONALD PUBLISHERS LTD
EDINBURGH

© Alan Lugton 1998

All rights reserved.
No part of this publication may be reproduced
in any form or by any means without
the prior permission of the publishers
John Donald Publishers Limited,
73 Logie Green Road, Edinburgh, EH7 4HF.

ISBN 0 85976 498 2

British Library Cataloguing in Publication Data.

A catalogue record for this book is available
from the British Library.

Typesetting & origination by Brinnoven, Livingston.
Printed in Great Britain by Bell & Bain Ltd, Glasgow.

FOREWORD

The Making of Hibernian
Is faith, hope and charity,
Bravery, romance, and giving,
Where the deeds of the dead,
Still speak to the living.

We are two lifelong Hibs-supporting sisters who live in Edinburgh, Doreen Devlin Whelahan Connolly aged 80, and Sheilah Margarita Whelahan Devlin aged 77. Another sister, Kathleen, also lives in Edinburgh while two other sisters, Eileen and Marie, are resident in Fresno, California, USA.

Our grandfather was Michael Whelahan, who co-founded Hibernian Football Club in 1875 with Canon Hannan of St Patrick's church, Cowgate, Edinburgh. Relatives of Canon Hannan still live in the home village of Balingarry, County Limerick, Ireland, and they visited Edinburgh recently to see the Hibees.

It gives us two old sisters in our twilight years, an enormous amount of pleasure to write the foreword to the last book of Alan Lugton's trilogy on *The Making of Hibernian – The Romantic Years*. We do this on behalf of all the Whelahan and Hannan clan, and indeed for all Hibs supporters.

This honour would have fallen to Michael Whelahan's daughter, Kathleen Harvey, our Auntie Kathleen, but unfortunately she died in Edinburgh, in May 1993, one month short of her 96th birthday. In 1991 Auntie Kathleen, at the age of 94, played an active part in the 'Hands off Hibs' campaign, and was 'Hibs Daft' to her last breath.

The Romance of Hibernian Football Club, however, lives on in every Hibs supporter today and Alan's three books on *The Making of Hibernian* are a valuable illustration of that romance. This third book, *The Romantic Years*, will, like the other two, be treasured forever by all who are 'Hibs Daft'.

Doreen Connolly
Sheilah Devlin

ACKNOWLEDGEMENTS

Once again I must thank fellow Hibee Donald Morrison of the publishers for producing such a wonderful third book on *The Making of Hibernian*; all three are a credit to our dear club.

Many 'Hibs old timers' who supplied a lot of information many years ago are sadly no longer with us but I am particularly grateful to the late Jeannie Rutherford, the late Tommy Joyce, the late Joe McMurray and also the late Stewart Brown of the *Edinburgh Evening New*s.

My thanks also to Rikki Raginia, Phil Thomson, John R. Mackay, Eugene McBride, Kathleen Whelahan, Doreen Connolly, Pat Stanton, Kate Stanton, Jimmy O'Rourke, Patrick O'Flaherty, Sean McPartlin and also Bob Gilchrist, who was ever ready to he helpful, and George Boyle of Hibernian Swimming Club.

I am very much indebted to His Eminence the late Cardinal Gordon Joseph Gray, the clergy of St Patrick's church in the Cowgate, St Mary Star of the Sea, Leith, The Right Revd Mark Dilworth OSE, Abbot of Port Augustus and formerly of the Scottish Catholic Archives, Dr Johnson of the Scottish Catholic Archives, The Mother Superior of Little Sisters of the Poor St Joseph's Home, Gilmore Place, Edinburgh and the Catholic Chaplaincy of Edinburgh University.

I also wish to thank the British Medical Association, Edinburgh and the General Medical Council, London, and staff of the Scottish National War Memorial, Edinburgh Castle.

More thanks for the special helpfulness of the staff of the National Library of Scotland, Edinburgh, The Central Library, Edinburgh, Leith Library and the Mitchell Library, Glasgow. Also to the staff of the archives department of Edinburgh City Chambers, City of Edinburgh Council Environmental and Consumer Services and Environmental Health.

I am particularly grateful to Hibernian's Sir Tom Farmer CBE, KCSG, Tom O'Malley OBE and Rod Petrie. Also Douglas Cromb, ex-director of Hibernian.

PREFACE

As I am near the end of these acknowledgements I must thank for their response, information and enthusiasm Hibernians from as far apart as Ireland to the USA, France to Canada.

Lastly, I wish to thank 'Hibs Daft' Senga Nicol of Kwik-Fit for all her expert efforts with so much manuscript work, Ruth Noble and Russell Walker for their editorial contribution and also Bill Murray of Brinnoven.

Alan Lugton

CONTENTS

Foreword	v
Acknowledgements	vii
Introduction	x
1. Hibernian and the War Years: 1914–1915 to 1918–1919	1
2. The Soldier's Return to Easter Road: 1919–1920 to 1920–1921	49
3. The Celebrated Team – Scottish Cup Finalists 1923 and 1924	69
4. Greater Easter Road: 1924–1925	96
5. In Memoriam – Michael Whelahan Hibernian's Golden Jubilee: 1925–1926	109
6. The Green Serene: 1926–1927	122
7. Jimmy Dunn – The Wembley Wizard: 1927–1928	127
8. A Space of Stars: 1928–1929 to 1930–1931	138
9. Relegated Hibs Harry Swan Arrives and Soon Departs: 1931–1932 to 1932–1933	149
10. Back in the First Division And Harry Swan Returns: 1933–1934	159
11. Enter the Bold McCartney: 1935–1936 to 1938–1939	169
12. Hibernian and the War Years: 1939–1940 to 1944–1945	189
13. In Memoriam – Owen Brannigan and Paddy Cannon: 1946	217
Epilogue	221
Hibernian Results 1914–1946	224

INTRODUCTION

This is the final book in the trilogy of the *Making of Hibernian*. We have already seen how Hibernian sprang from the poor Irish emigrant community isolated in Edinburgh's Old Town ghetto of Little Ireland and founded in 1875 by Canon Edward Joseph Hannan of St Patrick's RC church in the Cowgate and Michael Whelahan of the Catholic Young Men's Society attached to St Patrick's. It was St Patrick's CYMS who were to run Hibernian for the next 16 years.

Hibernian were surrounded by a constant anti-Irish bias but they rose above it all, becoming not only the champions of the poor with their charitable crusade but becoming champions of Scottish football by winning the Scottish Cup in February 1887 and a few months later, in August 1887, they also became no less than World Champions.

Due to various circumstances Hibernian's fortunes went into a steep decline and they even lost their original Easter Road home, their Holy Ground, Hibernian Park at the foot of Bothwell Street. The death of Canon Hannan in June 1891 heralded Hibs' decision to stop playing for 18 months while they put their house in order, due largely to the efforts of Fr J.J. O'Carroll OMI of St Mary Star of the Sea (Stella Maris) RC church Leith and the Stella Maris Catholic Young Men's Society, led by John and Philip Farmer the grandfather and great great-uncle of today's principal shareholder of Hibernian, Sir Tom Farmer CBE, KCSG. Other Stella Maris Leithers such as Dan McMichael and Barney Lester were involved, as were Michael Whelahan and Owen Brannigan of the St Patrick's CYMS and many others. It was Philip Farmer, however, that we have to thank for the successful resuscitation of the Hibernian who started playing again in February 1893 at their new Easter Road Holy Ground, our present Easter Road Stadium.

Hibernian were now a professional football club and although still in the hands of the 'ould Irish' they made it clear that the club had been saved for the whole community and not, as in the past, just for the 'recreation of young catholic men from the Irish slums of Edinburgh and Leith'. There was also an Irish ghetto in central Leith known as the Irish Barracks. Hibernian were very successful in this brave venture, but only among the under-class and when

INTRODUCTION

Hibernian issued a share offer their passionate pleas for businessmen to become involved was totally ignored so the 'ould Irish' shareholders and directors had to struggle on unaided.

By this time, Hibernian had quickly become founders of the Scottish Second Division, winning it twice in succession, but were only allowed into the First Division after a great deal of hostility against them. They contested the Scottish Cup final in 1896 but again only after an enormous amount of hostility which even involved a law battle in the Court of Session. In 1902 Hibernian were Scottish Cup winners and in 1903 Scottish League champions and respectable opinion said that 'it transformed Hibernian and their supporters from the despised Irishmen of Easter Road into an accepted member of the Scottish football family'. This acceptance however proved to be a mirage.

Even with the hugely successful rise of Glasgow Celtic, Hibernian, being the oldest 'Irish' club in Scotland, were still referred to as 'the premier club of the Irish in Scotland' but as the barren years passed, their status dwindled and Hibernian went on a 'mission' to regain it by contesting the 1914 Scottish Cup final, the last one to be played before the First World War, but they lost, to of all clubs Celtic. It was a forlorn but very brave Hibernian that entered the dreadful years of the Great War, a war they almost didn't survive.

So we now again take up our story of the third stage of the struggle that went into *The Making of Hibernian*: the third stepping stone to the Hibernian we all love and support today.

> You are the bearers of a proud tradition,
> Of a people once outcast,
> But if our foundations were firm,
> Then things are meant to last.
>
> Now see that wee lad there.
> Why does he look downcast?
> Will you lift him over the turnstile,
> Before his chance is past?
>
> He's come to see Hibernian.
> He is the future, not the past,
> Give him the lift of a lifetime now,
> Give him something to last.
>
> He will treasure the memory forever,
> In his heart keeps it fast,
> And he will know Hibernian's greatness,
> As we did in the past.

The tide is turning, turning again.
See how he runs so fast,
He runs to the future you give him,
As once you did in the past.

Take a hard look at the future.
Take a hard look at the past,
As your foundations are firm,
So then his dreams will last.

Yet even today we Hibs' supporters get a taste of the hostilities that surrounded our club in the past when only the generosity of Sir Tom Farmer in 1991 repeated John and Philip Farmer's life-saving act in 1891. We all lived through history that dreadful summer of 1991 when a smug Wallace Mercer tried to destroy our club and accused the 'Hands off Hibs' campaign of 'Hibernian tribalism'; for once he was dead right.

Mercer came and tried to teach us his ways,
And he scorned us for just being what we are,
But he might as well go chasing after moonbeams,
Or light a penny candle from a star.

The Making of Hibernian has been like the ripples from a stone dropped in a pond that have reached out and touched many people. For Hibernian supporters today, the 'Hands off Hibs' campaign was a rational continuation of the past that kept us anchored to reality.

Since the founding of Hibernian Football Club in 1875 with its christian charitable ethos, the survival of the Hibees' unconquered soul has been one long struggle against hostility but the good Lord had seen us before we were born and watched over us, recording all our days in His Book. Hibernian and its supporters have been troubled on every side but not distressed, cast down but never destroyed and we are the inheritors of the strength of past generations of Hibs supporters, for the Good Book tells us 'as thy days so shall thy strength be'.

So remember now the ould Hibees,
And remember to the new,
And remember how Hibernian's greatest strength,
Is always me and you.

– 1 –

HIBERNIAN AND THE WAR YEARS
1914–1915 TO 1918–1919

Leave George Whelahan here,
To his endless rest,
Fold Hibs' green flag
O'er his breast,
In the Battle's fire
He stood the test,
And his earthly work is done.

No ungrateful world
Shall sing George Whelahan's name,
Here he will lie, in a foreign field,
Unknown to fame,
A Scottish soldier
Who played the game,
And died beside his gun.

Hibernian Football Club had failed in their 'mission' the previous season to defeat Celtic in the Scottish Cup final which was to have been their first step in re-establishing Hibernian's long-standing jealously guarded reputation of being 'the premier football club of the Irish of Scotland'.

Hibs finances, however, were their healthiest for a long time and in the close season they made further improvements to Hibernian Park, increasing the capacity by a further 5,000. Land to the east, where the stand was situated had been incorporated and included a large exit for the convenience of Hibs' big Leith support. Directors John Farmer, Owen Brannigan and manager Dan McMichael had negotiated a further 11-year lease of the Holy Ground with the proprietors, the Trinity Hospital Trust; previously Hibs only had an annual lease. The rent was now considerably increased. Hibs had tentative ideas about demolishing the stand on the east side of the park and building a new stand on the west side, allowing them to convert the Holy Ground into a 100,000-capacity stadium. Only a pipe dream at this time but it did show ambition.

Hibernian, however, still had a lack of ambition on spending money to attract star players and their playing squad as always was small, usually numbering 15. To be fair, Hibs were very much a working-class club and normally strapped for cash. Hibs depended solely on the shrewd judgement of long-serving manager Dan McMitchell to bring talented young players to Easter Road to be nurtured and developed. Dan had certainly produced entertaining teams that kept Hibs safe but lack of money meant he bad never been able to repeat the Scottish Cup and League Championship successes of 1902 and 1903. Hibernian, being the oldest and bravest senior Irish club in Scotland, had always been recognised as 'the Irish top dogs' but in succeeding years wealthy Celtic were winning one national honour or another as Hibs slipped further behind and Hibs' massive Glasgow-Irish support gradually slipped away to their local heroes at Celtic Park.

Hibs had roused themselves last season with a 'mission' to reverse the damage to their once proud status but Celtic had beaten them in the Scottish Cup final. The Edinburgh Irishmen were shattered but still they lived on the east wind and refused to spend big money on players. In the Hibs Year Book for this new season we can clearly see what was described as 'the Irish philosophy of the Hibernian football school at Easter Road.' It tells us 'We have sought for no new stars, we don't need them. Hibernian bring out stars of their own. Football is a funny game. We did our best last season and if now and again we suffered unmeritedly there may have been a time or two when fortune favoured us'. So that was the unchanging 'Irish philosophy' of Hibernian Football Club going back to their founding in 1875.

For this new season 1914–1915 Hibs retained all their Scottish Cup final team with the exception of Jock Wood because of his age. Age, however, was no barrier to Hibs retaining Paddy Callaghan for his 16th season, 'Paddy Callaghan is pretty much an emergency man, but it would be like Paddy to show that he is not yet a spent force. He has been a good servant to the club, and Paddy Callaghan would be the first to admit that Hibernian have been a good master to him.' Dan McMichael reckoned all he needed was a good inside forward to add to his small squad but, as always, money was the problem. 'Good season or bad, extravagance in the signing line, at least at the end of one season or the beginning of the next, has never been an Easter Road failing, and not a big lot of players have been called up for training. The number on the books is 15, and not a new man has been engaged. Every one of the 15 has already donned the green jersey. Some may say there is want of enterprise here, but the fact is that the Hibernian have not been able to lay hands on the class of player they want, the inside forward of ripe experience, and they have not felt that they needed any others, though there are one or two juniors they have their eyes on'.

This was Hibs' 15-man squad: Willie Allan, Neil Girdwood, Bobby Templeton, Peter Kerr, Matha Paterson, Sandy Grosert, Bobby Wilson, Sam Fleming, Jimmy Hendren, Paddy Callaghan, Willie Smith, Stevenson, Connell McColl, Aitken and Reid.

In beautiful summer weather Hibernian prepared for the new season 1914–1915 with training starting on Monday 27 July 1914. One week later the 'usually secretive Irish Mafia set-up at Easter Road' allowed their working-class support into the Holy Ground to see the team being put through their paces under the expert eye of long-serving trainer Paddy Cannon and they were allowed to mingle with the players and chat about the prospects for the new season over a cup of tea – a wee treat for the largely unemployed Hibs support from the under-class of Edinburgh and Leith.

The following day, Tuesday 4 August 1914, the lives of these Hibs supporters were dramatically changed, indeed the history of the world was irrevocably changed, England declared war on Germany.

England declaring war on Germany meant of course that the Scots, Irish and Welsh were also sucked into it, as was every country of the empire. There was already tension and conflict in Europe, but England was not directly involved. The causes of the First World War were many and varied in the tangled web of European politics, kings and capitalists, aristocrats and diplomats, war-mongers and war-profiteers. The politically unrepresented working class, who were to suffer most in the war, were merely onlookers as the tragedy unfolded. England had a neutrality treaty with Belgium dating away back to 1839 and when Germany breached it this gave England the excuse they were looking for to declare war, which came as a great surprise to the general public.

In Edinburgh and Leith the socialists immediately held anti-war demonstrations, but the working class were fighting a rearguard action against England's propaganda and jingoism which soon turned any doubts into a 'popular war'. For example, the Scots working classes were given vague promises that their living standards and employment would improve with the defeat of Germany, and the Irish were promised their long-awaited Home Rule. After the bloodshed, however, these turned out to be empty promises. But everyone fell for the propaganda that told them, 'it will all be over by Christmas, so get some fighting in now'. What an adventure for the working class and the unemployed, the army would feed them, give them a proud uniform to wear and a shilling (5p) a day. You never had it so good! Unfortunately, the slaughter was to drag on for over four years and millions were to die, be mutilated, blinded and gassed.

The big Hibs support in Leith flocked to enlist in Leith's own battalion, the 7th Royal Scots (Leith's Own), and in Edinburgh the 9th Battalion Royal Scots (Dandy Ninth). The backbone of the Hibs support still lived in the Irish slum ghetto of Little Ireland, in Edinburgh's Old Town. Unemployment and discrimination against them were rife, but now they became a very valuable asset. Such was the clamour by these Hibs supporters to volunteer for active service that the military authorities harnessed and consolidated this 'Hibernian tribalism' and raised the Edinburgh-Irish Brigade which, after training, was allocated to various Scottish regiments.

> When the summons in the ears
> Of the Edinburgh-Irish Brigade was shrill,
> Unshaken in their trust they rose,
> And then flung a backward glance, and carefree still
> Went strongly forth.

A whole generation of doomed youth whose training, equipment and higher leadership were criminally abysmal. This Great War of the ruling classes was to be the biggest ever betrayal of the patriotism and bravery of the working class, who only had the trench poets to articulate the futility of the war to end all wars, and the pity of the lions led by donkeys.

> 'Good morning, good morning', the general said,
> When we met him last week on our way to the line.
> Now the soldiers he smiled at are most of them dead,
> And we're cursing his staff for incompetent swine.
> 'He's a cheery old card', grunted Paddy Jack
> As they slogged up to Arras with rifle and pack.
>
> But he did for them both in his plan of attack.

Hibernian Football Club immediately made the Holy Ground available to the military authorities for the training of recruits and it was there the Edinburgh-Irish Brigade players and Hibs players first drilled together. They were soon joined by Hearts players, as it would appear Tynecastle had not been made available for military training. Hearts players and others connected to the club such as shareholders, however, went on to make an immense contribution to the war effort, as did every other club.

The chairman of Airdrieonians Football Club was almost a lone voice in wanting to see wartime football being abandoned as he thought it was repugnant for it to continue. Other entertainments continued and the pubs stayed open, so the general opinion was that football should continue as it was a morale booster.

Wartime football, however, was modified. League football continued, but a hold was put on the Scottish Cup, the strange reason being that it was thought it would interfere with military recruitment. A stop was also put to all international matches, even between Scotland and England. Players were no longer allowed to make a full-time living out of the game and wages were limited to £1 minimum and £2 maximum at each club's discretion. No close season wages were permitted. Any player not connected with the armed forces had to work in a war-related industry and the government soon discovered that it took three war workers to support a member of the armed forces. Matches were restricted to Saturdays and public holidays and war-work overtime was not to be interfered with; this prevented players making matches on many occasions. Guarantees for visiting clubs were reduced from £50 to £30.

With the war 11 days old, Hibs opened their season on Saturday 15 August by travelling to Glasgow for a league match with Clyde at Shawfield Park and lost by the only goal of the game. Even allowing for the war, we are told it was a record crowd for a Hibs visit to Shawfield on league business. The Hibs team was: Willie Allan, Neil Girdwood, Bobby Templeton, Peter Kerr, Matha Paterson, Sandy Grosert, Bobby Wilson, Connell McColl, Jimmy Hendren, Aitken and Willie Smith.

The poor result reflected a poor Hibs league campaign, although four days later, in the Dunedin Cup semi-final at Easter Road, the Edinburgh Irishmen defeated Raith Rovers 3-0, with a hat-trick from Jimmy Hendren. As this was the first game of the season at the Holy Ground a collection was taken for the National War Relief Fund. This fund-raising was now to become a hallmark of Hibs.

Dan McMichael signed an inside forward called Robert Lennie for Hibs' first league match at Easter Road against Falkirk on Saturday 22 August. Matha Paterson scored the Irishmen's goal in a 1-1 draw. Hibs were very disappointing and we were ominously told, 'Hibs played like a team wearying for the close of a strenuous season'. Things were not to improve much.

Crowds throughout Scottish football had never been better and this caused sections of society to lament the adverse effect football was having on recruitment to the armed forces. It must be remembered that conscription was not to be imposed on the public for another two years: 'the people have not yet awakened to the seriousness of the international situation. When will the football public realise the magnitude of the present crisis and recruiting receive a much needed stimulus'. At least this criticism could not be levelled against Hibernian and their supporters.

It was at this time that the ever-popular old-time Hibernian player 'Juglin' Geordie Smith died. Geordie had been Hibs' left-winger in their 1887 Scottish Cup winning team and although in later years he was a semi-invalid, he was an Easter Road regular and was an active member of Michael Whelahan's Old

Hibs Association. The passing of Geordie was deeply mourned at the Holy Ground. Dan McMichael now signed Dan Fleming from Vale of Clyde. Dan was the brother of Sam Fleming who had been with Hibs for several years, had played in the Scottish Cup final last season and was described as 'a footballer of glorious, fashion', a popular entertainer at Easter Road. Brother Dan was good, but not that good, but he made a winning debut at the Holy Ground on Saturday 5 September when Hibs recorded their first win of the season, defeating Airdrie by the only goal of the game scored by Lennie in front of 7,000 fans.

Four days later, Hibs travelled out to Shamrock Park, Broxburn and played a benefit match for Broxburn Shamrock who had always been a rich source of players for the Easter Road men. That same day, Hibernian allowed the Holy Ground to be used for a match between the 7th Royal Scots (Leith's Own) and the 9th Royal Scots (Dandy Ninth) – many Hibs supporters were recruits to both battalions. The match was in aid of the National War Relief Fund, and Hibernian were praised by the military authorities for their 'patriotic and generous gesture which is always forthcoming from the Edinburgh Irishmen of Easter Road'.

Celtic's visits to Easter Road always brought out capacity crowds for 'the battle of the Greens', but on Saturday 19 September only 12,000 attended, showing the effect army recruitment had on 'both acts of patriotic Irish supporters'. Later in the war, Celtic player Peter Johnstone was to be killed in action in France and Willie Angus was awarded the Victoria Cross for rescuing an officer in trench warfare in France. Willie was severely wounded in this brave single-handed action, and he lost the sight of one eye. The league match was a 1-1 draw, with Hibs' young American right-winger Bobby Wilson scoring the Easter Road counter. Bobby Wilson had been an inspired signing by Dan McMichael the previous season, and Bobby's goals had been instrumental in Hibs reaching the Scottish Cup final.

Two days later was the September holiday and Hibs picked up two points against Clyde at Easter Road. The Edinburgh Irishmen were not to taste victory for another two months and found themselves at the bottom of the league causing an outcry, 'where is the ould Irish fighting spirit of Hibernian, the players are unworthy of the traditions and standing of Hibernian and the wonder is they got off so lightly in recent matches'. Hibs had, in fact, not got off so lightly in some of these matches, and it was puzzling as they had a talented, if small squad, but injuries had taken their toll.

Dan McMichael tried to freshen things up by doing a temporary swap of two players with Broxburn Shamrock. This drastic move immediately paid off on Saturday 14 November when 'the Irish strangers to victory' picked up two points against Queen's Park at Hampden, lifting Hibs off the bottom of the league. The following week at the Holy Ground two more points were collected with 2-0 victory over Dundee, Sam Fleming and Willie Smith being the scorers. Again at Easter Road, on 28 November, the Irishmen picked up two more points with a fine 4-1 victory over high-flying Partick Thistle. The Jags only had a late penalty goal to show against one from Sam Fleming and Jimmy Hendren and two from Robert Lennie, who was now regularly on Hibs' score sheet. The Green Jerseys that day were: Willie Allan, Neil Girdwood, Bobby Templeton, Connell McColl, Matha Paterson, Sandy Grosert, Robert Lennie, Jimmy Hendren, Sam Fleming, Clark and Willie Smith.

It was at this time that news reached Easter Road that two Leithers who had been on Hibs' books in previous years had been killed in action in France: Joe McBride, a signaller with the 2nd Royal Scots Fusiliers and piper George Robertson, 2nd Battalion Royal Scots. The response from Hibs was their left-half Leither Sandy Grosert becoming a recruit in Sir George McCreal's Battalion.

> I'll make you Leithers full of pride,
> For the Green in any weather,
> He's the Hibs' own Sandy Grosert,
> As regular a Leither
> That ever kicked the leather.
>
> And once again the lads o' Leith
> Go forward with a will.
> And laurel shall their brows bequeath,
> As their deeds of bravery thrill.

Hibernian picked up a good point at Cathkin against Third Lanark after being two goals behind at half-time. Robert Lennie equalised things with two grand second-half goals. The following week at Hibernian Park against St Mirren, Lennie again scored, but J. Hendren stole the show with the Irishmen coming back twice from behind to win 3-2. On Boxing Day, Saturday 26 December, Jimmy Hendren scored another two at Dens Park in Hibernian's 2-4 victory over Dundee.

So the war was not 'all over by Christmas' as England's propaganda had promised. With no conscription, more and more recruits were being called up as the fighting on land, sea and air became fiercer and the casualty lists grew longer and longer. Young men from Edinburgh and Leith had already paid a heavy price for their patriotism and bravery, making it a black Christmas in many a working-class home. One such home in Edinburgh's Old Town Irish ghetto of Little Ireland received a letter from their teenage son who had joined the Edinburgh-Irish Brigade and was fighting in the trenches in France. He asked after his family and 'how the Hibs were getting on', before he turned to the horrors and futility of war: 'Twenty-one days in the trenches we charge the German lines by day and night mown down by machine guns. We are repulsed every time with heavy losses but we are ordered to attack again and again and charge blindly hoping we will be shot and put out of our misery. This is not war it is murder.' It should be remembered that these ill-trained, poorly equipped and abysmally-led raw recruits were up against a full time professional German army over one million strong, superbly trained, equipped and led.

> I know a simple soldier boy
> Who grinned at life in empty joy,
> Slept soundly through the lonesome dark,
> And whistled early with the lark.
>
> In winter trenches, cowed and glum,
> With crumps, and lice and lack of rum,
> He put a bullet through his brain.
> No one spoke of him again.
>
> You smug-faced crowds with kindling eye
> Who cheer when soldier lads march by,
> Sneak home and pray you'll never know
> The hell where youth and laughter go.

There was still no enforced conscription at this time and the Scottish football authorities now decided to withhold the Scottish Cup as they thought it would interfere with recruitment to the armed forces. Strange reasoning, as league football was still allowed to continue.

Hibs won only two of the six league matches they played in January 1915 although Jimmy Hendren was still banging in the goals. It is interesting to note that when Hibernian played Partick Thistle in mid-January the match attracted a crowd of 12,000, the biggest crowd in Scotland that day including Celtic, Rangers and table-toppers Hearts.

Saturday 6 February was Leith Irish Flag Day for the Belgian Relief Fund. Fifteen thousand lapel flags taking the form of the green flag with harp which flew at Easter Road were on sale with 100 collectors taking donations from all over the port. Hibernian Football Club had helped to organise the event in conjunction with the Ancient Order of Hibernians, the United Irish League and the Irish National Foresters. The headquarters of the event was St Mary Star of the Sea RC church, Constitution Street, Leith and a handsome £83 18s 9d (£83.93) was raised adding to a total of £5,000 already raised throughout

Scotland. The Easter Road men as always made their own generous contribution and all the players and officials had their green flag in their lapels that day as they travelled to Douglas Park to play Hamilton Academically. Hibs were trailing 2-1 at half-time but Jimmy Hendren scored a great equaliser to gain a well-deserved point.

The following Saturday at the Holy Ground Hibs played Raith Rovers and the stand was packed with soldiers and sailors singing the full repertoire of Easter Road songs. Paddy Callaghan, who was still a Hibs player, but not a regular because of his age, was in the stand with Sandy Grosert, who had been injured during his inadequate army training. They were joined by two old Hibs players, Paddy Murray and Bobby Atherton the Welsh internationalist who was Hibernian's captain when they won the Scottish Cup in 1902 and league championship in 1901. They enjoyed the sing-song and talked about the 'good ould days' and Hibs' 2-1 victory that day. Sad to say, poor Bobby Atherton was to die at sea later in the war.

After taking a well-deserved point against Aberdeen at Pittodrie, Hibernian then picked up another point at the Holy Ground against Hearts who were sitting at the top of the league; this was a fine performance by the Irishmen. Hibs were lying ninth in a league of 20, having played 33 games and accumulated 29 points.

Hibs' close neighbours, second-division Leith Athletic, known as 'the Zebras', had a young left full-back of Irish extraction named Willie Dornan and Hibs had their eye on him all season. Hibs' astute manager, Dan McMichael, had a real eye for young talent and he managed to negotiate a loan of Willie Dornan. A fine move on Dan's part, for after the war Willie was to become a member of one of the most famous teams in Hibernian's history. Meantime, Willie made his debut for the Irishmen against Morton at the Holy Ground on Saturday 13 March 1915. Morton were a goal up at half-time and in the second half Hibs captain Matha Paterson missed a penalty before top-scorer Jimmy Hendren snatched a glorious equaliser. The Hibernian team was: Willie Allan, Connell McColl, Willie Dornan, Peter Kerr, Matha Paterson, Robertson, Robert Lennie, Sam Fleming, Jimmy Hendren, Clark and Willie Smith.

At this time three other Hibernian players joined Sandy Grosert in the armed forces; they were David Stevenson, Reid and the young American Bobby Wilson who had been a hero of the Hibs' fight for the Scottish Cup the previous season.

Hibs had a second stadium for many years at Northfield, off the Portobello Road, but it had only been used for greyhound racing, cycling and athletics meetings – the Irishmen had too romantic a connection with Easter Road to ever seriously consider moving there. Hibs had 'generously and periodically' leased Northfield to the army, who now demolished the stand that had cost Hibs £1,000; it had also cost Hibs £4,000 in laying out and equipping the ground and all this was now lost to the Irishmen. Hibs' main shareholders were families that still lived in Ireland but they never asked the army for compensation as they saw it as their patriotic duty to do all they could for the war effort, just as Hibs players and supporters had. This, however, had left Hibs financially weak and the fact that many of their working-class support had volunteered for army service meant that their gates were halved, which put more strain on Hibs' finances. Things were so bad that throughout the war years Hibs never bought a new set of strips for the players and by the end of the war the famous green jerseys were a much-washed mud- and sweat-stained faded yellow.

Willie Dornan continued to play well for Hibs and this continued when, on Saturday 3 April, the Green Jerseys put four past Third Lanark's famous international goalkeeper Jimmy Brownlie at Easter Road. Jimmy Hendren was again on the score-sheet. Again at Hibernian Park, this time Jimmy Hendren scored a hat-trick. As we shall soon see, poor Jimmy Hendren had only two months of his short life left to live. Meantime, three days after his hat-trick Jimmy Hendren played for an Edinburgh select against an International select in aid of the Belgian Relief Fund. Three other Hibernian players, Willie Allan, Matha Paterson and Willie Smith also played in the Edinburgh select team.

Hibs beat Bradford City 5-1 in a friendly at Easter Road and they made it to the finals of the East of Scotland Shield and the Rosebery Charity Cup but lost out in both. By the end of the first week of May, Hibs' first season of the Great War was over.

The First World War dragged on and the casualties of the 'doomed generation of youth' continued to mount, bringing great sadness to many homes in Edinburgh and Leith. Many of these families and their relatives had several members fighting at the front. A keen Hibs supporting family, Mr and Mrs David Page of Tolbooth Wynd, Leith, perhaps epitomise the situation. They had three sons fighting at the front, Davy junior in the 2nd Battalion Cameron Highlanders, Patrick in the Royal Fusiliers and Daniel in the 7th Battalion Royal Scots (Leith's Own). Three of their daughters' husbands were also at the front, as were four of Mrs Page's nephews, and a brother-in-law in the Black Watch had already made the supreme sacrifice. This was described by the military authorities as 'truly a remarkable tribute of devotion and patriotism gallantly contributed by one family to their country's cause in its hour of need'. Davy Page junior had gone to St Mary Star of the Sea RC school which Hibernian had largely helped to build in 1903, in the grounds of the church of the same name in Constitution Street, Leith, popularly known as Stella Maris (Star of the Sea). Davy and his family were members of the Stella Maris Catholic Young Men's Society which always had a close association with Hibernian and Davy was a regular attender at Easter Road. Work, however, was hard to come by and Davy joined the 2nd Battalion Cameron Highlanders in 1909 and four and a half years of his service were spent in India but now he was fighting at the front line in France. Davy was badly wounded but was now fit again and on 10 May he sent his mother and father a postcard saying he was being sent back to the front. As fate would decree it, the very next day Davy was killed during a German gas attack. The day Mr and Mrs Page received their son's postcard at their Leith home the army notified them of his death. It was Saturday 22 May 1915, and by coincidence that date was to be one of the most tragic in Leith's history, the Gretna Disaster.

The Gretna disaster involved only soldiers of Leith's Own 7th Royal Scots. The batallion was raised from the population of Leith and just about every soldier in it came from the port. A troop train carrying 500 officers and men of Leith's Own travelling south for embarkation to the trenches reached Quintinshill sidings near Gretna Green at 7 am on Saturday 22 May 1915, when, due to a signalman's error, it was involved in a catastrophic collision with two other trains. Many of Leith's Own were killed instantly while others were seriously injured, trapped in the burning wreckage which was burning fiercely. We are told that no fewer than eight of the soldiers killed in the Gretna Disaster had at one time or another been on the books of Hibernian Football Club. Of the 500 officers and men of the Leith's Own, 214 were killed and 224 seriously injured; only 60 were able to answer the roll call.

Leith was naturally-grief stricken and a few days later a massive military funeral was arranged through the streets of the port to Greenbank Cemetery, in Pilrig Street, where a mass grave had been prepared in the north-west corner to take 101 coffins. The rest of the dead were privately buried by their families, many in Easter Road's Eastern Cemetery in the shadow of Hibernian Park. At Rosebank there were distressed scenes of grief which turned to hysteria as the mass burial proceeded, with volley after volley crashing out from the honour guard as the 101 coffins were lowered. A lone piper played *Lochaber No More* and a bugler played the *Last Post*. An impressive Gretna memorial was raised over the men's grave in remembrance of Leith's Own.

> Towards crimson fields and trenches deep
> They journeyed on,
> Til fate decreed that they should sleep
> Much nearer home.
> But though their couch be far removed

From scenes of strife,
Still to the Land they dearly loved
Each gave his life.
For in the will, not in the deed
True courage lies,
And all had owned their country's need,
Great sacrifice.

As we shall see later, by the end of the First World War, Leith's service record was to be unparalleled anywhere in Scotland.

In Memoriam – Jimmy Hendren

Many a Hibernian home was in mourning after the Gretna Disaster, when only a few weeks later Hibs supporters and the club received another shock. Jimmy Hendren, the Hibs centre-forward, who had been signed by manager Dan McMichael in 1910 and who had been Hibs' top scorer during his five years at Easter Road, suddenly died in the Royal Infirmary on Saturday 19 June.

Jimmy was a Scot of Irish extraction who had a powerful physique and a fair turn of speed and he had played for a short time with Kilmarnock while carrying on his trade as a miner in the Ayrshire coalfields. Seeking a better life, Jimmy emigrated to America where he developed a love for golf and Baseball, but he returned to Scotland and worked in the Fife coalfields while playing for Cowdenbeath and it was in 1910 that Dan McMichael swooped to bring him into top-class Scottish football. Being of Irish extraction, Jimmy was soon imbued with a deep affection for Hibs and settled in Edinburgh and Jimmy refused several big-money moves from Easter Road. He played in the famous team in the 1914 Scottish Cup final. Jimmy and his wife Annie Gordon had a child round about the outbreak of the war and while playing for Hibs Jimmy did full-time war-work at Leith Docks. Having learned to drive, he volunteered for active service in the Army Transport Corps but his call-up was delayed as his wife had just given birth to their second child and it was only 12 weeks old when Jimmy suddenly died. Jimmy's Requiem Mass took place on Tuesday 22 June at St Mary's Roman Catholic Cathedral in Broughton Street, Edinburgh. Hibernian's floral tribute took the form of a traditional broken harp and Jimmy was buried at the Eastern Cemetery, Easter Road, lying in the shadow of the Holy Ground. Hibernian appealed to the football authorities for permission to play a benefit match for Jimmy's widow and children but the request was turned down because of the war conditions. Hibs, however, stayed true to their reputation of being a caring club and presented Annie with a very generous cheque directly from the club's dwindling funds. Perhaps this short tribute at the time summed up Hibernian's high regard for Jimmy as a player and a man:

> Jimmy Hendren was a faithful, conscientious Hibernian. Although a player of moods he was a real personality and Hibs top scorer which gladdened our supporters no end. Jimmy could not be described as a great player but he fulfilled his duties for Hibernian with excellent results, he simply got goals. In private life he was a modest, unassuming young man possessed of sincere Christian principles and was devoted to his wife and children. Jimmy's sudden death prevented him from defending in battle our country whose freedom is now menaced.

It is of interest to note the family connection between Jimmy Hendren and today's 'living Hibernian legend', Pat Stanton. Jimmy was an uncle of Pat's mother Bridgit.

It was all sad news for Hibs just now when news reached Easter Road on Friday 23 July of the death of Peter Meechan, an old full-back of the late 1880s. Peter had remained a regular attender at Hibernian matches and was an active member of Michael Whelahan's Old Hibs Association and he played many charity matches for them. Peter was a sad loss from the Easter Road scene.

There was, however, one bright interlude for Hibs playing in a five-a-side tournament in aid of the Red Cross War Effort. Hibs beat St Bernard's in the first round, Celtic in the semi-final and then took great satisfaction in beating favourites Rangers in the final. A vast crowd supported this worthy venture and many dignitaries from Edinburgh, Leith and from the armed forces were present. The five Hibernian players who were presented with commemorative medals were Bobby Templeton, Peter Kerr, Willie Smith, Robert Lennie, and King.

Dan McMichael was unable to find a proven centre-forward to replace Jimmy Hendren because Hibs were operating with a loss of £705 from the previous season. Dan, however, signed three promising juniors, Robert 'Barney' Smith from Rutherglen Glencairn and Robert Taylor and Robert Alexander from Parkhead Juniors. These three Roberts were in the Hibs team that opened season 1915–1916 in a league match with a 3-0 victory over Queen's Park at the Holy Ground. The Green Jerseys were: Willie Allan, Neil Girdwood, Bobby Templeton, Peter Kerr, Matha Paterson, Robert Smith, Robert Alexander, Sam Fleming, Robert Lennie, Robert Taylor and Willie Smith. At this match the army were recruiting hard among Hibs under-class support and the directors allowed the army to parade sergeant Ripley in full kilted uniform displaying his recently awarded Victoria Cross. Ripley VC was now attached to the army recruiting office in Cockburn Street, Edinburgh, and by all accounts the Hibs support were fairly impressed by this brave Scottish soldier.

The following week at Somerset Park, Hibs picked up another two points with a 2-3 victory over Ayr United. Unfortunately, victories were to elude Hibs for another two months. Hibs were basically under strength and with players missing matches because of war-work they had to make last-minute drastic positional changes and introduce more new faces from the junior ranks.

Hibs' third league match on Saturday 4 September saw them go down by the only goal of the game, at the Holy Ground against Clyde. Of the 6,000 crowd we are told there were over 2,000 soldiers in uniform present. The Hibs support had volunteered for active service in large numbers and Hibernian Football Club were always to the fore in helping any war effort and fund raising. They had a close association with the gunners of the Forth RGA at Easter Road Barracks and as a morale booster played many friendly matches with them. Not unnaturally the Irishmen always 'crushed the gunners', who always tried to find excuses and one soldier put it in a poem.

> The gunners of the RGA
> Have heard their country's call,
> And now they ofttimes feel inclined
> To chase the rolling ball.
>
> They've got the time, they've got the men,
> They've got the spirit too;
> But ah! one little thing they lack,
> Which makes their faces blue,
>
> They haven't got the bally ball
> Wherewith to shoot the goal,
> And bricks, you know, they cannot kick,
> As they degrade their soles.
>
> And so they write with hopeful hearts,
> Which beat against their ribs,
> That some kind gent may send a ball
> To let them beat the Hibs.

Hibs signed Meacher from Musselburgh Athletic and he was in the team that took a good 1-1 draw with Falkirk at Brockville. After the match the Hibs trainer Paddy Cannon somehow got separated from the rest of the party and was left standing at the rail station with the large team hamper for two hours until the next train came along. While on the subject of Paddy Cannon, when Hibs travelled to Rugby Park to play Kilmarnock on Saturday 9 October, Paddy inspected the pitch before the kick-off and his expert eye saw that one of the 18-yard lines was four yards short and the red-faced Kilmarnock officials had to redraw it to Paddy's and the referee's satisfaction. The match was a 0-0 draw.

Paddy probably had time for such technicalities as team training had almost ceased because of the players' war-work and many lived outside Edinburgh.

Most other clubs were facing the same problems as Hibs, who were sitting near the bottom of the league and excuses were wearing very thin. Patience ran out on Saturday 13 November when another lowly-placed club, Third Lanark, defeated Hibs 3-0 at Cathkin. A newspaper article by an old Hibs player who signed himself 'an Irish onlooker' started a lengthy comment by saying 'What has gone wrong with the Hibernians? This is a question that must be exercising the minds of those who take any interest in the doing of the Easter Road club. A lapse in form, more or less temporary, takes place in even the most noted of sides, but Hibernians falling off has been alarmingly consistent as serious. The climax surely was reached a week ago when one of the most unfortunate clubs in the league, Third Lanark, soundly whacked the Edinburgh Irishmen to the tune of 3-0. Let us hope that really was the climax, and matters having reached their worst, will take a turn and mend.'

Meantime, Hibs signed Tommy Kilpatrick and Newton from Kilsyth St Patrick's and Harry Hutchison from Falkirk and it was Hutchison's two goals that finally brought Hibernian victory 2-1 against St Mirren at Holy Ground on Saturday 20 November.

Hibs clinched a deal with Leith Athletic for left full-back Willie Dornan whom they had thought most highly of when on loan the previous season. Hibs paid the Zebras £10 down, with £10 to follow at the end of the season. Willie Dornan was in the team that travelled to Ibrox the following week and Hutchison again scored two goals but high-flying Rangers got four. Strangely, Hibs were the better team but we are told: 'Rangers might have lost this game had the Hibees forwards been more solicitous of their clubs reputation and less mindful of their own. No Rangers player reached the cleverness of Robert Tailor and Rangers' wingers never showed the same understanding as Sam Fleming and Robert Lennie.' All Hibs forwards were very tricky but it was Rangers that did the essentials.' The Green Jerseys that day were: Willie Allan, Neil Girdwood, Willie Dornan, Robert Smith, Matha Paterson, Newton, Robert Lennie, Sam Fleming, Harry Hutchison, Robert Taylor and Willie Smith.

Another bad result followed then on Saturday 11 December at Easter Road, second-bottom Hibs lost 0-1 to third-bottom Third Lanark in front of a crowd of only 2,000. In another newspaper article 'an Irish onlooker' again lamented: 'A few weeks ago I made a few observations regarding the terrible plight the Hibernians have got into, and it seemed at that time that they were about to pull themselves together and mend their ways. That idea, however, has been knocked on the head and one cannot help wondering if the Hibs have made up their minds that the faithful few who still stick to them, with all their faults and who continue to go to Easter Road, rather prefer to see them losing to winning their games. No wonder the gates are dwindling away. I've seen many Hibernian teams, but, upon my soul, never one to beat the present lot in ineffectiveness … Truly the Edinburgh Irishmen cannot go much farther back.'

Goalkeeper Willie Allan could not be faulted, but his confidence was suffering and he was finding it more difficult to get away from his war-work, so Hibs brought in Harry McManus from Parkhead Juniors. But, 'Hibs are rarely free from team trouble', and it continued when they travelled to Broomfield to play Airdrie on Saturday 18 December. Harry McManus was to play but his war-work delayed him and he didn't make the kick-off and right-half Peter Kerr was goalkeeper for the day. Hibs lost by the only goal of the game but we are told: 'Peter Kerr prevented Airdrie from recording a tall score'. The downward trend continued the following week when, on Christmas Day, at the Holy Ground, Hibs went down 0-2 against Dundee although we are told: 'Harry McManus had a good game in front of a 3,000 crowd'. One highlight for the Hibs supporters was the return of Sandy Grosert who was on 'farewell leave' before being shipped to the trenches in the Royal Scots Motor Machine Gun Service.

Sandy Grosert was again in the Hibs team that played Hearts at Tynecastle on New Year's Day, Saturday 1 January 1916, in the Wilson Cup final. There were no league points at stake but lots of pride in trying to win Hearts' own cup. Hearts were going strong second-top of the league while Hibs were second bottom and we are told: 'the Irishmen expect to be at the wrong end of some tall scoring'. Hibernian, however, suddenly found their true form and after the match everyone changed their tune, 'the Irishmen pulled off a truly sensational victory'. The match was played in dreadful wet windy weather, keeping the crowd down to 5,000. Hearts had a lot of pressure but they could not break down Hibs and goalkeeper Harry McManus was inspired. Centre-forward Hutchison scored a goal in each half as 'a determined Hibs pulled off the shock victory of the season so far'. The Green Jerseys that day were: Harry McManus, Sandy Grosert, Willie Dornan, Peter Kerr, Matha Paterson, Robert Smith, Robert Alexander, Sam Fleming, Harry Hutchison, Robert Lennie and Willie Smith.

The carnage of the Great War had continued now for a year and a half and Hibs supporters had paid a high price in the massive battles of the Western Front: Mons, Marne, Aisne, Ypres, Givenchy, Neuve Chapelle, St Elio, Hill 60, St Julien, Hooge, and Loos. The pity of it all was never far away from the Holy Ground which is situated beside the Eastern Cemetary. The following Saturday Hibs defeated Raith Rovers 1-0 in the league but word quickly spread through the cheering supporters that the 'Last Post' was being played in the Eastern Cemetery for a fallen soldier and the crowd fell silent. There was no escape from the reality of the war.

In Memoriam – Sandy McMahon

A death unrelated to the war soon reached Easter Road. Alexander 'Sandy' McMahon died in Glasgow Royal Infirmary on Tuesday 25 January. Sandy McMahon was the true genius Hibernian player of the 1880s, known as 'the Duke', 'the sand-dancer' and 'the prince of dribbles'. Sandy was a team-mate of that other Hibernian genius 'Darling' Willie Groves who had sadly died in 1908. Like all the early great Hibernian players Sandy was of Irish stock, born in Selkirk in 1871 before his parents brought him to the capital and Sandy was brought up in Edinburgh's Old Town Irish ghetto of Little Ireland. Hibernian were run by St Patrick's Catholic Men's Society and it was in one of their nursery teams, Leith Harp, that Hibernian discovered Sandy, a gawky six-foot tall left full-back. It was in this position that Sandy made a premature debut for Hibernian at Easter Road on Saturday 7 November in a 4-1 victory over St Mirren. Sandy didn't make a first appearance for another three months when again at Easter Road, on Saturday 27 February 1886, Hibs defeated Dumbarton 3-1. By coincidence that day 17-year-old 'Darling' Willie Groves made his Hibernian debut. The sheer genius of Willie Groves was immediately recognised but Sandy was playing out of position and his true genius as an inside-left was not realised by Hibernian for another three years. We are told:

> Sandy McMahon was just a shade behind Willie Groves but Sandy was without doubt another genius from the Hibernian football school. Scour the country from John o' Groats to Land's End and you'll not find men of greater merit than Groves and McMahon. Edinburgh may not be the most prolific nursery of players in the Kingdom, but at intervals a star appears in the East, and men and judges contemplating the luminary will tell you that nothing brighter ever showed on the football firmament. Sandy McMahon was a great Hibernian product and belongs assuredly to a class whose membership is very limited. There is not much doubt that McMahon modelled his play on that of Willie Groves, McMahon had the same close command of the ball.

Sandy was only a reserve when Hibernian won the Scottish Cup in February 1887 and the World Championship six months later, but that surely gives us an insight into the class of Hibernian in those days. Sandy was 'Hibs Daft' and after a night's socialising in St Mary's Street Hall, Hibernian's headquarters in these days, his team-mates would try and avoid him or he would keep standing in the street until the small hours bending their ears about the Hibs. Sandy would play football any time anywhere, and 6ft, 12st 4lb Sandy would look very incongruous in overcoat and hat playing street football with the Irish urchins in the Cowgate. Sandy lost his old pal Willie Groves when Celtic poached Willie and the cream of the Hibernian squad in the summer of 1888 but it heralded the breakthrough for Sandy when on Saturday 19 January 1889 at Beechwood Park, Glasgow, Hibs found his true position at inside-left in a 0-2 victory over Glasgow Thistle. Sandy, after a long mazy dribbling run, scored a brilliant solo goal. Hibs had their new genius to replace Willie Groves. Sandy McMahon was the most unlikely looking footballer ever, with a large drooping moustache to disguise the fact that he had no front teeth, we are told that:

...big, awkward, ungainly and gawky with a shambling gait but when he put on that Hibs jersey he was transformed, all ease and grace, Sandy could take out a whole defence with just one swerve of his body. When he got the ball he hunched over it with arms outspread and weaved his way past desperate defenders with eel-like grace. And nobody could score goals like him, especially with his head, it was one of his many specialities.

There is little doubt that Sandy McMahon and Willie Groves, the two Hibernian geniuses, actually changed the nature of the way Scottish football would be played in the future, from kick and rush to combined play interlaced with individual skills. Unfortunately, at this time Hibs' only two players of any standing were Sandy McMahon and captain James McGhee and the club was in disarray, even losing their Hibernian park at the bottom of Bothwell Street, off Easter Road. It is of interest that it was Sandy McMahon who stayed true to the Hibs 'til the last kick of the ball, as did James McGhee. No one could have asked any more of them; by January 1891 they were both at Celtic Park. Sandy went on to win many club and international honours before hanging up his boots in 1904. Unfortunately, we are told: 'Sandy had not the best of luck in recent years, affairs did not go well for him'. Now Sandy had died at the age of 45 in straightened circumstances. Sandy McMahon, the Hibernian genius, is one of the all-time greats of Scottish football as this tribute to him testifies:

You who did not see Sandy McMahon play know nothing about the weaving artistry of our football game, all ease and grace, as if born to make a football answer his will.

Hibs continued to have mixed results and goalkeeper Willie Allan reappeared in mid-February for two matches, both defeats. Harry McManus was back in goal on Saturday 26 February, when Hibs defeated Kilmarnock 1-0 at Easter Road with a Sam Fleming goal. It was a rough-house of a match and Hibs' Willie Smith and Kilmarnock's Goldie were both sent off. Hibs' other Smith, Robert 'Barny Smith joined his home town regiment, the Glasgow Highlanders, for war service.

With his departure and the playing duties of others being curtailed because of their war-work, Dan McMichael signed three juniors: Carrigan, Johnstone and Muirhead. There was so much chopping and changing that when Hibs lost 2-1 against Dumbarton at Boghead on Saturday 8 April, Peter Kerr was again back in goal.

On the Edinburgh Monday holiday 17 April, second-bottom Hibs faced high-flying Hearts in a league match at Tynecastle. The Irishmen were again written off and this time it seemed justified with the maroons leading 1-0 at half-time. It is not known exactly what manager Dan McMichael said to his Hibs team at the interval but the words 'pride' and 'tradition' featured several times and it certainly worked, for in a five-minute spell in the second-half Fleming, Lennie and Newton scored three times to bring off another Hibs shock victory over 'the ould inimy'. The Green Jerseys that day were: Harry McManus, Peter Kerr, Neil Girdwood, Robert Taylor, Matha Paterson, Newton, Robert Lennie, Sam Fleming, Harry Hutchison, Muirhead and Willie Smith.

Peter Kerr again had to play in goal for Hibs when they played their last league match of the season. This match against Hamilton Accies should have been played on Saturday 25 March but was postponed because of snow at Easter Road. It was now being played on Wednesday 26 April but because nearly the whole Hibs team were engaged in war-work in Glasgow it was arranged for this Hibs home fixture to be played at Celtic Park so they could put out a reasonable team. A Muirhead goal didn't stop Hibs going down 1-3 in front of only 1,000 spectators. The reshuffled Hibs line-up was: Peter Kerr, Neil Girdwood, Willie Dornan, Robert Taylor, Matha Paterson, Newton, Robert Lennie, Sam Fleming, Muirhead, Robert Alexander and Tommy Kilpatrick.

Hibs finished second-bottom in a league of 20, luckily we are told, 'No championship competition, no title attached, no winners medals and no relegation. It's all make believe on paper. It is stop gap football the kind of thing the public wanted in wartime'. It is strange that in such conditions an SFA Emergency Committee were forced to issue the following warning, 'Any director, official, player or manager or anyone connected to the management of a football club would be expelled from the game if they bet upon the results of football matches'.

By this time the Military Service Bill had enforced conscription on the general public amid an almighty outcry led by the Trades Unions and socialists who were totally opposed to the needless slaughter of the working-class in 'a war which is only being fought for the benefit of kings and capitalists'. In Scotland, England and Wales, violent revolt was threatened against the ruling class of the establishment with their introduction of military conscription. In Ireland, conscription was the straw that broke the camel's back. The downtrodden Irish working-class and republicans had no faith in England's empty promise to give them Home Rule (devolution) when the war was won and anyway it was complete independence they wanted from England's military and political occupation which had crushed Ireland for the last 800 years.

In Memoriam – James Connolly

James Connolly was executed before a firing squad on 12 May 1916 in Dublin's Kilmainham Jail. He was one month short of his 48th birthday.

Hibs' most controversial supporter was a loving husband and devoted father of a large family, three of his daughters were born in Edinburgh. James Connolly is misunderstood by some because he is seen just as an individual rather than a political leader of a whole new 20th century world trend who was an unrepentant international socialist. He was also the founding father of a new European country; not bad for James Connolly the wee barefoot Hibs supporter from the Cowgate slums.

> Once more James Connolly's grave is warm with memory's tears,
> And Easter lilies blaze in spring grace,
> And time with kindly hands along the years,
> Hath bound the broken hearts a little space.
>
> Grieve, grieve not for James Connolly dead,
> He rests fulfilled, rests unpersued by time,
> The very birds that carolled beneath the sun,
> Sing suddenly and sweetly overhead,
> Of sacrifice and triumph just begun.
>
> Make haste to glean again these lost sprays
> Of rosemary and rue, still strongly twined
> With deathless laurel of determined peace,
> Herald and home of a distressed mankind.
>
> Grieve not for James Connolly dead,
> But make no play of this remembering,
> Lest great intent seem strangely desolate,
> And that high ecstasy a formless masquerade.

It is ironic to note that the very same week in May 1916 when James Connolly was executed by the army, his brother John was given a full military funeral in Edinburgh's Merchiston Cemetery as an honourably discharged army veteran. That week a photograph of James Connolly appeared in the Edinburgh press under the headline 'Irish Rebel Leader' with information reminding the public that James Connolly was Edinburgh born, had worked for Edinburgh Corporation as a carter and had stood in the Edinburgh Town Council elections as a socialist candidate.

On Saturday 6 May at Easter Road in the Rosebery Charity Cup semi-final, Hibernian defeated St Bernard's 6-0. War-work kept Peter Kerr from playing and Hibs signed up a big Irish Guardsman, Paddy O'Connor, for this match and by all accounts he played well. The following Saturday Hibs were at Tynecastle to play Hearts in the final. Hibs had hoped to put out as good a team as possible but captain Matha Paterson could not get away from his war-work. Davy Gordon of Leith Athletic accepted Hibs' invitation to play for the Green Jerseys and was ready to take the field when Hearts, as petty as ever even in a wartime charity match, objected to him and Hibs kicked off with ten men. Manager Dan McMichael, however, was lucky enough to find big Paddy O'Connor sitting in the stand to bring Hibs up to full strength. Unfortunately Hearts won.

At the end of May a Benefit in Aid of War Funds was played between an East Select and a West Select. The East Select was made up of players from Hibs, Hearts, St Bernard's, Falkirk and Dundee and two Hibernians, Peter Kerr and Muirhead, played. It was also at this time that Hibernian Football Club continued to send 'comfort packages' to troops at the front line. These comforts included footballs which were sent to France, Egypt and Selonika. Hibernian observed the 25th anniversary of the death of Canon Hannan, the co-founder of the club, with a memorial holy mass being celebrated in St Patricks RC church, Cowgate, Edinburgh, the spiritual home of Hibernian.

In the summer of 1916 as Hibs manager Dan McMichael tried to put a squad of players together, conscription had been in force for six months and more of his players were in the armed forces, but they were able to play before being sent to the trenches on the Western Front. The slaughter of the Great War had now continued for two years and thousands of Hibs supporters were involved in the bloody conflict and many had made the supreme sacrifice.

It is of interest to note that manager Dan McMichael and trainer Paddy Cannon had between them seven sons in the trenches, two of whom had been severely wounded.

> I have a rendezvous with death
> At some disputed barricade,
> When spring comes back with rustling shade

And apple blossoms fill the air,
I have a rendezvous with death.

Other players were in reserved occupations such as munitions factories, shipyards, coal mines and the docks which restricted their playing and Dan McMichael had a major headache having them available with his soldier-players to field a presentable team. This particularly affected four of his top players, Peter Kerr, Willie Smith, Neil Girdwood and Robert Lennie.

Recently called up to the Royal Garrison Artillery was Hibs captain Matha Paterson and others now in the army were John Hume and Muirhead. Dan McMichael also swooped to sign a soldier, Willie Miller, from Cambuslang Hibernian. Willie Miller, like Willie Dornan, was a superb signing and these two would go on to be part of the great 1920s Hibs team. Dan McMichael was already building for the future.

Leith Athletic, known as 'the Zebras', who ironically did not play in Leith but in Edinburgh at Logie Green, had now gone defunct and Dan McMichael snapped up their veteran left-half Davy Gordon. Another good signing and, as we shall see later, Leither Davy Gordon would later become Hibs manager.

Others in the Hibs squad were Bobby Templeton, who was still struggling with a long term injury, Harry McManus, Willie Dornan, Newton, Robert Alexander, Sam Fleming, Tommy Kilpatrick, Robert Taylor and Davy Reid, a pre-war player who was not yet out of the army. Among others were Armstrong of Grimsby Town and two from Cowdenbeath, Charlie Campbell and Borthwick, who was the brother of a pre-war Hibs player who was not in the army. No longer with Hibs were Willie Allan, and also Harry Hutchison, who had gone back to Rangers from where Hibs had signed him.

For season 1916–1917 a season ticket covering the stand and ground was 11/- (55p) for a new applicant and 8/- (40p) for a previous holder. Ground only was 5/6 (27½p) and boys 3/- (15p).

Hibernian opened the season at the Holy Ground on Saturday 19 August with a league match against Airdrie. The directors made it an open day for wounded soldiers, all of whom were also treated to tea in the pavilion. Reynolds, the goalkeeper of Fulham FC had been recommended to Hibs by their old west of Scotland chief scout and former manager Phil Kelso, who was now manager of Fulham FC. Reynolds played for Hibs today, but Hearts, as petty as ever, even in wartime football, complained, 'controversy has raged concerning Hibs capture of Reynolds and a certain amount of irritation exists at Tynecastle. Indeed there is talk of a reference to the league'. Reynolds never played for Hibs again. Hibs and Airdrie drew one goal each in front of a crowd of 5,000; Charlie Campbell had equalised for the Irishmen then Matha Paterson threw away the chance of victory by missing a penalty. The Hibs team was: Reynolds, John Hume, Willie Dornan, Borthwick, Matha Paterson, Davy Gordon, Robert Alexander, Sam Fleming, Davy Reid, Muirhead and Charlie Campbell.

The following week we are told 'Scotland's two leading Irish combinations, Hibernian and Celtic both of whom have contributed so much to the war efforts, play their league encounter at Parkhead.' We are further told 'the patriotic Edinburgh Irishmen lost a one sided match by 3-1 to the patriotic Glasgow Irishmen.' Willie Miller made his debut that day in front of a crowd of 8,000. Willie played at inside left but in later years he would be developed by Hibs into a superb centre-half. The star man that day however was the veteran left-half Davy Gordon, 'a word of praise for Davy Gordon who reduced Celtic's elusive Patsy Gallagher almost to mediocrity.' Robert Alexander scored Hibs' counter and the team was: Harry McManus, John Hume, Willie Dornan, Borthwick, Matha Paterson, Davy Gordon, Robert Alexander, Muirhead, Armstrong, Willie Miller and Charlie Campbell.

Hibs picked up two points at Easter Road with a 4-3 win over Hamilton Accies. Tommy Kilpatrick was back in the team and he scored, as did Charlie Campbell and Armstrong got a brace, probably to celebrate his forthcoming marriage. Three defeats followed, all by the odd goal in three, but on Saturday 23 September at Rugby Park Hibs picked up two points in a 1-3 victory over Kilmarnock. This was a good win as Hibs had to play right-half Peter Kerr in goal, 'Kerr had to play in goal and he saved everything that came his way except a penalty.' A new face, Beveridge, scored for Hibs and Robert Alexander got two.

The following week at Easter Road Willie Miller opened his account for the Edinburgh Irishmen scoring in a 1-1 draw with Third Lanark. And on Saturday 7 October at Love Street against St Mirren, Hibs with five soldier-players in their team again drew one goal each, the Hibs counter coming from Willie Smith. The Green Jerseys were: Harry McManus, Peter Kerr, John Hume, Borthwick, Matha Paterson, Newton, Robert Alexander, Muirhead, Tommy Kilpatrick, Willie Miller and Willie Smith. Hibs were now lying 13th in a league of 20 having played nine games with only seven points to show for their efforts. It had also been a real effort for Dan McMichael to field a consistent line-up. In their other October games Hibs had a defeat, a win and a draw and also at this time signed Pat Mooney from Kirkintilloch Rob Roy.

In Memoriam – Paddy Hagen

Before the end of October a shocking piece of news reached Easter Road. Big favourite pre-war Hibs forward Paddy Hagen had been killed in action in

France on the Western Front. Paddy was a sergeant in Edinburgh's regiment the Royal Scots. Of Irish emigrant parents, Paddy was a born and bred Hibs supporter from Edinburgh's Irish slum ghetto of Little Ireland but had been in the Emerald Isle playing for Belfast Celtic from whom Hibernian signed him in 1905. Paddy Hagen was a very versatile goal-scoring forward, who played with Hibs greats such as Harry Rennie, George Stewart, Barney Breslin, Paddy Callaghan and the tragic Jimmy Main to mention but a few. Paddy was described as a 'temperamentally exuberant Hibernian whose vivacity and loquacity, combined with his football ability, rendered him a worthy member of one of the best collection of players the Hibs have had in recent times'. The enthusiasm of 'Hibs Daft' Paddy is particularly remembered in two very different incidents. In a Scottish Cup tie against Partick Thistle in Glasgow, which Hibs eventually won, Partick were awarded two penalty kicks and they missed both of them and Paddy rushed up to the penalty taker on each occasion and shook his hand while the poor Partick player 'stood inanimate and lost to the world'. In a league match at Easter Road against Aberdeen played in a howling gale the match was nearing its end with no scoring and all 22 players were completely exhausted. Aberdeen were shooting down the slope with the gale at their backs and Paddy stopped a certain goal with some heroics right on the goal line, then controlling the ball and with the gale raging against him, he ran right up the full length of the Holy Ground beating man after man and crashed home a glorious winner. Yes, these incidents typified the many facets of Paddy Hagen who endeared himself to the Easter Road faithful. He lived at 18 Nicholson Street, Edinburgh, and at the outbreak of the Great War in 1914 he joined the Edinburgh-Irish Brigade with many other Hibernian players and supporters and after training he was allocated to the Royal Scots. He was born and brought up in Edinburgh but with his Irish name and having played football in Ireland gaining Irish international honours, there was a slight misunderstanding in a tribute-poem to Paddy Hagen at the time he made the supreme sacrifice for Scotland in the trenches.

> I met Hibs Paddy Hagen,
> And I said to him said I,
> 'Your Irish to the backbone,
> And you will be till you die.'
> Said he 'In peace oi'm Oirish,
> Shure I cannot get away,
> But now the storm clouds gather,
> I'm a Scottish soldier today.'

Paddy had remained a regular attender at Hibernian matches, was an active member of Michael Whelahan's Old Hibs Association and his cheery presence at Easter Road was sorely missed.

As Hibs played on with five draws and a defeat over November and early December two other bits of tragic news hit the Edinburgh Irishmen. First, goal-scoring forward Robert Alexander, while engaged in war-work in Glasgow, fell off a ladder into machinery, tearing off his left arm, breaking his right arm and badly injuring both legs. Dan McMichael visited him regularly in the Glasgow hospital and was eventually able to report that young Robert Alexander was making good progress and very cheerful, even allowing for the loss of his left arm. A second tragedy followed when Hibs player-soldier full-back John Hume lost his wife when she fell from the third storey of their Aberdeen tenement home while cleaning the windows. Needless to say John Hume was devastated.

Meantime, Hibs signed a forward, John Meaney, from Cowdenbeath and in their three league matches up to the end of December they suffered three defeats conceding 13 goals. To be fair, Hibs had to chop and change line-ups due to the unavailability of players and Peter Kerr had to play in goal for one of the matches.

The third Christmas of the war, the 'soldiers' Christmas' arrived as the slaughter of the Somme and Verdun ended in bloody stalemate: more tens of thousands had died for nothing.

> Same old trenches same old view,
> Same old rats as blooming tame,
> Same old dug-outs nothing new,
> Same old smells the very same,
> Same old bloody war.

Wounded soldiers in Edinburgh Royal Infirmary, Leith Hospital and Seafield War Hospital were treated to special Christmas dinners and teas to which Hibernian made a generous donation. Also 'Santa Hibs' made sure that many a dead soldier's bairns didn't have an empty stocking on Christmas morning, thanks to the generosity of the directors, manager and the Irish families who were Hibs' major shareholders and who still lived in Ireland.

Christmas holly wreaths were in abundance at the graves of fallen soldiers in Mount Vernon Catholic cemetery, the Grange cemetery, Eastern cemetery off Easter Road and Rosebank cemetery where the Gretna memorial to 'Leith's Own' was a mass of holly wreaths.

Pub opening hours had been restricted and the price of drink increased. Hibs supporters from the Irish community had run their 'illegal Irish shebeens' in the slum ghetto of Little Ireland for countless years and now more were springing up. These Hibbys played an amusing if dangerous cat and mouse game with the police. With most of the young men from Little Ireland now fighting on the Western Front it was the old-timers and women who were the 'elusive shebeeners', a favourite haunt being the underground vaults which stretched for miles beneath the South Bridge and George IV Bridge, both of which stretched over the Cowgate.

The Derby Day match on Monday 1 January 1917 against Hearts was played at Easter Road. Hearts' own trophy, the Wilson Cup, was at stake but no league points. With Hibs' bad run of results in December, Hearts were expected to win easily but the Green Jerseys rose magnificently to the occasion and set the Holy Ground alight with a sparkling 3-0 victory, with two from Tommy Kilpatrick and one from John Meaney. The whole team played above themselves as 'the Irishmen knocked out Hearts who went to pieces. The Hibs were very good all over and gave a brilliant display while Hearts were very uneven'. Robert Wilson of Hearts handed over his own cup to Hibs director Owen Brannigan and the army was represented by Major Robertson who added his congratulations to the 'patriotic Irishmen of Easter Road.' The gallant Hibs team was: Harry McManus, Borthwick, Willie Dornan, Peter Kerr, Matha Paterson, Davy Gordon, Sam Fleming, John Meaney, Tommy Kilpatrick, Muirhead and Willie Smith.

Throughout January Dan McMichael had a hard time reshuffling with the availability of his soldiers, miners, dockers and munitions workers. Hibs lost two matches, in one the unfit full-back Bobby Templeton, had to play in goal and in the other the Irishmen suffered from poor refereeing. Hibs however won their other three matches and when they defeated Dumbarton 3-1 at the Holy Ground on Saturday 27 January they were lying 14th in a league of 20 with 21 points from 26 games.

The Green Jerseys recorded only one win in February, on Saturday 10 at Shawfield, defeating Clyde 1-2. Hibs had two special guests at the match. One was their forward Robert Alexander who had lost his left arm in a factory accident last November. He was now out of hospital and looking very well, cheerfully telling Dan McMichael how much he was looking forward to pulling on the green jersey again. Poor Dan didn't have the heart to tell him his playing days were over. Hibs other guest was Willie Donnelly, a grand goalkeeper from the 1890s. Willie had been badly wounded fighting in the trenches with the Dublin Fusiliers and was now working in a munitions factory. Willie Donnelly continued to be an active member of Michael Whelahan's Old Hibs Association.

On Saturday 3 March a weak Hibs team, further weakened by the absence of Matha Paterson and Peter Kerr, took a very well-deserved 1-1 draw with Third Lanark at Cathkin. Willie Dornan gave away a penalty but it was a very soft award and later Willie was the hero with an acrobatic flying header goalline clearance. Robert Lennie got Hibs equaliser.

The following week as Hibs had a 0-3 victory over Partick Thistle at Firhill, we are told that Patrick Connolly, a Hibs Daft street busker, a real character from Tolbooth Wynd, Leith, who entertained the crowds at Easter Road for many years, ended up in court. Charged with being drunk and incapable, all poor Patrick could explain to the court was, 'a met some o' ma ould Hibs pals an' we hid a wee drink, a cannae remember anythin' else'. It all sounds so familiar to Hibbys today.

Two more Hibs victories followed before they went down to Airdrie at Broomfield. Hibs were to have travelled to play Lochgelly United in a friendly on Saturday 7 April but it was postponed because of snow. The snow continued the following week but Paddy Cannon kept the Holy Ground playable, unfortunately Hibs went down very unluckily 0-1 to Celtic, who were at the top of the league. The snow continued that April and two days later on Monday 16, the Edinburgh Spring Holiday, a very weak Hibs team lost out 0-2 to Hearts with a snow-storm raging at Easter Road. Hibs' last league match was on Saturday 21 April going down 2-1 against Aberdeen at Pittodrie. It had been a 'patch-up Hibs' all season and not surprisingly not one player had been able to play in every league match. Hibs ended fourth bottom in the league.

The Rosebery Charity Cup semi-final against Hearts at Tynecastle on Saturday 5 May shows what manager Dan McMichael was up against in fielding a team of his soldiers and war-workers. He managed to organise an eleven but as luck would have it Dan was notified five minutes before the kick-off that the goalkeeper Harry McManus could not get away. Dan McMichael scoured the ground for a suitable stand-in, even although he knew Hearts would protest at a new face, but this time Dan was in luck. At first he could find no one to do the job for Hibs when he spotted a group of high-ranked army officers in the stand. Sitting beside Lieutenant-Colonel Inglis was Lieutenant Chaplin of the Royal Fusiliers whom Dan recognised as a useful amateur player. The bold Dan McMichael introduced himself, explaining his problem, and asked Chaplin if he was willing to play for the Edinburgh Irishmen. A surprised Chaplin said he would be delighted, modestly adding 'if no one better can be found'. Petty Hearts immediately protested at an unsigned new face in the Hibs team, then just as quickly withdrew their protest when whey were told he was an army officer. Hearts wanted to save themselves a red face in a wartime charity match. So old Dan was able to field a full team and Chaplin had a good game, even allowing for Hearts winning the match.

In the close season Hibs played in tournament for the benefit of wounded soldiers, war funds, Red Cross funds and in the Edinburgh Territorial Force Association Sports. Also during the close season Hibs tried to smarten up Hibernian Park a bit as it had been badly neglected because of the war conditions.

Following Leith Athletic, Edinburgh's St Bernard's had also been forced to close down and Aberdeen, Dundee and Raith Rovers withdrew from the league. Dan McMichael was determined, however, that Hibs would battle on no matter how near impossible his task would be.

The war was now entering its third year and the tactics of the higher command in their conduct of the conflict beggars description. Their out-dated suicidal tactics saw the lives of soldiers recklessly thrown away without any thought for them or their families; it was nothing short of mass murder. England had entered the war because of an 1839 Belgian neutrality treaty but this was never mentioned again throughout the war. The reasons for the war were now forgotten by the opposing countries who were killing for killing's sake. The ordinary soldiers in all the armies still thought they were fighting for a long-forgotten 'something', a 'propaganda something', it meant nothing to them, only the ruling-classes and war-profiteers. All the soldiers of every country needed to say was 'no more', we're going home, no one would lose face, there was nothing to lose.

But the ruling-classes insisted the conflict continue and in the summer of 1917 the slaughter reached new heights of horror in Flanders and the third battle of Ypres.

As Hibs manager Dan McMichael and trainer Paddy Cannon pondered season 1917–1918 one wonders what their thoughts were for the seven sons they had at the front and all the players who had passed through their hands who were now sharing the horror. Likewise Michael Whelahan, the co-founder of Hibernian Football Club and the leading light of the official Old Hibs Association, who helped out at Easter Road in any way he could, was deeply concerned about his youngest son George. George Whelahan had not long been out of school when he volunteered with the Edinburgh Irish Brigade at the beginning of the war and through the years he had so far miraculously survived.

Hibs started off the season with the following squad of players: Harry McManus, Bobby Templeton, Willie Dornan, Peter Kerr, Matha Paterson, Davy Gordon, Borthwick, John Meaney, Tommy Kilpatrick, Willie Smith, Willie Miller and McDougall. Recent additions were Logan (East Stirlingshire), McLean (Cowdenbeath) and Cresswell (St. Bernards).

Encouragement was heaped on Hibs for the new season 'with Leith Athletic on the shelf it's up to the Edinburgh Irishmen alone to uphold the honour of the Port of Leith on the football field and we wish Hibernian thumping good luck and lots of goals for the coming season.'

Unfortunately it was not to be for war-torn Hibs. Starting the season on Saturday 18 August, Hibs ran up five straight league defeats, losing nine goals without being able to score one. They even managed to lose to newly promoted Clydebank at Easter Road.

Fortunately, on the Monday Holiday 17 September in the East of Scotland Shield final at the Holy Ground, Hibernian found their shooting boots and beat Hearts 4-0.

During these weeks Dan McMichael took steps to strengthen the Green Jerseys, first signing Walker, a very brave soldier who had been wounded five times sustaining facial injuries. Next was a superb signing, McCandless, an Irish internationalist goal-scoring forward who had played for Bradford before the war. McCandless served in the Glasgow Highlanders, the same regiment as another Hibs player, Robert 'Barney' Smith.

After that good result against Hearts things generally improved for Hibs, and they immediately picked up two points at Easter Road against Airdrie. In a 2-2 draw with Partick Thistle at Firhill the Jags needed two soft penalties to take a point in a dirty game which saw Hibernian's Tommy Kilpatrick and Partick's Brough sent off. Willie Miller got both the Irishmen's goals. Willie Miller was scoring quite a few goals, including a hat-trick against Queen's Park in a 4-2 Easter Road victory and a brace against Clyde in a 2-5 Shawfield victory, which was to be Hibs' only win that season. It was also Hibs' first win at Shawfield for 17 years. Willie Miller scored lots of other goals as did McCandless, John Meaney and Tommy Kilpatrick. Dan McMichael still had to do a lot of chopping and changing with his soldier-players and war-workers and twice full-back Bobby Templeton had to play in goal when goalkeeper Harry McManus couldn't get away from his war work.

As Hibernian Football Club put in a lot of work for the Leith Hospital Flag Day and the King George Fund for Sailors, the slaughter of the war reached new heights, if that were possible, at Passchendale and Cambrai.

A 2-2 draw with Falkirk at Brockville and a 2-1 victory over Partick Thistle at the Holy Ground took Hibernian through the war-torn Christmas of 1917, which set them up for the Wilson Cup Derby Day match against Hearts at Tynecastle on Tuesday 1 January 1918. Hibs were without five of their first choice players: Harry McManus, Peter Kerr, Matha Paterson, Scottish internationalist Willie Smith and Irish internationalist McCandless. Full-'back Bobby Templeton had to play in goal and a new fac, Bishop, was played at right-half. Good news was the return of player-soldier Leither Sandy Grosert who was on leave from the trenches. As difficult as it was for manager Dan McMichael to put together a team with many playing out of position we are told 'the Irishmen retained the Wilson Cup and fully deserved to do so'. Hibs missed a first half-penalty but still went on to record a fine 1-3 victory over 'the ould inimy' with two goals from Willie Miller and one from Charlie Campbell. The Green Jerseys were: Bobby Templeton, Borthwick, Willie Dornan, Bishop, Davy Gordon, Sandy Grosert, Tommy Kilpatrick, John Meaney, Willie Miller, Moir and Charlie Campbell.

Hibernian chairman John Farmer, when accepting the Wilson Cup, complimented both teams on a fine match, pointing out that Hibs now had won Hearts' own cup eight times against Hearts' five. Today the Wilson Cup, engraved with Hibernian's beautiful harp, can be found in the directors' room at Easter Road.

John Farmer had taken over the chairmanship of Hibernian from his brother Philip in 1911. Philip Farmer was still a shareholder and still helped to run Hibernian but deteriorating health over the years affected this and his business. The tragedy of the war on him and his family put Philip Farmer at a low ebb, as did the sad news that one of his young employees, 18-year-old Tommy Douglas of Elbe Street, Leith had been recently killed in a sea battle while serving in the Royal Navy.

Amid all Hibs' trials and tribulations caused by the war they were complimented on their brave contribution to the war effort and their brave sporting struggle for survival.

> A great side the Hibernians are not. But they have furnished up some capital sport in various parts of the country as well as Easter Road where for a considerable time they have at all events escaped defeat. They are a sporting side Hibernian. True, their defeats just about tally with their wins and draws but five of the ten reverses came higglety-pigglety on the top of one another at the beginning of the season and that was a tremendously big handicap. We have had however a different Hibernian lot since then ... Dan McMichael's chief trials have been over the fixing up of teams and placing the players available into suitable positions. Because of their players war duties the same Hibernian team have never been able to play twice in succession and this has not applied to any other club in the country. The immense war effort by Hibernian Football Club has caused this extraordinary state of affairs and gives in itself a very fair idea of the difficulties they have encountered. With so many young men of the Hibs support away fighting in the trenches the 'gates' at Hibernian Park have fallen away but it is still an exception when there is not at least £50 for any team visiting Easter Road.

Players such as full-back Willie Doran were complimented, as was Willie Miller who had scored 12 league goals. Scottish internationalist Willie Smith was still a good turn, although not the player he once was, but as for McCandless we are told, 'there is always something worth seeing when the Irish internationalist is playing'. It was in fact the unending exhausting work of a determined Dan McMichael that had kept Hibs alive and he was not in the best of health, for unknown to most people he suffered badly from a kidney complaint.

Over January, February and March Hibs had mixed results and signed two right-halves, McNeilage and Bennett. A match at Easter Road against Ayr United was postponed because of nine inches of snow on the pitch and in another match at the Holy Ground against Rangers, Willie Smith was rather harshly sent off followed by a Rangers player.

On Saturday 6 April Hibernian organised a very successful collection at the Holy Ground for the Roman Catholic Fund for Scottish Soldiers Serving Abroad; the visitors to Easter Road that day were Celtic and they won 0-2.

In Memoriam – Dan Doyle

Two days later, news reached Easter Road that the great old Hibernian full-back Dan Doyle had died in the Glasgow Cancer Hospital at the age of 54. Dan was one of the many great Hibernian discoveries of the 1880s who was nurtured and developed into international status. Dan Doyle was of Irish emigrant stock and was born in Paisley in September 1864. The family moved eastwards and Dan played at centre-forward for Rawyard Juniors then Slamannan Barnsmuir, when it was discovered by sheer accident that Dan's best position was left full-back as Hibs discovered him and farmed him out to their prolific nursery team Broxburn Shamrock. Dan was developed by 'the Irish school of football philosophy at Easter road' but such was the wealth of Hibernian talent in these days he was only a reserve when Hibs won the Scottish Cup and World Championship in 1887. Dan gave great service to Hibernian but work for catholics in these days was hard to come by. He eventually went to England with the promise of steady work and he played for Grimsby Town with another great Hibs full-back, James Lundie. There was a tragic incident when Grimsby played Stevely: Dan clashed with William Cropper who was also a Derbyshire cricketer and the following day Cropper died in hospital. A shattered Dan Doyle moved to Bolton Wanderers then Everton, with whom he won a league championship medal. Next 'Celtic gold' beckoned as it had many Hibernian greats and he joined many of his old Easter Road team-mates at Parkhead to have a sparkling career winning many Scottish League and full international honours. Dan hung up his boots from professional football in 1904, was reinstated as an amateur and was president of Mossend Hibernian. Easter Road was Dan's first love and he was a regular attender at Hibs matches and was a member of Michael Whelahan's Old Hibs Association. Dan's whisky business failed and like many great players in these days, he ended up in poverty working as a labourer before his days came to an end ravaged by cancer. The day before he died in hospital he showed a visitor his emaciated legs and laughed 'ah, well they made a little bit of football history'. One of the many tributes to Dan summed him up in just a few words, it said it all:

> Dan Doyle was one of the great Hibernian discoveries who transformed our football game. There is little doubt he was the greatest full-back in the world.

Hibs defeated Hearts 4-0 the previous August in the East of Scotland Shield final which had been carried forward from season 1916–1917 and now on Monday 15 April they clashed in this season's final, drawing 1-1 and thus the Green Jerseys retained the shield.

By the following Saturday the Irishmen had the services of Harry Gough, the Sheffield United goalkeeper as Harry McManus was in the army and shipped off to the trenches. Hibs drew 1-1 with Airdrie at Easter Road. Hibs lost out to Falkirk in the final of the Dunedin Cup but on Saturday 18 May, in the Rosbery Charity Cup final against Hearts at Tynecastle, the Irishmen disposed of Hearts 0-2 with another new face in the team, W.T. Spink of Grimsby Town who was serving in the Royal Navy. So this season a badly weakened Hibs, with a chopped and changed team had beaten Hearts in three finals for local trophies, the Rosebery Charity cup, East of Scotland Shield and Wilson Cup.

Meantime four Hibernians, Peter Kerr, Bobby Templeton, Tommy Kilpatrick and Moir played in an East Select against a West Select in a benefit for the Army and Navy Benevolent fund and Hibs played in a June tournament for Red Cross Funds.

Joining Harry McManus on active service in the trenches that summer was Matha Paterson and Willie Miller and Peter Kerr was doing his duty with the Royal Air Force. It was also at this time Moir was rushed to Glasgow Infirmary after an accident in the munitions factory in which he worked and lost the sight of an eye.

The senseless blood-letting of the First World War had now continued unabated for fully four years. The higher command and politicians on all sides were now fighting a statistical war, a war of numbers. The ruling-classes now had down on paper the size of the combatants' populations, the death averages in the conflict, so that the last soldier standing would win the war. At no time was a negotiated peace considered.

Hibernian had unselfishly and to the detriment of the club made a massive contribution to the war effort but in season 1918–1919 their patriotism was almost betrayed by the Scottish football authorities led by 'a Glasgow Rangers clique' with the demand that Hibernian Football Club be 'discarded and excluded from the league'. That was the thanks Hibernian were to get for their four years of war effort, a war that was still raging and in which Hibernian were still making a tremendous contribution. Just about all of Hibs' pre-war and wartime players had served in the armed forces and Hibs' manager, trainer, directors, shareholders and club members all had immediate family and relatives serving at the front. Countless numbers of Hibernian's working-class support had made the supreme sacrifice on the field of battle. Hibernian's fund-raising for war causes had been never-ending and were as legendary as their community charity work. The war had just about exhausted Hibernian but they were far from finished, thanks largely to manager Dan McMichael whose single-handed efforts to keep a Hibs team on the park were well supported by trainer Paddy Cannon and directors Owen Brannigan and the brothers John and Philip Farmer. They had all lived through the near-destruction of Hibernian in the early 1890s and they were determined Hibernian would survive now. It was their responsibility to the thousands of their supporters fighting in trenches; they would return to a strong Hibernian Football Club to be enjoyed once more. The Scottish football authorities and the 'Glasgow Rangers clique' were knocked back on their heels by the violent reaction of the 'usually so silent and sanguine stony faced closed Irish corporation at Easter Road'. They made it totally clear to everyone that they were no 'soft mark' and under no circumstances were Hibernian going to lie down and die, 'the German army can't do it and no one else will'. The message was received loud and clear, so Hibs prepared for the new season but Dan McMichael had a mountain to climb to put together a squad of players. Old age was catching up with Dan, as was his kidney complaint, and with the benefit of hindsight it was this last struggle for Hibernian that put the final nail in Dan's coffin.

For the fifth season of the Great War Dan could only call upon a few of his soldier-players and war-workers occasionally but he scoured the country to add to his depleted squad. First Dan signed two goalkeepers, Harry Gough (Sheffield United) and Cunningham (Cambuslang); others included Abercrombie (Kilsyth St Patrick's), Galloway (Dumbarton Harp) and Spink (Grimsby Town) who was serving in the Royal Navy. Shrewd Dan, however, was not panicking and was still looking to Hibs' long-term future and had previously signed wartime players whom he had earmarked to be the backbone of Hibs after the war and now Dan brought to Easter Road two others who would be part of the celebrated Hibernian of the 1920s, Willie McGinnigle, a Cambuslang junior of Irish stock and Hugh Shaw, a Clydebank junior. The press tells us at this time 'Dan McMichael is picking up excellent young players, and we hope that some day, and that soon, he will have hit on the right men for the right positions'.

Meantime, however, it was a hotchpotch Hibs squad and sometimes Dan could not even field a full team but he had experienced this all through the war and nothing would stop Dan ensuring Hibs were kept alive and competing but it did put him under a lot of strain. 'It might almost be though that Dan McMichael had put the Hibernian players into a big pepper-box, shaken then out, and let them get along as best they could where they happen to drop.' We are further told 'Dan was always uncertain of fixing up a team and every week they were makeshift and scratch lot and sometimes a poor lot'.

In the first two and a half months of season 1918–1919 Hibs went through 33 players and of the 11 games they played, the best result they could get was a 0-0 draw. The Hibs support however stayed true and Dan was at the Holy Ground till eight o'clock in the evening successfully selling season tickets.

A crowd of 12,000 was at Easter Road for Hibs' first league match of the season against Celtic, and the Edinburgh Irishmen used this fixture as a fund-raiser in conjunction with the Caledonian Catholic Society for Scottish Soldiers Serving Abroad. Willie McGinnigle made his debut that day but it was the start of a dreadful run of results. Seven days later Hugh Shaw made his debut against Hamilton at Douglas Park. Dan had spotted 'Big Hugh' playing at centre-forward but was to develop him as half-back, we are told 'Hugh Shaw does not shape like a centre-forward but he does not lack for weight'.

As Hibs ploughed on they signed Duffy (Liverpool), James Halket (Croy Celtic), Dan O'Donnell (St Paul's), Robert Gilmour (St Mirren Juniors and Pollock) and Fleming (Musselburgh). No sooner had soldier-player Jimmy Williamson returned from the trenches to play for Hibs when he was immediately sent back to the front line. Captain Matha Paterson dropped Dan McMichael a line from the trenches asking 'how are Hibs getting on' and he also received a letter from Sandy Grosert who was recovering in hospital from wounds received in the trenches and the effects of gassing. Peter Kerr who was serving in the Royal Air Force also kept in touch with his old manager. At this time Bobby Templeton was also shipped off to the trenches as Hibs struggled on and in one game against Third Lanark at Easter Road Dan could only field nine men and with two then being carried off injured, Hibs finished the match with only seven men on the park.

Perhaps not surprisingly it wasn't until Saturday 26 October that Hibs recorded their first league win with a 2-1 victory over Airdrie at Hibernian Park. Moir, who had lost an eye in his factory accident, was welcomed back to Easter

Road and Dan signed Willie McCourt from Blantyre Celtic, who scored a first minute goal for Hibs against St Mirren at Easter Road but it was another defeat that Saturday 9 November. Hibs had played 14 matches, 13 of them league games of which they had lost 11, won one and drawn one.

As the slaughter of the final offensive proceeded at Picardy and Flanders, Germany's allies had thrown in the towel and Germany itself was racked by a socialist revolution forcing Kaiser Wilhelm to abdicate and a German republic was declared. On the eleventh hour of the eleventh day of the eleventh month, Monday 11 November 1918, the Armistice was signed. The First World War, the Great War, the 'war to end all wars' was over after four and a half years. It had been the most terrible war in human history; ten million combatants had lost their lives at the command of the ruling-classes in an utterly futile conflict. It achieved nothing except the rise of two new great evils, Communism and Nazism. The allies had won the war because of the overwhelming manpower and economic strength of America. There were no real winners, in fact only losers, and it was to herald the beginning of the end of the British Empire. All the countries of the empire had made terrible sacrifices in England's war and now saw themselves as equals to England, no longer would they be subordinate to London. The time was ripe for Scotland to make its bid for independence: 'the red flag flew all over the country' but there was a lack of will. There was however no lack of will by the Irish – they were sick of 800 years of England's military and political occupation of their country and it was the Irish who were the first in the British Empire to make their bid for freedom.

The Scots, like the Irish, had lost 'a whole generation of doomed youth' in the First World War and it is appropriate in this Hibernian book to record Leith's contribution to the war effort, which was unparalleled anywhere in Scotland. The Port of Leith was a separate burgh from Edinburgh at this time and of Leith's 84,000 population no fewer than 14,000 males enlisted for war service. Two won the VC and five the DSO. Over 300 high honours were won by the Leithers, including the sons of Hibs manager Dan McMichael and trainer Paddy Cannon. Leither Sandy Grosert, Hibernian's long-serving left-half was a particularly gallant soldier. Sandy was 'a Hibs Daft school laddie from Leith Academy' and he played for Hibs in the 1914 Scottish Cup final against Celtic. A native Scot, he did however at the outbreak of the war join his team-mates and Hibs supporters in the Edinburgh-Irish Brigade drilling at Easter Road. Sandy was then allocated to Sir George McCrae's battalion of the Royal Scots and in 1915 was transferred to the Machine Gun Corps, and in 1917 was granted a commission in the 6th Gordon Highlanders. Second Lieutenant Sandy Grosert was part of the famous 51st Storming Division at the victories of Rouex and Greenland Hill and he won the Military Cross for conspicuous gallantly in action. Badly wounded and gassed, Sandy never fully recovered but after the war he remained a regular in the Hibernian team. At least Sandy survived the horror, the male members of some families had been totally wiped out. Other Leith soldiers returning from the trenches were to find family and friends decimated and the Gretna Disaster was still deeply mourned.

> My soul is sick for the ould Leith Town,
> I've been so long away,
> I care not if the skies are dull,
> And the fog hangs thick all day.
> Though other skies are clear and blue,
> Whence Boreans blasts ne'er roar,
> I'd like to breathe the ould Leith wind
> That's blasting down the shore,
> Across the sea, across the foam,
> The voice of ould Leith calls me home.
> Beneath Leith's dark grey sky
> Easter Road shines clear before us,
> and Hibs green flag is flying high
> Proudly floating o'er us.
>
> A prayer beats hard at heaven's gate,
> When I think of Leith gone by,
> Watching Hibs at Easter Road,
> Beneath the ould grey sky
> With true friends all together,
> Now a shadow over life is cast,
> These friends are gone forever.
> But guid ould Leith like many other toun,
> Has sent forth o' her best,
> And Leith can boast a roll o' fame,
> As gallant as the rest,
> For Leithers left their hame sae brave,
> But to find a soldiers grave.

Shortly after the First World War the Port of Leith was swallowed up by the ever-expanding City of Edinburgh. Like Leith, many an Edinburgh home made tremendous sacrifices in the war, but for the purposes of this Hibernian book perhaps one young Hibs supporter epitomises the war tragedy of Hibernian Football Club.

In Memoriam – George Alexander Whelahan

George Whelahan was the youngest of the eight children of Michael Whelahan, the co-founder of Hibernian Football Club in 1875. We shall hear more of Michael Whelahan later in this book. George, being the youngest and being very clever with a happy disposition, was the family favourite. Naturally he was 'Hibs Daft' and never away from Easter Road with his family and pals but he was also a brilliant scholar with an eleven and a half years' unbroken attendance record at St Patrick's school in Little Ireland's Cowgate. George passed all the local Oxford Examinations in Mathematics, English, French, Latin, History, Geography and even Art. A bright university career beckoned for George Whelahan but for the outbreak of the First World War, with George immediately volunteering for active service and he was one of the first to drill with other Hibs supporters and players in the Edinburgh-Irish Brigade at Easter Road.

> They were all volunteers the Edinburgh-Irish Brigade,
> Doing their bit without brag,
> Brave heroes who history made,
> Preparing beneath Hibs ould green flag.
>
> Love of ould Scotland, others to save,
> they're ready to do or to die,
> Fighting like lions, honour the brave,
> Keep sacred the graves where they lie.
>
> As long as the Hibs flag is flying,
> And after the Germans are paid,
> I shall think with pride undying,
> Of the Edinburgh-Irish Brigade.

It was expected that George would be allocated to Edinburgh's own regiment the Royal Scots but out of respect for his father who had been born in the province of Connaught, Ireland, George joined the Connaught regiment who were known as the Devil's Own, with the motto 'Everywhere and Ever Faithful' and the harp was its regimental badge. Its ranks were made up of the hardy peasant farming stock of the west of Ireland and it was one of the oldest and fiercest regiments of the line. George was joined by four of his childhood Hibs pals from the St Patrick's parish in the Cowgate; they were John Pender, Frank Rooney, Frank Devlin and Willie Harvey. George and his four pals served on many of the major battlefields but only Willie Harvey was to survive the slaughter.

Private 4744 John Pender, battalion unknown the Connaught's, born

Edinburgh, died 10 February 1916 of wounds received in action against the Turks in Mesopotamia.

Private 3806 Frank Rooney, 6th battalion the Connaught's, born County Leitrin, Ireland, brought up in Edinburgh, died 3 September 1916, killed in action against the Germans in Flanders.

Lance sergeant 5995 Frank Devlin, 6th Battalion the Connaught's latterly 13233, 7/8 battalion Inniskillen Fusiliers, born Edinburgh, died 16 August 1917, killed in action against the Germans in Flanders.

Private 2658 George Alexander Whelahan, 6th battalion the Connaught's, born Edinburgh, died 21 March 1918, killed in action against the Germans in Flanders.

> In Flanders fields
> The poppies blow,
> Between the crosses
> Row on row.

George was the last of the young comrades who made the supreme sacrifice. He survived almost four years of hell and ironically died when peace was being discussed.

His father, Michael Whelahan, was utterly devastated when the army notified him of his youngest son's death.

> I am indeed sorry that such a young soldier should be taken so near to peace being achieved and I am indeed sorry for your loss. I think you should be proud he died a soldier's death on duty in the firing line serving his country and helping to keep safe our people at home.

Only Willie Harvey survived and when he returned to Little Ireland he married George's sister Kathleen in St Patrick's church. It was the men of St Patrick's church who had founded Hibernian in 1875 and today it is still the spiritual home of Hibernian Football Club. No fewer than 320 men of the St Patrick's parish made the supreme sacrifice in the First World War and inside St Patrick's a beautiful mortuary chapel was raised to their memory. In the mortuary chapel are large copper plaques with the names and regiments of all the fallen heroes and there you will find the names of George Whelahan and three of his pals. You will also find the name of the previously mentioned Hibernian player Paddy Hagan. Other names had been on Hibs' books at one time or another, officials, shareholders and ordinary supporters.

> They marched away so bravely, their young heads proudly held,
> Their footsteps never faltered, their courage never failed.
> Now we light a candle and say a prayer in a holy place,
> For they fought and died for Scotland and the honour of their race.

Oh George Whelahan, were you here at Easter Road
That I might grasp your hand,
And sing with you at the Holy Ground,
Green flag flying from the stand.

Though George and comrades died far from home,
I shall forget thee never,
And deep within St Patrick's walls,
Your names shall live forever.

So the war was over and Hibernian Football Club had survived its crippling events, thanks to the determination of Dan McMichael, who kept his promise to Hibs soldier-supporters in the trenches.

It was discovered that Dan's kidney complaint was now causing heart trouble and poor Dan was almost as exhausted as his beloved Hibs. Hibernian Park was in a run-down condition and the once-smart was now humorously described as 'the eggbox'. Understandably, no investment had been made at the Holy Ground throughout the war years, not even a new set of strips had been bought and the 'immortal Green Jerseys' were now a sweat-stained faded yellow. Dan's playing squad had to be restructured but at least he could look forward to the return of his soldier-players after demobilisation. For a sick old man, however, it would be another mountain to climb for Dan to get his squad back to pre-war strength and Hibs were just about broke.

During the war it had only been survival that had mattered to Hibernian and as things stood at this juncture of season 1918–1919 they were anchored at the bottom of the league, having played 13, lost 11, drawn one and won one having only three points. Hibs had lost 37 goals and scored only eight.

Hibs' first match after the Armistice was to have been on Saturday 16 November against Partick Thistle at Firhill but it was postponed because of dense fog. Hibs ploughed on with mostly bad results in the latter part of 1918. And bad as things were for the club, they never forgot their charitable birthright and arranged for a collection to be taken when Motherwell visited Easter Road and the Little Sisters of the Poor, who were tending badly disabled soldiers of all denominations, benefited by £14 17s 1d (£14.86).

After their service in the armed forces some Hibs players were gradually returning to the Holy Ground – Sandy Grosert, Matha Paterson, Peter Kerr, Tommy Kilpatrick, Bobby Templeton, and King. Others like Willie Dornan, Willie McGinnigle, Shaw and Davy Gordon continued to play well when they were available and the two goalkeepers, Gough and Cunningham did their best. Dan O'Donnell, Willie McCourt, Robertson and Kay ware regularly in the team but many players were in and out due to the uncertainties of life in post-war Scotland.

Scotland was in turmoil with violent strikers rioting and in the General Election in mid-December 1918 'democratic Britain' allowed women to vote for the first time. It was to be an election victory for the war agitator Lloyd George's Coalition Government and the Scottish working-class didn't expect their lot to improve any. In the whole of the Island of Ireland (there was no partition at this time) the republican/nationalist parties won no less than 83 per cent of the seats. At last the Irish nation expected their democratic voice at the ballot box would finally give them their freedom and England would peacefully withdraw her military and political presence from their island. And why not, England had promised this after the terrible sacrifices the Irish had made for England during the war. Unfortunately, England ignored Ireland's democratic voice and 'Lloyd George's New House of Commons', a child of England's imperialism instigated the Anglo-Irish War, the ongoing effects of which are still with us today but hopefully current peace negotiations will at last bring Ireland's tortured divided history to an end and the past will become the past for ever.

Unfortunately, this Irish War of Independence was to have an adverse effect upon Hibernian Football Club whose directors, shareholders, officials, management and supporters were largely Irish.

On Wednesday 1 January 1919 the New Year Derby with Hearts for the Wilson Cup came off at Easter Road in front of a crowd of 10,000. A good crowd and 'through the kindness and generosity of the Hibernian directors' a big collection was taken in aid of the Edinburgh East End Branch of the Federation of Discharged Soldiers. The teams shared four goals, Bobby Gilmour and King being Hibs' scorers. The Edinburgh Irishmen's team was: Harry Gough, Willie McGinnigle, Bobby Templeton, Hugh Shaw, Matha Paterson, Sandy Grosert, Spink, Willie McCourt, Bobby Gilmour, Kay and Campbell.

Hibs played four league matches in January and someone played an obvious hoax when Partick Thistle visited Easter Road on Saturday 18; every Partick player received a letter offering them £50 each if they would help Hibs win!

In Memoriam – Dan McMichael

On Saturday 1 February 1919 Dan McMichael carried out his last duties for Hibernian when he travelled with his team, or 'ma laddies' as Dan called them, for a league match against Falkirk at Brockville which ended in a 1-1 draw.

> Dan should never have travelled to Falkirk with his team as he was a very sick old man made worse by falling victim to the 'flu epidemic. You were wasting your breath trying to tell the stony faced old Irishman not to go, he lived and ultimately died for Hibernian Football Club.

On the return trip from Falkirk poor Dan collapsed and his players brought him to his home at 287 Easter Road to be cared for by his wife Jane Murphy who had borne him eight children. The doctors could do nothing for him and at eight o'clock on the morning of Thursday 6 February Dan passed away peacefully in his bed, fortified by the Rites of Holy Mother Church.

Dan McMichael was Irish born, of Ulster catholic stock emigrating first to the west of Scotland then on to Edinburgh's Old Town Irish ghetto, Little Ireland, before settling in the Irish Barracks which was Leith's Irish ghetto. For the rest of his life Dan considered himself a Leither. Dan was a Hibs supporter all his days, going back to the founding of the club in 1875 and he was one of the Stella Maris Catholic Young Men's Society of St Mary Star of the Sea church, Leith, who fought for the survival of Hibernian in the early 1890s and by 1895 he was a Hibs scout. Dan was a fair athlete in his youth, became an SFA referee and an expert physiotherapist which stood him in good stead all his years at Easter Road. Dan's expertise was also always available in the wider community and we are told that even his parish priest Fr Byrne, who had been seriously injured by a 'wild motorcyclist', was only able to carry on his parish duties thanks to the attention of Dan McMichael and two Hibs trainers, Paddy Cannon and Di Christopher.

From 1899 for the next 20 years Dan was treasurer, then secretary-manager with Hibs, winning the Scottish Cup in 1902 and league championship in 1903 and he was a shareholder when Hibs became a limited liability company. Dan was very shrewd and expert at bringing talented young players to Easter Road, personally coaching them to greatness, some to international honours. Cash-strapped Hibs could never give Dan much money to buy big name players but Dan always defended his directors about this and once when provoked the normally unruffled Dan snapped back, 'I don't need money to bring stars to Easter Road, Hibs bring out their own stars'. One of Dan's famous young players was the tragic Jimmy Main whom he had signed in 1904 when he was but a 'raw eighteen year old youth'. For five years Dan coached young Jimmy to Scottish League honours and then on to full Scottish international honours. Jimmy Main received serious injuries on the football field on Christmas Day 1909 and he died a few days later at the age of 23. Dan had stayed at Jimmy's hospital bedside with Jimmy's family and when the young man died the usually unemotional Dan sobbed 'he was like a son to me'.

Dan's grief was certainly genuine as he and the directors had built Hibs a great reputation of being 'a very caring club, a big happy family'. You would never have guessed it from 'the stony faced' Irish manager and directors of Hibernian who ran their own school of Irish football philosophy at Easter Road. An old supporter likened Dan McMichael's personality to that of the great Jock Stein, appearing serious and gruff but with a heart of gold and a sound football knowledge, gaining him genuine respect and affection. Dan served for ten years on the Scottish League management committee and was awarded a long service medal. Dan led Hibs on their 'mission' to re-establish them as 'the premier club of the Irish of Scotland' by taking them to the Scottish Cup final in 1914. As we have seen in this book, it was Dan who kept Hibs alive during the First World War while three of his sons served with distinction in the trenches. Dan McMichael led Hibs to the highest honours in Scottish football and fielded exciting teams but his claim to Hibernian's Hall of Fame in his 20 years as Hibs manager must surely be his pride, passion and unselfish hard work in keeping the club alive throughout the dreadful years of the war.

> More than any other club Hibs convey the impression that their difficulties in whipping up teams week in and out are almost insurmountable but Dan McMichael seems to manage somehow even when in the depths of despair to get 11 Hibernians.

When Dan died, he had, however laid the foundations of one of the most celebrated teams in Hibernian's history, having signed Peter Kerr, Willie Dornan, Willie Miller, Willie McGinnigle and Hugh Shaw. These great Dan McMichael signings were to pay off handsomely in the 1920s.

Dan's Requiem Mass took place in St Mary Star of the Sea RC church in Leith attended by Hibernians old and new and the club's wreath took the form of the traditional broken harp. Also in attendance were the Stella Maris and St Patrick's CYMS and the teachers and children of St Mary Star of the Sea school. Leithers of all denominations were there in great numbers. In the impressive funeral cortege every Scottish club was represented, as was the Scottish League, the SFA and the East of Scotland FA. Dan was buried in the Eastern Cemetery, off Easter Road, close to his Easter Road home and beloved Easter Road club.

> The peace I shall know
> In green grass I've found,
> Resting at Easter Road
> In the shadow of the Holy Ground.
>
> Hibernian Park, the green, the harp and Erin go Bragh,
> Hibs four immortal blends,
> Dan McMichael, faith, hope and charity,
> Hibs four immortal friends.

Dan McMichael was a tall, serious-looking man with a bushy moustache who was respected not only in football circles but in the general community and was held in high esteem by a wide circle of acquaintances. It is perhaps fitting to close this memory of Dan McMichael with tributes from two of these acquaintances.

> Dan McMichael was Hibs guiding star and Hibs have lost a good friend in him whose heart was in the club he has so long served. I never saw an approach to a smile on his face, and while I put it down to team worries, when all the time it was failing health, a malady, slow and insidious, that finally carried him off. Dan was an excellent judge of a player and saw many good young ones pass through his hands for he had not a Parkhead or Ibrox backing financially. It must have been a heartbreaking job to keep the green flag flying at Easter Road these four lean years of his life.

> It is difficult to think of Easter Road without Dan. I never knew anyone who had a hard or unkind word to say of him, nor did I ever hear Dan speak harshly or ungenerously of any living creature. It would have been against his nature to have done so. True he had his own way of doing things and at times he made mysteries when there need have been none, but that his heart was in the right place no one who knew him could ever have doubted. There will never be anyone more zealous and conscientious for the welfare of Hibernian Football club for which it is not too much to say, he died as well as lived. He never thought of himself when it was a case of doing something for the Hibs. Dan had come to be one of the institutions of the game in Edinburgh and Leith and those who knew him could not help respecting him and liking him. There was something in the nature of the man, something kind and considerate, that made it so, and he was ever ready, even at personal inconvenience, to give what help he could to anyone. Many a real good player he was responsible for bringing to Easter Road and got many good-going sided together. They were always a happy family at Easter Road, directors, manager and players. There was nothing of the marinet about old Dan, but he knew better than many others whose discipline was far more severe how to win not only the respect but affection of his men. Dan treated them with every consideration, and they regarded him more as a friend than a boss. Poor old Dan, he was a good kindly soul and will be much missed by many. With Dan McMichael away it would seem as if Easter Road would never be quite what it used to be.

It was a sad, shocked Hibernian who played Dumbarton in the league at the Holy Ground on Saturday 8 February. A minute's silence was observed to the memory of Dan McMichael, the green flag was lowered to half-mast and the players wore black armbands. We are told: 'The Edinburgh Irishmen's game was overwhelmed by the death of Dan McMichael but for all that it had to be played and not surprisingly it was a poor game but the Hibs did win 1-0.'

The following week, managerless Hibs crashed 9-2 against Morton at Cappielow. The match should never have been played as there was 'a lake' in the Hibs goal area and Morton did most of the damage in the first half. Seven days later Hibs, who were still without a manager, went down 1-2 against Hamilton at Easter Road. Hugh Shaw scored the Irishmen's goal.

After the match Hibernian officially appointed their new manager, none other then their 'indefatigable' 35-year-old left-half Davy Gordon. He remained a registered player but all his energies were now devoted to the management of the team. Hibs' Irish directors had made a very good and popular choice and they had the courage to select for the first time someone outside the Irish community of Edinburgh and Leith to guide the club forward. It was thought if anyone from the playing staff was to get the job it would have been long-serving Matha Paterson or Peter Kerr, but they too were delighted at Davy Gordon's appointment and of course gave him their full support. Like Dan McMichael, Davy Gordon was a joiner to trade and had done valuable war-work in the Leith shipyards. The popular Davy Gordon was to do a great job for Hibs, building on the foundation laid by Dan McMichael, signing more of the celebrated 1920s team.

Edinburgh-born Davy Gordon immediately made a 'real capture' in John Wood who had recently been demobbed from the Black Watch. Having no league match on Saturday 1 March, Davy Gordon arranged a popular friendly at the Holy Ground against a club they had inspired and whose ground they had in 1909, Dundee Hibernian, the great club we all know today as Dundee United. We are told: 'This Irish festival at Easter Road saw the Edinburgh Irishmen defeat the Dundee Irishmen by six goals to two.'

Davy Gordon also made another popular move by recalling to his team goalkeeper David Stevenson, who was a Leither and had been signed by Dan McMichael in the season before the war. Like all other Hibernians at the outbreak of conflict David Stevenson joined the Edinburgh-Irish Brigade drilling at Easter Road before he was allocated to the Royal Garrison Artillery with whom he served in France and David was badly gassed at the Somme. David Stevenson was highly decorated for his courage in action and later served as an instructor with the Royal Signal Corps. After the war David Stevenson rejoined his Easter Road team-mates while working as an insurance clerk with the Tailors and Fireman's Union in Leith. That Saturday 8 March Hibs lost 0-2 at Easter Road to Ayr United but young David had a sound game 'receiving much encouragement from a big Hibs crowd'. The Green Jerseys were: David Stevenson, Willie McGinnigle, Willie Dornan, Hugh Shaw, Matha Paterson, Dan O'Donnell, John Wood, Willie McCour, Tommy Kilpatrick, Bob Gilmour and Robertson.

The following week Hibs were to gain a quick and sweet revenge on Ayr United, The first national trophy since the outbreak of war was now being played for, the Victory Cup. Hibs had a bye in the first round but in the second they were by coincidence drawn against the men from Ayr at Easter Road. This time it was the Edinburgh Irishmen who won 1-0 in front of a 13,000 crowd. Tommy Kilpatrick got Hibs' late winner but it was another Hibs player who was the hero after a great 90-minute display: 'goalkeeper David Stevenson is of the do-or-die order and had a great reception from the Easter Road crowd after a good day's work.'

A puzzled Ayr United fan wrote to the press asking for clarification on Hibs' Edinburgh/Leith connections and was given the simple reply: 'Hibs are an Edinburgh club with its ground, Hibernian Park, at Easter Road in Leith. The name of the club is Edinburgh Hibernian.'

On Saturday 29 March in the third round of the Victory Cup luck smiled on Hibs, with another home draw against the highly-fancied Motherwell. There was nothing lucky however about Hibs' excellent 2-0 victory in front of 20,000 happy Hibs fans. Again David Stevenson was the hero: 'The Hibernian goalkeeper made some brilliant saves when all seemed over, the Irishmen have been fortunate to secure this youth to guard their goal.'

So Hibs surprised everyone, including themselves, in reaching the semi-final of the Victory Cup. If anyone deserved a little limelight it was most assuredly the Edinburgh Irishmen whose war efforts had almost run the club into the ground. The Victory Cup was a one-off competition to celebrate the winning of the war and it would have been wholly appropriate for Hibs to win it, unfortunately it was not to be. Luck continued to smile on Hibs when the semi-final draw saw them again get the home draw but their opponents were high-flying St Mirren who were very strong at this time both in football ability and physique. We are told: 'Hibernian really mixed it with their weightier opponents with native Irish elbows to the fore.' The semi-final came off at Easter Road on Saturday 12 April in front of no fewer than 30,000 hopeful Hibs supporters, the vast majority of whom were demobbed servicemen home from the trenches. Davy Gordon had kept Dan McMichael's wartime promise that a strong going Hibs would still be at the Holy Ground for them. The Newhaven Silver band entertained the crowd while a collection was taken for the Leith Branch of the Soldiers and Sailors Federation. Hibs scored first in this 'rough and tumble' match but at full time it was all square with St Mirren looking stronger. Thirty minutes extra time was played and almost immediately Hibs' Bobby Gilmour was carried off with a broken collarbone and a brave ten men Hibs eventually went down 1-3. Again the Irishmen's young goalkeeper David Stevenson was above criticism: 'His saving was brilliant by his sharpness and daring keeping out the opposites when all seemed lost.' There were ten soldiers and ex-soldiers in the Hibs team: David Stevenson, Willie McGinnigle, Bobby Templeton, Peter Kerr, Matha Paterson, Robert 'Barney'

Smith, John Wood, Tommy Kilpatrick, Jimmy Williamson, Bobby Gilmour and Horace Williams. Hibs' share of the £820 gate was £400 and at last they were able to buy a new set of green jerseys. St Mirren went on to win the Victory Cup, defeating Hearts 3-0 in the Parkhead final.

Monday 14 August and Hibernian travelled up to the Jute City to play the return friendly with Dundee Hibs and once again the Edinburgh Irishmen defeated the Dundee Irishmen, this time 0-3. Dreadful weather kept the crowd down for this 'Irish festival' as Jimmy Williamson scored two and John Wood one. In-form Easter Road goalkeeper David Stevenson saved a penalty.

Meanwhile Hibs manager Davy Gordon, building on Dan McMichael's foundations of a great 1920s team, made a superb signing in the shape of Henry McGill Ritchie. A natural left-winger, Harry Ritchie was however to eventually make his mark on the right wing, becoming one of the most popular players in the history of Hibernian Football club. Harry Ritchie made his debut for the Irishmen at the Holy Ground on Saturday 26 April 1919 in a 1-0 league victory against a much-fancied Queen's Park. We are told it was a shock result. We are further told: 'An old supporter who had seen all the Hibernian greats thought Harry Ritchie looked a wee bit slow and made the snap judgement that "Harry Ritchie niver wiz or would be a fitba'er." ' Just how wrong can you be, for Harry was to develop into an exciting winger of the best Hibernian tradition gaining unparalleled popularity and the unquestioned love of every Hibs supporter, and gaining international honours.

Two days later Davy Gordon had his old club Hull City at Easter Road for a friendly and the disappointingly small crowd saw a cracker of a match with the teams sharing six goals.

Hibs' last league match of the season on Saturday 10 May saw them travel to Broomfield, playing out a 3-3 draw with Airdrie after the Green Jerseys had been ahead by three goals. Hibs finished bottom of the league, thank God it was only make-believe wartime football with nothing at stake. The main thing was that Hibs had survived the crippling events of the war and the massive contribution the club and the supporters had made in the war effort. As we have seen, it was the unselfish heroes of the late Dan McMichael that every Hibernian had to thank for the club's survival and now it was up to Davy Gordon and the directors to keep faith with old Dan and get Hibernian back on a proper footing. The Hibs supporters had kept faith, as did the demobbed Hibernian soldier-supporters who didn't even know if there would be a Hibernian when they returned from the trenches. They now swelled the crowds at the Holy Ground, as seen nowhere more clearly than in the Victory Cup competition. It was up to everyone now to pull together.

The rest of this last wartime season ended on a low note for Hibs, who lost out to Hearts in the local cup competitions. In the case of the East of Scotland Shield final, which also had the Wilson Cup at stake, hundreds of Hibs supporters rioted and broke out into Tynecastle, causing a lot of damage and Hibs eventually went down 1-0 to a disputed penalty. When Hearts were presented with the trophies after the match in their pavilion we are told:

> John Farmer the stony faced Irish chairman of Hibs who was always very gentlemanly and sporting surprised everyone by declaring at the top of his voice 'Hearts didn't deserve to win'. Nobody could ever remember John Farmer ever making such an outburst before.

The Hibs team was: Willie Stevenson, Willie McGinnigle, Willie Dornan, Robert 'Barney Smith, Matha Paterson, Sandy Grosert, John Wood, Maxwell, Jimmy Williamson, Bobby Gilmour and Horace Williams.

In the close season, Hibs played in many charity five-a-side competitions and allowed junior clubs to play their cup finals at Easter Road free of charge. After a Hibs charity match for the Edinburgh Sick Children's Hospital, however, they had to call a halt to allow Paddy Canon to get the pitch in order and carry out much-needed maintenance and repairs to the Holy Ground.

As season 1919–1920 approaches let us look at the sorry state of the beloved Holy Ground, Hibernian Park, Easter Road. The sloping pitch was much more pronounced than it is at present. The small once-smart wooden stand was on the east side of the pitch and had fallen into disrepair during the war and was, as already mentioned, disparagingly known as 'the eggbox'. The wooden pavilion (dressing rooms) was a separate structure adjoining the stand up the slope to the south about level with the 18-yard line. There was no terracing, just earth banking on the north, south and west of the pitch which was surrounded by wooden palings. You would gradually slide down the banking, particularly on rainy days, tripping over beer bottles while trying to avoid a big navvy peeing on your legs. It was primitive stuff. The pitch, which was always in superb condition thanks to trainer/groundsman Paddy Cannon, was further west then at present and desperate clearances would land in Norton Park school yard. The only entrances were at the north end, the Leith end, at the bottom of the slope. These entrances, as today, faced immediately onto the wall of the Eastern Cemetery where many Hibs players, directors and supporters have been laid to rest. The fans put up with this without complaint for this was Easter Road their own Holy Ground and they, like the manager and directors, were more interested in the team on the park. Plans to modernise Hibernian Park had been on the table before the war but now the first priority was to get a worthy playing squad. It wasn't realised then but Hibs already had six players on their books who would become part of the celebrated 1920s team, one of the popular and entertaining elevens that were to wear Hibernian's immortal green jerseys that graced the Holy Ground.

> Dan McMichael kept his promise
> When you return from fields of blood,
> You would still find Hibernian
> Playing at Easter Road.
>
> The Cobbles of Easter Road lie before you
> And the Holy Ground of haunting charm
> With its memories comrades
> To keep you ever warm.

– 2 –
THE SOLDIERS' RETURN TO EASTER ROAD
1919–1920 TO 1920–1921

The florists were glowing with golden mimosa,
In Easter Road a blind soldier is playing a concertina.

Vendors – 'Hibs Rosettes' – vie and cry then
Clad tap to tae like medicine men.

In an air of banners, a light of oriflammes
'Git yer Hibs colours', 'half-times', 'programmes'.

So the stream jostles by – soldiers, buskers, jongleurs,
Past mounted police – aloof as centaurs.

To the holy ground, a world afore ptolemy's, sma', green, and galius
sea of faces rowe-in' roond – another oceanus.

And a blind soldier playing a concertina
brings a galaxy doun to a rise o' mimosa.

Season 1919–1920 saw Davy Gordon put together his squad of players. There were only two new faces, goalkeeper Jimmy Scott, signed the end of last season from Newtongrange United, and inside-right Willie Stage, recently signed from Middlesborough. The full squad was: goalkeepers David Stevenson and Jimmy Scott; full-backs Willie McGinnigle, Willie Dornan and Bobby Templeton; half-backs Peter Kerr, Hugh Shaw, Matha Paterson, Robert 'Barney' Smith, Dan O'Donnell and Sandy Grosert; forwards John Wood, Willie Stage, Jimmy Williamson, Willie Miller, Bobby Gilmore, Horace Williams, Harry Ritchie and Tommy Kilpatrick.

The league was made up of 22 clubs and there would be no automatic relegation/promotion. Outside of the Old Firm we are told clubs would be 'judged on paying not playing'.

After a public practice match at Hibernian Park at the beginning of August, Hibs played their first league match at Cathkin, going down 2-0 to Third Lanark on Saturday 16 August. Four days later at Easter Road, Hibs collected their first two league points by defeating Hamilton Academicals 3-0, thanks to a Jimmy Williamson hat-trick. The Green Jerseys were: David Stevenson, Willie McGinnigle, Bobby Templeton, Peter Kerr, Matha Paterson, Robert 'Barney' Smith, John Wood, Willie Stage, Jimmy Williamson, Bobby Gilmour and Tommy Kilpatrick.

This pattern of home wins and away defeats was to continue. The Hibs support kept faith with the crowds at the Holy Ground averaging 10,000, and season tickets quickly sold out and others were immediately printed.

On Saturday 23 August against St Mirren at Easter Road, goalkeeper David Stevenson, the 'Daring Leither', was carried off injured but ten-man Hibs went on to win 2-1 'in true Hibernian tradition'. David Stevenson was to pick up many injuries, usually the week before important matches, which ruled him out of the action. A most encouraging crowd of 15,000 were in the Holy Ground on Saturday 6 September and saw Jimmy Williamson's two goals give Hibernian a 2-1 victory over Aberdeen with the following team: David Stevenson, Willie McGinnigle, Willie Dornan, Peter Kerr, Matha Paterson, Robert 'Barney' Smith, John Wood, Willie Stage, Jimmy Williamson, Willie Miller and Tommy Kilpatrick.

Davy Gordon was using his small squad as best he could as injuries and illness took its toll; in the case of 'Leith's Favourite', Sandy Grosert, he had made only one appearance so far because of an appendix operation. Dan O'Donnell made the odd appearance but Hugh Shaw and Harry Ritchie were out of the picture. Willie Miller was to keep his place meantime at inside-left but as we shall see later he would be developed in a totally different position.

It was not until Monday 29 September that Hibs recorded their first away win, defeating Albion Rovers 1-2 at Cliftonhill. We are told: 'Hibs did something to remove the impression that they are a home team pure and simple.' The Irishmen were now lying eighth in the league with ten points. Centre-half Matha Paterson scored one of the Hibs goals in that game and he also got a broken nose. This brought Hugh Shaw into the team the following Saturday in a 3-3 draw with Dumbarton at Easter Road, in a match 'noted for its roughness and penalty kicks'. Goalkeeper David Stevenson was again carried off, this time with a broken ankle that was to sideline him for some time. Reserve goalkeeper Jimmy Scott was unfortunate enough to come into the team for Hibs' visit to Celtic Park the following week. Hibs scored three goals that day, which was 'unheard of against Celtic at Parkhead', but Celtic scored seven. Poor unfortunate Jimmy Scott, had, not surprisingly for a young reserve, a poor game.

Hibs' next match was on Saturday 18 October at the Holy Ground and they restored their pride in front of a crowd of 10,000 by defeating Partick Thistle

6-2 after Partick had actually led 0-2. That man Jimmy Williamson got four goals, while Willie Stage and John Wood got one each. Harry Ritchie was reintroduced on the left wing and had an excellent game, supplying much of the ammunition. A new goalkeeper also made his appearance that day – Willie Thomson from Kilsyth St Patrick's.

At the beginning of November Hibs were at Hampden to play a much-fancied Queen's Park in front of a crowd of 12,000. After going behind 2-0, Hibs dug deep and got one back through Jimmy Williamson before Harry Ritchie scored a glorious equaliser. Of fighting Hibs that day we are told, 'any team that took anything for granted against the fighting Edinburgh Irishmen is extremely foolish as Hibernian fought back to save a game that looked beyond saving'. The Green Jerseys that day were: Willie Thomson, Bobby Templeton, Willie Dornan, Peter Kerr, Hugh Shaw, Robert 'Barney' Smith, John Wood, Willie Stage, Jimmy Williamson, Willie Miller and Harry Ritchie.

Hibs' three other league matches in November were all at Easter Road and were all victories. Long-serving full-back Neil Girdwood was newly out of the army and he made an appearance, as did George Anderson, a new full-back signed from Penicuik Athletic. Goalkeeping problems still plagued Hibs and Willie Thomson picked up a pulled muscle, heralding the return of Jimmy Scott for the last match of November and Hibs, with a reshuffled defence beat Morton 1-0 with yet another goal from Jimmy Williamson. He had, in fact, earlier scored 'a beauty' and it was not until the ball had been re-centred that the referee decided to consult both his linesmen and it was ultimately disallowed for off-side. The referee's indecision and apparent lack of understanding caused quite a storm in the press. A reshuffled injury-hit Hibs team were however highly praised in their victory:

> Hibs injury handicaps ought to have put them of count against such a strong team as Greenock Morton. But Hibs teams never reckon any handicaps as impairing their chance of success and in their traditional manner the Irish forwards swept through the Morton defence.

There were 12,000 happy Hibs supporters in the Holy Ground that day.

Poor Jimmy Scott was just back in the team when he lost another seven, this time at Ibrox on Saturday 6 December. Hibs' other three December matches saw them win, lose and draw leaving them tenth equal with Hearts in the league, both having played 22 games with 22 points.

As the year 1919 comes to an end, it is fitting to recall that it was now that Paddy Callaghan, a 20-year club servant finally, had to call it a day at Easter Road. Paddy was of Irish stock and born in Riccarton, Ayrshire, in 1879 and Hibs signed him from the junior club Jordanhill in 1899. Paddy Callaghan was

'Hibs Daft' and Hibernian were to be his only senior club, with whom he won a Scottish Cup medal in 1902 and a League Championship medal in 1903. Paddy also gained Scottish international honours. So Paddy was now leaving but he kept in touch through Michael Whelahan's official Old Hibs Association and he was also a regular attender at Hibernian matches. As we shall see, Paddy was to be recalled by Hibs to play in and help run the reserves. He sometimes acted as a linesman in Lanarkshire football while working as a Wine and Spirit Merchant's Assistant before he died at the age of 80 in 1959. Paddy Callaghan was a great player and a great servant and is assured of a place in the Hibernian Hall of Fame.

Back to season 1919–1920 and with Hibs and Hearts neck and neck in the league, the New Year's Day derby match was eagerly looked forward to on Thursday 1 January 1920. A crowd of 18,000 streamed into Tynecastle and saw Hearts score three goals in the first half, luckily two of them were own goals, giving Hibs a 1-2 lead at half-time. Adventurous Hibs were the better team that day and Jimmy Williamson added a third in the second half, 'Hibernians surprising triumph was in the manner they defeated Hearts and the willingness of the Hibs forwards to take risks'. The Green Jerseys were: Jimmy Scott, William McGinnigle, Willie Dornan, Sandy Grosert, Hugh Shaw, Robert 'Barney' Smith, John Wood, Willie Stage, Jimmy Williamson, Willie Miller and Harry Ritchie.

Two days later, 14,000 turned up at the Holy Ground to give Hearts conquerors a warm welcome and the Green Jerseys defeated Clydebank 2-0, with Willie Miller and Jimmy Williamson being the scorers. Tuesday 6 January, Hibs played a benefit for long-serving Peter Kerr and the Irishmen defeated J. McDonald's XI 3-2. The scorer of all three Hibs goals was Hugh McClymont, recently signed from Douglas Water Thistle. Two league defeats followed and in one of them goalkeeper David Stevenson made his comeback after breaking his ankle at the beginning of last October, but the injury-prone dare-devil goalkeeper was carried off injured yet again.

This meant reserve goalkeeper Jimmy Scott was pitchforked back into action for an important away match, the Scottish Cup first round against minnows Galston from Ayrshire. The circumstances surrounding this match was nothing short of farce and it came off on Saturday 24 January. Galston was a mining village a few miles from Kilmarnock and their pitch was narrow, bumpy and sitting on top of mine workings. Two weeks previously, part of the pitch had subsided and Hibs made Galston a financial offer to switch the tie to Easter Road; Galston refused and put their pitch to rights as best they could, with the SFA taking no interest whatsoever. Hibs travelled down to Kilmarnock on the Friday and stayed there overnight. It was a night of torrential rain, causing more subsidence of the Galston pitch and when Hibs arrived several hours before the kick-off the Galston club, with the aid of local farmers were filling up pot-holes and patching up collapsed goalposts. It was a comic opera situation and Hibs' chairman John Farmer, with directors Owen Brannigan and Barney Lester, expressed to the referee that in their opinion the pitch was totally unsuitable for a Scottish Cup tie and was in fact downright dangerous. The referee, Mr A. Kirkland of Glasgow, incredibly thought otherwise and declared the match on. Hibs grumbled that all the old hostility they had always suffered from the football authorities was once more rearing its ugly head. To cut a long story short, what saved Hibs from defeat that day was the canal which ran alongside the ground. Galston had five footballs to their name and at one time 'Hibernians desperate clearances' had all five balls bobbing about in the water. In the circumstances, it was justified time-wasting tactics, but the 5,000 crowd and the referee were not amused. On their atrocious home pitch, which Galston were well used to, they played a tough rushing game but every Hibernian player was a hero, especially the defence, and goalkeeper Jimmy Scott was particularly brave. The game ended in a 0-0 draw and we are told: 'The Edinburgh Irishmen came through their trying ordeal with the green flag flying high.'

The replay at Easter Road should have been played on the Wednesday, but Galston appealed that their players could not get off work and this time the SFA did take an interest and ordered the tie to be played on Saturday 31 January. It was rumoured that Galston had the temerity to offer Hibs £150 to have the replay back at Galston. A curious Easter Road crowd of 12,000 saw Hibernian win 'a rugged match' 2-1. It was Harry Ritchie who got the winner with only six minutes to go.

Hibs' Scottish Cup nightmare continued the following week when they had to travel to Volunteer Park to play minnows Armadale who won 1-0, and so ended a really poor cup campaign.

It is, perhaps, interesting to note that there were several upsets by unfashionable teams in both the cup and league. For instance, before Armadale had put out Hibs they had disposed of Clyde in the first round and in the third round saw off Ayr United, before finally succumbing to Kilmarnock. Albion Rovers reached the final of the Scottish Cup, disposing of Rangers in the semi-final after two replays.

Albion Rovers lost out in the Hampden final to Kilmarnock in front of a crowd of no less than 96,000. Albion Rovers were anchored at the bottom of the league but in a league match that didn't stop them taking six goals off Hearts.

The Port of Leith was planning a war memorial but it was to be a practical memorial to the Leithers who had made the supreme sacrifice in the war. A fund was started for a new sick children's ward in Leith Hospital so Hibernian, in conjunction with their old friends the Stella Maris Catholic Young Men's Society of St Mary Star of the Sea RC church, Leith, organised a highly successful fund-raising Irish Concert in Leith Assembly Rooms. A female relative of Hibernian chairman John Farmer was one of several fine soloists. This fund-raising concert in February was just part of much work done by Hibernian and the Stella Maris men.

As the season continued, Hibs signed Borthwick from Gala Fairydean, Archie Young from Abercorn, George Verrill from Middlesborough, Davy Anderson, a junior internationalist from Newtongrange Star, and Alex Strange.

Hibs played two benefit matches for two long-serving players, Bobby Templeton and Sandy Grosert – both had played in the 1914 Scottish Cup final. Hibs played 16 other league matches but the best they could do was win one and draw four, leaving then 18th in the League with 33 points. The Green Jerseys lost out in the local cup competitions and at the end of the season, injury-prone goalkeeper David Stevenson was transferred to St Bernard's as was the very useful Willie Stage. Big Easter Road favourite, Leither Sandy Grosert, 'The Gallant Soldier', went to Aberdeen and top scorer Jimmy Williamson departed for Tranmere Rovers.

With Hibernian's strong association with the Port of Leith, it is appropriate to record that in the summer of 1920 Leith lost its independence and was absorbed into the City of Edinburgh. The Port of Leith had been a burgh independent of Edinburgh since 1832 and Leith, being an industrial centre along with its shipyards and docks, had done very nicely thank you. But now the burgeoning population of Edinburgh saw the city complete a pincer movement around Leith by acquiring Granton and Seafield. It was argued that the costs of running separate municipal functions was a strong case for Leith to be amalgamated with Edinburgh and become a district of the expanding capital. The fiercely proud and independent Leithers opposed this vigorously and an official plebiscite was taken.

> Leithers harken to my story,
> Noo it means defeat or glory,
> Whether socialist, whig or tory,
> Vote for Leith.

> Kirkgate and auld Tolbooth Wynd,
> Never yet were left behind,
> Let Auld Reekie ken yir mind,
> Vote for Leith.

Ye Hibernians at Easter Road do dwell,
Haste ye tae the booth pell mell,
Pit yer cross a tale to tell,
Vote for Leith.

When they speak o' amalgamation,
Show yir righteous indignation,
Leither o' whitiver station
Vote for Leith.

The result was 59,357 against with 29,891 for; a majority of 24,534 against the amalgamation. All Scottish affairs were of course decided in London and a House of Commons Committee passed 'The Edinburgh Boundaries Extension and Tramways Bill', ignoring the democratic voice of Leith, 'A certain democratic, independent people who dwell on the shores of the Forth were hauled before the autocracy of London and doomed to extinction.' London conceded that the regal title Port of Leith would be retained, as would Leith's ancient catholic coat of arms, the Virgin and Child Jesus seated in a Galleon with the motto 'Persevere'.

Leith alas your in Edinburgh's grips,
Edina's got you by the hips,
And soon she'll send you doon the slips,
She did before
She has shut democracy's lips,
And barred Persevere's door.

The amalgamation of Leith with Edinburgh had to be accepted by Leithers but it was largely ignored, 'you can take the man out of Leith but you can't take Leith out of the man.' The biggest effect Leith's Hibs supporters said was they missed moving from the Edinburgh side to the Leith side of the Boundary Bar for a late drink when the licensing hours became strictly observed.

For season 1920–1921 Hibs were the first club to issue their fixture list with signed players, at a cost of 2d (1p). Among several promising new signings were Paddy Hannigan from Dumbarton Harp, Paddy Maxwell from Stewarton Juniors, Davy Anderson from Newtongrange Star, John Cannon from Lochgelly United, John Gordon, late of Loanhead Mayflower and Bonnyrigg Rose, Hector Williams from St Johnstone, Wright from Alva and Strang from Arniston. A total of 19 players were on Hibs' books, more than they had had for many years. The Irishmen also applied for membership of the Scottish Alliance to run a reserve team in their league.

With 22 teams being in the first division and the chance of relegation being introduced, we are told Hibs manager Davy Gordon should have been more enterprising with his signings, 'the Hibernians will have to be careful or at the end of the season they may find themselves, vulgarly speaking, in the cart'. As it turned out, the relegation and promotion was delayed until next season.

In their first four league matches Hibs lost two, drew one and won one. The 1-0 victory over St Mirren at the Holy Ground on Saturday 21 August was achieved in front of a crowd of 10,000 with the following team: Willie Thomson, Willie McGinnigle, Bobby Templeton, Hugh Shaw, Matha Paterson, Johnny Cannon, Paddy Hannigan, John Gordon, Davy Anderson, Young, Willie Miller and Hector Williams.

At the end of August, manager Davy Gordon made two signings that were to prove to be among the best ever made by Hibs: Willie Harper, a goalkeeper from Hibs' nursery team Edinburgh Emmet and Jimmy 'Tim' Dunn, an inside-right from the Glasgow junior club St Anthony's. Two more players who would be part of the celebrated team.

Willie Harper and Jimmy Dunn made their debut at the Holy Ground on Wednesday 1 September, when Hibs went down 0-2 to Airdrie. The Green Jerseys were: Willie Harper, Willie McGinnigle, Willie Dornan, Peter Kerr, Matha Paterson, Johnny Cannon, Paddy Hannigan, Jimmy Dunn, Harry Ritchie, Willie Miller and Hector Williams.

As always, the Edinburgh Irishmen were to the fore for a charitable cause and they travelled to Newtown Park and defeated Bo'ness United 1-2 in a benefit for one of their players, Jimmy Watson, a miner who had been permanently disabled in a pit accident.

As Hibs collected four points from their next two league matches there was high praise for Willie Harper from Hibs old goalkeeper Willie Allan who had played in the 1914 Scottish Cup final. A run of three defeats followed and it is of interest to note that an article in the press about Hibs, under the heading 'the Unsettled Irish' was signed A.S.M. This was Alec S. Maley, whom we shall soon see would later this season be appointed Hibs manager.

One of these three defeats was at the hands of Rangers at Ibrox 1-0 but Willie Harper was again outstanding. He, and indeed the whole Hibs team, were unfortunately subjected to 'a new type of Ibrox hostility that had nothing to do with football'. The attitude of the Rangers support had drastically changed recently. With Harland and Wolff, the Belfast Shipbuilders, expanding their operations to Glasgow, large numbers of Ulster Orangemen followed to work there. They quickly attached themselves to Rangers who already had a big support and although they were less successful than Celtic, Rangers were their strongest challengers. These Ulster orange supporters readily influenced other Rangers supporters, turning enthusiasm for Rangers into a 'holy war' against catholics and Irish national influence. Initially Rangers could not be responsible for the bigoted supporters coming through their turnstiles, but their crowds were growing and the money was rolling in and they quickly took up the 'Orange theme' to such an extent that the Rangers management enforced a 'no catholics' policy at Ibrox, to curry favour with the social views of their support. We are told: 'By adopting a policy of religious apartheid Rangers Football club had given bigotry a seal of approval and tacitly endorsed the vicious sectarianism now manifesting itself on the Ibrox terracing.'

Back to our football story and, although Hibs only won two of the five league matches in October, manager Davy Gordon was particularly happy with his two signings, Willie Harper and Jimmy Dunn.

> Going along Princes Street the other morning I met Mr David Gordon and there was on his face that smile that it used to wear when he first ceased being a player and became manager at Easter Road … Despite Jimmy Dunn's lack of inches, he expressed the confident belief that the players will yet do great things for the Hibs. Dunn who wants some filling out badly, is a confident little fellow … with Willie Harper he is also delighted, the best recruit in his opinion that Hibernian have picked up for many a day, he is going to be one of the greatest players the Hibs have introduced to first-class football.

At the beginning of November, Davy Gordon swooped to make another great signing, John 'Hally' Halligan, an inside-left from Shawfield Juniors. Yet another member of the celebrated team was now at Easter Road and Johnny Halligan made his debut at the Holy Ground on Saturday 6 November, in a 5-2 victory over Albion Rovers in front of a 10,000 crowd. Davy Anderson and Paddy Hannigan got two goals each and Jimmy Dunn the other. The Hibs team was: Willie Harper, Wright, Willie Dornan, Peter Kerr, Matha Paterson, Johnny Cannon, Paddy Hannigan, Jimmy Dunn, Davy Anderson, Johnny Halligan and Willie Miller.

Two weeks later, Davy Gordon made yet another superb signing, John 'Darkie' Walker, an outside-right from Kirkintilloch Rob Roy. Hibs now had ten of the celebrated team on their books. 'Darkie' Walker made his debut at the Holy Ground on Saturday 20 November in a 2-0 victory over Dundee in front of a crowd of 15,000. The Green Jerseys were: Willie Harper, Wright, Willie Dornan, Peter Kerr, Matha Paterson, Hugh Shaw, John 'Darkie' Walker, Jimmy Dunn, Davy Anderson, Johnny Halligan and Paddy Hannigan. A collection that day was taken for the Royal Blind Asylum.

Hibs drew three and lost one of their next four matches. During one of these draws at Easter Road we are told of 'a very unusual incident of a Hibs supporter using a megaphone to cheer on the Irishmen'. The Irishmen's last match of

1920 was on Christmas Day at Clydeholm Park in a 2-2 draw with Clydebank. The point placed Hibs 16th in the league, with 20 points from 24 games.

Derby Day, Saturday 1 January 1921, and Hearts visited Easter Road for the first time since the hostile amalgamation of Leith with Edinburgh and 30,000 Hibs supporters greeted the Tynecastle players with good-humoured 'Hibs Daft' songs.

> Poor ould Hearts did knock their knees,
> And chatter at the teeth,
> So badly does the wind get up,
> When they play the Hibs in Leith.

After an almighty roar another 'Hibs Ditty' quickly followed.

> The divil walked through Leith,
> A Hearts supporter under each oxter
> An' another in his teeth,
> The divils deid, the divils deid
> An' he's buried in Tynecastle.

The band of the 7th Royal Scots were at the Holy Ground to entertain the crowd but the Hibs choir were doing nicely themselves. The Irishmen had already been written off by the press but 'Hibs played a methodical game' and Jimmy Dunn gave them a 1-0 half-time lead. In the second half 'the Irishmen were all over Hearts' and Johnny Halligan and 'Darkie' Walker made the final score 3-0. Willie Harper even saved a penalty, to add to Hearts' humiliation as 'the Irish recorded a decisive success over hot favourites Hearts'.

A dejected Hearts then trooped off the Holy Ground with another 'Hibs Daft' song ringing in their ears. It was set to a traditional Irish folk tune.

> Poor Leith has been rudely connected,
> Into part of the town up the way,
> But we're not in the least disconcerted,
> We're improving Auld Reekie each day,
>
> Since Leith joined Edina's fair city,
> Rumours are going around rife,
> But the city and port are Hibs home,
> And have been all of their life.
>
> Mush, Mush, Mush tooral-i-adi,
> Mush, Mush, Mush tooral-i-ay,
> You close Leith pubs by voting no licence,
> But you can't shut up Hibernians that way.

There were nine men in the Green Jerseys that day who would be part of the later celebrated team. The Hibs eleven were: Willie Harper, Willie McGinnigle, Willie Dornan, Peter Kerr, Matha Paterson, Hugh Shaw, Harry Ritchie, Jimmy Dunn, 'Darkie' Walker, Johnny Halligan and Paddy Hannigan.

Two days later, Hibs travelled to the Jute City and took a good 1-1 draw with Dundee. Because of injuries, Paddy Maxwell came into the team, as did Willie Miller who was Hibs' scorer.

After Hibs supplied six players in an East of Scotland Select team in a benefit match for a Hearts player, the Green Jerseys' next match was at Shawfield, where they went down 2-0 to Clyde. The conditions were atrocious and Willie Harper had made a goal-line save but the referee gave the goal 'amid strong protests by the Irishmen'. Davy Anderson had come in at centre-forward and he sustained a nasty head knock and had to be treated on the park by Hibs' own Dr Kivlichen, an ex-Celtic player, before poor Anderson was carried off.

Meantime, Hibs signed a young defender, Jim Cassidy from Duntocher Hibs, as the Green Jerseys played host to Ayr United in a five-goal thriller on Saturday 15 January. The Irishmen hit the woodwork five times, before winning 3-2 with two goals from Jimmy Dunn and an 'impossible' goal from Paddy Hannigan, direct from a corner kick, which had the 12,000 crowd buzzing.

Hibs were drawn away from home against Third Lanark in the first round of the Scottish Cup the following week. It was the big tie but Hibs' manager and directors kept preparations low-key with the Irishmen's traditional 'big happy family' approach. A billiards competition over two evenings, a night at the Lyceum theatre and even the night before the match, they were all at the Empire theatre. Two special trains were laid on for the Hibs supporters departing from Leith Central via the Waverley Station. A 20,000 Cathkin crowd saw Third Lanark take the lead but 'roared on by their good humoured Irish support Hibernian adopted cup-tie tactics and by fast, open, tireless play the Irishmen forced a well-deserved draw through Harry Ritchie.'

In the replay the following Wednesday afternoon, with 22,000 in the Holy Ground, the teams again drew 1-1. Hibs were ahead at half-time through a Jimmy Dunn goal but in the second half Willie Harper, as he had done in the Clyde game, pulled off a goal-line save but the referee gave Third Lanark their equaliser as 'Hibs appealed vigorously but to no avail.' It was perceived by Hibs supporters and the club that all the hostility they had suffered in the past was again rearing its head; the Hibernian war sacrifices had changed nothing.

The second replay of this prolonged Scottish Cup first round tie came off on Tuesday 1 February at neutral Ibrox, where Hibs had lost several such deciders in the past. A big Hibs support swelled the 30,000 crowd and this time the Irishmen were victorious 0-1, with a 65th-minute goal from Johnny

Halligan direct from a corner. Paddy Hannigan had done this in January against Ayr United and now Johnny Halligan did the 'impossible' as well.

In the second round of the Scottish Cup, Hibs were drawn at home against Partick Thistle who were a class act at the time, with three internationalists in their team. Hibs had no internationalists. The Easter Road crowd was 25,000 that Saturday, 5 February, and the directors took the opportunity for a collection to be taken for the convent of the Poor Clares, Liberton, Edinburgh. The match ended in a 0-0 draw and three days later, in the replay at Partick Thistle's Firhill ground, Maryhill, Glasgow, it was again a 0-0 draw. We are told that near the end of the game a Maryhill tenement chimney caught fire, pouring heavy smoke into the faces of the Hibs team, hampering their play badly. The fire was no sooner put out when another chimney caught fire, again causing heavy smoke to blow directly into the Hibee's faces. Some paranoid Hibs supporters grumbled that it was 'an Orange conspiracy'.

The second replay of this prolonged second round Scottish Cup tie came off on Tuesday 13 February at neutral Celtic Park, in front of a crowd of 30,000 and unfortunately, this time Hibs went down by the only goal of the game after a brave fight and a penalty save by Willie Harper. Hibs director Owen Brannigan had remarked before the game that whoever won this tie would go on to win the Scottish Cup; he was right – Patrick Thistle did just that.

In these two rounds of the Scottish Cup Hibs had played six games, four of them in Glasgow and the one satisfying aspect for them was 'the large numbers of Hibs Glasgow-Irish friends who game them great support.' It was quite remarkable, considering the massive success of Celtic, that Hibs still had 'many old supporters in the west of Scotland'.

Meantime, Hibs had been trying to buy their Holy Ground, which was only leased from the Trinity Hospital Committee of Edinburgh Town Council, but the Trinity Hospital Committee refused to sell. The Edinburgh Parks Committee had no objections to the purchase but the Trinity people, for their own reasons, never had good relations with Hibernian, but they conceded a long lease of 30 years.

During the protracted Scottish Cup ties, Hibernian also played two away league matches against Queen's Park and Albion Rovers, and the Irishmen won both of them. Against Queen's Park Willie Harper saved a twice-taken penalty and against Albion Rovers he had another penalty save; Willie Harper was certainly building a reputation for himself. Hibs had fielded very weak teams for both these matches and the SFA later fined the Irishmen £50 for doing this even allowing for the fact that the Green Jerseys won both the matches.

Throughout March and early April Hibs had mixed results in the league. Two days after a good 1-1 draw at Easter Road with table-toppers Rangers, the Hibs played a benefit match on Monday 11 April for the building fund of St Cuthbert's RC church and school, Slateford Road, Edinburgh. Hibs played another benefit match on Monday 18 April, this time for long-serving centre-half and captain Matha Paterson. Celtic won this Easter Road match by the only goal of the game but it was a big success for this great Hibernian servant.

It was also in April that the Irishmen lost the services, temporarily, of Willie Harper and Paddy Maxwell, both of whom were army reservists and were called up to the Scottish Defence Force. Baillie took over in goal from Willie Harper.

A week or so later, Hibs manager Davy Gordon unexpectedly resigned because of personal reasons. This was a great pity as he was a very able and popular man and in his short reign he had signed no less than six of the great players who would later become part of the celebrated team.

The Hibernian directors, however, quickly made another excellent appointment to the post of manager – Alec S. Maley, the boss of Clydebank, who was the brother of the legendary Celtic manager Willie Maley. It was the first time in Scottish football that brothers managed opposing clubs and it caused quite a stir.

In the early part of May the Irishmen dumped Hearts 1-0 in both the Wilson Cup final and the East of Scotland Shield final, a satisfying double over the 'ould inimy', before new manager Alec Maley took Hibs on a foreign tour for the first time in their history.

A 15-day three-game tour/holiday of Denmark was arranged, the Hibs party being made up of directors John Farmer, Owen Brannigan and Barney Lester with manager Alec Maley and a 12-player squad. A strike by ships' stewards and cooks delayed Hibs' departure by 24 hours but, on Friday 13 May, the Irishmen sailed out of the Port of Leith for Copenhagen on the MV *Weimar*. Hibs played two matches against a Copenhagen Select, winning one and losing one, and they drew with an Aarhus Select. Unfortunately, Johnny Halligan broke his collar bone during the tour. Hibs were impressed with the quality of Danish football and they were also impressed by the beautiful country on their sight-seeing trips. The Green Jerseys returned to Leith on Sunday 29 May on the MV *Coblenz*, where they had met up with the Queen's Park team who had also been on tour in Denmark.

It was a very warm, dry summer and as season 1921–1922 approached we are told:

> The grass, usually so green and luxuriant, has suffered from the drought and the heat, and when I visited Hibernian Park the other day it was just recovering its verdant hue after heavy rain. There has been no growth upon it in the close-season and Paddy Cannon, the trainer/groundsman told me that never in 20-years

experience has he had so little grass-cutting to do. It's an illwind that blaws naebody guid.

The all-important relegation/promotion issue was now in force this season, and manager Alec Maley had 22 players on his books to cover his first and reserve team and he had his eye on some juniors when required. Before Hibs' league campaign started, the Irishmen went along to Wood Park and played Portobello Thistle in a benefit match for the sea-side men. Old-timer Paddy Callaghan officiated as referee.

Saturday 20 August was Hibs' first league match playing Celtic at Parkhead and going down 3-1 in front of a 15,000 crowd. The Edinburgh Irishmen, however, did play a good game and Jimmy Dunn had a goal harshly ruled offside when a draw looked a likely result. Celtic's manager Willie Maley, the brother of Hibs' manager Alec was very impressed by Willie Harper, Jimmy Dunn, and Harry Ritchie. The Hibs team was: Willie Harper, Willie McGinnigle, Willie Dornan, Peter Kerr, Matha Paterson, Hugh Shaw, Harry Ritchie, Jimmy Dunn, Young, Halligan and 'Darkie' Walker. At Easter Road, however, Hibs Reserves beat Celtics Reserves 2-1 with the following team: J. Baillie, Bobby Templeton, Jim Cassidy, Johnny Cannon, Paddy Maxwell, Alex Strang, Jimmy Buchanan, John Gordon, Davy Anderson, Willie Miller and Callaghan.

Two days later, Hibs were playing in Little Ireland at 'the grass roots of Hibernian Football Club' in a benefit match for their nursery team Edinburgh Emmet, in recognition of them having supplied 'the Easter Road big boys' with superb goalkeeper Willie Harper. Edinburgh Emmet had been founded by Hibernian as a nursery team dating back to the 1880s and they were named after Robert Emmet, the famous, tragic Irish patriot. They played at Bathgate Park which was situated at the east end of the north back Canongate that is now Waverley station railway property. Bathgate Park was named after Bailie Bathgate, the Edinburgh Town councillor, who was fondly known as 'a good friend of the Irish of this city'. He had always taken a great interest in the welfare of the downtrodden Irish community in the Little Ireland ghetto and had been a great ally to Hibernian, particularly in their fight to retain their Easter Road home. Bathgate Park and Edinburgh Emmet were famous throughout Scottish junior football and were run by 'Hibs Daft' Paddy Kelly, a fishmonger from Little Ireland's St Mary's Street. Hibs fielded a strong team and won the match 0-2. Only 3,000 spectators could be safely crammed into Bathgate Park to see this 'Irish festival' but hundreds more got a view from the tenement windows and roofs. Hundreds of others got a more distant view from the 'Jews Gallery' up on Regent Road.

Hibs' first league match at Easter Road was on Saturday 27 August, with a

1-1 draw with St Mirren, the Irishmen's scorer being Harry Ritchie, in front of 14,000 spectators. Hibs' first league victory came two weeks later, with a 3-0 victory over Queen's Park. The green flag at Easter Road was lowered to half-mast, marking the death of Mick Dunbar, an old player from the 1880s.

On Saturday 10 September, Hibs and Hearts clashed at the Holy Ground in front of a crowd of 22,000. The Irishmen brought in reserve centre-forward Davy Anderson and he did the damage in a 2-1 victory. We are told, 'two green clad ladies were hugging and kissing when Hibs scored, is this a new football fad?'. Having played six games, the Hibs had five points and were lying in the middle of the league. Hearts were near the bottom with three points.

With there now being automatic relegation, this was foremost in the minds of clubs, outwith Celtic and Rangers, and this observation was made:

> ...sufficient time has elapsed to enable some of the effects of the new system of relegation in the league competition to be observed. Everywhere it is recognised that the play has been speeded up and the players are more intense ... The enhanced value of league points has imbued the players, prompted by officials with the nightmare of relegation looming ahead, with the conviction that nothing else matters.

There was a quick return league match against Celtic on Monday 19 September, 'The Edinburgh Autumn Holiday was the occasion for the Edinburgh Irishmen to play host to the undefeated Glasgow Irishmen and attempt to reverse their earlier defeat.' Manager Alec Maley moved centre-half Matha Paterson to centre-forward to add more weight and punch to the forward line and it paid off, with the Hibs captain opening the scoring, much to the delight of 18,000 supporters. Celtic, however, immediately replied with the truly remarkable goal from their truly remarkable inside-right Patsy 'The Mighty Atom' Gallagher. He simply waltzed through the whole Hibs team – and he was no speed merchant – and picked his spot behind an unprotected Willie Harper. For years later, Willie Harper would speak about this goal, which he could hardly credit. Hibs, however, 'dug in' and got the last laugh in the last minute of the game, with a winning goal from the head of 'Darkie' Walker. The Hibs team that pulled off the 'shock result that had the whole of Scotland talking' was: Willie Harper, Bobby Templeton, Willie Dornan, Peter Kerr, Hugh Shaw, Alex Strang, Harry Ritchie, Jimmy Dunn, Matha Paterson, Johnny Halligan and 'Darkie' Walker.

The catholic press, however, didn't see this as a shock result:

> ...in the Green Derby the all green Hibernians were not a shock or a surprise to us. Hibs strong, bustling, fearless game, their undoubted skill and their 'Leith Persevering' follow up were bound to cause trouble to Celtic. The unbreakable spirit of Hibernian asked no quarter and gave none.

It was at this time that the Irish War of Independence saw catholics in Belfast fall victim to Orange pogroms and Hibernian tried to organise a benefit game to help relieve family hardships, but even Celtic would not oblige for this worthy cause. Hibs, however, put in more 'Leith Persevering' and finally got an exciting Scottish Junior Select to play them at the Holy Ground in a hugely successful benefit. Hibs' controlling shareholders lived in Ireland and they saw to it that the money went to the most needy riot-torn Belfast families, their bread-winners having been expelled from their places of employment simply because they were catholics.

It was also at this time that Hibernian supplied five players for a benefit match in aid of the Hearts War Memorial Fund.

Over October, November and December, Hibs picked up a lot of league points. Harry Ritchie's form on the right-wing was brilliant and Newcastle United showed a lot of interest in him as he was selected to play for the Scottish League against the Irish League at Shawfield, Glasgow. This was a fine honour for 'Big Harry' and for Hibernian who had nurtured him under the manager Alec Maley and trainer Paddy Cannon. Harry Ritchie, however, almost lost out on his first international honour when he missed the train to Glasgow and had to persuade a taxi to take him there and he arrived at Shawfield two minutes before the kick-off.

Hibernian Football Club had very close associations, going back to 1887, with Hibernian Amateur Swimming and Humane Society and everyone at Easter Road was the swimmers' guests at their annual gala at Infirmary Street Baths.

Some incidents at Hibs league matches, during these three months are worth a mention. When Hibs pulled off a surprise 1-2 win over Aberdeen at Pittodrie there was an unusual and comical incident. A very well-dressed Aberdeen supporter sitting in the reserved seats in the stand was ordered to leave the ground by the famous referee Mr Dougray of Bellshill, as he took great exception to the rude remarks that were being shouted at him. A referee was again the centre of attention, this time at Easter Road when Hibs and Dundee drew one goal each; it was no laughing matter for Hibs, it was daylight robbery. Willie Harper was clearing with one of his mighty kicks which 'inoculated the Easter Road turf', when the ball rebounded off a Dundee player, almost pole-axing him and the ball sailed back well over the crossbar. The referee awarded the Irishmen a goal-kick but, after being badgered by the Dundee players who claimed a goal, the referee consulted a badly-positioned linesman who thought it was a goal. The weak referee then examined the goal net and found a hole in it 'that even a tennis ball could not get through' and he, incredibly, awarded Dundee their equaliser. The Hibs players were furious and the Hibs supporters were raging as they saw the ball go clearly over the bar but we are told 'perhaps they were not the most impartial of witnesses, to put it mildly.' This was particularly tough luck on Willie Harper, but another feature of his play at this time was his continuing knack for saving penalties.

Hibernian made many collections at the Holy Ground for the Edinburgh Lord Provost's Unemployment Fund for Rent Relief and in a football tournament for this worthy cause, Hibs disposed of Leith Athletic 7-0 in the semi-final. The final against Hearts would be played much later in the season. It is of interest to note that Leith Athletic had recently been reformed after going out of business during the war and they had now been admitted to the Western League for smaller junior-type clubs.

On Christmas Eve, Hibs picked up a good point against Rangers in a 0-0 draw at Easter Road. The only dark cloud was Matha Paterson picking up a serious injury, adding to a long list of injured Hibernians. A week later on New Year's Eve, again at Easter Road, Hibs again had to settle for one point in a 1-1 draw with Ayr United.

The Derby Day match against Hearts at Tynecastle, on Monday 2 January 1922, saw Hibs in a very weak situation with five first team regulars out through injury. So confident were Hearts of victory over the 'badly weakened Irishmen', they said 'if Hearts don't beat this Hibs team we'll give away our jerseys'. Well, as it turned out, Hearts had to buy a new set of strips as 'they worked at the collar against eleven very determined Irishmen and Hearts broke down under the strain.' Jimmy Buchanan and Jimmy Dunn gave Hibs a 0-2 victory 'to the delight of the raucous supporters of the green who were well represented in the 22,000 crowd.' The Green Jerseys were: Willie Harper, Bobby Templeton, Willie Dornan, Peter Kerr, Willie Miller, Alex Strang, Harry Ritchie, Jimmy Dunn, Jimmy Buchanan, Johnny Halligan and 'Darkie' Walker. Hibs now stood fifth in the league with 30 points.

Hibs' four other league matches in January saw them collect four points and during this month Alec Maley took his team on a couple of weekend breaks, first to Skelmorlie and then Wemyss Bay.

In the Scottish Cup first round on Saturday 28 January, Hibs were drawn at Easter Road against the team who put them out last season, Armadale. A crowd of 15,000 came along to the Holy Ground to see a still weakened and changed Hibs get revenge and this they did by three goals to nil, the counters coming from Jimmy Dunn, 'Darkie' Walker and Young. Revenge is sweet and it was put in verse.

> At Easter Road the green brigade,
> Put Armadale clean in the shade,
> The second half had just begun,

> There came a goal twas doubly 'Dunn',
> In bowling speech a first time chalker,
> Soon followed up by one from Walker,
> And then a cheer from every lung,
> When came the third and last from Young.

There was, however, to be no cup run and Hibs went out to Motherwell 3-2 at Fir Park in the next round. The rest of Hibs' league results were mixed and they wound up their league campaign at Easter Road on Saturday 29 April with a 6-0 victory over Clydebank. Manager Alec Maley had come to Hibs from Clydebank and the Bankies presented him with a silver tea service in recognition of all the good work he had done for them. Hibs ended up seventh in the league with 46 points.

Meantime Hearts' war memorial at Haymarket was unveiled on Sunday 9 April and everyone at Hibernian was there to pay their respects: directors, manager, trainers and playing-staff, and the traditional Hibs wreath in the form of the harp was laid at the memorial. The Irish families who were Hibs' chief shareholders made the trip from the strife-torn Emerald Isle to be there, in a show of Hibernian solidarity. Afterwards, the Hibs party retired to Hibernian's spiritual home, St Patrick's RC church in the Cowgate, for a war remembrance Holy Mass. Four days later, on Wednesday 12 April, Hibs were at neutral Tynecastle, defeating Falkirk 0-1 in the final of the Dunedin Cup, having disposed of Raith Rovers in the semi-final. On their way to Tynecastle that day, the Irishmen again laid a harp wreath at the Hearts war memorial. As a matter of interest, it was the first time Hibernian had ever won the Dunedin Cup.

Hibs went on to win all the other local cup competitions. After disposing of Hearts in the East of Scotland Shield semi-final, they beat St Bernard's 3-2 in the final. In the Wilson Cup final, Hibs were victorious over Hearts 2-4. In the Rosebery Cup final, Hibs disposed of Hearts 0-1 and then in the final, beat Leith Athletic 0-3. In the Edinburgh Lord Provost's Unemployment Fund for Rent Relief tournament final, Hibs disposed of Hearts 0-1. In all, Hibernian had played Hearts six times this season and the Irishmen had defeated them on every occasion and a sporting Hearts supporter paid tribute to Hibs in verse.

> It would be ill-disposed o' me
> Gin I laid doon my rhymin' pen
> Withoot a word o' praise to gie
> To Easter Road and Maley's men;
> Thou I ne'er look through glasses green,
> An' my pet colour be maroon,

A sportsman puir I'd be, I wean,
Gin I your merits didna' soun'.

See here's my han' to ane an' a'
Frae goal to centre-ilka line,
Oor minds gae back to Powderha',
The Powderha' o' auld langsyne.
An' though six times ye beat the Hearts,
I carena' though 'twere twice the same,
They simply socht their ain deserts,
Noo theirs the sulks and yours the fame.

An' mair than that, ye scooped the pool
O' a' the local trophies granted;
Ye met ilk team wi' judgement cool,
An' gied them mair than what they wanted.
Raith Rovers found ye far ower wide,
An' syne the Falkirk bairns ye routed;
Ye Leith Athletic brushed aside,
An noo your worth's nae longer doubted.

Ye've struggled weel, ye've struggled sair,
Ye've had your anxious times like ithers,
But ower it a' the secret's there,
Ye helped each ither on like brithers.
An' though the Flag ye didna' win,
Nor yet attained the Scottish Cup,
In this we gratefu' comfort fin',
Ye kept Auld Reekie's pecker up.

For a 'wee treat' the Hibs directors and manager took their playing squad on a coach trip, taking in St Margaret's Loch and Dumfries. The traditional way of running Hibs as a 'big happy family' still continued, as did their tradition of 'looking after their own', making a gift of £50 to Dan McMichael's widow.

The previously mentioned Bailie Bathgate had presented Michael Whelahan's Old Hibs Association with a silver cup to be played for annually in the furtherance of Michael's charity work for old players. It was first played for this close season between Ould Hibs and Auld Hearts at Hibernian Park. The Ould Hibs fielded a very interesting team which included internationalists Paddy Murray and John Kennedy, from Hibs' 1895 Scottish Cup final team. Hibernian also played several five-a-side competitions and won the Hearts tournament at Tynecastle.

The most best-remembered and popular attractions at Easter Road in the close season were top-class athletics meetings, which were the brainchild of manager Alec Maley. It must have given Hibs trainer/groundsman Paddy Cannon a lot of hard work laying out the park for field events and steeplechases with water jump obstacles. Among the many athletics heroes of the time to compete at the Easter Road competitions were E.D. Mountain, the Cambridge half-miler and Jack London, the coloured sprinter. The most fondly remembered and loved, however, was Edinburgh's own Eric Liddell of *Chariots of Fire* fame, an Olympic champion and minister of religion who was later to tragically die in China on missionary work.

As we end this chapter there were at Easter Road ten particularly outstanding players. The late Dan McMichael had signed five of them and building on Dan's foundations, Davy Gordon had signed the other five. They had still not been moulded together properly, in fact one was being developed by manager Alec Maley who saw him in a totally different position and he was in the reserves more than the first team. Alec Maley now had to sign just one player, a centre-forward, the final link that would produce one of the most celebrated and popular teams in the history of Hibernian Football Club. This team was not just popular or 'heroes', they were gods to the Hibs supporters. Strangely, as great an eleven as they were, with many international honours, they would never win a national competition.

– 3 –

THE CELEBRATED TEAM –
SCOTTISH CUP FINALISTS 1923 AND 1924

Harper, McGinnigle and Dornan,
On St Patrick's Day in the mornin',
Kerr, Miller and Shaw,
For the harp and Erin go Bragh.
Ritchie, Dunn and McColl,
Keep Hibernian on the ball,
Halligan and Walker,
Sweet as a Blarney talker.

Season 1922–1923 saw Hibs scrap their reserve team because of financial restrictions, a decision that would rebound on the Irishmen in later years. A strong 16-man squad was retained. Last season's injury to centre-half Matha Paterson had seen manager Alec Maley continue to develop one-time inside-left Willie Miller into a centre-half, a great example of Alec Maley's visionary coaching. The centre-forward position was, however, Alec Maley's biggest headache, trying out several players last season without the desired result. He now even bought Paddy Allen from Clyde, an experienced man, but he was now past his best. With four 'eager young bloods' in the forward line, Alec Maley saw Paddy Allen as 'steadying the line' but as one unnamed Hibs player, probably the joker Jimmy Dunn, later said, 'he damn near stopped us a' thegither'.

Paddy Allan made his debut as Hibs opened the season with a league match at the Holy Ground on Wednesday 16 August, defeating Falkirk 1-0, with a second-minute goal from Peter Kerr in front of 17,000 supporters. The Green Jerseys were: Willie Harper, Willie McGinnigle, Willie Dornan, Peter Kerr, Willie Miller, Hugh Shaw, Harry Ritchie, Jimmy Dunn, Paddy Allen, Johnny Halligan and 'Darkie Walker'.

Hibs' next three league matches were also victories, with Jimmy Buchanan replacing Paddy Allen at centre-forward. In the East of Scotland Shield semi-final, the Irishmen disposed of Leith Athletic 4-0 and in the final drew 1-1 with Hearts; the final replay would have to wait until the end of the season. Hibs were also back in Little Ireland, playing a friendly with Edinburgh Emmet, with the Easter Road men winning 0-1 with a lot of trialists in their team.

Hibs were at the top of the league with eight points before they were hit with two defeats, one being a 0-3 reverse against St Mirren at Easter Road, in which Harry Ritchie missed two penalties, but Harry would get away with anything so loved was he by his Hibs supporters.

On the Edinburgh holiday, Monday 18 September at the Holy Ground, Hibernian defeated champions Celtic 1-0 with a goal in the last minute from Jimmy Dunn, in front of a crowd of 18,000. The following Saturday at Tynecastle, in front of a crowd of 30,000, Hibs took a 2-2 draw with a late equaliser from Harry Ritchie. The Irishmen were top of the league with 11 points from eight games. A week later, against Kilmarnock at Easter Road, a 1-1 draw was fought out, with Harry Ritchie again scoring a late equaliser for the Irishmen.

Hibernian had largely avoided injuries and were able to field almost the same side since the start of the season, except for the centre-forward position. Paddy Allen, Jimmy Buchanan, Jimmy Young and Davy Duncan had all been given their chance, without convincing manager Alec Maley. It was now that the Hibernian manager acted to solve the problem, bringing in the final link in his celebrated team. Alec Maley's target was ex-Celtic Jimmy McColl who was now with Partick Thistle. Although Hamilton Accies had put in a higher bid than Hibs, and Celtic had also tried to entice Jimmy McColl back to Parkhead, Jimmy insisted he only wanted to sign for the Edinburgh Irishmen and he did so on Wednesday 4 October. Hibs paid a big fee to get Jimmy McColl – we are told it was, 'more than the cost of the rest of the team put together'. Hibs supporters, while recognising the goal-scoring prowess of Jimmy McColl, thought he was now 'getting on a wee bit' but his signing was to be an Alec Maley master-stroke.

So one of the most entertaining and celebrated teams in the history of Hibernian Football club was now complete. These 11 players would always be Alec Maley's first choice without any question, only injuries would prevent Alec Maley from showing his utter loyalty, devotion and confidence in these 11 Hibernians, of whom we are told 'more than half of them were true Hibernians being of Irish stock'.

Goalkeeper *Willie Harper* came from Winchburgh, born in January 1897, and he first played juvenile football with Winchburgh Violet. Following his father and brother, he worked as a blacksmith in Winchburgh Oil Works. Moving up to junior football, he played for Broxburn St Andrews, who had connections with Hibernian and as early as before the First World War, Hibernian director Barney Lester had already noted the name of the 6-foot, 12-stone goalkeeper. At the outbreak of the war, 17-year-old Willie Harper enlisted in the Scots Guards and was their heavyweight boxing champion and he actually knocked out Joe Beckett, the British heavyweight boxing champion of the time. Later in the war, Willie served with the Royal Flying Corps as a leading aircraftsman. After the war he returned to his blacksmith trade and played in Winchburgh junior football before the 'Hibs network' fixed him up with the Irishmen's junior nursery team, Edinburgh Emmet, who were known as the 'pride o' the Canongate' by everyone in Little Ireland. Edinburgh Emmet played at Bathgate Park, off the Canongate, and Willie was paid 10/- a week by the junior club for about seven or eight games before Barney Lester, who was still a Hibernian director and fancied himself as an amateur scout, brought glowing reports to Easter Road of his fantastic new 'discovery'. His fellow directors, John Farmer and Owen Brannigan, had heard it all before from Barney Lester, but this time he had hit the jackpot and Hibs manager Davy Gordon signed Willie Harper in August 1920. Willie became a Hibernian legend and a regular Scottish internationalist and was never on a losing side against England. Strangely for such a big man, Willie's only apparent weakness was his tendency to fist out cross-balls, perhaps echoes of his boxing days in the army. Big Willie was not a showy goalkeeper but, as we shall see later, he was to create a sensation with a goalkeeper's 'new dress fashion'. Willie was a great goal-stopper with hands like shovels, massive clearances and an expert penalty saver, 'Willie Harper fills the goal well. A big strapping chap, he has wonderful agility for his height and weight and all sorts of shots come alike to him'. The Hibs team would sometimes be described as 'Harper and ten others' which was a wee bit unfair to his ten other great team-mates.

Right-back *Willie McGinnigle* was signed by Dan McMichael in August 1918 from junior club Cambuslang and he was a stocky, compact defender who tackled like a demon. Willie's full-back play was also away ahead of its time, an early version of John Brownlie and Danny McGrain. In the days when full-backs were judged on the distance they could clear the ball upfield, Willie McGinnigle would run with the ball and was skilled at setting up attacks. Willie's play was a revelation and he would gain international honours.

Left-back *Willie Dornan* was also signed by Dan McMichael in August 1918 from Leith Athletic. As a 15-year-old, he played with Pumpherston Violet before moving to the Hibs-connected Broxburn St Andrews. Willie was recommended to Easter Road but Leith Athletic stepped in first, before Dan McMichael swooped to sign him. Willie Dornan was a quiet but tough superb full-back with great positional play, clever, neat and effective without being dashing. He did, however, have a fine turn of speed and was famous for hitting wingers with his renowned 'scissor tackles'. Willie Dornan rarely came out second-best in a clash.

Right-half *Peter Kerr* was another Dan McMichael signing away back in November 1910 from Wemyss Athletic. Peter came from the Musselburgh/Prestonpans area and was born in 1891. He had also played for Prestonpans and Wallyford Bluebell before Easter Road received the tip-off from their long-standing friends in the Tranent lodge of the Irish National Foresters. Peter Kerr played in Hibs' 1914 Scottish Cup final team and, as we shall see, Peter was to appear in two other Hibs' Scottish Cup final teams, the only Easter Road player to date to appear in three separate Scottish Cup finals. The First World War interrupted Peter's Hibs career but when he returned from the trenches he staked his place in the Hibernian Hall of Fame. Peter's rock-solid dependability saw him described as 'the best uncapped half back in Scotland'. He was to develop a formidable triangle with the right side of the forward line of this celebrated team.

Centre-half *Willie Miller* was again another Dan McMichael signing in August 1916, from junior club Cambuslang. Originally a goal-scoring inside-left, before Dan McMichael started to develop Willie in the half-back line and Alec Maley finished the process by patiently coaching him into a superb centre-half. On the face of it, this seems a most unlikely recipe for success but Willie Miller rose magnificently to the challenge. This unlikely centre-half was known at the Holy Ground as 'The Holy Ghost' because of his uncanny knack of seeming to appear from nowhere at the most crucial times to coolly clear danger in the Hibs goalmouth. Willie Miller was so cool, even in the most hectic of situations, that his team-mates and Hibs supporters would almost die of fright as he casually cleared in the last split second. Tall, with a pale complexion and fair hair, which was always in place no matter how tough the match, added to his nickname 'The Holy Ghost'. Willie Miller was the son of a director of Partick Thistle.

Left-half *Hugh Shaw* was yet another great Dan McMichael signing, bringing Hugh from Clydebank Juniors in August 1918. He had a massive physique and woebetide any opposition who took unfair advantage of his lighter team-mates, but Hugh's real strength was the calm and skilful way he could switch play in an instant. A powerful player of great presence, Hugh Shaw would later be the manager of Hibernian during the magnificent Famous Five era.

Right-winger *Henry McGill Ritchie*. Harry Ritchie was signed by Davy Gordon from Perth Violet in April 1919. Harry was born in Kirkcudbright in October 1898, brought up in Scone and grew to be a 6-foot 13-stone strapping

Hibernian right-winger, Scotland's original 'Yogi'. Harry served in the Royal Navy during World War One and shortly after his demob he came to Easter Road. A naturally left-footed player, he was equally good with the right and it was on the right wing he made his mark. Harry was so idolised by the Easter Road support he could get away with anything. What a sight he was, thundering down the wing in unstoppable fashion, 'Jeysus here comes big Harry, sumbiddy open the bliddy gates'. His speciality on the right wing was to suddenly switch the ball to his left foot and cut in with a slashing shot at goal. Another speciality was his pin-point crosses. For all his height and weight Harry was not just a 'mow 'em down player', he was a class act, and the only criticism being 'Big Harry mibby lacked a wee bit o' the divil'. Without doubt, Harry was on that not so long list of most dearly loved Hibs players ever to grace the Holy Ground. I personally remember as a young lad walking out of the Holy Ground in the late 50s with my much-loved late father, when he bumped into an old Easter Road pal, Paddy 'Kipper Baldy' Flannigan, who he hadn't seen for over 30 years and they greeted each other by simultaneously shouting 'Harry Ritchie'. Harry Ritchie went on to gain international honours.

Inside-right *Jimmy Dunn*, with the nicknames 'Tim' or 'Ginger', was a junior internationalist with St Anthony FC when Davy Gordon signed him in August 1920 for the princely fee of £20, the bargain of the century. Jimmy was only 5 foot 6 inches in height – what we would describe today with political correctness as 'diminutive'. On his arrival at Easter Road, however, in the 1920s he was described as 'a red-haired Irish leprechaun wi' a heid like a fifty shillin' kail post'. Yes, wee Jimmy was the most unlikely-looking super-hero, but super-hero he certainly was, 'wee "Tim" Dunn was a Hibs player of glorious fashion, an artist and prolific goal scorer.' Jimmy Dunn would gain many international honours and, as we shall see, he became not only a legend of Hibernian Football Club but a Scottish international legend when as a Hibs player, he was one of the unforgettable Wembley Wizards.

Centre-forward *Jimmy McColl*, as we have just seen, was signed by Alec Maley in October 1922 from Partick Thistle. Like Jimmy Dunn, Jimmy McColl also started his career with junior club St Anthony FC before being signed by Celtic and it was Jimmy McColl who did most of the damage to Hibs in the replay of the 1914 Scottish Cup final. Later, Jimmy went to England to play for Stoke but he could not settle there and he returned to Scotland to sign for Partick Thistle, many thinking just to finish his football career. Alec Maley thought otherwise, as did the Hibs directors John Farmer, Owen Brannigan and Barney Lester, who clearly remembered Jimmy McColl from the 1914 Scottish Cup final. It was, of course, thought that Jimmy McColl might just be 'past it', but Alec Maley was convinced that he was 'just the man for Easter Road', so the 'cash-strapped stony-faced Irish directors of Hibernian made every penny available to get Jimmy McColl from Partick Thistle.' Jimmy McColl was to be a prolific goal scorer for Hibernian for the next nine years, showing everyone he was not 'past it'. In later years, Jimmy would team up with Hugh Shaw again, to be the head trainer at Easter Road during the Famous Five era.

Inside-left *Johnny Halligan* was signed by Davy Gordon in November 1920 from Shawfield Juniors. 'Hally' was the Hibernian playmaker with 'a superb command of the ball nobody could "kill", control and pass the ball like Johnny Halligan, he was the perfect foil for Jimmy Dunn.' Johnny Halligan, however, was no prima donna and he was a tremendous fetch and carry work-horse, always putting in a power of work. Strangely for such a fine ball player, his trade mark was his perfectly timed 'sliding tackles'. In later years, Johnny Halligan would become Hibs manager.

Outside-left *John Walker* was signed by Davy Gordon, also in November 1920, from junior club Kirkintilloch Rob Roy. John Walker's nickname was 'Darkie' because of his dark swarthy skin and jet-black hair. He was the only player in this celebrated Hibs team to be referred to constantly by his nickname. In fact it came to pass that Hibs supporters forgot his name was John. He was very much a left-sided player, 'yon "Darkie" Walker kid oanly uses his richt fit fur standin' oan'. He had, however, a great turn of speed and was the scorer of many vital goals. 'Darkie' Walker was like Harry Ritchie in the true tradition of great Hibs wingers.

Manager *Alec Maley* coached and moulded together this great Hibernian team. Alec was a member of a famous footballing family. Two of his brothers, Tom and Willie, played for Hibernian in the 1880s and Tom had been a reserve in the victorious Hibs Scottish Cup final team in February 1887. Tom and Willie later played for Celtic and became legends on the park and in the boardroom. Willie was now manager of Celtic. The Maley family name had been anglicised from O'Maley by their father, who was a regular soldier. Only one of the family, a brother Charles who was a priest, retained the original name O'Maley. Hibs manager Alec Maley had wide managerial experience on both sides of the border and had been manager of Clyde in their 1912 Scottish Cup final. When Hibs appointed Alec Maley as manager in April 1921, the family connection with Celtic was well known, but Alec was quick to point out that Tom and Willie were both ex-Hibs players and had been Hibs supporters long before Celtic had ever even been thought about and as for himself: 'I've been a Hibs supporter all my days'. The late Dan McMichael used to call his Hibs players 'ma laddies'; Alec Maley called them 'ma family'.

It is of interest to note that old-time supporters tell us that it was Alec

THE CELEBRATED TEAM

Maley's celebrated team that really popularised Hibernian's nickname Hibees. The 'ould Irish support' had used 'Hibees' for countless years but it was lost among a plethora of other nicknames: the Hibs, the Bhoys and the Leithers, only to mention a few. The press still preferred to refer to Hibernian as the Irishmen or the Hibs but for the supporters, Hibees was now here to stay. Hibees was a romanticised version of Hibs (Hi-bs) and we are told it meant 'the colour of the grass', but one suspects that is lost in the mists of Edinburgh-Irish folklore.

It was at this time that a Hibs season-ticket holder took up an official position with Hibernian as club doctor. He is another of these dedicated long-serving but long-forgotten servants of the Hibees. He was an Irishman and served Hibs for 40 years and as he takes up his duties in 1922, it is well worth recording a little about him: his name was Dr St John Cogan.

Dr St John Cogan

Dr St John Cogan was born in Cork, Ireland in the early 1880s and as a young man he gained international rugby honours for Ireland. In 1908 he arrived in Edinburgh to continue his medical studies and in 1910 graduated from the Royal College of Physicians and the Royal College of Surgeons in Edinburgh. He was also a graduate of the Royal Faculty of Physicians and Surgeons in Glasgow. Having fallen in love with Edinburgh and the Hibees, where he was a season-ticket holder, the Irish doctor decided to work here. Dr St John Cogan was highly qualified but his vocation in medicine was to work as a humble general practitioner among the working-class of Leith and he opened his practice first at Links Place and then Duke Street.

The First World War saw him volunteer for service and not only did he tend wounded Commonwealth Soldiers on the battlefield of Salonica but also in the Turkish concentration camps. After his horrific war experiences he returned to his practice in Leith and continued his love affair with Hibs as a season-ticket holder. Always a great sports enthusiast, Dr St John Cogan was appointed the Medical Officer of Health for amateur and professional boxing in Leith and Edinburgh. Professional boxing was in its heyday and he had the pleasure and honour of looking after greats such as Tansy Lee and Alex Ireland, both of whom happened to be 'Hibs Daft'.

Now in 1922, the Irish doctor was appointed the official Hibernian physician, described by himself as 'an extremely great honour'. For the next 40 years, Dr St John Cogan tended the celebrated team of the 20s, the struggling teams of the 30s, the war-team of the 40s and the magnificent championship teams of the Famous Five era. During that era, not only was the Irish doctor looking after Smith, Johnstone, Reilly, Turnbull and Ormond and all their great teammates, who picked up many serious injuries, he was also tending a full Hibernian playing staff of 75. Yes, 75 – such was Hibernians prominence in these days. By the mid 1950s, Dr St John Cogan was in his early 70s when carrying out his expert work for Hibernian and he was still a general practitioner for the people of Leith. A tremendous work-load for a man of his age. A member of the Famous Five remembered him fondly:

> Aye, auld 'Doc' Cogan, wi did'nae half keep him busy but only an extreme emergency kept him fi missing a Hibs game, home or away. He loved Hibs dances and functions wi' his wife and a big glass o' good malt whisky and him an' his wife would regularly hiv players doun ti their hoose at Hermitage Place in Leith for dinner and drinks. Aye, auld 'Doc' Cogan and his missus were a lovely auld pair; great Hibees ye ken.

In closing this short reminiscence of Dr St John Cogan, it is of interest to note that Leith-born Tom O'Malley, OBE, the present-day chairman of Hibernian, was brought into the world by the Irish doctor, as was fellow Leither, John Gibson, the famous 'Hibs Daft' journalist of the *Edinburgh Evening News*.

Due to injuries, Alec Maley could not field his first choice team for four months and players such as Matha Paterson, George Murray, Paddy Allan, Paddy Moore, Davy Duncan, Bobby Templeton and Jimmy Buchanan all made appearances. The last-named player was at centre forward when Hibs defeated Celtic 1-0 with a Jimmy Dunn goal, on Monday 18 September.

The Scottish League played the Irish League at Celtic Park on Wednesday 18 October, with Hibernians Willie Harper, Harry Ritchie and Jimmy Dunn all playing in the Dark Blue and Peter Kerr was a reserve. We are told 'everyone from a proud Easter Road was at the game'.

On Saturday 21 October against Raith Rovers at the Holy Ground, Jimmy McColl recorded his first goal for Hibernian in a 2-0 victory in front of 10,000 supporters. We are told: 'McColl's first goal for the Irishmen received the appropriate recognition from the Easter Road crowd.' Perhaps this rather polite description reflected the fact that 'the wild Irishmen of Easter Road' were now not as wild as they used to be. The sacrifices made by Hibs under-class support in the First World War made them feel more accepted as part of society and less like outsiders. Certainly, the big Irish section of the Hibs support had this perception.

When Hibs' goalkeeper Willie Harper ran out on to the Holy Ground on Saturday 9 December, he caused a sensation throughout Scottish football. The harmless reason was that he wore a bright yellow jersey instead of every goalie's usual black, grey or brown. We are told: 'Willie Harper was transformed from a sparrow into a canary.' This fashion, however, was soon to catch on with every club. The Irishmen defeated Hamilton Accies 2-0 that day, with goals from Jimmy Dunn and Jimmy McColl.

Also in December, plans for Hibs new stand were awaiting the approval of the Edinburgh Dean of Guild Court. Of course, as in the past, anything the Irishmen wanted to improve met with obstruction and it would be another year and a half before things got moving. The name of the late great Hibernian genius, 'Darling' Willie Groves, appeared once again at this time, when Hibs showed an interest in his teenage nephew Paddy McGrogan, a pupil at Holy Cross Academy, Leith. Willie Groves in his heyday could sprint 100 yards in 10.4 seconds, young McGrogan was also fast, but not that fast, unfortunately Hibs' interest came to nothing.

As the year 1922 came to an end the country's post-war economic depression was biting hard and unemployment was rife. The New Year's Day derby game with Hearts at Easter Road on Monday 1 January saw Hibs organise with the St Vincent de Paul Society, a catholic charitable organisation, a very successful collection to aid poor relief of all denominations. The Irishmen picked the right day for the collection with 28,000 in the Holy Ground. We are told:

> It was a wise move by the Hibernian club to open the gates shortly after 10 o'clock. Even at that hour the crowd entered the ground and as the hour for the start approached the roads leading to Easter Road were practically impassable. A special force of mounted police, however, kept the crowd in some semblance of order.

The Hibees were below form that day and missed a lot of chances when Hearts took the lead in the second half. Stung into action Johnny Halligan immediately equalised and later 'Darkie' Walker the chief culprit of the earlier missed chances hit the winner to send the big noisy Hibs support away happy. The Green Jerseys were: Willie Harper, Willie McGinnigle, Willie Dornan, Peter Kerr, Willie Miller, Geordie Murray, Harry Ritchie, Jimmy Dunn, Jimmy McColl, Johnny Halligan and 'Darkie' Walker.

Due to continued injuries, there was one face missing from Alec Maley's first choice team and this was to continue a little longer, much to the manager's annoyance, as the Scottish Cup ties were fast approaching and he was determined to make a concerted effort to lift the 'greatest prize in Scottish football'. Hibs certainly had the players capable of doing it and, just like the late Dan McMichael in 1914, it became an obsession with the ambitious Alec Maley and his directors John Farmer, Owen Brannigan and Barney Lester. Once again, Scottish Cup success took the dimension of a 'mission', a 'mission of redemption' to restore Hibs' proud but lost status of being 'the premier club of the Irish of Scotland'.

Alec Maley could not field his first choice 11 in the first two rounds of the Scottish Cup but at least they were not difficult ties. In the first round, the Irishmen were drawn away to Clackmannan but Hibs made them a financial offer to play the tie at Easter Road. On Saturday 13 January, 9,000 were in the Holy Ground to see the Hibees win 4-0, with two goals from Jimmy McColl and one each from Johnny Halligan and Harry Ritchie.

In the second round at Easter Road, on Saturday 27 January, the opposition was Peebles Rovers and a 14,000 crowd saw a disappointing 0-0 draw. Hibs did not play well, to put it mildly, but it could have been worse for the Irishmen, considering that day Bo'ness disposed of Hearts and Ayr United saw off Rangers. For the replay, Peebles Rovers accepted Hibs' financial offer for it to be played at the Holy Ground and on Tuesday 30 January, 9,000 saw Hibs win 3-0 with goals from Harry Ritchie, Jimmy McColl and Willie Miller. So Hibs were through to the next round draw of the Scottish Cup and Hearts' humiliating exit at the hands of Bo'ness was remembered in verse:

That the draw is no sae piquant,
A' among us will confess,
Since puir auld Herts sair wir sickened
By the lads o' black Bo'ness.

In the third round of the Scottish Cup, the Hibees got a home draw against Queen's Park, known as the Spiders, who were still 'the oldest and most respected club in Scotland because of their magnificent past achievements in the Scottish Cup.' With Edinburgh's two other clubs Hearts and St Bernard's out of the cup, only the Irishmen represented the capital as they continued their 'mission' to bring the cup to Easter Road.

In preparation for this big game, Alec Maley took his players to Gullane for 'golf and the sea breezes'. Paddy Cannon, Hibs' long-serving 67-year-old trainer/groundsman, was left at Easter Road to make sure the Holy Ground was in perfect condition as always. His son Tommy was now a trainer and he, with another long-serving trainer, Di Christopher, were with the players 'to tone them up with massage sessions and light training'.

This third round Scottish Cup tie came off at Easter Road on Saturday 10 February and, for the first time, the Irishmen were able to field their celebrated team: Willie Harper, Willie McGinnigle, Willie Dornan, Peter Kerr (captain), Willie Miller, Hugh Shaw, Harry Ritchie, Jimmy Dunn, Jimmy McColl, Johnny Halligan and 'Darkie' Walker. There were 22,000 singing Hibs supporters in the Holy Ground that day as the legend of this great team was born with a 2-0 victory, the goals coming from Jimmy Dunn and Jimmy McColl.

There was still a long way to go for Hibernian to accomplish their 'mission' and in league games Alec Maley 'rested some of his superstars'. In the case of Willie Harper and Harry Ritchie, they could not play in one league match as they were on international duty when the Scottish League played the English League, on Saturday 17 February at St James Park, Newcastle. Willie Harper had played 86 consecutive games for Hibs before this interruption. It was Harry Ritchie's 23rd birthday when he turned out for the Scottish League that day and although he did not have an inspired game, Newcastle United were very keen to sign him as they had been in the past, but Big Harry had no intention of leaving Easter Road and Hibs had no intention of selling him.

The Irishmen were back at Gullane to prepare for their quarter-final tie in the Scottish Cup which was a real tough one against 'the granite men o' Aberdeen', but again the Hibees had a home draw. On Saturday 24 February, Hibs were able to field their celebrated team and 28,000 'green clad madmen' went delirious when 'in the first minute Jimmy Dunn brought the house down with an unsaveable goal high in the net after a cross from "Darkie" Walker.' It was a really tough cup-tie and it was not until the 84th minute that Harry Ritchie made sure of victory with one of his 'specials', to put the Hibees safe and sure into the semi-finals. With regard to the 'green clad madmen' observation it must be recorded that Hibs boasted a very large number of female enthusiasts, we are told at this time: 'No football club in Scotland has such numerous faithful supporters of the fair sex than Hibernian.'

The following Saturday, Aberdeen were back at Easter Road, this time on league business and the Irishmen again dumped them 2-0, with goals from Johnny Halligan and Harry Ritchie. Willie Harper was unable to play that day as he was on international duty for Scotland against Ireland in Belfast.

The Scottish Cup semi-final draw was between Hibernian, Third Lanark, Motherwell and, of course, Celtic. We are told: 'The Irish clubs of Edinburgh and Glasgow avoided each other in the draw and Hibernian will face the strong going, plucky Third Lanark at neutral Tynecastle. All the Hibernian ties have been in Edinburgh.' Hibs went back to Gullane to prepare for this crucial match.

> The gallant Hibs for battle keen,
> Will thereby find their mate;
> And they wha trounced the Aberdeen,
> Will come frae Gullane tig and clean
> Wi' little fear o' fate;
> Wi' every sort o' staunch support,
> Their optimism's great.

Alec Maley was optimistic in an interview which started with him giving a short history of the Hibs and his vision of the proposed new stand and complete upgrading of the Holy Ground. He recalled his days as a referee and how he officiated at the benefit match at Easter Road in September 1901 for Hibs' long-serving internationalist Paddy Murray. Alec Maley also rattled off name after name of all the great Hibs players he had watched as a spectator at Hibernian Park and he confirmed now, as Hibs manager, that his squad were just as enthusiastic as the 'ould brigade'. He went on to comment about the 'Hibs happy family' which was legendary throughout Scottish football.

> The one outstanding feature of the Hibernians that has always appealed to me was the wonderful comradeship which always existed between directors, manager, trainers and players. There always seemed to be a bond of good fellowship between them all. Old players coming in after years of absence from the game were always received in a spirit that betokened respect, affection, aye, and sometimes awe. Their names had been handed down from team to team and it seemed as if the younger men felt that it was 'up to them' to uphold the old traditions. Hibernian have always had a hard uphill fight, but who can deny that they have fought boldly against almost overwhelming odds. Hibernian have made themselves respected in Scottish football on and off the field and if the fates be kind Hibernian will have at least a sporting chance of overcoming Third Lanark in the semi-final and may yet win the Scottish Cup. You can be sure the play of The Bhoys will honour Hibernian in their "mission" to bring the cup into its own again.
>
> Come Maley's men ye bravely ken
> Hibs pride is in you noo;
> On you our fondest hopes depen'
> Sae to yoursel's be true noo.

Hibernian and Third Lanark played out their Scottish Cup semi-final at Tynecastle on Saturday 10 March, as 30,000 Hibs supporters turned Gorgie Road green. The celebrated team again filled the green jerseys and Jimmy Dunn, the smallest man on the park, headed home the only goal of the game after 15 minutes, to give Hibs a hard-fought victory. 'Both teams played grand cup-tie football but the Volunteers could not break down the Irish defence in which Willie Harper played his part. The Hibernian forwards were smarter than the very able Third Lanark attack and the Irishmen won narrowly but deservedly.' So Alec Maley's celebrated Hibernian team were in the final of the Scottish Cup.

Over the next two weeks, Harry Ritchie gained his first full Scottish international cap when he joined Willie Harper in the Scottish team that played Wales at Love Street, Paisley. Also at this time in Scottish international trials, Willie McGinnigle and Peter Kerr played for the Home Scots against the Anglo-Scots.

THE CELEBRATED TEAM

Having got these international interruptions out of the way, Hibs prepared at Gullane for the Hampden final of the Scottish Cup. Alec Maley and his celebrated Hibernian team were only 90 minutes away from accomplishing their 'mission' to start the re-establishment of Hibernian as 'the premier football club of the Irish of Scotland'. But fate decreed, just as it had done in the 1914 cup final, that Hibs opponents were the 'Mighty Celtic' who had claimed this title for themselves through having appeared in 15 previous cup finals and having won nine of them. The Hibees had only contested four previous cup finals, winning two, although one of these victories was over Celtic in 1902.

As when Hibs and Celtic previously met twice in the final, this 1923 final was again billed as the 'all Irish Scottish Cup Final' with other embellishments such as the 'all green final', the 'all Irish affair' and 'the 'Irish pair make a popular fancy'.

> Pompous the boast
> Yet the truth it speaks
> When Hibernian meets Celtic at Athens (Hampden)
> Greek meets Greek.

We are further told: 'In a Green Final it hardly matters which side wins, the great thing is the two great Irish teams have conquered all opposition and stand face to face for the closing tussle.' It did, however, matter very much to Hibernian who just had to regain their lost status.

The Hibs support were in a ferment and special trains from Musselburgh, Leith Central, Waverley Station and Caledonian (Princes Street) Station carried 13,000 of them to Glasgow. The notorious 'brake clubs', an early version of supporters' buses, carried thousands more, we are told, 'from Edinburgh, Leith, East Central Scotland and The Borders'. It is almost forgotten today just how widespread and popular these 'notorious Hibernian brake clubs' were. Drunkenness and violence surrounded these clubs with the carrying of Hibs banners, Irish banners and socialist banners and an assortment of fearsome weapons. Male Hibs supporters in the brake would have razor blades concealed in the peak of their pulled-down bunnets while 'the ladies' could do a lot of damage with a screwtop concealed in their handbags. In Glasgow the situation was even worse. Anyway, between the trains, the brake clubs and Hibs' Glasgow-Irish sympathisers it was estimated that there were 30,000 Hibs supporters among the 80,000 crowd on 'the classic slopes of Hampden'. The police, however, were clamping down on supporters, especially from the brake clubs, and it took away much of the colourful spectacle from the terraces. We are told:

Owners and drivers of vehicles who allowed passengers to carry flags, banners etc must be prepared to give the names and addresses of all passengers whom they carry. Passengers who carry flags, banners, rattles, bugles, whistles or other noisy instruments into the football field will incur the danger of police proceedings.

Hibs manager Alec Maley and his brother Willie Maley, manager of Celtic, both agreed on one thing, 'The final shall be played in a most sportsmanlike manner'. The Celtic team were an experienced class act and were at the top of their form after an indifferent start to the season but Alec Maley was confident 'my Hibernian bhoys' would carry the day. Alec Maley was able to field his full-strength celebrated team, a younger team than Celtic, and it was packed with talent, class, inventiveness and toughness. He felt his half-back line would be the difference in Hibs securing a victory or else the only other difference would be luck or a mistake.

> We don't know which we like the most,
> The dashing runs of Harry,
> Or 'Darkie' with his man on toast;
> Or Harper's brilliant parry.
> Our faith is in McColl – again
>
> We can't decide if we prefer,
> McGinnigle or Dornan,
> And some go wild on Peter Kerr,
> Or Hughie if his form's in.
> For Shaw's a giant on his day,
> And be the pace a killer
> There's one who's studied in his play,
> You can't whack Willie Miller.
>
> 'Tis all for one and one for all,
> A happy band of brothers,
> Who play the game and stand or fall,
> All helping one another.
> This is the secret of success,
> A team without a shirker,
> A good tip for the Cup I guess
> For every man's a worker.

On Saturday 31 March, 'Hibernian the refreshed Irish giant' clashed with 'Celtic the giants progeny' in the final of the Scottish Cup at Hampden. It was not a classic final but Hibs had the best of the first half, with Harry Ritchie coming closest to scoring. In the second half, the Edinburgh Irishmen were still looking good before Celtic started to exert pressure, when a cross fell in the Hibs goalmouth, bobbling between two defenders as Willie Harper hesitated and Celtic's Cassidy pounced to head the only goal of the game. So it was just a mistake that separated the two teams. Later, a shot from 'Darkie' Walker had the Hibs support roaring 'goal', but it hit the side net. Almost on time Jimmy McColl fired in a fine shot and it was stopped by the hand of Cringan, the Celtic centre-half, but, you've just guessed it, the referee waved play on as the Hibs players appealed in vain for a penalty. So the Hibernian 'mission' to re-establish themselves as 'the premier football club of the Irish of Scotland' had failed again, just as it had in the 1914 final. It was all very disappointing for all the 'Hibernian family', especially for Alec Maley and his celebrated team, but 'the defeat was taken in true Hibernian sporting fashion' in a game that 'was contested in an admirable spirit from start to finish'. We are further told: 'The Hibernians made a desperate bid for the equaliser and went down fighting gloriously in one of the cleanest and most creditable finals on record.' A verse of the times shows the good spirit that existed between Hibernian and Celtic:

> I went to see last Saturday
> The Battle of the Greens,
> On the world renowned enclosure
> That's the glory of the Queen's.
> There was very little in it,
> It was quite an even fight,
> Till a head gave the victory
> To the Celtic Green and White.
>
> So here's three cheers for Celtic
> And three more for the Hibs,
> They couldn't share the trophy,
> But they shared the glittering dibs.
> The Cup is on the sideboard
> Of the Glasgow club which means
> That the losers were the greener
> In the Battle of the Greens.

Two days later, it was a deflated Hibernian who travelled to Kirkcaldy and drew two goals each with Raith Rovers, the Greens goals coming from Harry Ritchie and a Jimmy Dunn equaliser. An injured Willie Dornan was replaced at full-back by veteran Bobby Templeton.

One week after the final, on Saturday 7 April, Alec Maley was able to field his first choice team at the Holy Ground in a 1-0 match against 'the mighty Rangers who were well on their way to being this seasons champions'. The talented Hibs were desperate to redeem themselves in the eyes of their supporters and this they did with 'a magnificent 2-0 victory forcing Rangers to put their championship celebrations on hold'. We are told it was a real surprise result and the goals from Hugh Shaw and Jimmy McColl had the 16,000 Hibs supporters singing at the top of their voices once again. All was quickly forgiven of this talented Hibs team of 11 individual stars.

A week later, Willie Harper was in goal for Scotland against England at Hampden. In the league Hibs finally finished eighth, having played 38 games with 41 points. In the local cup competition, Hibs won the East of Scotland Shield final, defeating Hearts 1-2 at Tynecastle at the end of April. The building of the new stand, and redevelopment of the whole of the Holy Ground, we are told, would not proceed for another year.

For season 1923–1924 Alec Maley still had all his celebrated team and his useful squad, as a whole, was still the same. Hibs directors John Farmer, Owen Brannigan and Barney Lester were applauded for refusing many big offers for their great players, especially goalkeeper Willie Harper. These players could have earned a lot more money elsewhere but we are told, 'no one wanted to leave the happy family at Easter Road'. Others, while complimenting the Hibees on retaining their team, reasoned it was only because 'the players know when and where they are well off'. It was, however, agreed that 'of the two Edinburgh clubs Hibernian and Hearts, the Irishmen are doing most to maintain the prestige of football in the capital'. There was some criticism in the press that 'a man of enterprise and ambition like Alec Maley should be content to leave the side as it were'. This criticism was unjustified but what was justified was Hibs being criticised by their supporters for not running a reserve team. A lot of finances had been set aside for the new stand but the false economy of not running a reserve team would in a few years time rebound on the Hibs. Meantime, Alec Maley planned another 'mission' to win the Scottish Cup.

By the time Hibs started training at the end of July, chairman John Farmer achieved a long-held ambition of the Irishmen: he had managed to negotiate the purchase of Hibernian Park from the Trinity Hospital Committee of Edinburgh Corporation. This was wonderful news for Hibernian Football Club and John Farmer's plans for the new stand and redevelopment of the Holy Ground; echoes of what his grandson Sir Tom Farmer, CBE KSG is doing for Hibernian today. The vision of John Farmer's countless years of hard, unpaid work was now about to pay off. Unfortunately, all his efforts had taken their toll on his health and tragically, as we shall soon see, he would not live to see the fruits of his labour.

After a successful sports and five-a-side tournament at Easter Road, Hibs opened their season on Wednesday with an East of Scotland Shield semi-final at Logie Green, the home of St Bernard's, and after surprisingly going two goals behind, a replay was forced, with goals from Jimmy Dunn and 'Darkie' Walker.

Three days later, the Irishmen travelled to Cathkin Park for their first league game and dumped Third Lanark 1-4. Harry Ritchie gave the Hibees a goal lead at half-time and Jimmy McColl scored a magnificent second-half hat trick.

As usual, Hibs were on charity business and on Tuesday 21 August they invited Celtic through to Easter Road to play a benefit in aid of St Ninian's RC Church Extension Fund. The Hibees won by a single Johnny Halligan goal and the fund benefited by a handsome £100. St Ninian's, which is still thriving today, is in the ancient parish of Restalrig which bordered Hibernian Park and the Church had been built by parish priest Monsignor Miley, a brilliant and 'Hibs Daft' priest who had been born in the Cowgate, the centre of the Little Ireland ghetto. In our story later we shall hear more of Monsignor Miley and his close association with Hibernian Football Club and his close friendship with Harry Swan, who became Hibs' chairman in the 1930s.

The following day, and more charity business when Hibs travelled out to Winchburgh and played a benefit against Winchburgh Thistle to aid their funds. Winchburgh Thistle was one of Willie Harper's early junior clubs.

After disposing of St Bernard's 5-1 at Easter Road in the replay of the East of Scotland Shield semi-final, Hibs drew 1-1 with Hearts at Tynecastle in the final, the replay of which was held over till the end of the season.

Hibs had not done too well in their league matches, and on Saturday 8 September, they again drew 1-1 with Hearts in their Easter Road encounter. The following week in the league at Broomfield, it was another 1-1 draw, this time with Airdrie who were a real class act at this time and were sitting at the top of the league. Airdrie would loom large in Hibs' story this season.

By the time Hibs played Rangers on Saturday 20 October, the Ibrox club were table-toppers, with Airdrie lying second. There was a crowd of 22,000 for Rangers' visit to the Holy Ground and Hibs made what many thought was an unwise decision to choose this match to take a collection for the Convent of the Good Shepherd, Colinton, Edinburgh. But there was always a big crowd and not too many Rangers supporters showed face at Easter Road in these days. Some nuns were involved in the collection and Hibs took no chances by ensuring there was a strong body of Hibee supporters, 'the angels with broken noses', to stand guard close by them in case there was any unpleasantness from 'the orange tin hats'. The Hibs also laid on the Broxburn Roman Catholic Band to play selections at the match. An injured Willie Harper should never have played and Hibs lost 1-3. Willie's injured leg muscles were to keep him out of the team for a while. A stop-gap goalkeeper, Mason, was signed from St Bernard's – but he had a poor match.

Three days later, five Hibs players; Willie McGinnigle, Peter Kerr, Hugh Shaw, Harry Ritchie and Johnny Halligan, played in a select in a benefit for The Samaritan Hospital for Women, Glasgow. The five players received gold watches as mementos.

On Wednesday 31 October, Hibs long-serving captain Peter Kerr and Harry Ritchie played for the Scottish League against the Irish League at Belfast. Willie Gowdie, who played for the Irish League, would in later years be signed by Hibernian.

Hibs had only 11 fit players as injuries took their toll on Alec Maley's small squad of players but this didn't stop him from transferring long-serving Matha Paterson to St Bernard's. Matha Paterson was a great 16-year servant of Hibernian and had been captain for many years including the 1914 Scottish Cup Final. Even allowing for the injuries, four Hibernians played in a select team in a benefit for the Edinburgh Poor Fund. With Willie Harper's continuing injury problem, Alec Maley signed yet another goalkeeper, Hughes, from Celtic and he did Hibs proud. Considering the partial changes in the team, Hibs did reasonably well in the league up to the end of 1923.

The New Year's Day derby match, on Tuesday 1 January 1924, only attracted 14,000 to Tynecastle and it looked like Hearts had won by a single goal until the last kick of the ball when 'the never-say-die Irishmen' scored through 'the Wee Magician' Jimmy Dunn, to share the points with the 'Gorgie men'. Injury problems had prevented Alec Maley fielding his full celebrated team for some time and there were three changes that New Year's Day. The fighting Hibs team was: Willie Harper, Willie McGinnigle, Bobby Templeton, Peter Kerr, Willie Miller, Geordie Murray, Harry Ritchie, Jimmy Dunn, Jimmy McColl, Davy Duncan and 'Darkie' Walker. Hibs had played 22 league games and were placed 13th with 20 points – disappointing, but things were to improve.

In the Hibees' next four league games they picked up seven out of eight points, which was good form for the run-up to the Scottish Cup campaign, which was to be another 'mission' by the celebrated team as they tried to restore Hibernian as 'the premier football club of the Irish of Scotland'. The obsession of Alec Maley and his directors to restore Hibs' lost status was as strong as ever and there was no doubt his team were 'bonnie cup fighters'. This cup campaign was to push Alec Maley's men to the limits of their determination, toughness and skill. Alec Maley also had a 'wee ace' up his sleeve, a squad player called Geordie Murray, who was more than just useful when called upon.

Hibernian had been instrumental and inspirational in the founding of Dundee Hibs in 1909. The club from the Jute City had, after a long struggle, gained admission to the Second Division. Hibernian had to insist with the football authorities that the Dundee Club would have to change its name and they now operated under the name Dundee United, the great club we all know today. This change had only just happened and, by coincidence, they were drawn against Hibernian at Easter Road on Saturday 26 January in the first round of the Scottish Cup. The Hibs made heavy weather of defeating them 1-0 with a Harry Ritchie 'special', in front of a crowd of 18,000. This great Hibernian team had, of course, built up quite a reputation for themselves and other clubs always raised their game against them.

It was going to be a very tough cup 'mission' and Hibs made even heavier weather of the second round when, on Saturday 9 February in front of 10,000 at Easter Road, Alloa took a 1-1 draw after Hibs had led at half-time with a Geordie Murray goal. Three days later, however, in the replay, the Hibees redeemed themselves with a 0-5 victory, the goals coming from the famous forward line of Ritchie, Dunn, McColl, Halligan and Walker.

Meantime, Hibs won all their league games and Willie Harper played for Scotland against Wales at Cardiff, when in the third round of the Scottish Cup the Edinburgh Irishmen landed the plumb tie against table-toppers Rangers at Ibrox. With all their league success, Rangers had not won the Scottish Cup since 1903, something that really rankled with them, so they were on their own 'mission'. Before a ball was kicked, Hibs were completely written off against this superb Rangers team but we are told 'it is a dangerous thing to forget the cup fighting qualities and skill of Hibernian and even if the tie is to be played at "the temple of hate" we are sure the Edinburgh Irishmen will keep the green flag flying high.'

Hibs 'crack centre-forward' Jimmy McColl was out through injury and this could have spelt disaster for the Irishmen but Alec Maley pulled off a tactical master-stroke and surprised everyone by playing reserve half-back Geordie Murray at centre, with instructions to run non-stop at the Rangers defence. It was a calculated gamble that was to pay off handsomely. A crowd of 54,000 packed Ibrox on Saturday 23 February.

It was a classic Scottish Cup tie between two talented teams with their reputations at stake and, although Hibs found themselves down by a goal at half-time, they were playing magnificently, but it is goals that count. Alec Maley gave the Green Jerseys 'a wee pep talk' at the interval about tradition, pride and attitude and reminded them, 'wur a better team than that blue lot'.

It paid off for, early in the second half, 'Darkie' Walker equalised after Geordie Murray caused panic in the Rangers defence. The tie was now wide open and very hard but Hibs continued to play a 'sweet game'. The Hibees defence stood up to everything Rangers threw at them with Willie Harper, as always, playing his part. Left-back Willie Dornan also played his part when, in a goalmouth scramble while lying on his back, he grasped the ball between his knees before clearing the danger. The forwards were fast and tricky and Harry Ritchie was causing Rangers havoc on the right wing when, with only seven minutes to go, after one of his 'thunderous runs' he squared the ball to stand-in centre Geordie Murray who rapped in the winner, sending the 15,000 Hibs supporters wild with delight. We are told: 'Of all the exploits of this great Hibs team this was their finest moment.' An old timer tells us:

> Hibs, since my earliest recollections of them, have always struck me as the personification of dash. The famous All-Greens have borne a noble part in the making of Scottish football history. They have had pattern-weaving wonder-workers such as Groves, McMahon and Blessington of old and Ritchie, Dunn and Halligan of today. The recognised and traditional Hibs game is of the breezy, buoyant, quick-darting and sturdily aggressive type summed up in the word dash. Good old Hibs.

Rangers supporters took this cup exit very badly; the least offensive and stupid thing they could say was: 'We didnae want the Scottish Cup oanywie, it was made in Dublin.' This great Scottish football event was turned into a 'religious war' by Rangers hooligans, or rather cowards, who violently turned on any isolated Hibs supporter. We are told:

> Scandalous misbehaviour of the notorious Blue supporters...disgraceful scenes at the sensational cup-tie with Hibernian...attacks directed brutally by bands of self-styled Rangers supporters against lone Hibs supporters wearing green rosettes, split heads were bandaged under the grandstand...Hideous uproars were disgustingly ferocious and the epithets with an Orange Party implication were horribly obscene...A young Hibs supporter standing on his own cheered when Murray scored the winner. He was seized and punched, thrown down and kicked and finally flung headlong down the steep terracing to lie bleeding and bruised at the rails. This was bad enough. What followed was, in a way, more offensive. Some Good Samaritan Rangers supporters went to the young lads aid only to be greeted with the Orange hooligans shouting at them 'take him to Carfin'. You only hear from these bullies when they are in an overwhelming majority...The place for these bullies is the nearest police cell but why are they allowed to commit such acts with so many police present both in uniform and plain clothes. It begs the question where are the police?

Anyway, Hibernian were through to the next round of the Scottish Cup, 'their "mission" was alive and as green an ever'. The Hibees' moment of triumph, however, turned to tragedy when four days later their long-serving chairman John Farmer died.

In Memoriam – John Farmer

Leither John Farmer was a born and bred Hibs supporter. As a member of the St Mary Star of the Sea (Stella Maris) Catholic Young Men's Society, Leith, he was, in his late teens, a Hibernian committee member in the late 1880s with his brother Philip. John and Philip were leading lights of Hibernian's resuscitation in the early L890s, so John Farmer's official connection to Hibernian spanned 36 years as a committee member, director, shareholder, president and chairman. He was also on the Scottish League Management Committee for many years. In private life he was married to Mary Kavanagh, had a son, and was a Leith wine and spirit merchant. With Hibernian Football Club being a proprietary concern, John Farmer took over the chairmanship of the club in 1909 when his brother Philip retired. John was a tireless, unpaid servant of Hibernian all his life and it had taken its toll on his health for a long time and for the past month he had been confined to his bed, tended by Hibernian's Dr St John Cogan. Now, at the early age of 54, John had died on Wednesday 27 February 1924, fortified by the Rites of Holy Mother Church in his home at 39 Hermitage Park, Leith. This was just a stone's throw from the Holy Ground where, by coincidence, Hibs had played a league match earlier that day, defeating Kilmarnock 3-1. Of this great Hibernian servant we are told: 'John Farmer was one of the most familiar figures in Edinburgh football circles and an enthusiastic follower and worker of Hibernian all his days. Although one of these traditionally stony-faced Irish directors of Easter Road he was a man of genial personality.' We are further told of John Farmer in this affectionate tribute:

Possessed of a quiet, pawky humour, John Farmer was a man of retiring disposition; he did not push himself forward in any way, but he always took the warmest interest in the affairs of Hibernian and Scottish football generally, and with his knowledge of the game, and natural shrewdness, his advice was always treated with the utmost respect by his colleagues. His death, which was not unexpected, will cause a dampner at Easter Road in Hibernians great period of triumph in the Scottish Cup and when the club are on the eve of launching out on their big scheme of ground reconstruction which was a vision of John Farmer's. It would have been a great delight to him to have been at the head of the club in the event of Scottish Cup success, and the new Easter Road scheme was a matter very dear to his heart. John Farmer will be greatly missed by manager Alec Maley and his old Irish co-directors Owen Brannigan and Barney Lester. The old Irish brigade are gradually dwindling away.

After his requiem mass at St Mary Star of the Sea RC Church, Constitution Street, Leith, on Sunday 2 March, which was attended by Hibernians old and new and representatives of Scottish football, John Farmer was laid to rest in Seafield cemetery.

> Will you forget John Farmer
> When the Hibees fight is done?
> Will you forget John Farmer
> In defeat or victory won?
> Will you forget John Farmer
> And his Hibernian pride?
> Will you forget John Farmer
> Now that he has died?
> Will you forget John Farmer?

John Farmer is the grandfather of Sir Tom Farmer, CBE KSG, the saviour and principal shareholder of today's Hibernian Football Club.

It was expected that John Farmer's son would now become a director but he, with admirable honesty, felt he could not do the job justice, and as we will see it would be Hibs' manager, Alec Maley, who would be appointed to the board.

At the beginning of March, Willie Harper and Peter Kerr played for Scotland against Ireland at Celtic Park. In the quarter-finals of the Scottish Cup the Hibees were drawn against Partick Thistle at Easter Road. The Jags were a class act in these days, with internationalists in their team, and as Hibs' 'mission' continued this tie was to become a match marathon. The green flag at Easter Road had been flying at half-mast for over a week in respect for John Farmer and when Hibs and Partick Thistle met on Saturday 8 March, a minute's silence was observed. There were 20,000 in the Holy Ground to give 'Rangers' Conquerors' an ecstatic welcome but Partick hadn't read the script and at half-time were leading 0-2 although Hibs' play had been superior. It took another Alec Maley 'pep talk' at the interval to do the trick and a replay was forced with goals from Geordie Murray and Jimmy Dunn. We are told: 'It was a case of the old horse and the hard road for the seasoned Hibernians refusing to "get the wind up" because they were two goals down. Their recovery was a masterly thing in a way. It brought out the best in a clever team and carried hope for the replay in Glasgow.' By the way, Hearts were dumped out of the cup by Falkirk that day.

Four days later at Firhill, the mid-week replay attracted a crowd of 40,000, many of whom were Hibs' 'old Glasgow-Irish supporters'. A great crowd and a great game, with 'Darkie' Walker giving the Edinburgh Irishmen an early lead but Partick Thistle, who were the last Glasgow club left in the Scottish Cup, got a second-half equaliser when it looked as if Hibs were going to win the game. Thirty minutes' extra time was played with no more scoring. We are

THE CELEBRATED TEAM

told: 'Brilliant work marked the second meeting of Hibs and Partick Thistle. Jimmy Dunn has brains, a real football genius, he kept the green flag flying nobly.'

The second replay came off at neutral Celtic Park on Tuesday 18 March. With the extra games and mid-week travelling to Glasgow, it was biting hard on the unemployed Hibs supporters' dole money, but there was still a 27,000 crowd. We are told: 'Hibs had a very big support from Edinburgh and Celtic Park was hardly a neutral venue for the Edinburgh Irishmen it was more like a home tie with so many of Hibs Glasgow-Irish support in attendance.' Hibs took a grip of the game immediately and goals from the 'sheer genius' of Jimmy Dunn gave them a 0-2 lead at half-time. Partick tried to come back but the Hibees were in command and, although an unfortunate own goal glanced off Willie McGinnigle's head gave the Jags some hope, there was no way back for them and the celebrated Hibs team, which was fully represented, marched into the semi-finals of the Scottish Cup. These three games with Partick Thistle had been very hard but played 'in the best sportsmanlike fashion' and we are told that 'Hibernian are a team of class and determination straight out of the school of all the Easter Road cup fighting greats.'

When the team arrived back at Caledonian Station/Princes Street, Edinburgh, 1,000 Hibs supporters were waiting to greet them with old favourite songs – 'God Save Ireland' and 'The Green Flag' – ringing round the station followed by the chant, 'well done Dunn'. The crowd broke through strong police lines and carried the players shoulder-high. But someone was missing, the two-goal hero Jimmy Dunn, 'where's Dunn went up the shout'. Joker Jimmy had expected there to be a boisterous welcoming party so, without expressing his misgivings to the rest of the team, he had sneaked off the train at Merchiston Halt, Gorgie. A laughing Jimmy said later, 'well ye see am jist a wee guy an' a didnae fancy gitin' thrown aboot the shoudders a' the big navvies; an' oanywie a thought it wud be nice to strut through Gorgie like the cock o' the walk an' let that lot see a real conquering hero.' Jimmy Dunn was the most unlikely-looking hero but be always lived up to his reputation of being a joker.

The long Scottish Cup 'mission' of Hibernian Football Club became even more gruelling when they were drawn against Aberdeen in the semi-final: it was to take another three games to settle the tie. On Saturday 22 March at neutral Dens Park, 'the Edinburgh Greens and the Black and Gold of Aberdeen (their jerseys were black and gold stripes in these days) fought out a no-scoring draw in a hardy dour struggle that was played in the best of spirits in front of a crowd of 20,000.'

Four days later, again at neutral Dens Park, it was the same story and even 30 minutes' extra time did not produce a goal. We are told: 'It was gratifying to see such a clever footballing team as Hibs "digging in" when required against such robust opposition.'

This really was a gruelling time for the players and, besides all the cup matches, they had been playing league games and several of the players had also been involved in Scottish international trials and fixtures. A 'well-deserved wee break away from it all' was quickly organised by Alec Maley and the directors, in conjunction with the Irish families who were Hibs principal shareholders and who still lived in Ireland. Dublin was the destination and a big Hibs party of 30 including some wives, had a calm ferry crossing and on the evening of Friday 28 March they had dinner with Dublin Bohemians FC and played them in a friendly at Dalymount Park the following day. "Sixteen thousand Dubliners availed themselves of the opportunity to see the "homecoming" of the famous Edinburgh Hibernians one of Scotland's top football clubs which has such close associations with the Emerald Isle.' The Hibs won 1-2, with goals from Jimmy McColl and a brilliant Johnny Halligan solo effort. The whole Hibs team put on an 'exhibition' but Jimmy Dunn was the star, pulling out every trick he knew. That evening, the Dublin Bohemians laid on an 'Irish ball' for the Hibees, who danced the night away.

It was an enjoyable and welcome break in Dublin, for Hibs were soon back on league business before they had to face Aberdeen for the third time at Dens Park, in the second replay of the Scottish Cup semi-final on Wednesday 9 April. 'It was a match of the most crucial importance' to the Edinburgh Irishmen. Both Hibs and Aberdeen had agreed to play the match at neutral Tynecastle where the 35,000/40,000 crowd was guaranteed but the SFA knocked this back and as 'the dole money could only stretch so far' there was only a crowd of 12,000 at Dens Park. Again it was a hard, entertaining game with both teams 'opening up a bit which favoured Hibernian' but Willie Harper still had to pull off some fine saves, one of which 'showed Harper to be the best goalkeeper in Scotland'. The Hibees put Aberdeen under a lot of pressure which mounted as the match got older, 'in 85 minutes Dunn's shot hit the upright with great force. It was a first time effort and easily the best shot of the match.' Then, two minutes later, 'Harry Ritchie went on an unstoppable run down the right wing and the Aberdeen goalkeeper could not hold his thunderbolt shot leaving "Darkie" Walker to ram home the winning goal.'

Hibernian had reached the Scottish Cup final for the second consecutive year. It was a great achievement by a great team, with all the 'ould Irish fighting spirit of the Easter Road club'. To reach this final, Hibs had played no less than ten games and played no less than 16 hours of football. The Hibees were now only 90 minutes away from accomplishing their 'mission'.

The train carrying the victorious Hibs team back to Edinburgh was this

THE CELEBRATED TEAM

time destined for Waverley Station and it was thronged with ecstatic singing Hibs supporters to 'welcome the bhoys home'. They were, however, to be disappointed as Alec Maley wisely ordered the team off the train at Haymarket, straight into taxis.

Hibs opponents in the final were Airdrie, a highly talented team who were only to be pipped by Rangers for the league championship this season. By coincidence, three days after defeating Aberdeen, the Hibees played Airdrie in league match at the Holy Ground in a 'final rehearsal'. Hibs were badly weakened by the fact that Willie Harper was playing for Scotland that day against England, in the first match between the two countries to be played at Wembley. Right-half Peter Kerr played in goal for Hibs and there were other changes in the team but 12,000 saw the Hibees win easily 2-0, with goals from Jimmy McColl and 'Darkie' Walker. Neither Hibs, nor Airdrie took much account of the result – a Scottish Cup final was a different proposition.

With regard to that first ever Wembley international against the Auld Enemy which ended in a 1-1 draw, it is interesting how some players from 'unfashionable' clubs filled the Scottish jerseys in these days. There was, of course, Willie Harper from Hibernian in goal, both the full-backs played for Ayr United, the centre-half was from Raith Rovers and the left-half was provided by Partick Thistle.

This Ibrox Scottish Cup final was the last time for over 70 years that Hampden would not be the venue. The Airdrie team 'were in the midst of a Golden Age'. This season they were to have three internationalists in their ranks who were soon to be joined by another four. A team with seven international-class players, and they were second only to Rangers in the league championship – in other words they were a 'class act'. Two of their players were to become Scottish football legends, Hughie Gallagher and Bob McPhail.

Hibs, however, were tipped as slight favourites, for they too were a 'class act' with their own two legends of Scottish football, Willie Harper and Jimmy Dunn. Manager Alec Maley created a wee bit of Scottish football history by fielding his same celebrated 11 for successive cup finals: Harper, McGinnigle, Dornan, Kerr, Miller, Shaw, Ritchie, Dunn, McColl, Halligan and Walker. A lot of emotion was involved in Alec Maley's decision to give his celebrated favourites another crack at the Scottish Cup final, they certainly deserved it. But Jimmy Dunn and Willie Dornan both had aggravated ongoing ankle injuries and, as it turned out, should not have played.

A crowd of 60,000 packed out Ibrox on Saturday 19 April and we are told: 'Green was everywhere there must have been at least 40,000 favouring the Edinburgh Irishmen. Rosettes, balloons, streamers and hats of every description were seen and they were all the one colour – green.' Perhaps these

Hibees had a premonition of another disappointment for we are told ,'the Hibernian supporters were confident "we can do it this time" but it was a quiet confidence and their singing was not as loud as we know it can be.' In only two minutes, Russell of Airdrie headed the Lanarkshire team into the lead. The Hibees kept their composure and played a 'scientific combined game' but soon Willie Dornan's injury saw him limping. There was worse to come because the injury to the 'wee Magician' soon saw him break down and Hibs' potential match winner was consigned to the wing as a passenger, with Harry Ritchie forced to go to the inside-right position. We are told: 'When Hibs lost Jimmy Dunn, Hibs lost the cup.' Ten minutes before half-time, Russell headed his and Airdrie's second goal.

Another Alec Maley 'pep talk' at the interval saw Hibs go 'full tilt' at Airdrie and, early in the second half, Johnny Halligan was right in on goal when he was blatantly chopped down. The referee had no choice but to award Hibs a penalty and as Johnny Halligan received treatment, Harry Ritchie placed the ball on the spot. Suddenly the referee seemed to dither, ran over to a linesman, and incredibly changed his mind and awarded Airdrie a goal kick. Even the Airdrie players and supporters were stunned. What was disquieting from a Hibs point of view was that all three match officials were from Lanarkshire, Airdrie's home county. This had been the disgraceful decision of the SFA and was a fierce bone of contention, both before and after the final. Hibs played on manfully and Harry Ritchie was the Greens' most dangerous forward bringing out several great saves from the Airdrie custodian and one 'special' slid past the post, when it looked like going in. No sour grapes, Airdrie were worthy winners of the Scottish Cup for the first, and, to date, only time in their history. It is of interest to note that Hibernian's right-half and captain, Peter Kerr, had made his third appearance in three separate Scottish Cup finals: 1914, 1923 and 1924, the only Hibs player to date to have ever done this.

It was bitterly disappointing for Hibernian to have once again failed in their 'mission' at the final hurdle, especially after such a long, hard, heroic cup run that season.

Hibs finished seventh in a league of 20 and before the season was over the Hibees were victorious over Hearts in both the East of Scotland Shield final and the Rosebery Cup final. Although Hibs had their setbacks over the last few seasons we are told: 'Hibernian have kept the Edinburgh football flag flying which should be welcomed by all the capital's football followers.'

It is of interest to record that at this time in Edinburgh, on Saturday 24 May 1924, arguably the greatest ever Hibernian player was born: his name was Gordon Smith.

At the end of May Alec Maley took Hibernian on a tour of Austria and

Germany. It was very successful and Hibs kicked off with a superb 1-3 victory over Rapide Vienna. Other matches were played in Austria and in Germany the Hibees played in Munich, Dresden and Cologne, where they played a British Army XI.

We are told there were 'incidents galore' on the tour – here are a few of them.

> On one journey the kit hamper was lost and Hibs turned out in weird and wonderful garb. Willie Harper was reported to have been arrayed in a violet jersey and yellow shorts. What was no joke was the fact that the whole team had to wear purchased boots and play on a ground so sun-drenched that an Austrian official kindly suggested that substitutes would be allowed if any player collapsed from sun stroke. Though the Hibees avoided that calamity there were plenty of 'sair feet' when the game was over. On a overnight train journey a player in the top sleeping berth found a handle protruding from the roof and found it very handy for levering himself in and out of the berth. He did this three or four times and each time the train screeched to a halt causing an unholy row, he had unknowingly been pulling the communications cord. In one game the referee wanted to try the old continental habit of changing the regulation ball to smaller lighter ball at half time. Hibs captain Peter Kerr was too canny for that. 'Na, Na', said Peters, 'Ja, Ja', expostulated the referee. 'Na, Na', replied Peter, 'ba' ower sma' ' (in his best German) but the referee gathered what he meant and the regulation ball was used.

After the tour Alec Maley was appointed to the board of directors, joining Barney Lester and Owen Brannigan who was now chairman.

In the close season, elderly Michael Whelahan was still very active in Hibs' affairs and with his Old Hibs Association he put together a great team of 'Ould Hibees'. A charity match between Ould Hibs and Auld Hearts on Saturday 5 July came off in Little Ireland at Bathgate Park, the home of Hibernian nursery team, the junior cracks Edinburgh Emmet. The Bailie Bathgate Cup was at stake and the Auld Hibs were victors 4-1. Among the Hibee veterans were ex-manager Davy Gordon, ex-internationalist Paddy Murray, Paddy Kennedy, Paddy O'Brien, John Meaney and John Morton, who scored all four goals. The 2,000 crowd reserved a special welcome for ex-internationalist Paddy Callaghan, a 20-year Hibernian servant.

So this chapter ends with Alec Maley's celebrated team having reached two successive Scottish Cup finals, but the long-held dream of restoring the Hibees' lost status as the 'premier football club of the Irish of Scotland' was as far away as ever. The complete modernised reconstruction of the Holy Ground with a large, impressive new stand was progressing throughout the summer, and it was time for the celebrated team to make a concerted effort at the league championship.

– 4 –

GREATER EASTER ROAD
1924–1925

The Hibs rin oot a skeely team
The colour o' the grass,
Herts dander in a seely team
And ridder nor the roan.

Hibernian, Hibernian, the colour o' the grass,
Hibernian, Hibernian, the wearin' o' the green,
Hibernian, Hibernian, the first to wear the green.
The Hibs, the Hibs, the cabbage and ribs,
The Holy Ground, the Holy Ground, with forty shades of green,
Easter Road, Easter Road, the green flag is seen.
Hibees, Hibees, o' the emerald class,
Hibernian, Hibernian, the colour o' the grass.

The Hibs rin oot a skeely team
The colour o' the grass,
Herts dander in a seely team
and ridder nor the roan.

The complete reconstruction of the Holy Ground continued throughout the summer of 1924, with the old wooden stand on the east side being swept away and a new 5,000-seater steel structured stand being built on the west side stretching the whole length of the pitch. That stand is still there at Easter Road today.

The resiting of this super new stand gave Hibernian the space also to expand the standing room. We are told:

There will be a new stand to seat 5,000 and high embankments surrounding the rest of the pitch with standing room for 45,000. Access to this greater Easter Road will be made through 25 new entrance gates situated at both the north (Leith Irish Barracks end) and the south (Edinburgh's Little Ireland end). A stone boundary wall will surround the pitch. Greater Easter Road will soon be in apple pie order. A tremendously big job is the reconstruction scheme and a huge sum of money in excess of £25,000 is being expended. When the embankments are terraced the transformation will be complete and the ambition of the Irishmen deserves the warmest congratulations.

From greater Easter Road the views of Fair Edina, the Queen of the North, the Modern Athens, were breathtakingly spectacular with Arthur's Seat, the architecture of Calton Hill and the skyline of the Old Town there for all to see.

> Fling open Easter Road's high casement
> And see Edinburgh lie
> On shining slopes of verdant hills
> Brushed by a pearl-strewn sky.
> Her Emerald domes and pinnacles
> Her chanting turquoise spires
> Clean with eternal lustre, blaze with immortal flame.

A year previously Portobello Power Station had been opened, with its giant chimney becoming another landmark seen from greater Easter Road.

> Near half the height o' Arthur's Seat
> There rises from the sea
> From Portobello's golden sand
> The mightiest chimney in the land
> A shaft resplendent, God-like, grand
> As from antiquity
> And lo, at our ecstatic feet
> Lie sea and city spread,
> The Castle and the Port o' Leith
> And the grey sky overhead.

Portobello was Edinburgh's popular holiday resort in these days, attracting huge crowds from all over Scotland. There was a beautiful large beach with donkey rides and rowing boats. Portobello's pride and joy was its pier stretching no less than 1,250 feet into the Forth. It was the very first of its kind in Scotland with restaurant, tea rooms, camera obscura and a magnificent concert hall which featured the best variety acts of the time, including Portobello-born Sir Harry Lauder. There were also sightseeing ferry trips on the Forth from the pier. Later, the popular open air swimming pool was opened on the promenade, supplementings the indoor one. Today nearly everything has been swept away, as Portobello as a holiday resort went into a swift decline.

> At Portobello the soft glow
> Of Azure tide expands,

For there the waves of ocean flow
On its smooth shelving sands.

My song,
My shanty east-coast town,
East resort
Of the terminally out of season.

From greater Easter Road there were, of course, also spectacular views of the Port of Leith and the river Forth where 'deathless Hibernian memories roll on to an ageless sea' with the ten islands of the Forth 'like an emerald island rosary'.

A couldna bide in Gorgie,
There's nothin' there I care,
Gie mi Hibs and Easter Road
And guid ould Leith sae fair.
For the spell o' Leith holds mi
Always longing ti be there,
An' I'd give the world for the Port o' Leith
An' a breath o' it's fresh salt air.

I digress; back to the reconstruction of greater Easter Road and the work being done to reduce 'the Easter Road slope' which is today still held in great affection by Hibs supporters. The slope of the pitch was more vicious in these days and we are told.

The levelling of the pitch is an extra burden on the Irishmen and a serious one. It is going to be a huge undertaking in itself to reduce the slope. It is an extraordinary state of affairs that the south end is 6 feet higher than the north end, the highest point being at the Norton Park school side corner. The average gradient is one foot in 58 feet. It seems hardly credible that there should be such a difference in the levels. But it is a fact nevertheless. No wonder Hibs are always so dangerous when playing downhill in the second half. It is little wonder that the Irishmen are always so keen to win the toss and they always seem to do so with the Hibs captain always calling harps (instead of heads) so that they can choose to 'kick up the hill' in the first half leaving visiting teams to 'kick up hell' at their misfortune.

This was and still is all part of 'the romance of Hibernian Football Club and their 'Holy Ground'. Another part of the romantic feelings of Hibs supporters in these days was that parts of the demolished old wooden stand and its palings were carried off by them to build little enclosures and 'shrines' at the graves of deceased family members. This 'act of devotion' was particularly carried out at the Eastern Cemetery beside Hibernian Park, Rosebank Cemetery and Mount Vernon Catholic Cemetery. Also even after all these years, you can still find back green fences made from the old Hibs stand at the tenements in Easter Road, Albion Road, Albion Terrace and Albion Place.

For this very ambitious creation of a greater Easter Road, the Hibs tried to attract investors in the club as they had done previously in 1905 when they became a limited liability company. At that time no individuals or businesses outside the Irish community of Edinburgh and Leith took the slightest bit of interest in becoming involved with 'an Irish organisation'. It was now hoped, particularly after the sacrifices the Irish of Edinburgh and Leith had made in the First World War, that a more mature attitude would prevail among native Scots business people, just as it had among Hibs working under-class support which was now a very big Irish/Scots melting pot. Hibernian issued a prospectus open to all. Amid some unhelpful and hostile sniping in the press, 'for a present day football club Hibernian is a very Irish, very closed and very private concern'.

The Hibernian Football Club
Limited
(Incorporated Under the Companies Acts 1862 to 1900)
Capital £2000
Divided into 2000 Shares of £1 Each
Issue of £20,000 6 Per Cent Debentures.
Directors
Owen Brannigan, 13, Jeffrey Street, Edinburgh.
Bernard Lester, 50, Albion Road, Leith, Edinburgh.
Alexander S Maley, 62, Brunstane Road, Joppa, Edinburgh.
Secretary
Alexander S Maley, Easter Road Park, Edinburgh.

The company has recently concluded negotiations with the Governors of Trinity Hospital, Edinburgh, for the purchase of the ground, which has been tenanted by the company since its inception. In order to meet the demand of the public, and to thoroughly secure their comfort and safety, the Directors have resolved to erect a new Grand Stand, with suitable offices and accommodation for the proper conduct of the Company's business, and to make extensive alterations and improvements on the Ground. On the completion of the proposed scheme it is estimated that the Ground and Stand will comfortably hold not less then 50,000 people.

To meet the cost, the Directors have resolved to issue Debentures of £50 each, bearing interest at the rate of 6 per cent per annum, to the amount of £20,000. In addition to the said interest, the Company undertake in each year to provide each person, whose name appears in the register as a holder of a Debenture or Debentures, with a season ticket admitting the holder to the Ground and a specially numbered seat in the new Grand Stand, at a charge of £1 10 shillings (inclusive of entertainment tax).

THE MAKING OF HIBERNIAN 3

The above is only an extract from the prospectus that this time did bring a response from businessmen outside the Irish community. One was a Hibs supporter, some said a most unlikely Hibs supporter, but his name was to find its place in Hibernian's Hall of Fame: Harry Swan. We shall, of course, hear more of Harry Swan later in this book. Meantime, Harry Swan was just another Hibs supporter who had shown his faith in Hibernian Football Club as a Debenture holder. The major investment was still left to 'Hibs Irish directors and Irish supporters who were better-off.' We are further told 'it has once again been left to the Irish families who still reside in the Emerald Isle to be the principal financial backers of Hibernian Football Club who are still very much in Irish hands. But the breakthrough which the Irish dearly wanted had been made, as illustrated by Harry Swan's involvement, albeit minor at this time.

A builders' and joiners' strike delayed the opening of greater Easter Road and Edinburgh Corporation, who were the landlords of Tynecastle Park, forced Hearts to allow the Hibees to use the Gorgie ground for their home matches in August.

Before Hearts had played at Tynecastle Park they had played across the road from it at a place called the 'Stibble Park'. But for many years now they had been at Tynecastle Park, which was built on the site of an old sand pit. Unlike greater Easter Road, which afforded beautiful panoramic views of the City of Edinburgh and Port of Leith, Tynecastle Park was hemmed in by industrial and municipal buildings and tenements with no views whatsoever and not one endearing feature. Also unlike Hibernian's Easter Road Park, affectionately called 'The Holy Ground', the Hearts' Tynecastle Park was derisively referred to an 'The Hole'.

Anyway, it was at 'The Hole' Hibs opened season 1924–1925 with a league match against Partick Thistle on the evening of Friday 15 August in front of '18,000 green-clad singing Hibernian supporters'. It was a terrific match and with the score standing at two goals each and with only two minutes to go, the teams were 'neck and neck in the tussle for supremacy', when the brilliant Jimmy Dunn rattled home Hibs' winner. It was the unchanged celebrated side that did the business.

Hibs had been training at Portobello beach and at Woods Park, the home of Portobello Thistle and the Irishmen played a friendly/benefit match against the seasiders at Woods Park on Monday 18 August as a 'wee thank you'.

That Saturday the Hibees travelled to Rugby Park on league business and 'Kilmarnock failed to penetrate a stout Irish defence' and a goal from 'Darkie' Walker gave Hibs both points.

Wednesday 27 August and Hibs were back at Tynecastle, this time to play

Hearts in an East of Scotland Shield semi-final in front of a crowd of 17,000. Hearts' 'kicking back tactics' spoiled the spectacle, which ended 0-0. The replay was held over until the end of the season.

Two days later the Irishmen were back again at Tynecastle for their evening league match against Motherwell and 'rain fell in copious torrents, keeping the crowd down to 9,000 but they saw a great game between 'two clever teams', with Hibs victors by a Jimmy McColl goal. So Hibs had played their second and last 'home' league match at Tynecastle and we are told: 'Thank you Hearts. The "Hole" was lucky for Hibernian.'

St Johnstone were new to the 'charmed circle' of the first division and on Saturday 6 September Hibs travelled to Recreation Park, Perth, on league business and defeated St Johnstone 2-3. Jimmy Dunn notched two and 'Darkie' Wallace scored a brilliant solo effort.

Three days later Harry Ritchie was married in Edinburgh greeted by 'sunshine and showers of confetti'. We are told: 'Harry's bride carried a rather worn looking lucky horseshoe complete with green ribbons. The rather sorry state of this bridal accessory was because it had travelled for several years in Hibs kit-hamper courtesy of the new Mrs Ritchie.'

The long-awaited match to open the completely restructured greater Easter Road with its new stand came off on Saturday 13 September in a league match against Scotland's oldest club, Queen's Park. The only thing not finished to Hibs' high standards were the dressing rooms, so meantime the Hibees and their visitors changed in a local hotel and were driven to Easter Road.

Interest was naturally high among supporters:

> many people will no doubt be attracted to Easter Road out of curiosity to see the new ground. And it is well worth seeing. A complete transformation has been effected. The old place is hardly recognisable, and when everything has been got into ship-shape order and cleaned up the 'New Greater Easter Road' will be one of the tidiest and most commodious enclosures in the country.

Also a tribute was paid:

> Changed days at Easter Road when the late manager Dan McMichael a joiner to trade used to go round the Holy Ground with a hammer and nails doing repairs and the late chairman John Farmer was his labourer. Greater Easter Road was their brainchild for many years and what a pleasant surprise it would be for these late great Hibernians if they could see their old haunt now. The reconstruction was very dear to them, what a pity they did not live to see it, it would have brought a smile to their stony Irish faces and a tear to their old Irish eyes.

We are also told:

It may be a changed Easter Road but some things never change. Built into the impressive main South Entrance is Hibernians crest. It in a massive affair of emerald harp surrounded with clusters of emerald shamrocks. Hibs charitable efforts also never change for at the Queen's Park game a collection will be taken for the St Vincent de Paul Society, a catholic charitable organisation who do magnificent work among the poor folk of the city irrespective of denomination. Little Ireland's Grassmarket Silver Band will play selections before the kick-off and at half-time.

It was a 'green gala' as 25,000 swarmed into greater Easter Road . It was appropriate that the full favourite celebrated team did the opening honours, Harper, MacGinnigle, Dornan, Kerr, Miller, Shaw, Ritchie, Dunn, McColl, Halligan and Walker. 'Though grounds change however and teams come and teams may go, the Hibs seem to go on for ever. No doubt in 1974 when the new stand celebrates its jubilee Mr Maley will hand "the usual' to the press and Peter Kerr will lead out the same Grand old eleven.' The celebrated team 'appeared to an almighty roar to display their skills on the best playing surface in Scotland. But it has always been so at Easter Road. The verdant Irish turf must have given groundsman Paddy Cannon an enormous amount of work in laying as the pitch has been moved several yards to the west. His loving care however has paid off.' Hibs defeated a 'stubborn Queen's Park' 2-0, with goals from Jimmy McColl and Jimmy Dunn. So Hibs had won their first five league matches, a promising start to their 'big push' for the league championship.

That day Harry Swan had walked under the harp and shamrocks at the main South Entrance and, as a debenture holder, took his reserved numbered seat in the new stand. He was very impressed by greater Easter Road, Hibs' performance and the whole gala affair. Many years later he recalled, 'Harry Ritchie was brilliant, not even Gordon Smith has given a better exhibition.'

Hibs picked up five league points from a possible eight over the next few weeks and Jimmy Dunn's photograph appeared in the Hibs programme as he was the top scorer so far. The main development, however, was the news that Alec Maley, while remaining a director, had decided to relinquish the managerial post when a replacement could be found.

On Saturday 4 October at the Holy Ground the Hibees rattled seven past Ayr United, with three braces from Jimmy Dunn, Jimmy McColl and Johnny Halligan and Harry Ritchie got one. When Hibs beat Dundee at Easter Road 4-2 a collection was taken for the Convent of the Good Shepherd and Harry Ritchie was limping badly at the end of the game. This injury prevented him from playing for the Scottish League against the Irish League at Tynecastle on Wednesday 29 October; however, Willie McGinnigle was free of any injury and kept his place at full-back.

Harry Ritchie, Willie Harper and Hugh Shaw missed several games between them, hindering Hibs' league challenge, but generally the Irishmen's form was good and Jimmy Dunn got a hat-trick against Aberdeen and Jimmy McColl did the same against St Johnstone. Willie Harper was soon back in the thick of things and pulled off a vital penalty save against Airdrie at Easter Road and Jimmy McColl at his best scored with a 40-yard drive in a 1-1l draw.

In Memoriam – Andrew Sinclair

On Thursday 25 December a life-long Hibs supporter, 52-year-old Andrew Sinclair, who had served with his sons in the First World War, left with his wife and family their slum tenement second floor home at 13 Blackfriar Street, in Little Ireland, and went to Christmas Mass at St Patrick's RC church in the Cowgate. In the afternoon the Sinclair clan attended Easter Road for Willie Dornan's benefit match in recognition of the full-back's ten years' service to Hibernian. The following morning, Boxing Day, Andrew went to early morning Holy Mass at St Patrick's as he did every day, before going out to work as a street sweeper for Edinburgh Corporation. His duties that day took him to Great Junction Street, Leith, and there he was knocked down by a tram-car. Seriously injured, Andrew was taken to Leith Hospital but the following day he died of his injuries, fortified by the Rites of Holy Mother Church.

So who was Andrew Sinclair, the anonymous Hibs supporter, the anonymous street sweeper? He was, in fact, the father of Margaret Sinclair, a nun in the Order of the Poor Clare Colettines. Margaret, over the years, became the focus of world-wide catholic devotion and we shall hear more of Margaret soon in our story.

One day after the death of Andrew Sinclair, the anonymous Hibs supporter, one of Hibernian's most famous supporters and ex-directors died. He had become a Hibernian legend in his own life-time for, without this man, there may not even be a Hibernian Football Club today. His name was Philip Farmer.

In Memoriam – Philip Farmer

Leither Philip Farmer was the elder brother of the recently deceased Hibernian chairman John Farmer. Their lives, private and with Hibernian, ran almost parallel. In his early 20s Philip was on the Hibernian committee, in the late 1880s with his brother John. Philip was also president of the Stella Maris Catholic Young Men's Society of St Mary Star of the Sea RC church, Constitution Street, Leith, when the Stella Maris men led the fight to resuscitate Hibernian from its near destruction in the early 1890s. It was the leadership, determination and personal generosity of Philip Farmer which undoubtedly kept Hibs a living reality. Without fear of contradiction, it was a never-say-die Philip and his single-mindedness that saved Hibernian Football Club for future generations to enjoy. In the decade of the 1890s Philip Farmer was Hibernian's treasurer, building up the club's strength and he was Hibs' president when they won the Scottish Cup in 1902 and league championship in 1903. He became a leading shareholder when Hibs became a public limited company which was due to much hard work by Philip in 1905. He was Hibs' chairman until 1909 when, due to poor health, he handed over the reins to his brother, John, who was a director. Philip's unpaid labours for Hibernian spanned 25 years in the most trying circumstances as a committee member, saviour, treasurer, president, shareholder and chairman. In private life, like his brother John, he was a popular Leith wine and spirits merchant and was married with a son and daughter. Philip was in poor health for a long time and only a few months before he died he lost his wife, which hastened his own demise. Until the day he died, Philip Farmer remained active in the affairs of Hibernian Football Club when, on Sunday 28 December at the age of 59 he died, fortified by the Rites of Holy Mother Church, at his home at 3 Hermitage Place, Leith. An affectionate short tribute was paid to 'Philip Farmer the saviour of Hibernian in 1891 and the father of the modern club':

> Philip Farmer was Hibs keenest enthusiast and like his brother John was one of those quiet, unassuming stony faced Irish directors you find at Easter Road. It was Philip's determination not to be baulked in his object that Hibernian Football Club owe their existence today. He always tended the affairs of Hibernian with the greatest diligence and was also for many years on the Scottish League Management Committee. Hibernian have lost a hard worker, generous benefactor and a true friend.

On Hogmanay, Wednesday 31 December 1924, after his Requiem Mass at St Mary Star of the Sea church which was attended in great numbers by Hibernians old and new, representatives of Scottish football and the general public of all denominations, Philip Farmer was buried in Rosebank Cemetery close to the Gretna Memorial.

> Philip Farmer what have you given,
> Bold spirit free
> In earth or Heaven,
> You left Hibernian for me.

> What can I give
> Philip strong and brave,
> As long as I live,
> Respect the life you gave.

It was no accident that Philip Farmer's Hibernian life-saving act in 1891 was repeated exactly 100 years later in 1991 by his great grand-nephew Sir Tom Farmer, CBE KSG. A unique Hibernian family connection encompassing 100 years of Hib's history. Yet another part of the halo of undiminished romance of Hibernian Football Club.

Twenty-four hours after Philip Farmer was laid to rest, the New Year's Day derby match on Thursday 1 January 1925 against Hearts saw Easter Road in mourning, with a minute's silence being observed, the green flag lowered to half-mast and the Hibs team wearing black arm-bands. Hibs had one change from their usual celebrated team, with long-serving old war-horse Bobby Templeton coming in at left full-back in place of the injured Willie Dornan and the 24,000 crowd saw Hearts take a one-goal lead at half-time. However, we are told: 'Superior work by Hibernian in the second half saw "Darkie" Walker equalise then the head of Jimmy Dunn gave the Irishmen a well deserved victory.' In the 'big push' for the league championship Hibs were lying third with 31 points, having played 22 games. With the same number of games played, Airdrie were second with 35 points and Rangers top with 38 points.

Following this victory over Hearts the Hibees picked up full points against Kilmarnock in a two-goal victory which featured a Harry Ritchie twice-taken penalty. Then a 0-1 win on a visit to Aberdeen which featured 'Darkie' Walker 'doing the impossible' by scoring direct from a corner. A point was dropped in a 0-0 draw against Falkirk at Brockville, but two points the following week at Easter Road in a 2-1 over Hamilton kept Hibs challenge on song.

In the first round of the Scottish Cup at Easter Road, on Saturday 24 January, Hibs played Aberdeen, the team they had recently beaten at Pittodrie. There was no Scottish Cup run for the Hibees as they surprisingly went down 0-2 in a disappointing display.

The following week it was back to league business and a point was collected against Celtic at Parkhead, in a 1-1 draw after Hibs had gone a goal behind. More points were collected and that was with Willie Harper and Jimmy Dunn being rested for and playing in a Scotland international victory against Wales on Saturday 14 February. The great Welsh captain Billy Meredith was quoted as saying that Hibernian's Harper and Dunn were Scotland's best players. Harper and Dunn were again the Scottish stars in an international against Ireland in Belfast on Saturday 28 February; Jimmy Dunn scored a beauty. Other internationals were coming up and Hibs could ill-afford to rest and lose players, as the Hibees needed all their players for their league matches. Hibernian Football Club, however, always put country first.

Hibernian were, however, able to field their full celebrated team for the 'crunch league match' at the Holy Ground against Rangers on Wednesday 11

March. We are told: 'In arranging for a five o'clock start Hibs manager Alec Maley was indulging in a little gamble with the weather. He was however rewarded for his optimism as the light held. Not only were the conditions perfect but a crowd of fully 20,000 turned out.' Hibs ran amok and had a three goal lead at half-time with counters from 'Darkie' Walker, Jimmy McColl and Johnny Halligan. In the second half Jimmy McColl added a fourth as 'Hibernian set about their work with renewed vigour and always looked certain winners even if they continued to miss chances at the rate they had been doing. The score was not at all flattering to the Irishmen, with better finishing the score against Rangers could have been overwhelming.' We are further told:

> The Ibrox men were a very leg weary lot and therein lies the chief reason for their heavy defeat. Rangers just could not last the pace set by a great Hibernian team that was full of energy and enterprise. The Irishmen were after everything they could get, every man-jack of them put his back into the work. Rangers were soundly thrashed by the Irish combination and there can be nothing but credit for the spirited display of the Hibernians.

Hibs were now second in the league, having pushed Rangers into third place, Airdrie were now top of the league but it was all very tight.

Injuries were now hampering Hibs and they lost Willie Harper who played for the Scottish XI against the English league at Liverpool on Saturday 14 March. That day, with three reserves in the team, Hibs lost 3-1 to Partick Thistle at Firhill, thus denting their league challenge. The following Saturday, the first rugby international to be played at Murrayfield between Scotland and England saw Hibs put their Easter Road league match with St Mirren off until Tuesday 24 March and the Hibees collected both points. Over the next two weeks Hibs dropped a point at Cappielow against Morton in a 2-2 draw; Hibs had been two goals down after only ten minutes so at least it was a fighting point. Worse followed at Dens Park. Willie Harper was out, as he was playing for Scotland against England at Hampden and after only a few moments of the Dens Park game Hibs lost Willie McGinnigle with a cut eye which needed stitches. Ten-man Hibs went down 3-0, with reserve goalkeeper McAlpine having a poor games

Too many injuries and the loss of key players to international duty and Hibs' chances of being league champions disappeared. Another problem was Hibs still not running a reserve team and keeping their squad to only 15 or 16 players but they did battle to the bitter end. Their last league match, on Saturday 18 April, was against the strong-going Airdrie at Broomfield and the Hibees lost 2-0. Hibs ended up third in the league and Airdrie threw away their chance of the championship and finished second behind Rangers.

Meantime Hibs travelled to draw 2-2 with Aberdeen in a benefit for the Dons' Willie Grant; an experimental 40-yard offside area was used. At Easter Road a friendly was played against a Glasgow Junior Select and a friendly was also played against Gala Fairydean at Eastlands Park, Galashiels – a weak Hibernian XI, which featured Alec Maley's son in the Hibs goal won 1-5.

The Hibees also played a benefit match at Easter Road for their nine-year servant, centre-half Willie Miller. We are told:

> It was one of these Easter Road Irish galas with recent Scottish Cup winners Celtic providing the opposition. In the true sporting tradition of Easter Road the Hibs groundsman Paddy Cannon paraded Celtic's cup round the Holy Ground and it was greeted with applause from all. Tommy Milligan the European professional boxing champion and local Leith professional Alex Ireland gave an exhibition boxing match under the watchful eye of Hibernian's Dr St John Cogan who was also Edinburgh's boxing medical health officer. The Irishmen of Edinburgh and Glasgow drew 1-1 in an exciting football match in this hugely successful benefit for Hibs Willie Miller.

Hibs scorer was the newly signed Alex Love from West Lothian junior club Blackburn Rovers.

In the local cup competitions Hibs did well. In the Wilson Cup final they disposed of Hearts 1-0 at the Holy Ground and in the replay of the East of Scotland Sheild, Hibs beat Hearts by the same score at the same venue, before defeating Leith Athletic in the final at Easter Road with a Jimmy Dunn hat-trick. In the Rosebery Charity Cup semi-final at Easter Road, Leith Athletic were again Hibs' victims, this time 4-0 and against Hearts in the final at Tynecastle the Hibees again beat them 0-1. Hibs also invited the great Newcastle United, 'a team of many talents', to play a friendly at the Holy Ground and the Hibees surprisingly beat them 3-1.

So Hibernian's celebrated team were again this season a very entertaining and popular lot but were again the 'nearly men'. They had nearly won the Scottish Cup twice and this season nearly won the league championship. It was not for the want of trying, they had 'character' and in their day were 'the toughest, talented and most entertaining team in Scotland'. This team and the new greater Easter Road saw record crowds and gate receipts and the Irishmen were spending some of that money on improving the drainage system at the new stand side.

In the summer Harry Ritchie had a successful appendix operation and Willie Dornan had his tonsils out. A summer tour of Poland had been arranged by Hibs but had to be cancelled because of problems on the Polish side of things.

THE MAKING OF HIBERNIAN 3

Michael Whelahan's Old Hibs Association was still going strong, as was Michael himself, and his Ould Hibs drew 1-1 with Auld Hearts in the Ballie Bathgate Old Hibs Association Charity Cup at Little Ireland's Bathgate Park in the Canongate, the home of Hibs' junior nursery team Edinburgh Emmet. As always, Michael Whelahan was able to call on lots of old famous Hibernians such as Archie 'Baldy' Grey, Paddy Callaghan, Neil Girdwood, John O'Hara, Davy Gordon, Willie Donnelly, Jimmy Buchan, Willie Combe, John Kennedy, John Sharp, Richard O'Brien, Paddy Douglas and Paddy Murray. The sons of Paddy Murray and John O'Hara were causing a lot of signing interest at Easter Road at this time.

The name of Michael Whelahan, the co-founder of Hibernian Football Club in 1875, was to tragically loom large next season, Hibs' Golden Jubilee season of 1925–1926.

– 5 –

IN MEMORIAM – MICHAEL WHELAHAN HIBERNIAN'S GOLDEN JUBILEE SEASON 1925-1926

We are not native here or anywhere,
We are the Irish wave that broke over Scotland
And ran up this beach among these stones,
But when the tide ebbed were left stranded here
In crevices and ledge protected pools
That have grown saltier with the drying up
Of the great common flow that kept us sweet
with fresh, cold draughts from deep down in the ocean.

Season 1925–1926 was the Golden Jubilee season of Hibernian Football Club, which was co-founded by Canon Edward Joseph Hannan of St Patrick's Roman Catholic Young Men's Society attached to St Patrick's. Hibernian was launched on Friday 6 August 1875 at the Catholic Institute more widely known as St Mary's Street Halls, the headquarters of the CYMS, during their celebration to mark the centenary of the birth of Daniel O'Connell, the champion of Catholic Emancipation.

Fifty years after the founding of Hibernian, Michael Whelahan was still alive and actively involved in the affairs of the club and was also the founder and leading light of the official Old Hibernian Association which kept ex-players in touch with Hibernian and they were renowned for their charity work.

Hibernian celebrated their Golden Jubilee on Saturday 6 August 1925 with a Holy Mass of thanksgiving in St Patrick's, their spiritual home. There was an overspill congregation of 2,000 Hibernian officials and players old and new and supporters of all denominations. The modest Michael Whelahan was special guest of honour and it was his son Father Michael, the priest in charge of the catholic mission of Armadale, who celebrated the Holy Mass. A moving tribute was paid to Cannon Hannan who had died in 1891.

It was fitting that Hibs' Golden Jubilee should be celebrated with a church service and the club was founded on and had functioned for the last 50 years on the Christian principles of faith, hope and charity.

It was also fitting that the 'stony faced Irish director of Easter Road' chose not to celebrate this special season by spending club finances on dinners or parties but instead made generous donations to church charities and those of Edinburgh Corporation. They also made arrangements to award benefit matches to no fewer than four of their players: Willie McGinnigle, Hugh Shaw, Peter Kerr and Harry Ritchie. Hibernian, as always, were famous for looking after their players.

There was a major change by the Scottish football authorities to the offside rule, which was now altered so that only two rather than three defenders had to be between a forward and his opponent's goal line. The idea was to produce more goals, and it did, and also confusion among players and match officials, as illustrated in Hibs' first match of the season in the league on Saturday 15 August against Celtic at Parkhead, billed as 'the battle of the Greens, Scotland's match of the day'. We are told: 'The chief interest is concentrated on the working of the new offside rule, the innovation promises to be an unqualified success.' It certainly wasn't for Hibs. No one seemed to know who was offside and who was not and the referee and linemen had to consult their written instructions at half-time. Of course every hesitant, dubious decision went Celtic's way as the Hibees crashed 5-0, with the Hibs players and officials declaring 'not one of the goals should have stood'. Hibs had their full celebrated team out that day in 'a rout as complete as it was unexpected'.

Two days later, the same team played Partick Thistle at Easter Road in Willie McGinnigle's benefit match marking his seven-year service to Hibernian. Would the new offside rule work for the Hibees this time? Well, in the first half Jimmy Dunn and Jimmy McColl scored and early in the second half, two more were added from the head of Johnny Halligan. The Hibees were up 4-0 and everything looked good when the roof fell in and Partick ran riot and scored no fewer than six. A remarkable comeback by the Jags and we are told: 'The Hibs defence are going to find the new offside rule a source of great worry to them.'

Five days later, on Saturday 22 August, Hibs played a league match against Kilmarnock at the Holy Ground in front of 17,000 of the faithful 'who did not know what to expect'. They need not have worried, for Alec Maley must have done some homework with his celebrated team as they went on to win 8-0. Poor Killie, it would appear, also had their problems with the new offside rule. Hibs' scorers that day were 'Darkie' Walker with a hat-trick, two from Jimmy Dunn and one each from Jimmy McColl, Harry Ritchie and Johnny Halligan.

No one realised it then, but this match would be the last time the full eleven of Hibernian's celebrated team; Harper, McGinnigle, Dornan, Kerr, Miller, Shaw, Ritchie, Dunn, Halligan and Walker would ever be able to play together.

Injuries would cause constant team changes and eventually transfers would take their toll.

It was now Alec Maley resigned as manager, to take up his duties full-time on the board of directors which had been further strengthened by the earlier appointment of Sean Meagher, the ex-president of Hibernian's nursery junior club Edinburgh Emmet. Sean Meagher had been appointed as treasurer of Hibernian.

It was hotly tipped that Paddy Travers of Clyde would be appointed Hibs' new manager but the job went to Bobby Templeton, a full-back with 15 years' service to the Hibees. It was a popular choice but Peter Kerr of the celebrated team, who was a servant of even longer standing, must have been disappointed at being overlooked.

Bobby Templeton remained a registered player and it was just as well, as he had to select himself on many occasions as injuries mounted on his small squad which included George Murray, Alex Love, Mellon and Clerk, all of whom had to be called upon. Hibs' new manager was determined to build up his squad and run a reserve team, something that had been neglected by Alec Maley because of his double obsession with his celebrated team and the need to save Hibs' money on reserve players; it was in the long run to be a false economy. Bobby Templeton was still fortunate to have a strong backroom staff of Paddy Cannon, Paddy's son Tommy and Di Christopher. Tommy Cannon, following in his father's steps as a Hibs trainer, was also an athlete of considerable standing and famed throughout Scotland. Di Christopher had also been a great athlete in his day and a Hibs trainer for countless years and he had also played professional rugby league in England as a wing three-quarter with Swinton. As for 69-year-old Paddy Cannon who had been Hibs' trainer/groundsman for 28 years, he had in his day been a British and European champion professional runner, setting records that still stood at this time. Paddy had become a Hibernian legend in his own lifetime and he still had 21 more years of service to Hibernian in him.

The day after Bobby Templeton's appointment, Hibs played St Bernard's on Wednesday 26 August at the Holy Ground, in the East of Scotland Shield semi-final and the tall scoring continued with Hibs victors by 9-0. 'Darkie' Walker recorded another hat-trick as young Alex Love replaced the injured McColl at centre.

On Wednesday 2 September, seven-year servant Hugh Shaw was afforded his benefit match against Hearts at Easter Road and to mark the occasion the Hearts team were presented with crystal rosebowls.

The 'ould inimy' were the Hibees' opponents again two weeks later at Tynecastle, in the final of the East of Scotland Shield. The Green Jerseys were victorious 1-2, with goals from Jimmy Dunn and Clerk. Hibs' long-serving director Barney Lester was presented with the shield in Hearts' pavilion after the match. Barney had expected Hearts to use this charity affair to express their congratulations to Hibs on their Golden Jubilee but none were forthcoming. Barney had prepared a neat, humorous 'thank you' in sporting terms, with praiseworthy comments about his city rivals but he never had to take it out of his pocket and as it turned out it remained there as Hearts, throughout the season, never acknowledged Hibs' 50 years.

Injuries plagued Hibs and sometimes the team included four reserves; Bobby Templeton himself was forced to play in goal, full-back and inside-right. Hibs lost six of their next seven league matches and in six of them failed to score a single goal. Their best result was a 0-0 draw with Hearts at the Holy Ground. By the end of October Hibs were second-bottom of the league, just as news reached Easter Road of the death in America of Leither Barney Fagan, Hibs' left full-back when they had won the Scottish Cup in 1887. Barney's descendants in Edinburgh today are the proud possessors of his cup medal.

During this run of bad results, Hibs supporters were up in arms as usually half the players on the park were unfit and eventually Willie Harper could not be fielded any longer – as we are told, 'Harper will need crutches soon'. A thigh injury was giving him a lot of trouble and kept him out of the team for several weeks. Bobby Templeton signed a goalkeeper, James Sharp, from Dalkeith Thistle and he played in five of the games in that bad run but we are told, 'Jimmy Sharp could not be faulted'. Jimmy Sharp was in goal when Hibs finally recorded a 3-1 league victory over Falkirk at Easter Road on Saturday 31 October.

Seven days later, on Saturday 7 November, Willie Harper was back in goal when Hibs travelled to Cowdenbeath in the league and suffered a 3-1 defeat. It was Willie Harper's last game for the Hibees because, on the following Monday, he was transferred to London giants Arsenal. We are told:

> Every football follower in Edinburgh can tell you the amount of Harper's transfer fee but no two stories are alike, the amounts ranging from £3,000 to £6,000. Herbert Chapman the Arsenal manager says the fee must remain private but we can draw our own conclusions as Mr Chapman rates Harper as the best goalkeeper in Britain.

Comments from 'a very old Hibs follower' suggested that the transfer fee be immediately spent on strengthening the team, 'It is about time Hibs did something to lift themselves out of the rut they are in. Defeat after defeat will not pay for the new stand.' So the first of the celebrated team that it was thought would go on forever was away. Hibs president Barney Lester, manager

Bobby Templeton and captain Peter Kerr saw Willie off at Waverley Station for the goalkeeper's big adventure in London. Willie Harper had gained many Scottish international honours during his five years' service at Easter Road and was a highly respected favourite of the supporters. Today it is still arguable that he was Hibs' greatest goalkeeper ever to grace the Holy Ground.

Hibs were at the bottom of the league but struggled on, picking up some points. Two league victories at Easter Road were high-scoring affairs, 5-1 against Clydebank and 8-4 against Hamilton. A right full-back, Bertie Stark, was signed from Murrayfield Amateurs.

We have read how Andrew Sinclair, the 'anonymous Hibs supporter', died 11 months ago and now, on Tuesday 24 November 1925, his 25-year-old daughter Margaret died. Margaret was just another 'anonymous Hibs supporter' but today she is known throughout the world as 'The Edinburgh Wonder Worker'.

In Memoriam – Margaret Sinclair

There is too much to be said of Margaret's short life for this book, and a very brief outline has already appeared in *The Making of Hibernian 2*. We have also read in this book of her father.

Margaret was one of the six Sinclair children, a poor anonymous 'Hibs Daft' family from Little Ireland. She worked on Edinburgh's factory floor, but also had a great generosity of spirit, spending much of her spare time helping those less fortunate than herself. Margaret also had a strong religious vocation, and, in 1923, became a nun in the order of the Poor Clares Colettines at their convent in Notting Hill, London. Her religious life as a nun was as unremarkable as her secular like in Edinburgh. Margaret developed tuberculosis and died on 24 November 1925 at the early age of 25.

In Edinburgh's Little Ireland, Margaret was remembered through prayer. Miracle cures which baffled the medical profession were attributed to her and so, after investigation by Rome, she was elevated in 1978 to the title 'The Venerable Margaret Sinclair'. Margaret may one day be canonised, becoming Scotland's first modern-day worker saint.

What was so special about 'the anonymous wee Hibs supporter'? The answer appears to be in the generosity of spirit of Margaret's every-day life, something very few of us ever attain.

> I remember the devotion of your youth,
> How you followed me as a bride,
> Following me in the desert,
> In a land unsown.
>
> Text. Jeremiah 2.2.

THE MAKING OF HIBERNIAN 3

Through the end of November and the beginning of December, Hibs had mixed results when, on Christmas Day 1925, a great old Hibernian player died – Paddy Murray.

In Memoriam – Paddy Murray

Paddy Murray, we are told, died with 'tragic suddenness'. Paddy had played for Hibs after their resuscitation in February 1893. 'Hibs Daft' Paddy was a class act and Celtic wanted him, but Paddy was determined to play his part in restoring Hibs to a force in Scottish football. This he did, playing in two successive Division 2 championship teams, playing in the 1896 Scottish Cup final and gaining international honours. Paddy resisted two big money moves to Celtic and Liverpool, staying true to the Hibees, his only senior club. Hibs rewarded him with a benefit match when he hung up his boots in 1901. He was a great eight-year servant as Hibs struggled back to the top and he surely deserves his place in the Hibernian Hall of Fame.

The following day, Boxing Day, Saturday 26 December, Hibs travelled to Dens Park and with three reserves in a positionally reshuffled team they surprisingly defeated Dundee 1-4.

Thank God Hibs had found a little form because they were third-bottom of the league and their next match was against third-top Hearts at Tynecastle. A polite observation tell us: 'Hearts, who have championship ambitions and who have recorded ten successive wins on home territory anticipate that ground advantage will turn the scales in their favour in their game with Hibernian.' There was, as always, the usual hostile observation telling us, 'High flying Hearts and their confident support expect not only to win handsomely but to no less than thrash the ragged Irishmen of Easter Road.' On Friday 1 January 1926, the New Year's Day Derby match between the bitter city rivals saw them clash at 'The Hole'. Highly-fancied Hearts must have wished they could have dug a hole for themselves that day for it was 'the ragged Irishmen of Easter Road' who handed out the thrashing, 'a Golden Jubilee thrashing of the Hearts'. A goal from long-serving captain Peter Kerr, a double from Harry Ritchie and a second-half counter from Johnny Halligan gave Hibs their 1-4 victory. Hearts idol of the times Jock White was first booked, then finally sent off for persistent fouling, as Hearts took their 'bad beating' with a poor display of sportsmanship. Hearts, supporters and indeed all the pundits, expected Hearts to run up a big score against Hibs and the Hearts support left Tynecastle bewildered and asking each other 'how did that Irish lot beat us?' The Irish lot that day were: Jimmy Sharp, Bertie Stark, Willie Dornan, Peter

Kerr, Willie Miller, Hugh Shaw, Geordie Murray, Jimmy Dunn, Jimmy McColl, Johnny Halligan and Harry Ritchie.

Mixed results again followed and Hibs could have won a 0-0 draw with Aberdeen at Pittodrie when Harry Ritchie scored with a penalty, but the referee ordered it to be retaken and this time the goalkeeper saved it. In a match at Easter Road the Hibees defeated Morton 4-1 and Jimmy McColl, who had been coming under a lot of criticism, scored two in the last five minutes.

On Saturday 16 January, table-toppers Celtic, who would go on to be the league champions, were the visitors to the Holy Ground and 25,000 saw 'a magnificent battle of the Greens in the best tradition of Scotland's two Irish combatants'. The first two minutes set the tone of this high-scoring match, Celtic immediately scored and Hibs immediately equalised. To cut a long story short, the final score was four goals each after Hibs had kept their noses continually in front. It was a see-saw match that the Hibs probably deserved to win:

> Both sets of the Irish forwards were very clever but the Hibs half-backs were superior to such an extent it should have turned the game in favour of the Edinburgh Irishmen but for a fatal weakness in their goalkeeper Sharp who was a contributory cause of two of Celtics goals. Hibs however have improved their poor showing in the league table.

Johnny Halligan scored with two headers and 'Darkie' Walker and Jimmy McColl got the other two.

That evening, Hibernian's directors Owen Brannigan, Barney Lester, Alec Maley and Sean Meagher, along with several players and members of the official Old Hibs Association, headed together for Edinburgh's Chalmers Hospital to visit the seriously ill 72-year-old Michael Whelahan, the co-founder of Hibernian Football Club. They had always been regular visitors, keeping Michael up-to-date with Easter Road developments and match reports, and that evening they told him about the exciting 4-4 draw with Celtic. Michael was very weak but his old Irish eyes lightened momentarily and he murmured in his laboured breathing, 'I wish I had been there at Easter Road the day.'

In Memoriam – Michael Whelahan

Four days later, on Wednesday 20 January 1926, Michael Whelahan died in Chalmers Hospital, Edinburgh, fortified by the Rites of Holy Mother Church.

Michael was born in 1854 in the tiny parish of Kilglass, County Roscommon, but he and his older sister, Marie, both grew up in grinding poverty among fellow Irish exiles in Little Ireland, an area whose population never exceeded 25,000. Nevertheless they made up one third of the population of Edinburgh's Old Town. The total population of the capital at this time was 250,000, so the Irish were never seen as a 'threat' or 'feared' by their fellow citizens, but they were ignored when it came to housing, education and employment, and they were subjected to an irrational racial and religious hostility:

> Indeed were a native of the Emerald Isle to drop from the clouds some Sunday evening into the Cowgate, he might easily be pardoned for imagining himself at home. There he would find the same unmistakable names, the same O'Donnells and O'Gormans, the same uncouth brogue, strange oaths and picturesque attire, the same lanthorn jaws, hunger-bitten and woe begone by day and lighted up with the glass of reckless intoxication by night and to crown it all, the same servility to the priest, crouching before his frown and fondly licking the hand that has scourged them into submission.

So these were the social conditions in which Michael Whelahan, the co-founder of Hibernian, grew up.

St Patrick's church in the Cowgate was opened in 1856, and five years later Canon Edward Joseph Hannan, a professor of Classics, was appointed to St Patrick's to start a crusade to improve the lives of the Irish exiles. This he did very effectively, and he was to go on to be the co-founder of Hibernian Football Club with Michael Whelahan.

Michael left St Patrick's Boys' School at the age of ten and found a job as a factory labourer in the Miller and Richard Type Foundry situated behind Nicholson Street where he was to serve the firm for over 60 years. He was a tall, strong, handsome, hard-working young man, and he was promoted to foreman – an almost unknown achievement for a Catholic in these days, and the firm gave him the house attached to the foundry. It is of interest to note that as Michael grow up in the Cowgate he rubbed shoulders with other Edinburgh-Irish greats who were later to find fame, among them William McGonagall, James Connolly and Arthur Conan Doyle, who later received a knighthood. Michael was also acquainted with Scotland's giant of literature, Robert Louis Stevenson, who sought refuge in the slums of Little Ireland, where he found the haunted romanticism of his later literary genius.

Whelahan was a member of Canon Hannon's St Patrick's Catholic Young Men's Society and when association football arrived in Edinburgh it was this unlikely partnership that founded Hibernian Football Club in 1875. The almighty struggle to do so has been covered in Book 1 of *The Making of Hibernian* and need not be repeated. Suffice it to say that Michael Whelahan named our club *Hibernian*, from the old Roman Latin meaning 'Irishmen', and he was the club's first captain, leading them through their early struggles and successes. Hibs won the first and second XI Edinburgh FA cups three years in a row and they were awarded them to keep outright. Thereafter they remained in St Patrick's church for safekeeping, and today they are still to be found in the spiritual home of Hibernian. In 1880 Michael Whelehan and Canon Hannan established Hibs at Easter Road, and by 1887 Michael was the president of Hibernian when they won the Scottish Cup and World Championship. Due to player and financial troubles Hibs lost their Holy Ground at Easter Road, but Michael and the men of St Patrick's along with the driving force of St Mary Star of the Sea (Stella Maris) CMYS Leith re-established Hibernian at Easter Road in 1893, thanks to the hard work and generosity of Philip Farmer, president of the Stella Maris CYMS. Michael also founded an organisation first called the 'Auld Associates' for ex-Hibernian players in the unlikely venue of Airds pub in Lothian Street – but Michael and his colleagues were all teetotallers. The Hibs Daft socialist revolutionary James Connolly, himself a non-drinker, and his family had a slum flat in Lothian Street. He offered them his home for meetings and it was there that the Old Hibs Association was formalised as an official part of Hibernian Football Club.

Meantime Michael met a lovely Scots girl, Isabella Robertson, and although both families had their misgivings the happy couple married in St Patrick's and their union produced eight children.

We have heard how Michael Whelahan's youngest son George was killed in the First World War and how George's friend Willie Harvey, on returning from the trenches, married Michael's daughter Kathleen. Kathleen, in her late 90s, was a strong supporter of the Hands Off Hibs campaign in 1990/91 and received a lot of press publicity for the Hib's cause.

It is of interest to note that Whelahan's elder sister Marie married a certain Andrew Stanton, another Irish exile living in the Cowgate. It would seem that heaven decreed that Michael Whelahan, the first captain of Hibernian in 1875, would be the great-great-great-grand uncle of Patrick Stanton, the Captain of Hibernian, when they celebrated their centenary in 1975. This was a unique family connection, encompassing 100 years of Hibernian Football Club. Pat Stanton's free scoring Hibs team-mate, Jimmy O'Rourke, came from a similar Little Ireland background as did Tom O'Malley, OBE, the present day vice-chairman of Hibernian. Philip Farmer saved Hibs from extinction in the early 1890s and his great-grand nephew, Sir Tom Farmer, CBE KSG, did the same exactly 100 years later in 1991. These unique family connections are all part of the halo of romance of Hibernian Football Club, a halo of romance that can never by diminished.

The late Theresa McGurk, who herself came from a Little Ireland background and was a life-long Hibs supporter, paid tribute to Michael Whelahan's relative Pat Stanton, the 'Hibees King':

Whenever you are thinking of the Hibees
There's one name springs to mind more than the rest;
To the fans he'll always be 'King of the Hibees'
Of all our football heroes, he's the best.

Pat Stanton is his name – the one and only –
He's known and he's respected near and far,
You can keep your Greig's, your Cruikies and your Bremer's –
For Paddy he outshines them – he's a star.

He came from Holy Cross to join the Hibees
A shy young lad of only seventeen
He hasn't changed – he's the 'quiet man',
But he can hold his own playing for the green …

So thank you Pat, for all those hours of pleasure
We've enjoyed it, even in the snow and rain
We can boast that we have seen the Great Pat Stanton
The likes of him we'll never see again.

Michael Whelahan continued to work for Hibernian in many capacities and became a shareholder in 1906. When Hibernian became a limited liability company his charitable work with his Old Hibs' Association entered the realms of legend. Michael's wife 'my beloved Isabella' died in 1910, and with the further loss of George in the Great War, Michael's health started failing, but he continued to work for Hibernian and for the Miller and Richard Type Foundry, until his death on 20 January 1926.

Two days later, the East of Scotland FA convened a special meeting and passed a motion of sympathy to Michael Whelahan's family and paid tribute to Michael and his single-mindedness with Hibernian in defeating Hearts in the 1880s on the issue of the local player rule that had brought Edinburgh out of the backwaters of Scottish football. Hibernian had been the first club to bring the Scottish Cup to Edinburgh, breaking the west of Scotland monopoly. Michael Whelahan's work with Hibernian was the biggest contribution to the success of football in Edinburgh.

The following day, Saturday 23 January, Michael Whelahan's Requiem Mass was celebrated in St Patrick's church by his son, Father Michael. The congregation spilled out of the church into the grounds, and it was estimated that over 3,000 were present. Joining the family were everyone from Hibernian Football Club, along with countless old players and officials. The SFA and the

HIBERNIAN'S GOLDEN JUBILEE

Scottish League were represented, and John Williamson represented the West of Scotland FA. Walter and John Miller Richard, his employers, were also there to pay their respects to a 60-year employee. Hibernian's wreath in the form of the traditional broken harp was almost lost in a mass of floral tributes. At the request of the family, Michael's interment was a private affair at the family plot in Mount Vernon Cemetery.

> And who will steep Michael Whelahan's senses in the flowers?
> And who will feed his spirit on the fruit?
> And who will fill his veins with the Great Wine?
> Michael shall see no winters and feel no rains,
> But joy perpetual in the land of God.

Michael Whelahan had lived through the first 50 years of Hibernian, from his co-founding of the club in 1875 through to the Golden Jubilee season 1925–1926, and Michael's Hibernian had exerted a profound effect on Scottish football. Without Michael and his Hibernian there would be no Glasgow Celtic or Dundee United today. Michael had made Hibs a household name throughout Scotland. It must have given Michael great satisfaction that Hibernian had come so far in 50 years, from their most humble beginnings as 'an Edinburgh-Irish slum football club for the recreation of young catholic men' and were now an integrated community club for all the population of Edinburgh and Leith. One wonders just how proud Michael would have been in later years when Hibernian would play throughout the world: Europe, Scandinavia, South America, Central America, the USA, Canada and even darkest Africa.

It was Michael Whelahan who gave Hibernian their name. His founding of the club has been like the ripples from a stone dropped in a pond that have reached out and touched many, many people giving them so much enjoyment and timeless memories, making them proud to be known as 'Hibs Daft'.

So Michael was gone. Like so many of his 'Hibernian ould guard', they had left the stage one by one to go to their reward and meet again at the gates of Heaven. Hibs chairman, Owen Brannigan, and president, Barney Lester, were two of the few surviving 'ould guard', and they were asked if Michael's death was a particular landmark for Hibernian. 'Naw', said Owen, 'Michael's life was one big landmark from the cradle to the grave, an' he never took Hibs romance tae the grave wi' him; that romance lives in every Hibs supporter.' Barney, deep in thought, added, 'Aye yur right Ownie and a' the ould deid yins still seem tae live among us.'

> Hibernian ghosts raise their eyes to greet
> The green flag where they stood,

They see me walking in the street,
Easter Road quietude.

I pass into the Holy Ground – Hibernians olden shrine,
Not as a stranger, not unknown,
And though I feel no hand in mine
I'll never walk alone.

By Little Ireland's crooked wynd and Leith's sullen gate,
My footsteps echo clear,
And though the streets are desolate,
Hibernian ghosts are near.

Ye phantom figures wreathed in green,
Wider grows the pilgrim pathway ye trod,
Through star cut night 'til the vaults of heaven seen,
In the Easter lilly fields of God.

O Hibernians past that will not be denied,
The green, the Harp our birthright be,
Is it Hibernian ghosts walk by my side?
Or some dead ghost of me?

That Saturday, 23 January, after Hibernian had attended Michael Whelahan's requiem mass, they played their Scottish Cup first round tie at the Holy Ground against second division Broxburn United. The green flag was already at half-mast and the team wore black arm-bands and a minute's silence was observed. The match ended in a 1-1 draw and three days later the replay was again at Easter Road, after a financial agreement was reached with Broxburn and the promise that their supporters would be admitted free of charge. The Hibees won by a single goal and a new goalkeeper, Hislop from Shawfield Juniors, made his debut. We are told: 'He was quite good but a bit on the wee side.'

On Saturday 30 January, Hibs played Airdrie in the league at Easter Road. Airdrie were a very strong outfit and were to be league runners-up this season for no less than the fourth successive time. They beat the Hibees 1-4 and by coincidence they were back at Easter Road the following week for the Scottish Cup second round and they won again, this time 2-3

Mixed league results followed for the Hibees and they signed Jimmy Hutchison from Cadzow St Anns and Bobby Barr from Queen's Park. A crazy 1-2 defeat by Cowdenbeath at Easter Road is worth a mention – Hibs missed three penalties. In the first half the Fife goalkeeper saved Harry Ritchie's penalty. In the second half, Jimmy Dunn hit the crossbar from a second penalty and near the end the goalkeeper saved the third penalty, again from Harry Ritchie.

Hibs were in deep relegation trouble, as were Clydebank, and the Green Jerseys travelled down to Clydeholm Park on Saturday 13 March for a match they just had to win. There was no scoring when Hibs were awarded a free kick 30 yards out. Hugh Shaw dummied it and Peter Kerr drove the ball into the net but the referee ordered it to be retaken. This time Big Hugh took it himself and he drove it home, with the goalkeeper leaning away back to try and keep it out but the referee this time awarded the goal – the only goal of the game. At the end of Hibs league campaign, they were fifth from the bottom with 30 points. Hibs had won the East of Scotland Shield at the beginning of the season but now they lost out in all the end of the season local competitions.

Harry Ritchie's benefit match was postponed until next season but Peter Kerr's, against Celtic at Easter Road, was a roaring success and every member of the Celtic team was gifted with a solid silver tea service to mark Peter Kerr's 16 years with Hibs, and also to mark Hibs' own Golden Jubilee 50 years. Peter's playing days were now nearing an end, so Hibs gave him a free transfer, the second of the celebrated team to leave Easter Road. Willie Harper had been the first to go earlier in the season to Arsenal, and now the Hibees travelled to play the Londoners in a friendly in which Willie Harper was, unfortunately, not able to play because of injury.

In June, just as Hibs chairman Owen Brannigan was re-appointed as an SFA councillor, he was mourning the death of another old Cowgate friend, Stephen J. Cooney. Stephen had run Hibs' most successful nursery team Harp Athletic since the 1880s, bringing a lot of talent to Easter Road, including the genius James Blessington. We are told:

> Stephen Cooney was a famous athlete in his day when he ran Hibernians Harp Athletic and later he was president of Hibernians junior nursery club, Edinburgh Emmet and president of Michael Whelahan's Old Hibs Association, but more and more the ould Irish guard of Hibernian are dwindling away.

The death of Stephen Cooney also saw the death of Bathgate Park, the home of Edinburgh Emmet, as the land was taken over by the railway authorities of Waverley station. Even allowing for all the recent events, Michael Whelahan's Old Hibs Association still functioned and Easter Road was made available for the Ould Hibs to play the Auld Hearts in the Baillie Bathgate Charity Cup.

And so this chapter on Hibernian's Golden Jubilee season comes to an end, just as the death of Michael Whelahan brought a chapter in Hibernian's history to an end. It was the end of an era.

– 6 –

THE GREEN SERENE
1926–1927

Ma granddad I'd like you to know
Arrived in Edinburgh over a century ago.
He drank pints o' porter ate cabbage an' ribs
An' wi' thousands o' fellow Irishmen followed the Hibs.

The Green Serene hailed oot by Samson's ribs,
An' his folk far back fair followed Hibs.
Of a' his tunes sprang yin that he would stress,
Come away Hibernian the colour o' the grass.

Hibs had not solved their goalkeeping problem after the loss of Willie Harper and just as they started training at the end of July, manager Bobby Templeton swapped left-half Hugh Shaw for Rangers' international goalkeeper Willie Robb. The departure of Hugh Shaw, the third member of the celebrated team to leave Easter Road, was not popular with the Hibs supporters as he had been a big favourite of theirs. We are told: 'Only Willie Miller is left of a great half-back line but he is the coolest most collected Hibernian I have ever saw. Now bhoys, forget the past and look to a bright future and turn out in your thousands for the start of the new season.' Bobby Templeton had, however, got his much needed top-class goalkeeper.

Left-winger 'Darkie' Walker had been late in re-signing and meantime Bobby Templeton stepped in and signed 'a talented young Irish lad', Jackie Bradley, from Glasgow junior club St Roch's and he was to keep 'Darkie' out of the team. Two half-backs were also signed, Willie Dick (now there's an unfortunate name!), from Airdrie, and a 'Celtic cast-off', Eddie Gilfeather who had 'the pass-back down to a fine art'. Never a popular tactic in Edinburgh, but Eddie Gilfeather became a bit of a personality who always gave 100 per cent effort, except when playing against his old club Celtic, when he gave 110 per cent.

At the end of July an old Hibs centre-half, Jimmy Norton, died in his home at 2 Murano Place, Edinburgh. He had been an enthusiastic member of the Old Hibs Association and had played countless charity matches for them.

The Hibees opened season 1926–1927 with a league match at Easter Road on Saturday 14 August against St Johnstone; it was a shocker for the 15,000 Hibs supporters. Jimmy McColl gave Hibs a seven-minute lead but by the end of 90 minutes the Perth men had scored five which was, we are told, 'not an exhilarating experience for Willie Robb, Hibs new international goalkeeper, even although he was faultless with all five'. The sluggish Hibs team that day was: Willie Robb, Willie McGinnigle, Willie Dornan, Willie Dick, Willie Miller, Eddie Gilfeather, Harry Ritchie, Jimmy Dunn, Jimmy McColl, Johnny Halligan and Jackie Bradley.

On Wednesday 8 September the benefit match for the hugely popular Harry Ritchie came off at the Holy Ground against Hearts 'to do honour to an international player who has faithfully served Hibernian Football Club for six years'. All the Hearts players were given commemorative gifts to mark the occasion.

Three days later, Hibs played their third home league match and it was third time lucky in front of 18,000 supporters with a fine 2-1 victory over Scottish Cup holders St Mirren. Versatile utility player Geordie Murray, known as 'Sticker', played at right-half and he got Hibs' opener which 'The Buddies' equalised. Hibs then had a goal disallowed before Harry Ritchie put the Irishmen ahead with a twice-taken penalty. By now Hibs had played five league matches, won two, lost three and were lying 12th with four points in a league of 20.

Having disposed of the Scottish Cup holders, the Hibees soon took on the current league champions, Celtic, at Easter Road on Saturday 25 September, in front of a crowd of 25,000. A newly-signed centre-forward, Pat Heggarty, from Whitrigg United, played for Hibs as cover for the injured Jimmy McColl. Young Pat was keen to show the Hibees what he could do, as was ex-Celt Eddie Gilfeather, who today was to 'wear his feet down to his ankles for Hibernian as the Edinburgh Irishmen pulled off a shock 3-2 victory'. Celtic were twice in the lead but 'the Irish squadrons of Easter Road' scored three times through Harry Ritchie, Jackie Bradley and a great winner from Pat Heggarty. Hibs captain and centre-half Willie Miller had a great game against Celtic's legendary centre-forward Jimmy McGrory, even allowing for the 'Mighty McGrory' scoring twice.

The following Monday Hibs were hosts to St Roch's in a friendly/benefit match as part of the deal for the transfer of Jackie Bradley. On the Wednesday, Rangers were the visitors to the Holy Ground for Jimmy Dunn's benefit match. An unpopular choice of opposition and 'Wee Tim the Hibernian Magician' managed to miss a penalty. Hibs continued with mixed league results, during which time Willie Robb saved a penalty and Jackie Bradley still kept 'Darkie' Walker out of the team.

On Saturday 30 October Hibs visited Tynecastle for a league derby game with Hearts. In one incident Eddie Gilfeather, the pass-back specialist, was taking a free kick inside the Hearts half and was greeted by a torrent of abuse from the Hearts supporters. Eddie gave them a smile and a wave and duly passed the ball all the way back to goalkeeper Willie Robb, sending his abusers into further paroxysms of rage; manager Bobby Templeton wasn't too pleased either. Hearts took the lead twice but goals from Harry Ritchie and Jimmy McColl gave Hibs a well-deserved point. Of goal hero Jimmy McColl we are told: 'he is getting on a bit but Jimmy can still produce the goods and he will be staying with Hibs and honouring his contract although he has gone into the restaurant business in Glasgow.' The Hibs team was: Willie Robb, Bertie Stark, Willie Dornan, Willie Dick, Willie Miller, Eddie Gilfeather, Harry Ritchie, Jimmy Dunn, Jimmy McColl, Johnny Halligan and Jackie Bradley. Two weeks later, the same team took another good point when they played out another 2-2 draw with Rangers at the Holy Ground in front of a crowd of 18,000 and Jimmy McColl was on the scoresheet again.

Mixed league results continued up to the end of 1926 and Hibs had a Mr W. Bruce Sutherland, a physical training instructor, on a short contract giving the players a course of special exercises. Hibs signed Findlay, a defender from Dundee United, but due to an irregularity he was suspended from playing for a month and the Hibees were fined £1. Jimmy Sharp, Hibs' reserve goalkeeper, was transferred to Dunfermline. There was also trouble at Tynecastle at the end of the year with the Hearts directors stupidly banning the Edinburgh press because of their recent 'harmful and sarcastic criticism of the running of the club'.

On Saturday 1 January 1927, the New Year's Day derby match came off at the Holy Ground between Hibs and the 'petty criticismed Hearts'. Maybe Hearts felt they had something to prove, for they took the lead, Harry Ritchie equalised, but again a strong Hearts scored to take a half-time lead and they were looking good. The 'sea of green', however, roared on the Hibees who fought like terriers, but they left it late, with Johnny Halligan scoring with only five minutes to go. The cheering was wild as the Hearts goalkeeper was left looking helpless, giving rise to a daft Hibs song.

> My old man's a Hibee,
> Wears green ribbon in his hat,
> He took me doun tae Easter Road
> To see the Derby Match.

> Where wiz the Herts goalie,
> When the ba' went in the net?
> Hingin' fae a lampost,
> Wi' his breeks aroond his neck.

It was an unchanged Hibs team and they were lying 11th in the league with 21 points from 21 games.

James McLaren of Hibs' Scottish Cup winning team of 1887 died in Canada on Monday 3 January and his memoriam has been recorded in Book 2 and need not be repeated here. That day the Irishmen travelled up to Pittodrie and crushed Aberdeen 2-5. It's a pity they didn't save some of these goals for the Scottish Cup first round when they travelled to play Cowdenbeath and went down tamely 3-0 in a shock result.

Hibs got back on the rails on Wednesday 2 February when at Parkhead they made it a league double over Celtic with a 2-3 victory. We are told: 'Hibernian's surprising if not amazing victory over Celtic was due to the magnificent display of Jimmy Dunn. He at times bewildered the Celtic defence by his mystifying footcraft and was the inspiration of the forward line.' Willie Robb was out injured and Hibs' goalkeeper was listed as 'Douglas' who turned out to be none other than manager Bobby Templeton who 'made no fatal mistakes'. Hibs' scorers were Jimmy Dunn, Jackie Bradley and Johnny Halligan and the team that recorded this unexpected double were: Bobby Templeton, Willie McGinnigle, Bertie Stark, Findlay, Willie Dick, Geordie Murray, Harry Ritchie, Jimmy Dunn, Jimmy McColl, Johnny Halligan and Jackie Bradley.

Jimmy Dunn played for Scotland against Ireland in Belfast on Saturday 26 February and three weeks later Harry Ritchie played for the Scottish League against the English League at Leicester. On Saturday 2 April Willie Robb was reserve goalkeeper when Scotland played England at Hampden.

The Hibees finished ninth in a league of 20 having played 38 games with 39 points. Hibs won only one of the local cup competitions when at the Holy Ground they defeated Hearts 2-1 in the Wilson Cup. Chairman Owen Brannigan was again re-elected unopposed to the SFA council. John 'Darkie' Walker was the fourth member of the celebrated team to leave Easter Road, when Hibs gave him a free transfer in recognition of his seven years' service and he was signed up by Swindon Town.

Among several five-a-side tournaments Hibs hosted in the close season one was a benefit for the Edinburgh University Settlement and another for the East of Scotland Harriers. The Old Hibs Association in one of their charity games fielded a great team that included Scottish Cup winners, league champions and internationalists among whom were Paddy Callaghan, Willie Donnelly,

Bobby Glen, Geordie Rae, John O'Hara, Sam Fleming, Neil Girdwood, Willie Smith, Richard O'Brien, Davy Gordon and John Rafferty.

Hibs also made three close-season signings, a very young Willie Martin from the Edinburgh Juveniles, Jimmy Preston from the west of Scotland junior club Benburb and a certain James McPartlin from Hibs' own junior nursery club, Edinburgh Emmet. Jimmy McPartlin was a born and bred Hibs supporter of Irish stock from a Little Ireland family and was an interesting character.

Jimmy McPartlin's family had emigrated from Country Leitrim, Ireland, and settled with Edinburgh's Southside Irish. They had a house and grocer's shop in Buccleuch Street. Jimmy's father was a keen Hibs supporter and with Jimmy himself being born in Edinburgh he was one of the thousands of the 'Paddy Macs' who were also devoted to the Hibees. When he wasn't at Easter Road, Jimmy as a young lad would push his delivery cart to the posh residences of Newington and Liberton but he would always be late back to the grocer's shop and his angry dad would find him practising his football on the Meadows. Jimmy developed into a fine footballer like so many of the 'Paddy Macs' who played for Hibs, although his sojourn at Easter Road was only to last one year. Football was not to be Jimmy's life as he had a very strong religious vocation and joined a Franciscan seminary in the English Midlands as a novice to train for the priesthood. There was another Scottish ex-professional footballer at the seminary and he and Jimmy caused an outcry in English amateur football circles when they were discovered playing for an amateur club.

Jimmy McPartlin went from Hibernian footballer to Franciscan priest – Father Giles OPM – and until the day he died he remained a keen Hibs supporter and was known as the 'Footballing Friar'. He died in 1960 and is buried in the Franciscan Friary, Dundee.

Lastly, in the close season Jimmy Dunn resisted a fabulous offer to play in, of all places in these days, America. Big English clubs, especially Everton, were also after Jimmy Dunn and, with so much interest being shown in this truly great Hibernian, a mischievous rumour spread that he was on the verge of signing for Hearts. We are told: 'when Jimmy Dunn heard of the rumour 'Wee Tim' jist aboot laughted his ginger heid oaf his shooder'. Jimmy the 'Hibs Daft Joker' said: 'Whit a nightmare, sign fur that lot? If it wisnae sae bliddy funny a wid bliddy cry.'

For the last seven years we are told: 'Jimmy Dunn's ball juggling, trickery and multitude of goals had the Easter Road crowds laughing and applauding loudly.' Next season Jimmy Dunn would be a member of the most famous and legendary team in Scottish international football history. Jimmy Dunn, the 'Hibernian Magician', would be transformed into a 'Wembley Wizard'.

– 7 –

JIMMY DUNN – THE WEMBLEY WIZARD
1927–1928.

Jimmy Dunn, Jimmy Dunn, Jimmy Dunn,
Down Easter Road he'll run, run, run,
Playing for the Hibees is such fun, fun, fun,
Pullin' rabbits oot o' hats,
Jimmy's never done.

Now the Hibernian Magician
Is a Wembley Wizard
The legend had just begun.
All Scotland sings your praise,
Well done Jimmy Dunn.

Besides the three junior signings at the end of last season, Hibs added defender Hugh McFarlane, the brother of 'Jean', a great Celtic player, and another defender, Hector Wilkinson from juniors Vale of Grange. Hector would become a great Hibs servant, being described as 'the best uncapped half-back in Scotland'. Manager Bobby Templeton built up the numbers in his playing squad to field a team in the Alliance reserve league, Hibs having 'departed from a policy of running a first-class football club with only about sixteen men'.

Hibs' first league match at Easter Road for season 1927–1928 was on Saturday 20 August with a 3-0 victory over Cowdenbeath, who found

> the Irish forwards in almost irresistible mood and their plight in coping with such a band of artists was not an enviable one. Jimmy Dunn was the ringleader with his medley of trickery and ball control. Dunn's two goals emphasised what a great little forward he is. One goal revealed his power as a shot the other his aptitude for springing into the air to head the ball home.

Jimmy McColl scored Hibs' other goal and he hit the post, 'overall Hibs could have doubled their score so dominant were they in front of 14,000 of their noisy supporters'. The Green Jerseys were: Willie Robb, Willie McGinnigle, Bertie

Stark, Findlay, Willie Dick, Geordie Murray, Harry Ritchie, Jimmy Dunn, Jimmy McColl, Johnny Halligan and Jackie Bradley.

It is interesting to note that every other club in Scotland kicked off at 3 pm except Hibernian who insisted on 3.15 pm and this came under criticism from other clubs. The decision was, however, defended by Hibs supporters as this was the doing of director Barney Lester, who had an interest in several pubs around Easter Road, and this gave Hibs supporters 'a wee bit more drinking-up time'.

After defeating St Bernard's 7-1 in the semi-final of the East of Scotland Shield at the Holy Ground, the final against Hearts at Tynecastle was a 2-2 draw. That day Hibs played a new signing, James Keenan, a lance corporal in the Cameron Highlanders, the six-foot goalkeeper taking the place of injured Willie Robb. In the replay back at the Holy Ground Hibs won 2-1 but left it late using 'the back pass craze' too much. However, this must have given Hearts a false sense of security with their one goal lead, for in the very last two minutes of the game Harry Ritchie equalised 'with one of his hardest and deadliest shots' then after 'wonderful wing-work' big Harry laid on the winner for Jackie Bradley. 'What would Hibs do without Harry Ritchie, the most forcing winger in Scottish football with the hardest shot.'

Meantime, seven-year servant Johnny Halligan had his benefit match, as did five-year servant Jimmy McColl. Jimmy was not getting any younger but he was still banging in the goals and when he scored a hat-trick against Partick Thistle in a 4-1 league victory at the Holy Ground on Saturday 1 October, it took his tally of league goals to 11. The Hibs programme that day had an interesting caution to supporters: 'Our patrons are requested to look carefully at their change when entering the Holy Ground. A lot of bad money appears to be in circulation just now.'

The Holy Ground, with 30,000 in it, was the venue for the first league clash of the season on Saturday 15 October between Hibs and the 'ould inimy' Hearts, who were making a strong challenge for the championship and were already six points ahead of the Hibees. Jimmy McColl put Hibs ahead but Hearts got a penalty and it was all even at half-time. In the second half the great Jimmy Dunn managed to miss a penalty as the Hibs appeared to struggle, and Willie Robb had to be at his best in goal before left-half Eddie Gilfeather rapped home a 25-yard drive high into the Hearts net 'to give the Irishmen a somewhat sensational victory that dented Hearts league challenge'. Hibs were now lying 14th in a league of 20 with eight points.

The following week in the league at Shawfield, cheeky Clyde deserted their traditional red and white jerseys and wore maroon as Hibs beat them 0-2 with a Jimmy Dunn brace. We are told: 'Shawfield is a real bogey ground for Hibs but the sight of these maroon jerseys inspired the Edinburgh Irishmen.'

On Saturday 29 October Scotland's first international of the season came off at Wrexham against Wales. Neither Jimmy Dunn or Harry Ritchie had been selected, which surprised many, but goalkeeper Willie Robb was. Scotland went two goals up then collapsed, with Wales coming back to take a draw. Several players who were to create the Wembley legend later in the season were in the Scottish team that day but overall it was a disappointing performance and it took Willie Robb of 'unfashionable Hibs' to prevent a defeat. The SFA selectors, however, had grave misgivings about the quality and spirit of the team for future internationals.

In these days the league programme was not interrupted because of internationals and Hibs defeated Hamilton 5-1 at Easter Road. Jimmy McColl scored a hat-trick and Jackie Bradley and Pat Heggarty got one each. James McPartlin made his league debut for Hibernian at inside-right that day but it was on the right-wing that he played in several reshuffled teams over the next few weeks as forwards Dunn, Ritchie and Halligan struggled with injuries. James McPartlin, however, did catch the eye, particularly in a 3-1 victory over Falkirk at Easter Road on Saturday 26 November, 'young McPartlin gave a promising display and merits being retained at outside right'. To keep Harry Ritchie or Jimmy Dunn out of the team was, of course, mission impossible even for the 'Hibs Daft pluckily clever McPartlin'. Another 'talented Hibernian', Pat Heggarty, was in the same situation.

Mixed results continued for reshuffled Hibs but in one game on Saturday 10 December, after going behind twice against Raith Rovers at Easter Road, the Hibees won 3-2, with the winner coming from left-back Bertie Stark, who scored with a prodigious drive from the half-way line.

On Chistmas Eve, Saturday 24 December, the battle of the greens between Hibs and Celtic at the Holy Ground was a 2-2 draw in front of a crowd of 16,000. We are told: 'Besides Jimmy McColl scoring yet another two goals bringing his total to 20L, he brilliantly led the forces of the Edinburgh Irishmen.' The following Saturday, 31 December, Hogmanay, it was another 2-2 draw at Broomfield against Airdrie, with Jimmy McColl and Jackie Bradley scoring for Hibs.

Two days later, Monday 2 January 1928, at Tynecastle, against Hearts, yet another 2-2 draw was played out. Jimmy McColl scored after only three minutes, but by the middle of the second half the Green Jerseys trailed 2-1, when we are told:

> Jackie Bradley was surrounded by three Hearts defenders and numbers it seemed must tell but they did not. Bradley fought off all three and screwed the ball past the Hearts goalkeeper for a glorious equaliser, as bravely a fought for goal as ever was.

Those three draws over the Christmas and New Year period were performed by Hibs' strongest team: Willie Robb, Willie McGinnigle, Bertie Stark, Geordie Murray, Willie Dick, Eddie Gilfeather, Harry Ritchie, Jimmy Dunn, Jimmy McColl, Johnny Halligan and Jackie Bradley.

Hibs made a brave fight for the Scottish Cup this season but their home draw on Saturday 21 January was never played, as opponents Dykehead decided to withdraw. In the second round two weeks later a big Hibs support travelled to Cathkin to see Harry Ritchie and Jimmy Dunn give the Hibees an excellent 0-2 victory over Third Lanark. In the third round, on Saturday 18 February, at Easter Road, 18,000 saw a hard 0-0 draw with Falkirk, and hopes were not high for the Brockville replay four days later. After 90 minutes there was still no scoring and 30 minutes extra time had to be played. Hibs looked stronger but the match could have gone either way until five minutes before the end, as Jimmy Dunn's 'magic' began to tell along with the 'forcing strength' of Harry Ritchie, which took him past three Falkirk defenders before he passed to Jimmy McColl, who rapped home the only goal of the game in 'a gruelling fight in the best traditions of Hibernian in a Scottish Cup tie.'

Three days after this stamina-sapping cup-tie Willie Robb was overlooked by the Scottish selectors, but this time Harry Ritchie and Jimmy Dunn formed the right-wing partnership for Scotland against Ireland at Firhill, Glasgow. Ireland won by the only goal of the game due to an inspired game by their goalkeeper Elisha Scott. In the Scottish team were four from Rangers and two from Celtic, and they came in for a lot of criticism with Scotland being 'let down at centre and on the left'. It was the 'unfashionable Hibs pair' who won any praise: 'Harry Ritchie was a success in the right wing partnership with Jimmy Dunn and Dunn was the artistic and polished player of the match. His methods were as practical as they ware attractive and Dunn without doubt served Scotland assiduously and subtly.' Four top Anglos were unable to play that day and the overall team performance only added to the Scottish selectors' headaches, as the 'big one' against England at Wembley was only five weeks away.

A week later, on Saturday 3 March, Hibs carried a very big support over to East End Park for their Scottish Cup quarter final against Dunfermline. We are told: 'In the 15,000 crowd the green flag and green rosettes were to the fore.' Many wore green bowler hats inscribed 'Well Done Dunn', 'That's the Way Harry' and 'Hurry up Hibs'. Like their supporters, the Hibs team were in 'cup tie mood' and Hibernian 'fireworks' gave them a 0-4 victory, with goals from Johnny Halligan, Jackie Bradley and two from Jimmy Dunn. We are told:

> Dunfermline's greatest trouble was Dunn. Every flick of his foot seemed to guide the ball as he wanted it and he kept Harry Ritchie going well. Ritchie's response was likewise good, both his crossing and cutting-in were in his best style.

The Scottish selectors' problems worsened a week later when the Scottish League crashed 2-6 against the Irish League in front of a disillusioned 60,000 at Ibrox. There was no Willie Robb or Jimmy Dunn in the team and Harry Ritchie was only a reserve. There were six Celtic and Rangers players, two from Motherwell, one from Partick Thistle and Cowdenbeath's goalkeeper. Although this was an annual fixture in its own right, it had been treated by the Scottish selectors as a 'trial' for the 'big one' at Wembley and a Scottish League team could not include Anglos and it was seen they were badly missed. Another 'trial' was quickly fixed for three days later on Tuesday 13 March and the Home Scots drew 1-1 with the Anglo-Scots in front of an abysmal and further disillusioned 6,000 at Firhill, Glasgow. Again, the three Hibernians were overlooked, but four of the Anglos showed up well as did the young amateur Jack Harkness, the goalkeeper of Queen's Park, who played for the Home Scots. To say the Scottish selectors were in a turmoil is putting it mildly; and they now had so little time to search their souls and choose the best 11 to represent Scotland at 'the most important fixture of the season at Wembley' and the players, like the supporters, had spirits which were 'at their lowest ebb.'

Meantime, on St Patrick's Day, Saturday 17 March, the Holy Ground had 20,000 inside for the league match between Hibs and Rangers who were challenging at the top of the league. Being St Patrick's Day the Hibs support were bedecked in even more green than usual and 'the shamrock was in abundance on the "Paddy Macs" in the vicinity of Easter Road'. In the first minute of the game a Rangers' cross glanced off the crossbar and was kicked clear by Hibs' Willie Dick but, to everyone's surprise, including the Rangers players, the referee awarded them a goal, sparking a near riot among the Hibs support and only a massive police presence (because it was St Patrick's Day) prevented a pitch invasion and the referee being lynched from the offending crossbar. Things soon calmed down, however, because it took Jimmy Dunn only five minutes to score a beautiful goal. Every Hibs player was a hero that day but Jimmy Dunn was the super-hero, when with only ten minutes left he crashed home an unstoppable winner. Of 'Hibs the underdogs' we are told:

> Jimmy Dunn spread his passes with fine effect and his two goals were gems of opportunistic art. Dunn was the outstanding personality of the game but Willie Robb was an inspired goalkeeper and Harry Ritchie was his old thrusting self. St Patrick's Day at Easter Road has been a serious set-back to Rangers' championship hopes. The Hibs support, the 'Paddy Macs', were in full voice with their 'St Patrick's Day Hibee Song':
>
> Well I woke me up this morning
> To great almighty roar,
> From the throats of trusty Hibee men

Twenty thousand strong,
Sure it was the Hibernian brigade
Winding up for to join the big parade,
So I put me on my bunnet
And the scarf I love so well,
And I bought myself a shamrock
Just to wear in my lapel,
Don't you know that today's March 17
It's the day for the wearin' o' the green.
Oh it's a great day for the Hibees
It's a great day for the green,
Sure the emeralds and the shamrocks are the order
Sure there's not a finer team across the border,
Oh it's a great day for the Hibees
Oh their green flag's flying high,
Ev'ry Paddy Mac is singing
And the bells they all are ringing
It's a great, great day
Go tell the Rangers, it's a great, great day.

Seven days later, Hibs' opponents were again Rangers and this time they got their revenge in the Scottish Cup semi-final at neutral Tynecastle. It was almost unknown then, as today, for Rangers to be ordered to play such a match outside of Glasgow and, after last week's league defeat, we are told: 'Rangers came to the capital to kick the Edinburgh Irish off the park.' Well, that's just what they did, 'in the most disgraceful and unsporting manner conceding no less than 27 free kicks crippling several of the Green Jerseys and not one Rangers player was sent off or booked or even spoken to by the referee.' The Hibees went down 3-0 as Jimmy Dunn took some brutal treatment and, although he had some good tries at goal, he was forced to defend a lot and only the strength of Harry Ritchie saw him make good headway against the brutality. Willie Robb had a poor game in goal for Hibs and gave Rangers an early soft goal in front of a crowd of 44,000.

The Wembley Wizards

The following Saturday the most important international match, which is so crucial to Scottish pride came off at Wembley against England. We all know the intense rivalry that exists but it was even more intense, if that is possible, 70 years ago. All Scotland was desperately hopeful but there were grave misgivings about the team that was to have the honour of representing the pride and passion of Brave Caledonia. Scotland's performances this season had inspired no confidence and the Scottish selectors had sleepless nights turning over in their minds the best line-up to face the Auld Enemy, who were indeed a class act which included 'Dixie Dean the Goal Machine'. Scottish pride was everything, but the Scottish press were forced to articulate what every Scottish supporter dared not say: 'We are on our knees and we know it.'

The Scottish selectors drew up a list of 37 players from which they would choose the 11 to play at Wembley. Three players from Hibernian Football Club were on that list: goalkeeper Willie Robb, outside-right Harry Ritchie and inside-right Jimmy Dunn. There was not a Hearts player anywhere to be seen.

The nine Scottish selectors, led by SFA president Robert Campbell of St Johnstone FC, met at SFA headquarters in Glasgow to make their final deliberations and announce to a mass of waiting press the wisdom of their team selection. It took them only 40 minutes to announce their team and Hibernian's Jimmy Dunn was one of the 11 who would face England at Wembley.

Jimmy Dunn, 'Wee Tim', had never played against England before but he did have several full international honours and several Scottish League honours. Also, when Hibernian had signed him from St Anthony he was a Scottish Junior Internationalist. In his eight years at Easter Road 'Jimmy Dunn the Edinburgh Irishmen's playmaker' had scored over 100 league and Scottish Cup goals. 'Wee Tim' certainly had the credentials but the scorn poured upon his selection and the selection of his Wembley team-mates would have withered lesser men.

The waiting newspaper reporters were surprised at the speed of the selectors' decision and their gasps turned to groans when the team was announced, as every Scotman's worst nightmare had been realised. Only three of the team were home-based players; the other eight were Anglos and in these days Anglos were looked upon as 'Scottish traitors' for playing their football in England. For two of the team it was their very first cap and for another only his second. Of 12 possible Celtic and Rangers players, only one was selected. The goalkeeper was a Queen's Park amateur. To make matters worse, the selected centre-forward had not kicked a ball in earnest for two months and the forward line as a whole were midgets, the smallest forward line in Scottish international history. 'The towering English defence will simply hammer this Scottish forward line into the ground and there's every possibility that Hibs Jimmy Dunn will be buried beneath the Wembley turf.' Cocky Jimmy Dunn, however, was too much of a joker to take offence and he prophetically reminded his critics that 'speed and skill can make up for lack of inches'.

Never before had a whole Scottish team been no severely criticised as 'inexperienced incompetents' and they were written off before a ball was kicked. A team spokesman, however, was later to say: 'We were given no chance but we were never discouraged. We were determined to show the critics that they could not have been more wrong.' The following is the much criticised Scottish team that would later be hailed as the Wembley Wizards:

Goalkeeper: Jack Harkness, (Queen's Park); Right-back: Jimmy Nelson (Cardiff City); Left-back: Tommy Law (Chelsea): Right-half: Jimmy Gibson (Aston Villa); Centre-half: Tom Bradshaw (Bury); Left-half and Captain: Jimmy McMullan (Manchester City); Outside-right: Alec Jackson (Huddersfield Town); Inside-right: Jimmy Dunn (Hibernian); Centre-forward: Hughie Gallacher (Newcastle United); Inside-left: Alex James (Preston North End); Outside-left: Alan Morton (Rangers).

When the dust had settled after the announcement of the 'shock' Scottish team some Scots sports reporters with a little more insight recognised the 'class' of the team but they hedged their bets with 'what might happen' as 'a humiliating defeat is a distinct possibility'. Strangely, it was the English press that thought the Scottish II were 'remarkably well-balanced'; they were right.

Wembley Stadium (the Empire Stadium, London) was barely five years old in 1928 and Scotland had played there only once before in 1924, drawing 1-1 with the Auld Enemy. Hibernian Football Club was represented then too, as Willie Harper was Scotland's goalkeeper. In 1924 only 5,000 Scotland supporters were able to afford the expensive trip to London. Unemployment and low-paid work was rife and most supporters could hardly afford to follow their clubs to away matches – that was a treat. A trip to London for the vast majority was just a dream. Finances had not changed for the better but the magic of the Wembley occasion had caught the imagination of the Scottish supporters and this year 10,000, a vast number in those days, were to make the trip to London.

This was, in fact, the birth of the Tartan Army and it's good to know that about 300 Hibs supporters, the 'Paddy Macs', were part of it. An old Hibs supporter tells us:

> Money wiz awfie tight then an' ye hid tae save hard tae make it tae Wembley. An' wi' Jimmy Dunn playin' mair o' us jist hid tae go an' the hooskeepin' wiz jiggled somethin' terrible. A loat o' us fi the Coogit (Cowgate) took some o' oor savin's oot St Pat's Catholic Young Man's Society savin's bank an' oot o' St Pat's church burial fund. The priest knew whi wir up tae, bit he nivir said anythin'. It cost aboot 25 bob (£1.25) fur a third-class return train tickit an' if ye hid a suit ye wore it wi white shirt, collar an' tie. That's the wi it wiz in these days. A suppose wi mast hiv a' looked a bit daft 'coz wi hid huge tartan tammies that wir far too big far oor heids. Some o' us Paddy Macs, Hibs supporters ye ken, wore thir faithirs kilts fi the Great War an' some played the bagpipes. Ach whit the hell if wi looked daft, wi wir gaun tae cheer Scotland. Jimmy Dunn wiz a Paddy Mac ye ken, an' so wir some o' the other 'Wembley Wizards'.

Jimmy Dunn, the two other home-based Scots players and officials travelled down to London on the famous train, the *Royal Scot*. The eight Anglo players made their own arrangements from their respective English towns and the team met up together at the Regent Palace Hotel in Piccadilly Circus, hardly the best location. There was no country hide-away for the players, no manager or coach, no team-talk, no tactics and the players were almost strangers to each other. There was of course no television, but neither the radio, or the press, held interviews or gave the much-criticised Scottish team any publicity. Their only friends were the Scottish supporters but that Saturday, 31 March 1928, that fledgling Tartan Army was to see these 11 players take Scottish football to new heights which arguably have never been reached again.

In their hotel the night before the match the Scottish captain, Jimmy McMullan, a 'Paddy Mac' who had played for Denny Hibs in his junior football days, was instructed by the president of the SFA to take the players upstairs and 'talk about tomorrow's game'. Jimmy McMullan was not one for great tactical discussion. He gathered his players on the first floor landing and made a few remarks about conduct. 'Now I don't want any unnecessary talking. Get on with the game and don't talk to opponents or the referee.' He continued with the now famous words: 'I think you all know as well as I do what the whole of Scotland expects from you tomorrow. So get off to bed, put your head on the pillow and pray for rain.' Their prayers were answered. Jimmy McMullan knew that with such a small, lightweight forward line a wet, treacherous surface, would give the Scots a distinct advantage.

The Wembley crowd of 80,682 was a record for a London international and the Duke of York and his guest, King Amanullah of Afghanistan, were presented to the teams. The whole occasion seemed to badly affect a 'nervous looking Scots team', but Jimmy Dunn, a notorious joker, kept up a string of wise-cracks to ease the strain. Just before the kick-off, Scotland's 21-year-old amateur goalkeeper, Jack Harkness, had to grab hold of a goalpost as he lost his composure and nearly fainted.

All the misgivings about the Scots team almost became a reality when, in the very first minute of the match, England hit the woodwork but the legend of the Wembley Wizards was born two minutes later when Alec Jackson headed home the first of the three goals he was to score. Alex James scored two, and Scotland won the match 1-5 as they 'annihilated England with science, skill and pace ... a dazzling Scottish machine that teased and toyed with England making them look ludicrous.'

The performance of the forward line was particularly outstanding but every player played as a team and they were all heroes, Scottish heroes, none more so than the 'Hibernian Magician' Jimmy Dunn. He probably had the least

THE MAKING OF HIBERNIAN 3

glamorous role of the magnificent forward line. 'Wee Tim' was the 'fetch and carry workhorse' but while doing this his amazing dribbling skills would easily draw three and four English defenders out of position, leaving all the space for his team-mates to whom he would pass the ball 'timed and weighed to perfection' and 'Dunn's pace was non-stop, he must have covered 10,000 miles of the Wembley turf striking up a magnificent partnership with hat-trick hero Alec Jackson.'

The press, both Scots and English, had a field day.

To the skirl of the bagpipes Scotland caused the rose of England to wither and die at Wembley.

England were not beaten at Wembley. They were routed and outpaced by Scotland and thrashed by 5-1. And the wonder is that the score was not bigger.

In the annals of international football I do not think there is a parallel to this match.

Each man was playing to the top of his form, the skill and judgement was a delight to watch.

The success of the Scots was primarily another demonstration that Scottish skill, science and trickery will still prevail.

The Wembley Wizards opened everyone's eyes as to how football should be played and in this day and age of outrageous wage bills it is of interest to note the mid-field maestro Jimmy Dunn was paid only £6 for that 'unforgettable day of magic'.

It in also of interest to note that the Wembley Wizards had never played as a team before, and, quite incredibly, they were never to play together again. But that one afternoon of 'unique Scottish football' was theirs and theirs alone for all time, and Jimmy Dunn of Hibernian Football Club was a glorious part of it.

While the Wembley Wizards were weaving their magic, Hibs were at Brockville on league business and even without Jimmy Dunn they forced a good 2-2 draw with Falkirk. By the end of the league campaign Hibs were lying 14th with 35 points.

Jimmy Dunn had attracted a lot of interest from big English clubs over the last few years but Jimmy and Hibs had rebuffed all approaches, but now after his display at Wembley he went to Everton for a whopping £5,000 transfer fee; Everton still got a bargain. Jimmy Dunn is certainly assured of his place in Hibernian's Hall of Fame, even although he never won a league or cup medal with them. With Everton, Jimmy won two league medals and one cup medal. His son, also named Jimmy, won an FA cup medal in a brilliant

Wolverhampton Wanderers team in 1949. Jimmy Dunn, the 'Hibernian Magician', died of cancer in 1963 at the age of 62.

'Wee Tim' was the fifth of Hibernian's celebrated team to leave Easter Road, and at the end of the season two others, Willie Dornan and Willie Miller, were given free transfers. Only four of the celebrated team, Willie McGinnigle, Harry Ritchie, Jimmy McColl and Johnny Halligan, now remained at Easter Road, as an exciting era of stars slowly came to an end. A swift decline in Hibs fortunes lay ahead.

– 8 –

A SPACE OF STARS
1928–1929 TO 1930–1931

A space of stars
Between the chimney pots
Crowds Easter road.

On comes another Saturday night,
Wives at their sinks the dishes dyte,
As one by one the windies light.

The Hibs game is endin' dour,
On the Holy Ground the moon leans oor
And the tenements lean like Pisa's tower.

Sleepless Hibernians crowd the street,
Heavy their thoughts,
Restless their feet.

Grant Hibernian's walled-in soul
A mute benediction,
A space of stars.

As season 1928–1929 approached, Hibs were in long negotiations with Everton who wanted Harry Ritchie to join Jimmy Dunn at Goodison Park. So Harry did not feature in the first 1-0 match at Easter Road, on Saturday 11 August, when two goals from Jimmy McColl could only give Hibs a draw with St Johnstone.

The press pointed out the obvious by saying: 'Hibs need strengthening', but the reverse happened a few days later when Harry Ritchie was transferred to Everton for 'a big fee which will not be divulged by Easter Road'. Harry Ritchie had been one of the most talented and popular players ever to grace the Holy Ground and his nine entertaining years assured him his place in the Hibernian Hall of Fame. Harry was the eighth member of the celebrated team to leave Easter Road.

The three remaining players of the great team were regulars for the rest of the season and they played well in the first league victory on Saturday 25 August, when 9,000 at Easter Road saw Hibs defeat Aberdeen 4-1. Johnny Halligan scored two and Jimmy McColl and Jackie Bradley got one each. The Hibs team was: Willie Robb, Willie McGinnigle, Bertie Stark, Geordie Murray, Willie Dick, Eddie Gilfeather, John Frew, Findlay, Jimmy McColl, Johnny Halligan and Jackie Bradley.

Meanwhile, in the East of Scotland Shield semi-final at the Marine Gardens, Portobello, Leith Athletic and Hibs drew 0-0 and in the replay at Easter Road the score was the same, as Hibs toiled. In the second replay, however, the Irishmen got it right at Easter Road, on Wednesday 29 August, with a 5-0 victory. A week later in the final at the Holy Ground the Hibees recorded a surprise 3-2 victory over Hearts.

Hibs won four and drew one of their next five league matches and they played a benefit match for six-year utility-man Geordie Murray, who had always been the 'worthy twelfth man of the celebrated team'.

Suddenly there was a disastrous 0-1 defeat against Queen's Park at Hampden, and even although Johnny Halligan was carried off injured in the first half, ten-man Hibs should not have collapsed in that way and the following week, Saturday 20 October, the Hibees had to face Hearts at Tynecastle. Harry Brown made his first-team debut for the Irishmen at inside-right and scored in a 1-1 draw in front of a crowd of 28,000. The following week it was Hibs' turn to score six against Third Lanark at Easter Road and Harry Brown notched another two goals.

On Saturday 3 November, at the Holy Ground, Hibs played table-toppers Rangers – 'two teams keyed up to the highest endeavour'. As usual, it was the Irishmen against 12 men, tough Rangers, and the referee. Harry Brown gave Hibs a one-goal half-time lead. To cut a horror story short, the referee first tried to help Rangers by giving them a hotly disputed soft penalty but Willie Robb saved it. Willie McGinnigle was carried off injured, as was Geordie Murray with a broken leg after Rangers had equalised. The Referee took action against Rangers' dirty play, then with only nine Hibernians on the park he gave Rangers 'the winner that never was'. The ball passed across the Hibs goalmouth, hit a post and rebounded into play, the referee awarded Rangers a goal and sparked a riot with 'the Paddy Macs giving the Rangers supporters an awfie hammerin' but it was the referee that really deserved it'. The riot spilled out into the streets and it took the police, with hastily called reinforcements, a long time to restore order. It had been a long time since 'the wild Irishmen of Easter Road' had behaved in this way and it was sad, as they had built up a reputation of being 'the best humoured support in Scotland'.

Dr St John Cogan, the Hibs doctor, tended Geordie Murray's broken leg and had him admitted to Leith Hospital, while Willie McGinnigle's twisted knee was given electric heat treatment by the Irish doctor.

A mixed bag of results followed up to the end of the year with several team changes and Dalziel from Hibs' junior nursery team Edinburgh Emmet was introduced at the beginning of December. It was an unsettled Hibs for the New Year's Day derby game at the Holy Ground on Tuesday 1 January 1929 against second-top of the league Hearts. A crowd of 28,000 saw the Irishmen pull off a 'surprise' 1-0 victory with a goal from Jimmy McColl. After 90 minutes, however, no one was surprised, we are told: 'Hearts were inferior to the Irishmen. The margin of Hibernians victory should have been greater, Hearts getting off lightly on the run of play.' We are also reminded: 'Hearts have not won a league match at Easter Road for nine years and not won any New Year's Day match since the end of the Great War. Hibs were now lying eighth in the league, having played 21 games with 23 points. The Hibs team was: Willie Robb, Hector Wilkinson, Bertie Stark, Findlay, Willie Dick, Eddie Gilfeather, Dalziel, Harry Brown, Jimmy McColl, Johnny Halligan and Jackie Bradley.

Five other January matches saw Hibs win only one and lose four including their Scottish Cup first round tie against St Johnstone at Easter Road. Hibs should have spent some of the big transfer fees for Dunn and Ritchie on 'class' players but they didn't, they did however stay true to their charitable birthright and donated 50 guineas (£52.50) to Edinburgh's Lord Provost for the Miners Distress Fund. The miners had been on strike for some time.

February's results were little better as Hibs signed Danny Kelly, the son of Celtic director, ex-Hibernian James Kelly. Young Danny was also a cousin of Hibs left-winger Jackie Bradley. The Hibees did have a 'big occasion' victory, on Saturday 23 February, when at the Holy Ground they defeated Celtic 2-1, their two goals coming from reserve right-winger Preston. A generous collection was taken for the convent of the Poor Clares, Liberton, Edinburgh.

More bad results followed but again Hibs rose to the 'big occasion' on Saturday 13 April by defeating Celtic again for an unexpected league double. The match should have been played at Parkhead but Celtic Park was under repair after fire damage so it was played at the Holy Ground. The Hibs team was not in good shape because of injuries and four reserves were drafted in, three defenders and one forward. Hibs should have had little chance but Celtic's superb, tragic international goalkeeper John Thomson had a 'very uncharacteristic bad game', selling two goals and Celtic's international full-back Willie McStay scored an own goal. Jimmy McColl got Hibs' fourth goal. Hibs won 4-1 without having to do a lot, in fact the Edinburgh Irishmen even missed a penalty. The Hibs team was: Harris, Hector Wilkinson, Duncan Urquhart, Findlay, Willie Dick, Eddie Gilfeather, Frew, Harry Brown, Jimmy

McColl, Johnny Halligan and Jackie Bradley. At the end of their league campaign Hibs lay 14th in the table with 32 points.

In the final of three local cup competitions, all against Hearts and all played at Tynecastle, Hibs lost a total of 18 goals and scored only four. Certainly, there was team reshuffling and reserves given a chance but the writing was on the wall for the Hibees and manager Bobby Templeton didn't read it.

It is of interest to note a wee bit of trivia from the past season handed out by the 'crazy' Scottish League authorities. All teams playing away from home would have to wear black or navy pants rather than their usual white. The strange reasoning of the Scottish League was that neutral supporters could identify the home team at a glance – what nonsense. This only lasted for the past season as most Scottish clubs hated dark shorts. Mind you, the original plan by the Scottish League was even more unpopular – they wanted to scrap club colours altogether with all teams playing at home in red jerseys and away teams in blue. There was an almighty outcry against this led by Hibs, who told them under no circumstances would they forfeit their immortal green jerseys and rob the club of its birthright and rob their supporters of their famous battle cry 'come away the colour o' the grass'. The Scottish League soon backed down.

As season 1929–1930 approached Hibs played two public practice matches. We are told:

> The innovation of witnessing a practice match between the Hibernian players attracted fully 3,000 spectators to Easter Road last night. Admittance was free and the crowd who were not even asked for a collection were treated to a bright exhibition of football, there will be another on Monday evening.

For the second public practice match, admission was again free but this time the Hibs directors had a collection for Edinburgh's Catholic charities.

Hibs were reasonably pleased with the practice matches and long-serving Johnny Halligan and Jimmy McColl showed up well, while all the others showed themselves to be 'able', there were no new 'stars' and as the first league match loomed we are told:

> Once more there are fears for the Hibernians this season, but they have been doomed often before and come through – threatened clubs, like threatened men seem to live long – and they seem to have a tolerable chance of coming out on top and confounding their critics.

Sure enough, Hibs got their two points that Saturday 10 August, in a 3-1 victory over Airdrie at Easter Road in front of a good 14,000 crowd. It would be a poor season and the Hibees needed every point they could get. Old war-horse Jimmy McColl scored two that day and Bob Sclater from junior club Polton Welfare got the other. The Green Jerseys were: Willie Robb, Hector

Wilkinson, Bertie Stark, Taylor, Willie Dick, Eddie Gilfeather, Johnny Halligan, Harry Brown, Jimmy MoColl, Bob Sclater and Jackie Bradley.

Hibs travelled over to Fife and played at East End Park in a benefit for the Dunfermline and West Fife Hospital Fund. In the semi-final of the East of Scotland Shield Hibs beat St Bernard's 3-4 at the Royal Gymnasium Park which was situated at Canonmills, along from Stockbridge. In the final against Hearts on Tuesday 3 September at Tynecastle the teams drew 4-4 and in the replay at the Holy Ground it was 1-1 but Hearts led by nine corners to five.

Hibs lost the next three league matches and when they played Cowdenbeath on Saturday 7 September at Easter Road in front of a faithful 14,000, they could only manage a 1-1 draw, thanks to a second-half 25-yard free kick from centre-half Willie Dick. There were three changes in the Hibs team, with Duncan Urquhart coming into the defence and Archie Connell and Preston in the forward line. Having played five league games, Hibs were 15th in a league of 20 with three points.

As Hibs struggled on with lots of bad results and team and positional changes, right full-back Willie McGinnigle signed for Irish club Colraine. Willie was the ninth of the celebrated team to leave Easter Road, only Johnny Halligan and Jimmy McColl were left. The Hibees were second bottom of the league when they recorded their second league win on Saturday 12 October with a 3-0 victory over Partick Thistle at the Holy Ground. Leither Frank Dobson, who had been signed from Tranent Juniors at the beginning of the season, got two goals and Harry Brown the other. The Green Jerseys were: Willie Robb, Hector Wilkinson, Bertie Stark, Eddie Gilfeather, Willie Dick, Hugh McFarlane, Johnny Halligan, Harry Brown, Frank Dobson, Jimmy McColl and Preston.

Two weeks later 20,000 uneasy Hibs supporters were in the Holy Ground for the visit of Hearts. We are, however, told:

> Heart of Midlothian are to meet their bogey team, the Hibernian, and despite the fact that Hearts are still championship challengers and the Hibernians in grave danger of deposition it is very open to question how the game will go. Hibs never fear Hearts who have good reason to be nervy as it is ten years since Hearts won a league game at Easter Road and Hearts folk are full of anxiety about the result. Hearts however on this occasion should not fail to win.

Well, once again they didn't, although they were a goal up at half-time a solid Hibs support roared on the Green Jerseys and Frank Dobson scored a great equaliser for the points to be shared. It was the same team that had beat Partick Thistle which put up the brave fight against the 'Ould Inimy'.

Up to the end of the year Hibs picked up only seven points from a possible

18 and when they clashed with Hearts at Tynecastle on New Year's Day, Wednesday 1 January 1930, we are told: 'The Irishmen remain Hearts bogey by again taking a one all draw after again being a goal behind at half-time.' So Hibs had shown 'all the ould pride and passion against Hearts' but they were third bottom of the league.

Hibs internationalist goalkeeper Willie Robb was out injured early in January and the Hibees introduced a new keeper, '6ft, 13½st Geordie Blyth from junior club Newburgh West End and he could look after himself.' Big Geordie was to keep Willie Robb out of the team.

In the Scottish Cup the Hibees put out Leith Amateurs and Ayr United but in the third round, on Saturday 15 February at Easter Road, Hearts finally got the better of Hibs 1-3. Hibs, however, did beat Hearts in the Dunedin Cup final and the Wilson Cup final, both played at Tynecastle Park, both won by the same team: Geordie Blyth, Hector Wilkinson, Willie Lauder, Taylor, Willie Dick, Hugh McFarlane, Harry Brown, Jimmy McColl, Frank Dobson, Tommy Lauder, and Jackie Bradley.

At the end of their league campaign Hibs finished fourth bottom and we are told: 'As in the past the Irish brigade at Easter Road are living on the east wind and sailing very close to it.' The disaster of relegation was staring Hibs in the face but the board and manager didn't seem to be able to shake off 'the traditional Irish philosophy of Hibernian – the bhoys will keep us safe'.

In the close season the Hibs directors did not invest in any new 'class' players but they did invest in improving the terracing. Goalkeeper Willie Robb was put on the transfer list with an asking price of £1,500 which was soon reduced to £500 but it was English non-league club Aldershot that signed him and Hibs got nothing. The Old Hibs Association played charity games as always, with a galaxy of old stars turning out for them and Hibs director Owen Brannigan was re-elected to the SFA Council. Ageing Paddy Cannon was still Hibs head groundman and his son, Tommy, was now head trainer. It was normality itself; God was in his heaven and 'the green flag fluttered at the Holy Ground. Edinburgh's little piece of Ireland at sanguine Easter Road.' As season 1930–1931 approached worried Hibs supporters were reminded: 'Hibernian have the youngest and most inexperienced squad of players in the country.' This season was to be a disaster for the Edinburgh Irishmen and Dr St John Cogan was to be kept busy.

Hibs played two public practice matches at the beginning of August and Willie Clelland, whom Hibs had signed from Glenboig St Joseph's last season, showed up well. He played in the first league match of the season at Love Street on Saturday 9 August when St Mirren won 1-0, their goal coming when Hibs' Tommy Lauder was off the pitch having a cut eye stitched by Dr St John

Cogan. The Hibees were: Geordie Blyth, Hector Wilkinson, Willie Lauder, Taylor, Willie Dick, Eddie Gilfeather, Harry Brown, Willie Clelland, Jimmy McColl, Tommy Lauder and Hugh McFarlane.

Things got worse on Saturday 23 August at Parkhead, when Celtic took six off the Hibees. It was particularly embarrassing for director Owen Brannigan who had invited his lifelong friend, Joe Devlin, the hardline Irish nationalist MP from Belfast, over for the match. The heavy defeat was due mainly to the fact that injured goalkeeper Geordie Blyth was not playing and Bobby Templeton quickly threw in a juvenile goalkeeper, Willie Dudgeon, from, would you believe, a club called Tynecastle Rangers. That poor performance from Dudgeon gave rise to a joke from the good-humoured Hibs supporters, 'Hibs have eleven players all with the same name, Dudgeon in goal and ten dud yins a' in front of front of him.' The good humour of the Hibs support this season, however, was to be stretched to breaking point.

The Hibs team was chopped and changed but few points won and to their credit the directors gave Bobby Templeton 'big money' to buy 'class players' but all approaches were rebuffed by several clubs. So it was back to the juniors scene and Willie 'Ginger' Watson, a centre-half, was signed from Stoneyburn Juniors; he was to develop into a fine and popular servant of the Edinburgh Irishmen.

Meantime poor results continued and the supporters' patience finally broke. On Tuesday 14 October a meeting of supporters, including the influential debenture holders, was convened in Leith. There was a lot of discussion about their total dissatisfaction at the progress, or rather lack of progress, of Hibernian: 'The followers of the club are undoubtedly seething with indignation at this Easter Road football travesty.' A debenture holder raged: 'The directors should get on or get out. Those of us who have money invested in the club are extremely dissatisfied, with the position of affairs.' Harry Swan, a leading debenture holder, followed up on this:

> Debenture holders once lifted the club out of the rut. The club, however, are ignoring us, apparently considering that if we are paid a dividend we should be satisfied. Do they forget that we as followers of the Hibernians, are desirous of seeing the team in a higher and more fitting position?'

At the conclusion of a passionate meeting 'it was agreed to write to the Hibernian management, and ask that a deputation be received. Failure of the club to accede to this request will result in another public meeting.'

Two weeks later, on Monday 27 October, all seven shareholders of Hibernian, which included the directors, met in Edinburgh. Over the past few years there had been changes on the board which was now Barney Lester (chairman), his wife, and Owen Brannigan. Mrs Lester was not a shareholder but her husband Barney and Owen were, and along with five other families they totally controlled Hibernian Football Club. At that time, as in the past, Hibernian was described an 'a closed Irish corporation in the hands of a few Edinburgh-Irish families who still lived in Ireland.' So important was this meeting that an influential shareholder travelled over from Ireland for the meeting and we are told: 'It was indeed the fact that he came over from Ireland which upset the old regime.' The 'closed corporation' remained but we are told: 'The Lester family had a bad day.' Barney was deposed as chairman but remained a director. Mrs Lester was voted off the board altogether. Owen Brannigan was appointed chairman and Alec Maley was brought back as a director. So it was now three shareholders on the board responsible for themselves and the other four. We are told:

> The old order of things was not satisfactory; neither is the new, and this is probably fully recognised. But it has always been thus with the hostility that has surrounded Hibernians history and their need for 'guardians' to keep the club safe.

As it turned out this was to be their last throw of the dice; after so many brave, brave years, they found it impossible to keep safe relegation-haunted Hibs.

Three days later, on Thursday 30 October, the reconstructed Hibs board received a deputation from the debenture holders led by Harry Swan. Director Barney Lester was conspicuous by his absence but manager Bobby Templeton was present. The debenture holders said they were 'unhappy at the unsatisfactory state of the club' and, although pleased with the board changes, they wanted 'new blood introduced' as Hibernian were too much of a 'closed corporation' and suggested that two debenture holders should be 'introduced to the board.' They also suggested the company (shareholders) should be 'opened up to the public' but the directors said they could 'not discuss such a matter at the moment.' Meantime, they asked that it should be seen 'what they could do to improve Hibernians position' and this was agreed to. The board then invited the debenture holders to be part of 'Hibs' official party' at Hampden that Saturday for the match against Queen's Park. For the record, the match ended in a 2-2 draw.

Director Alec Maley had his eye on Irish international half-back Joe Miller, who was on Middlesborough's transfer list and was meantime assisting Dublin Dolphins FC. Alec Maley took the ferry to Dublin and liked what he saw and on Wednesday 12 November Hibs paid a record £1,000 to Middlesborough for Joe Miller. A great signing, but one man could not save Hibs. Joe Miller made his debut that Saturday at Pittodrie and, as luck would have it, he broke his hand and Dr St Cogan had to take Joe to hospital for x-rays. Sad to say, Aberdeen went on to take seven goals off ten-man Hibs.

Hibs tried without success to sign other 'big money' players as more mixed results followed and in their last league match of 1930, on Saturday 27 December at Fir Park, the Hibees lost six goals to Motherwell.

The New Year's Day derby match five days later on Thursday 1 January 1931 was awaited with trepidation by the Hibs supporters. However 28,000 of them were in the Holy Ground and again Hearts could not beat 'bogy Hibs' on a New Year's Day, with the Green Jerseys taking a brave 2-2 draw.

Two days later, again at the Holy Ground, Hibs got another much-needed point in a surprise no-scoring draw with Celtic. A week later another point was picked up in a 1-1 draw with Leith Athletic at the Marine Gardens, Portobello. Hibs were missing Johnny Halligan, whose broken leg was being tended by Dr St John Cogan, so manager Bobby Templeton signed a replacement, Jimmy 'Brick' Wallace from Burnley. He was to be a good servant to Hibs but even by now the Hibs programme admitted 'the club is in deep relegation troubles'.

In the Scottish Cup Hibs first put out St Cuthbert's Wanderers from Kirkcudbright, then Hamilton Accies after a replay but in the third round at Easter Road a crowd of 33,000 saw Motherwell win 0-3. There was a lot of swaying in the crowd and crash barriers collapsed, causing a lot of injuries but none serious. The size of the crowd showed how much the Hibs supporters were keeping faith with the club.

Meantime, in the league, Hibs picked up some valuable points, especially from Ayr United with whom they were locked in the relegation battle. East Fife, who were anchored at the very bottom of the league, beat Hibs 1-0 at Methil on Saturday 28 February. A dreadful performance by the Greens and only a great performance from goalkeeper Geordie Blyth kept the score down.

Dr St John Cogan was working overtime on an injury-hit Hibs squad and at Ibrox on Saturday 18 April Geordie Blyth took a terrible kick in the face. He had to be tended off the park by the Irish doctor who recommended he should not return to the fray, as the big goalkeeper was half blind. Return he did however, but could not prevent a 1-0 defeat in a brave Hibs perfomance. Dr St John Cogan raged 'reckless Rangers will kill someone soon'.

East Fife were doomed to relegation – but who would join them? – it was neck and neck between Hibs and Ayr United. Hibs' last league match was at Brockville on Saturday 25 April and they took a fighting point against Falkirk in a 2-2 draw. The Green Jerseys were: Geordie Blyth, Hector Wilkinson, Willie Dick, Joe Miller, Willie 'Ginger' Watson, Hugh McFarlane, Harry Brown, Ross, Jimmy McColl, Jimmy 'Brick' Wallace and Jackie Bradley.

Four days later, on Wednesday 29 April, Ayr played their last league match on their home ground, Somerset Park, against local rivals Kilmarnock. Hibs and Ayr both had 25 points but Hibs had a better goal average, 0.6 against

0.56 and we are told the obvious: 'nothing less than the defeat of Ayr will save the Greens. It is a day of hope and fear for the Hibernians, the hope being that the future of the Easter Road club as a first division combine depends on the defeat of Ayr and the precarious thread of goal average.' Since their founding in 1875 Hibs had operated on the principles of faith, hope and charity but that day hope deserted them. Ayr won and the Hibees were relegated.

We are told:

It is a sad downfall for a club with such a history and such a tradition as the Hibernians, who in their day have been right at the top, both in the Cup and the League competitions, and have brought out many famous players. It is a sore blow to Edinburgh football which will be all the poorer because of Hibernians fall.

The following day a traumatised Hibs played Hearts at the Holy Ground in the Wilson Cup final and when it didn't matter the Hibees won 3-2.

In the middle of May the Hibs board made a long-awaited decision:

The directors of Hibernian Football Club have agreed to place unissued capital of 1093 shares before the public at par. It is understood that Alec Maley is mainly responsible for this action and the extension of the share capital should mean the addition of new directors. It was further agreed that no outsiders, only directors, debenture holders, the general support and Hibernian friends would have shares allotted to them should they wish to purchase.

The debenture holders held a meeting in Leith on, Friday 22 May and Hibs chairman Owen Brannigan had to bravely 'face the music' alone regarding the new shares, the financial position of the club and the distasteful possibility of greyhound racing being held at Hibernian Park. Harry Swan of the debenture holders had a lot to say about 'the flimsy structure of Hibernian' and 'if ever there was a time for every Hibernian to be pulling together it is now. All personal interests must be put aside even among the board who do not see eye to eye on these issues. The old Irish gang however cannot retain absolute control of Hibernian.' It was plain that an infusion of new blood into the club was required to prevent it from sinking into the depths beyond salvage. He would be the last man to advocate that men like Owen Brannigan and Barney Lester, who had rendered long service to the club, should sever their life-long connection with it, but events of recent years showed beyond doubt that matters were getting beyond them. Harry Swan went on to talk about the new shares and said it was 'childish' of the directors to propose to issue blocks of £1 to £10 which would only keep Hibs 'a closed corporation'. What was required was blocks of £100 to £300 to give a supporter-shareholder some weight in the deliberations of the club. The debenture holders had already showed faith in

Hibernian with large financial commitments and they would show more faith by taking up large blocks of shares. The debenture holders were the real friends of Hibernians and he was sure the general body of Hibs supporters would agree with this. It would also make way for at least two new directors who were fervent Hibs supporters.

With regard to the possible introduction of greyhound racing at the Holy Ground to help ease Hibs' financial situation, Harry Swan had been 'thunderstruck' at its contemplation and his voice was shaking with emotion when he stated:

> There in such a thing as sentiment, and I am sure we would all be loath to see this so-called sport introduced into the home of our dear old club. I would rather see the Hibs cease to exist than its existence being maintained by dog racing. If Hibernian Park, so rich in memory and tradition should be become the resort of yelping dogs and the worst element of the gambling fraternity it would be a very sad day.

Owen Brannigan leaped up to support Harry Swan 100 per cent, 'you can take it from me that there is as much chance of dog racing getting into the Holy Ground as there is of me jumping off Arthur's Seat.'

Debenture holders Mr Murphy and Mr West supported Owen Brannigan and Harry Swan on this emotive issue and a motion was put forward against greyhound racing at Easter Road using phrases such as, 'the consequent evils being introduced into the Holy Ground' and 'Hibernian Park, Easter Road, is for football only and always will be. Greyhound racing would be inimical to the best interests of the club and offensive to the general body of supporters.' It was John Farmer junior, the son of the late great Hibs director John Farmer, who seconded the motion, which was carried unanimously. So the meeting closed.

Director Barney Lester had not replied to the debenture holders' invitation to this meeting but this was no surprise as everyone knew he wanted to keep Hibs as 'a closed corporation of the old Irish gang'. Barney knew that 'opening up the club' with new blood and money would take Hibs forward but he was never convinced that 'new guardians' would have the same passion and commitment to Hibernian's birthright, maybe they were only in it for 'filthy lucre.' Poor Barney was still caught in a time warp, a prisoner of Hibernian's history. Alec Maley had written his apologies for not attending because of business commitments but he, like the ageing Owen Brannigan, who had an unbroken connection with Hibs since first playing for them in 1880, supported Harry Swan on bringing new money and talent on to the board.

The wheels were now in serious motion and all would be revealed in a few months as relegated Hibs played in the second division.

Paddy Hagen, who was killed in action in France, in October 1916, while serving with the Royal Scots.

George Whelahan – a St Patrick's School photograph.

Davy Gordon, who was appointed manager in February 1919.

J. M'GINNIGLE	W. HARPER	P. DORNAN
P. KERR	W. MILLER	W. SHAW
H. RITCHIE		J. HALLIGAN
T. DUNN	J. M'COLL	D. WALKER

The 'celebrated' Hibs team of the mid-1920s.

Harry Ritchie.

Jimmy 'Tim' Dunn, the Hibernian magician and Wembley Wizard.

Alec Maley, manager of the 'celebrated' team.

The Hibernian team of 1932, who were fighting to return to the First Division. Back row (left to right): Langton, Wilkinson, Watson, Blyth, Urquhart and McFarlane. Front row: Walls, Marshall, Flucker, Wallace and Polland.

Willie McCartney.

Harry Swan.

Tommy Brady, who signed for Hibs in 1935.

Davy Logan, photographed in 1938 wearing Hibs' new strip of green jerseys with white sleeves.

'McCartney Babe' Bobby Nutley, who was awarded the DFM during World War Two.

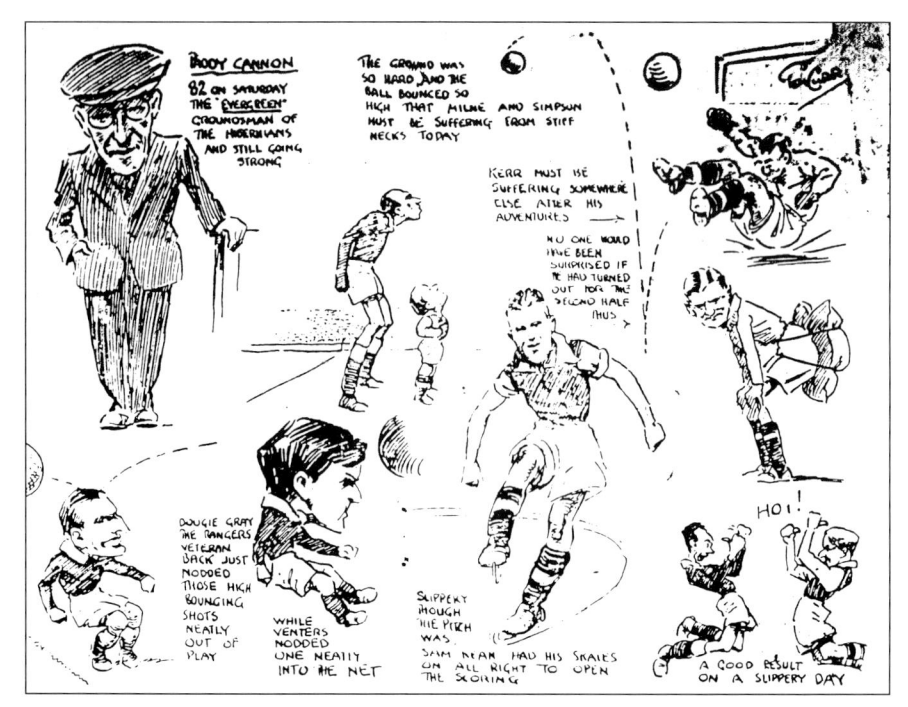

This cartoon was entitled 'The Low-Down on the High Spots', and was drawn following the League match between Hibs and Rangers at Easter Road on 14 January 1939. The game ended in a 1-1 draw.

Hibs 1939 team. Back row (from left to right): Logan, Shaw, Birse, Rice, Kerr and Prior. Front row: McIntyre, Finnegan, Milne, Davidson and Nutley.

In April 1939 Hibs reserve team won the 2nd XI Cup. Here, reserve team captain Davy Shaw shows the trophy to 'ould Irish' director Owen Brannigan.

The Hibs' party at Hampden after their Summer Cup triumph in 1941. Back row (left to right): Gallacher, Anderson, Smith, Cummings, Gilmartin, Fleming and Cuthbertson. Middle row: Mr J. Drummond Shiels (Director), Adams, Shaw, Busby, Milne, Kean, Kerr, Hall and McColl (Assistant Trainer). Front row: Nutley, Caskie, Mr H. Swan (Chairman), Baxter, McCartney (Manager), Finnegan, Combe and Shaw (Trainer).

Hibs 1943–1944 team with the Southern League and Rosebery Charity Cups. Back row (from left to right): J. McColl (Assistant Trainer), Milne, Smith, McCartney (Manager), Downie, Bogan, Kean and Shaw (Trainer). Front row: Finnegan, Nelson, Fraser, Baxter, Hall and Caskie.

Hibs team, November 1944. Back row (left to right): Finnegan, Hall, Kean, Downie, Baxter, Shaw, Bogan. Front row: Smith, Milne, McCartney (Manager), Nutley, Caskie.

– 9 –

RELEGATED HIBS –
HARRY SWAN ARRIVES AND SOON DEPARTS
1931–1932 TO 1932–1933

Comes the tansy hours, the ways of slow-go summer
with the Hawthorn lingering long for every lover
Blind thistledown groping along Easter Road.
Hibernian park stands, the gates of Eden shut.

Posters flame colour round Easter Road embankments
Comic as casey courts doze balcony'd tenements
Under the Bridge o' Sighs the cushie-doos retreat.
Hibernian Park stands, the gates of Eden shut.

Clouds of July shadow bare and empty terraces
Waiting and wondering, the lowly barriers
An on-ding shower its dancing stanzas beat.
Hibernian park stands, the gates of Eden shut.

The Holy Ground looks lost, remote as far-off Faroes
The frost-fired faces, where? the vanished heroes
Or can enchanted grass bring back the eager feet?
Hibernian Park stands, the gates of Eden shut.

In the close season, nine-year servant, high-scoring centre forward Jimmy McColl was given a free transfer and he signed for Leith Athletic as player/manager. That left only Johnny Halligan of the celebrated team to fight for Hibs in the second division and the press reminded everyone 'it will be a stiff fight ahead for Hibs and the Irishmen's task is not to be envied, it will not be an easy one'. That turned out to be an understatement.

Hibs brought in a trainer, Harry Rae, an ex-captain of Clyde, and at the end of July and beginning of August Hibs played two public practice matches at the Holy Ground which were attended by a total of 9,000 supporters. The Hibees organised a collection for the *Edinburgh Evening News* Shilling Fund for the Royal Infirmary and Leith Hospital.

THE MAKING OF HIBERNIAN 3

Some of the new faces played well in those matches and Hibs also signed a right-winger, John Friar from Bradford City, who had played his junior football with Carluke Rovers. Season 1931–1932 with Hibs determined to get out of the second division at the first attempt, opened at Easter Road on Saturday 8 August against Alloa Athletic in front of 4,000 disillusioned supporters. New face Paddy Burke who had come from Leith Emmet, another Hibs 'feeder' club scored the only goal of the game as 'Hibs scrambled through'. The Green Jerseys were: Georgie Blyth, Clark, Duncan Urquhart, Thomson, Willie 'Ginger' Watson, Paddy Burke, John Friar, Harry Brown, Andy Main, Johnny Halligan and Jackie Bradley.

The other Edinburgh clubs, St Bernard's and Edinburgh City were in the second division with Hibs and three days later Hibs played St Bernard's, not in the league, but in the East of Scotland Shield semi-final at the Royal Gymnasium. The Hibees, with Johnny Halligan injured, were swept aside 3-0. We are told: 'Hibs got a rude awakening and a taste of what lies ahead for them in the second division. There must be many combinations as robust and active as St Bernard's in the new sphere.'

All the warning signs were to go unheeded, even when, on the following Saturday in the league, Hibs travelled to Forfar and lost 1-0. Hibs scored some useful wins with six goals against St Johnston and Dunfermline but on a trip to Larbert they lost 2-1 to Stenhousemuir.

On Saturday 5 September in the league at Easter Road, Hibs went down 2-4 against St Bernard's. Goalkeeper Geordie Blyth broke his leg giving away a penalty and Dr St John Cogan had to rush him to the Royal Infirmary.

That Saturday was a day of accidents in Scottish football. An Alloa player also broke his leg, an Ayr player broke his nose, the Airdrie goalkeeper picked up a bad injury and a Motherwell player suffered bad facial injuries. But there was much worse when Dr St John Cogan's prediction about 'reckless Rangers' came tragically true at Ibrox. Johnny Thomson, Celtic's 22-year-old international goalkeeper was accidentally kicked on the head by Sam English, the Rangers centre-forward. Young Johnny was carried from the field and that evening he died from a depressed fracture of the skull in a Glasgow hospital. Thomson lived with his mother, father and brother in the small Fife mining village of Cardenden, and there, on Wednesday 9 September, his funeral took place. First, in the garden of the Thomson house a Mr Adamson of the Church of the Christ, the denomination to which Johnny belonged, held a service before the burial at the local Bowhill cemetery, where another service was held by a Mr Howie. The death of Johnny Thomson had sent shock waves through Scottish football and every club was represented, none more so of course than Celtic and their supporters. Hibernian were officially represented by chairman

Owen Brannigan and captain Johnny Halligan who both carried wreaths in the form of Hibernian's traditional broken harp.

That day the Hibs board and shareholders were to have held their Annual General Meeting but it was postponed out of respect for Johnny Thomson and held the following day, Thursday 10 September, and the AGM turned out to be a landmark in the history of Hibernian Football Club. Again, a forward-looking representative of the Irish family shareholders travelled over from the Emerald Isle. Alec Maley did not stand for re-election to the board because of heavy business commitments. The new board was to consist of five members: chairman Owen Brannigan and Barney Lester and three new directors were elected – Sean Martin, Mick Donoghue and Harry Swan. The Hibs landmark was Harry Swan because, for the first time in the club's 56-year history, someone from outside the Irish community had been elected by 'the ould Irish guard of that closed Easter Road corporation' to have a say in the running of Hibernian. We are told: 'the Ould Irish guard thought most highly of the abilities and commitment of Harry Swan to put new life into Hibernian given time.' Time, however, as we shall see, was initially to be short at Harry Swan's own choice.

Harry Swan, we are told, 'was an unlikely Hibs supporter', being a protestant businessman but he was certainly a staunch Hibee. He showed his commitment by investing in the club as a leading debenture holder helping towards the building of the new stand in 1924 and the development of greater Easter Road. Harry Swan, a master baker to trade, also helped Hibs financially by advertising his business round the track of the Holy Ground. 'Have your lunch and tea at Littlejohns restaurant & cafe, 33 Leith Street. Rooms available for private parties.' It must be remembered that Hibernian was a totally non-sectarian club in players, managers, back-room staff and supporters but this was the first time a protestant businessman had shown any interest in having a say in the running of Hibs, a club that still had a very 'Irish Catholic ethos'. The arrival of Harry Swan was a definite landmark both for the club and for the 'ould Irish guard' who had elected him on to the board.

As Hibs ploughed on they could only draw with Armadale, Montrose, and East Stirlingshire, to mention three bad performances, then on Saturday 10 October against Edinburgh City at Powderhall the Green Jerseys really let themselves down by losing 2-1. Certainly, Hibs lost Paddy Burke with a broken leg but they should not have lost to such poor opposition. We are told: 'Hibs are sacrificing good football for force and already promotion looks doubtful for the Irishmen.'

Hibs had signed a young goalkeeper, Hill, from junior club Yoker Athletic while Geordie Blyth recovered from his broken leg and now, to replace Paddy

Burke, they signed Bobby Marshall from Renfrew Juniors. Some victories were recorded but on a trip to play Bo'ness a point was dropped again. When Hibs travelled to Forthbank Park, Stirling, only 60 Hibees supporters went with them to see a 1-4 victory. It was remembered: 'The Hibees had never played at that ground before but the reserves had a few years back and the gate money was 11d (5½p).'

We don't knew if there were more or less than 60 Hibs supporters when the Green Jerseys travelled to defeat Alloa Athletic 1-2 on Saturday 19 December but there was trouble from the Alloa supporters in a crowd of less than 2,000. In the second division the referee was neutral but the two linesmen were supplied by the teams on the park and the Hibs linesman had the Alloa supporters 'in some doubt about his partiality'. We are further told: 'The electric state of the spectators in the closing stages of the match caused an ugly situation and the game ended with Alloa hotheads attempting to assault the Hibernian linesman and the referee before the police intervened.' Emotions obviously ran high in the second division, even in Alloa.

The emotions of the Hibs team were to run high in the New Year's Day derby match against local rivals St Bernard's at the Royal Gymnasium on Friday 1 January 1932. So far in the league, John Friar had scored 12 goals and Frank Dobson 11 and they were to feature in this tousy game for all the wrong reasons. John Friar missed a first-half penalty and in the second-half, as passions soared, Frank Dobson was sent off. Tempers became even more frayed and Hibs were reduced to nine men with 'Ginger' Watson also being went off. St Bernard's won by the only goal of the game and we are told: 'The game was so dirty there may be a Scottish League enquiry but Hibs who appear to be the main offenders are disgusted at St Bernard's tactics and the weak referee and would welcome any enquiry.' The Hibees were lying sixth in a league of 20, having played 23 games with 29 points; they were seven points adrift of the leaders East Stirlingshire.

Hector Wilkinson had not re-signed for Hibs until last October and it was only now that another defender, Hugh MacFarlane, re-signed. The board had dithered over wage agreements and MacFarlane was still studying at St Andrews University. These two were now joined by Andrew Leslie, who had travelled all the way from New Zealand to sign for the Hibees.

Things did not improve and in the first round of the Scottish Cup at Easter Road, on Saturday 16 January, Hibs lost 2-3 to Dundee United. Five weeks later tragedy struck a toiling Hibs.

In Memoriam – Barney Lester

Hibs' long-serving director Barney Lester died in his home at 50 Albion Road, beside Hibernian Park. Barney was one of the old Edinburgh-Irish who had been present at the founding of Hibernian in St Mary's Street Halls in 1875. He was an early supporter who eventually became a member of the committee that ran Hibernian and he was one of the St Patrick's Catholic Young Men's Society who, along with the driving force of the St Mary Star of the Sea (Stella Maris) CMYS, Leith, resuscitated Hibernian from its death throes in the early 1890s. Later Barney was a director and shareholder, one of those famous 'stony faced Irish directors of that closed Irish corporation at Easter Road.' Barney's wife was also a director, the first woman in Scottish football. It was never recorded if she was also 'stony faced'. Barney was a telephone linesman to trade and later he became a publican and was proprietor of the Albion Bar in Albion Road where he lived. The day of Barney's death, Hibs had to play Edinburgh City in the league at Easter Road and the Green Jerseys wore black armbands, the green flag was lowered to half-mast, and two minutes' silence was observed. The Hibees won 3-1 that day. On Thursday 23 February, after Requiem Mass at St Mary Star of the Sea RC church, Leith, attended by Hibernians old and new, Scottish football officials, Hibs supporters and the general public of all denominations, Barney was buried in the Eastern Cemetery off Easter Road, where so many Hibernians have been laid to rest in the shadow of the Holy Ground. The pall-bearers were Barney's 20-year-old son, of whom we shall hear more later, and five members of the Old Hibs Association. A seven-foot-high granite Celtic cross was raised over Barney's grave which is situated behind the tenements and his pub in Albion Road.

> Softly Barney's days did pass
> Silent, and slow of pace,
> Linking Hibs past with present grace,
> Now Angels at Love's behest,
> Place upon his breast,
> A Rosery of rest.

Barney was the most 'shadowy Hibernian of the ould Irish guard' as found in a short reminiscence:

> Barney Lester was a original, a proud 'Paddy Mac' who lived and worked for the Hibees all his life. He hated publicity, Hibs business was their own business and the club would be run by the directors their way. He never accepted that what he called 'outsiders' could really have the same passion for Hibs, He saw himself as the last caretaker of Hibernians birthright. Barney's fellow director old Owen

Brannigan was even steeped more in the club's history but he was forward looking and he welcomed the idea for what was called 'new blood' coming on to the board but Barney always resisted the idea. For all the 'stony faced' reputation there was not a mean bone in Barney's body and he was one of the Hibs saviours in the early 1890s who insisted that the club must be strictly non-sectarian and he did much to build up Hibs famous reputation for being 'a big happy family'. His wife was a director of Hibs as well and they ran the Albion Bar where they were very popular with a multitude of stories about the 'guid ould days'. Barney maybe lived too much in the past in not trusting people like Harry Swan to help take the club forward. In the short term it turned out Barney was right and you could imagine him saying from the grave 'I told you so.' The long term eventually proved otherwise but maybe Barney was right, who can say? After all that is said and done all Barney cared about all his life was the welfare of the Hibees.

The demise of Barney Lester should have strengthened ambitious Harry Swan's position on the Hibs board but it didn't. Struggling Hibs failed to gain promotion, failed to spend money on 'class' players and dragged their feet in wage negotiations for the new season. Harry Swan was furious he could not get his own way; he had always advocated investment in players and wages and Hibs were stuck in the second division for a second season. Harry Swan resigned in June after being on the board for only nine months. Among the Hibs support their talk was of 'Harry's desertion'. The 'ould Irish' members of the Hibs board were shattered at Harry Swan's decision as they had the highest regard for his ability and and thought that he was being too hasty. 'Rome wasn't built in a day.' Maybe Barney Lester had been right and the determination of the 'ould Irish' saw them buckle down with a determination that Hibs would win promotion next season and they would do it 'their way'.

Before we move on it is of interest to record that at the same time Barney Lester died, the death also occurred of ex-Hibernian Scottish internationalist, James Kelly, who was a director of Celtic. Also last season Hibs signed the son of Jimmy Quinn, another Celtic legend, unfortunately he did not match up to his famous father. Another Celtic legend, Patsy Gallagher, guested for Hibs in a local cup competition.

Before season 1932–1933 got underway trainer Harry Rae resigned and the Irishmen brought back 30-year servant Di Christopher. Tommy Cannon was still an assistant trainer and his old dad Paddy Cannon, with almost 40-years service behind him, was still groundsman, 'tending the beautiful turf of the Holy Ground with his usual loving care.'

Some players were put up for transfer and John Friar went to Portsmouth for a fee of £1,000. Most key players were retained, as was Nickey Langton, a good full-back signed last season from East Fife, and excellent signings were made, Johnny Polland, 'Brick' Wallace, James Hart, Rab Walls, Peter Carruthers and McPherson. Manager Bobby Templeton held two public practice matches attended by 10,000 supporters and he sorted out a strong squad of dour defenders and forwards with a reputation for high scoring. The Hibs directors had made some money available to Bobby Templeton with whom they had kept faith and he spent it wisely. It was absolutely vital to win promotion this season.

On Sunday 7 August, the Hibs directors and shareholders held their annual general meeting at Easter Road; again an influential Irish shareholder travelled over from the Emerald Isle to lend his weight to this important meeting. Hibs chairman Owen Brannigan officially recorded 'the loss of my old friend and colleague Barney Lester has been a severe loss sustained by Hibernian Football Club, he was a great worker for countless years.' An official vote of sympathy was also extended to the Lester family. Another loss was £557 in the financial report and 'no dividend would be paid to the shareholders'. This was nothing new and anyway the shareholders had not invested for profit but out of emotion to help 'keep Hibs safe'. Two new directors were voted in to replace the late Barney Lester and the resigned Harry Swan. Again the 'ould Irish' were determined to keep the momentum of 'new blood' on the board and in a vote they defeated the bid of Liam Devlin, 'an ould Glasgow-Irish Hibs supporter and debenture holder' in favour of electing an Englishman, Thomas Hartland, from Bristol, who had settled in Edinburgh and had been 'Hibs Daft for the 18 years. He was a debenture holder and friend of Harry Swan. Thomas Hartland was 'to be a very able director for over twenty years helping to make Hibs a force in Scottish football once again.' We are told: 'He was a quiet man who makes few speeches and none in public but has a vigorous zeal for Hibernian.' The other director voted on to the board was none other than Barney Lester's 20-year-old son Edward, the youngest director in Hibs history.

Hibs kicked off their campaign to win the second division championship on Saturday 13 August with a 2-0 victory over Dundee United in front of a 10,000 Easter Road crowd. By the end of September the Hibees had accumulated 13 points from a possible 18 and they signed a fine centre-forward, Peter Flucker, from Queen of the South and he popped in a few goals. On Saturday 1 October he scored again in a 0-3 away victory against Arbroath, the Green Jerseys were: Geordie Blyth, Hector Wilkinson, Duncan Urquhart, Nickey Langton, Willie 'Ginger' Watson, Hugh McFarlane, Rab Walls, 'Brick' Wallace, Peter Flucker, Johnny Halligan and Johnny Polland.

The Irishmen won their next eight league matches with a 'super fit squad of players' and they took seven goals off Bo'ness and eight off Armadale. As we shall see, these two clubs were forced to drop out of the second division later in the season as they could not meet financial guarantees. During these two months of October and November, classy left-half Hugh MacFarlane 'of deer-like speed' received his Master of Arts degree from St Andrew's University and Johnny Polland broke his leg which, along with other team injuries, kept Dr St John Cogan and trainer Di Christopher busy. A great old goalkeeper also died.

In Memoriam – Pat O'Brien

Pat O'Brien was one of the early 'Paddy Macs' present at the founding of Hibs in 1875 and he played for the club in the late 1870s and early 1880s, helping to establish the Irishmen as a football force. Later he was one of the most long-serving members of Michael Whelahan's Old Hibs Association, taking a great interest in their activities and playing in countless charity matches over the years. Pat lived at 209 Bank Street, off the Lawnmarket, at the top of the Mound and worked for Edinburgh Corporation Water Trust before he died on Sunday 20 November, in the Royal Infirmary, fortified by the Rites of Holy Mother Church. His Requiem Mass was attended by Hibernians old and new in St Patrick Church with the Hibees' official wreath taking the form of the traditional broken harp. The burial at Newington Cemetery was, at the family's request, a private affair where the pallbearers were six of Pat's ex-team mates from the Old Hibs Association. Another one, like so many others of the 'ould guard', was now gone.

On Boxing Day, Monday 26 December, Hibs took a break from league business and 12,000 were in the Holy Ground to see the Irishmen pull off a surprise 3-2 victory over Hearts in the Wilson Cup final.

On the last day of 1932, Saturday 31 December, it was back to league business at the Holy Ground and the Hibees disposed of Albion Rovers 2-1. Two days later, Monday 2 January 1933, at the Marine Gardens, Portobello, the Hibs gained another two hard-fought points in a 0-1 defeat of Leith Athletic. The Hibs team was: Geordie Blyth, Clarke, Duncan Urquhart, Nickey Langton, Willie 'Ginger' Watson, Hugh MacFarlane, Peter Carruthers, McPherson, Peter Flucker, 'Brick' Wallace and Rab Walls.

Three more league victories followed before the Scottish Cup came along and a first-round 2-2 draw with Forfar Athletic at Easter Road. Hibs travelled north for the replay on Thursday 26 January and they made no mistake with a 3-7 victory. The Hibees had to travel further north for the second round and took a brave 1-1 draw with Aberdeen 'with a big green support backing them loudly'. The replay on Wednesday 8 February saw a terrific mid-week crowd of 24,000 at the Holy Ground and the old war-horse Johnny Halligan scored the only goal of the game with six minutes to go, to give the faithful Hibs support something to celebrate. The press tells us: 'Hibs goalkeeper Blyth is evidently a believer in mascots, he had a youngster in full Hibs uniform and he carted about with him several harps and horse-shoes and they did him good.'

In the third round, Hibs had a home draw against Hearts, causing a lot of interest and a Hibs supporter cancelled a booking to sail to America so as not to miss the match. In the interests of crowd safety the Irishmen spent a lot of money in installing upgraded steel crush barriers and we are told: 'The Holy Ground looked like an archaeological excavation site with all the digging that was going on.' The match on Saturday 4 March was a 0-0 draw and the crowd of 34,000 were well-behaved, with the exception of a few who 'said it with bottles and fists before being sorted out by the long arm of the law'. Four days later Hibs lost the Tynecastle replay 2-0.

It was only the second division league championship that mattered to Hibs and during these cup ties they continued to pick up full points. They took seven goals off Edinburgh City and signed ex-Celt Paddy Connolly who had been playing in Ireland. The Hibs went on to be second division champions with 54 points. With Bo'ness and Armadale having withdrawn from the league, Hibs lost the six points they had accumulated against them and if this had not happened the Irishmen would have had 60 points, creating a second division record.

So the 'ould Irish' kept their promise to the supporters and did it 'their way' and there was a huge sigh of relief that they had taken the Hibees back into 'the charmed circle' of the first division. The prestigious catholic spiritual brotherhood, the Knights of St Columba, threw a 'Hibernian championship carnival supper-dance' at the Palais de Dance in Fountainbridge, attended by the directors, shareholders, debenture holders, backroom staff and, of course, Bobby Templeton and the victorious players who were 'feted like the heroes they were all evening'. It was a huge light-hearted success, that evening of Tuesday 25 April.

As the season drew to a close, five Hibs players, Geordie Blyth, Duncan Urquhart, 'Brick' Wallace, James Hart and Johnny Halligan, took part in a Hibs/Hearts Select against a Celtic/Rangers Select in a benefit match in aid of the recent local Granton Trawler Disaster.

In the past season, Hibs chairman Owen Brannigan was off the SFA council for the first time in almost 30 years, although he was now voted back on. Hibs director Nick Donoghue, however, was voted off the British League Management Committee. Hibs hadn't run a reserve team but now they were readmitted to the Alliance League.

The boardroom and manager's office at Easter Road was fitted out in oak panelling, the stand was repainted, as was the main south entrance with the club's name and harp in a beautiful mosaic. The Holy Ground was ready for Hibs' return to the first division.

– 10 –

BACK IN THE FIRST DIVISION AND HARRY SWAN RETURNS
1933–1934 AND 1934–1935

So here's a hurrah
For Erin-go-Bragh,
And one for the Hibs and the green,
An another hurrah
For Erin-go-Bragh,
And the harp on the Hibs flag is seen.

With the Holy Ground smartened up for Hibs' return to the first division, it was decided that it was time to smarten up the players' kit. The old collarless dark green jerseys were replaced by a slightly brighter green with a white collar. Shorts remained white and socks were updated to black with green tops. Sometimes the Hibees would wear green and white hooped socks. The smartness and quality of the Easter Road pitch was never in question and we are told: 'The verdant swath of the Holy Ground is in prime condition as always from the devoted attention of veteran groundsman Paddy Cannon, who seems unimpaired despite his 78 years.' Paddy had already given Hibernian 38 years' service and incredibly there were another 12 years' service in him.

Manager Bobby Templeton retained his main playing squad although it did take several weeks for Hugh MacFarlane to re-sign. The public practice matches were played at the beginning of August and of several juniors who had been signed, Somerville of Tranent Juniors showed up best.

Hibs' first home league match of season 1933–1934 came off at the Holy Ground on Saturday 19 August with a tough test against Rangers in front of a crowd of 21,000. As old war-horse captain 13-year servant Johnny Halligan, the last of the celebrated team led his men out:

> Hibs chairman Owen Brannigan raised the championship flag amid great cheering as the Irishmen said goodbye to the second division. Hibs also said goodbye to the old type of jerseys, and introduced collars to the wearin' o' the green. Johnny Mulligan must have hardly known himself in the new style.

In a 0-0 draw Hibs had the better chances and hit the crossbar. It was a good performance against a top team, considering that Hibs were back from the second division. The 'new Green Jerseys' were: Geordie Blyth, Hector Wilkinson, Duncan Urquhart, Clark, 'Ginger' Watson, Peter Langton, Rab Walls, 'Brick' Wallace, Peter Flucker, Johnny Halligan and Somerville.

Hibs picked up four points from a possible six before their next big test came along against Hearts at Tynecastle on Saturday 9 September. In the build-up to the match the press commented:

> The green flag is back at Tynecastle, probably the Hibernian followers would have preferred the battle at Easter Road. Sentimentally Hibs return to league battles with Hearts should be celebrated at the Holy Ground and because, frankly, the Irishmen would have a better chance of winning. Quite frankly, how much does the sentimental part matter? Well, so be it, Tynecastle. When were the Hibs ever afraid of Tynecastle? Haven't Hibernian gone out to Tynecastle before now and laid the Hearts low? Aye, many a time. In other words the followers of the Hibs are in good spirits.

The Hibs followers were also in good voice and their large numbers brought a 'Hibs Daft Sunny Leith' song with them.

> I'm not goin' tae Gorgie,
> I'm no' goin' again,
> I'm no' goin' tae Gorgie,
> It ayeways come oan rain.
>
> It's no' because ma shirt's no' clean,
> It's no' because a've nane,
> I'm no' goin' tae Gorgie,
> It ayeways come oan rain.
>
> Old Easter Road once more,
> That's the place that I adore,
> An' I hope to see an' I hope to be,
> In the Holy Ground once more.
>
> God bless the Hibs

It was a no-scoring grim struggle in which 'centre-half "Ginger" Watson was outstanding for the Irishmen with hand and foot or his whole self just butting in.' It was however, 'another good point for battling Hibs.'

Five days after the Hearts match Hibs signed Motherwell's versatile forward Willie Moffat, spending a club record of about £1,000. A few weeks previously Hibs had signed Celtic's Peter Kavenagh, so the directors showed that they were willing to spend in their efforts to keep the Hibees in the top division.

BACK IN THE FIRST DIVISION

This was applauded at the shareholders' AGM on Wednesday 27 September, which recorded a credit balance of £2,436. Bobby Templeton was reappointed team manager, director Sean Martin was re-elected to the board and old Owen Brannigan was re-elected as chairman. Again it was agreed that no dividend or directors' fees would be paid. An honorarium of £100 was, however, unanimously voted to be granted to Owen Brannigan 'for services to the club'. Owen Brannigan had been at the founding of Hibs at St Mary's Street Halls in 1875 and had an unbroken official connection with the club since signing for them as a player in 1880. It should be remembered that for years Hibs directors worked for the club seven days a week without any payment and the shareholders hardly ever got any dividend on their 'emotional investment'. Only the newer debenture holders like Harry Swan were guaranteed a return on their money.

In recognition of 'Ginger' Watson's superb form he got the well-deserved honour of playing for Scotland against the Irish League in Belfast on Saturday 30 September. Hibs badly missed him that day, as they dropped both points in a heavy defeat from St Johnstone at Easter Road.

A few weeks later, after mixed results, 'Ginger' Watson was sidelined with a very bad septic throat, Carruthers and others were also out with injuries and Dr St John Cogan was kept busy as Hibs neared the bottom of the league. Pat Malloy, a junior from Arthurlie, was brought in and he did very well in the forward line but soon captain Johnny Halligan was being treated by the Irish doctor for badly torn ligaments, sidelining him for a few months. This injury was in fact to end Johnny Halligan's playing career. Willie Moffat was appointed captain and he scored two brilliant goals in a vital 0-3 victory over Airdrie at Broomfield. Nicholson was signed from St Johnstone and he scored goals as Hibs picked up more points. A defeat at Ibrox in their last match of 1933 and a defeat from Hearts at Easter Road on New Year's Day, Monday 1 January 1934, kept Hibs in the danger zone and in their next three games they collected only two points. The directors splashed out more money, paying 'a substantial fee' to rivals Hearts for inside-left John J. Smith just in time for the Scottish Cup. In the Hearts programme they tried to make out the were helping Hibs in their time of trouble but the fact was they had charged almost £1,000 for the player.

John J. Smith, 'J.J.' to the Hibs supporters, was however an excellent player and he made his debut at the Holy Ground in the first round of the Scottish Cup against Clyde on Saturday 20 January. It was to be a remarkable debut in a remarkable game. A crowd of 17,000 saw Clyde take the lead but Rab Wall equalised things with a cheeky back header. Clyde went ahead again, then a penalty gave them a third and by half-time the score was Hibs 1, Clyde 4. The

Hibs supporters, we are told, 'were weighing up the relative merits of going home early for tea or waiting for the pubs to open to get the taste of the game out of their mouths.' We don't know what manager Bobby Templeton said to his players at half-time but they came out for the second half 'with all the fighting spirit of the ould Irish brigades as if defeat was out of the question for them.' Rab Walls got his and Hibs' second goal and new boy 'J.J.' Smith got a brace to make it four goals each. With 15 minutes to go a beautiful head flick from 'J.J.' gave young Paddy Malloy the opportunity to crash home the winner. We are told:

> The Hibs supporters were transformed from silent witnesses of doom into raving maniacs acclaiming their heroes with wild abandon. Total strangers threw each others' bunnets in the air and clung around each others necks and wept for joy and relief as Hibs electrified the big cup-tie crowd at the Holy Ground.

It was sheer bedlam and:

> The tie had at its conclusion some of the ould Hibernian ring. It reminded ould timers of the ould Hibernians who were never beaten until the final whistle blew and who pulled many a game out of the fire. Nothing finer has been done by Hibernian for several years.

The Green Jerseys who performed that great fight-back wore: Geordie Blyth, Hector Wilkinson, Duncan Urquhart, Peter Langton, 'Ginger' Watson, Tommy Egan, Rab Walls, Willie Moffat, Paddy Malloy, 'J.J.' Smith and Peter Kavenagh.

'J.J.' Smith's two-goal debut was celebrated in song:

> D'ye ken John Smith
> In his Jersey green?
> He went through Clyde
> Like a submarine.
> He scored twa goals
> He was sae keen
> An' the Hibs live to fight
> Anither mornin'.

Tommy Egan, who had signed for Hibs earlier in the season, played well in that famous victory and he would later go on to be an excellent servant. Paddy Malloy, who had scored 'the glorious winner' against Clyde, scored four of Hibs' six goals against Alloa in the Scottish Cup second round at Easter Road two weeks later. In the third round, again at Easter Road, on Saturday 17 February against Aberdeen, the goals dried up and Hibs lost 0-1 in front of 26,000 expectant supporters. What was annoying was that Hibs had taken three goals off the Dons in the league only a few weeks previously.

BACK IN THE FIRST DIVISION

Two league defeats followed before Hibs travelled to Love Street and pulled off a surprise 0-3 victory over St Mirren. Portobello-born entertainer Sir Harry Lauder was at the game and we are told: 'He was very impressed by the Edinburgh Irishmen's surprise victory.'

The following week was St Patrick's Day, Saturday 17 March, and Hibs played Celtic at Easter Road in the 'battle of the greens'. Always a big occasion in Scottish football, and more so with the clash being on St Patrick's Day, bringing out from the Edinburgh press such headlines as 'St Patrick's Day at Easter Road, wigs on the green', 'Hibs against Celtic, when Irish and Irish come together', 'St Patrick's Day, the wearing o' the green in Edinburgh'. The headlines were followed by tit-bits of information:

> In Roman Catholic churches in the city special services were held in connection with the Saint's anniversary. By the workings of coincidence Easter Road football ground will be given over entirely to the 'wearin' o the green', the meeting of the Hibernian and Celtic clubs being an event at which one might expect the local Irishmen to turn out in force to support the Hibs in this game between these two 'Irish' clubs. Wherever Irish people have gone on leaving their native land their families still gather round the fire to tell the stories of St Patrick and this is done as assiduously in Edinburgh as anywhere else

Before the kick-off the Hibs directors presented both teams with clusters of shamrock with a harp tied up in green ribbon and to entertain the supporters we are told: 'On St Patrick's Day at Easter Road we had an all Irish celebration with a most novel Irish band thrown in.' The match was played in poor weather but we are told it was 'exciting fare' with Celtic unfortunately recording a 1-2 victory. The Hibernian team was: Geordie Blyth, Hector Wilkinson, Duncan Urquhart, Peter Langton, 'Ginger' Watson, Hugh MacFarlane, Rab Walls, 'Brick' Wallace, Peter Flucker, 'J.J.' Smith and Peter Kavenagh.

Four more league defeats followed one after another as 'Hibs faded badly near the bottom of the league.' Their second last league match, on Saturday 21 April against Third Lanark at the Holy Ground, was crucial and the Irishmen won 3-1 to keep themselves safe. Hibs lost their last match at Dens Park against Dundee where the crowd only numbered 300. The Hibees finished 16th in a league of 20.

Hibs went on a three match tour of the north of Scotland winning two and drawing one. In the local Edinburgh cup competitions the Hibees were unsuccessful. Rab Walls and Duncan Urquhart had played in every match this season and they re-signed for the next, as did most of the squad.

So Hibs had survived their return to the First Division but it had been a struggle and the directors assured the supporters that they were 'working very hard to make improvements.' What they did was soon revealed and we are told:

'It was brave, unselfish, forward looking and indeed revolutionary for that ould Irish guard of that so closed Irish corporation of Hibernian down at Easter Road.'

The Annual General Meeting of Hibernian was coming up soon and the 'Irish gang of nine' (directors and shareholders) held a 'council of war' which included 'new blood' director Thomas Hartland, as they were positive he would back the revolution they were planning. Their plans were laid and the orchestrated AGM was held at the Holy Ground on Tuesday 12 June. The subdued financial report actually showed a profit of £191 18s 9d (£191.94) but as usual no dividends or directors' fees would be paid. The directors' report indicated that the return of Hibs to the First Division had not been as successful as hoped. Right on cue, director Nick Donoghue indicated as he was the retiring director by rotation he would not seek re-election, stating 'I originally joined the board to help Hibs fight out of the second division and re-establish themselves in the first, this has been achieved and I am now more than happy to step aside for a younger man.' Harry Swan of the 60 debenture holders was immediately and unanimously appointed back to the board by the 'Irish gang of nine'. He accepted the appointment. So far the plan was working like clockwork but the most revolutionary part was still to be realised. After the AGM Harry Swan joined his fellow directors in a private meeting and right on cue Owen Brannigan stated he would be remaining a director but was resigning the chairmanship of Hibernian because of 'old age' (Owen was 72 years old) so as to make way for a younger man. Swan assumed the younger man would be Edward Lester, the son of the late Barney Lester, so that the Hibs would remain in 'Irish hands' but the 'ould Irish' had a surprise for the stunned Harry Swan by, as pre-arranged, unanimously electing him to the chairmanship of Hibernian Football Club. Almost in a daze, Harry accepted. The plan of the 'ould Irish' was complete, in one fell swoop that evening they had brought back Harry Swan not only as a director but as chairman, with their full confidence that he was the man to take Hibs forward with his energy and enthusiasm. They were proved right, Harry Swan was to be a great chairman for the next 29 years.

This was a long overdue decision by 'Irish' Hibernian who were most certainly non-sectarian but this was the first time in the club's 59-year history that a protestant from outside the Irish community of Edinburgh and Leith would be the 'Easter Road supremo'. To be fair, of course, no one from outside the Irish community before Harry Swan had shown the slightest interest in running 'Irish Hibernian' and this had kept Hibs 'a closed Irish corporation' but now it was the Irish themselves who had finally buried that accusation.

Before our story moves on, we should briefly look at some of the myths about Harry Swan's chairmanship, which were stirred up by 'elements from outside Hibernian', but even today some of these myths survive among Hibs supporters. Basically, the myths are that he wanted to 'move Hibs away from their Irish roots' yet reality seems to be the reverse of this. It is said he wanted to change the club's colours to red but what he in fact did was enhance the jerseys to a bright emerald green with the addition of white sleeves to make Hibs the smartest turned out team in Scotland. Later in our story we shall see when he did this. He supposedly wanted to change the club's name to 'something' but there is no evidence of this and of course he never did although he had the power to do anything he wanted. He did, however, introduce green goal nets which were even unknown at Celtic Park. Another myth is that 'Harry Swan took down the harp' yet during the first 22 years of his chairmanship the harp remained at the north entrance and at the main south entrance and all the great players, including the Famous Five, all walked under it to sign, train and play for Hibs and that massive main entrance harp was surrounded by clusters of Shamrocks. With ground reconstruction in the mid-1950s these entrances had to be demolished. An expensive new mosaic harp was commissioned from a craftsman in Ireland and shipped over to Easter Road where it was hung in the boardroom. When Harry Swan died it was gifted to his widow. Perhaps the most unkind myth is that Harry Swan was 'anti-Irish', which didn't really add up when you consider he was a Hibs supporter long before he invested hard-earned cash as a debenture holder in the mid-1920s when the club was a 'closed Irish corporation' and it was the 'ould Irish' who welcomed him on to the board and unanimously elected him to 'supreme power' as chairman of Hibs. Hardly reasons to be anti-Irish. And to mention only three of the 'ould Irish', director Owen Brannigan, groundsman Paddy Cannon and medical officer Dr St John Cogan, Harry Swan valued and worked with them all through the years; he never removed them and he could have at any time. It is also of interest to note that when Harry Swan was just another season ticket holder at Easter Road he struck up a close friendship with another season ticket holder, a 'Hibs Daft' Roman Catholic priest, Monsigner Miley, of whom we shall hear of later in our story, and when Harry was appointed chairman he made Monsigner Miley the players' counsellor, the first and very forward-looking post of its kind in British football.

Having said that, another complete myth was that Harry Swan withdrew complimentary admission to the many RC priests and ministers of other denominations. With the huge demand by season ticket holders for seats in the Easter Road stand, Harry could no longer reserve seats for these clergymen but they still received complimentary admission to the stand.

Everyone has their own opinion of Harry Swan; for instance a member of the Famous Five, who must remain nameless, said 'the players didn't like him', but there in no denying that Harry Swan was a great visionary for Hibernian and Scottish football in general. He brought Hibernian into the European Cup, the first club in the whole of Britain, when everyone else thought it was a dead duck idea. He brought Hibernian into a British league, bringing all the great English clubs to Easter Road, and he built a 60,000 capacity stadium with a revolutionary state of the art floodlight system. These are but a few of his achievements as chairman of Hibernian Football Club. It is of interest to note that as a young lad Harry Swan followed the fortunes of Leith Athletic.

At the start of season 1934–1935 Dr St John Cogan had to advise 14-year servant Johnny Halligan, the last of the celebrated team, to stop playing because of badly damaged ligaments but 'Hally' remained at Easter Road as a coach/scout. He was joined by an old team-mate, Hugh Shaw, who was recalled to the Holy Ground as an assistant trainer. 'Big Hugh' had been manager of Elgin City, one of the clubs Hibs played on their Highland tour last season.

Most of last season's playing squad was retained, with Duncan Urquhart being appointed captain but others, Wallace, Kavenagh and Malley, were released. As always, promising juniors were signed up and at a public practice match at the beginning of August Harry Borland, John Davie, Hill and Crawford showed up well.

Harry Swan made a popular move with fellow director Owen Brannigan and manager Bobby Templeton by taking them and all the players to a day's golfing at Gleneagles. Harry Swan, however made a very unpopular move among the supporters by changing the Easter Road kick-off time from 3.15 to 3 o'clock. We are told: 'the ould Irish directors had always kept to the later kick-off because it suited the Hibs supporters' drinking habits' but now the Hibees were the last senior club to embrace the 3 o'olock kick-off and so it was for their first league match of season 1934–1935 at the Holy Ground on Saturday 11 August, when the Irishmen defeated Hamilton 3-1. The Hibs team was: Geordie Blyth, Hector Wilkinson, Duncan Urquhart, Crawford, 'Ginger' Watson, Tommy Egan, Rab Walls, Willie Moffat, John Davie, 'J.J.' Smith and Harry Borland.

As two more league victories followed, left-half Hugh McFarlane was put up for transfer, so Harry Swan splashed out a Hibs record of £1,700 to sign Celtic's classy veteran right-half Peter Wilson who, after 11 years, had become and still is a 'Parkhead legend'. Peter had won every club and international honour but had now maybe lost a yard of pace and he good-humouredly put it down to his big ears. One man does not make a team, but Peter Wilson was to help Hibs improve their position greatly this season, as did another new signing at this time, Alfie Anderson from junior club Yoker Athletic.

On Saturday 8 September there was a crowd of 30,000 in the Holy Ground when the Irishmen played Hearts. Hearts were awarded an early penalty which Geordie Blyth saved and in the second half Harry Borland gave Hibs an unexpected 1-0 victory over the 'ould inimy'. Peter Wilson had replaced Crawford in the half-back line and Peter Flucker came in at centre-forward in place of John Davie.

It was mostly bad results that followed and goalkeeper Geordie Blyth was, surprisingly, dropped in favour of Hill and also another junior goalkeeper, James Culley, was signed from Camelon Juniors. Another signing was centre-forward Willie Black from Wishaw Juniors. It was also at this time that Hibs caused a 'minor sensation' by playing some games in short-sleeved jerseys: 'they are surely a bold lot these Edinburgh Irishmen'.

Every Wednesday the Hibees had a golf outing at Edinburgh's Kingsknowe course and they started to put together a good run of seven undefeated league games, which set them up nicely for the 'battle of the greens' against Celtic at the Holy Ground on Saturday 15 December. A crowd of 25,000 saw Hibs take a well-deserved 3-2 victory with goals from Alfie Anderson, Rab Walls and 'J.J.' Smith. The Hibs team was: Hill, Hector Wilkinson, Duncan Urquhart, Peter Wilson, 'Ginger' Watson, Tommy Egan, Rab Walls, Willie Moffat, Willie Black, 'J.J.' Smith and Alfie Anderson. This was not a bad Hibees team and they lay exactly half-way in a league of 20 with 23 points.

Director Owen Brannigan was presented with a gold watch from the East of Scotland FA as he retired after 30 years service in office for them.

In the Scottish Cup first round at the Holy Ground Hibs took five goals off Vale of Atholl from Pitlochry and in the second round, again at the Holy Ground, seven were scored against Clachnacuddin. The third round was a tough tie against Aberdeen at Pittodrie on Saturday 23 February. On the Friday night Bobby Templeton took his players to the first house at the Royal Theatre to see *Robinson Crusoe* and in the morning it was a train journey to Aberdeen and a big Hibs support went north as well. Rab Walls missed a penalty but the 0-0 draw was celebrated on the pitch by this big support, in expectation of a victory in the replay at Easter Road four days later. With the replay standing at 1-1, Hibs thought they had scored a last-minute winner but the referee ruled offside; it was a very tight decision and both players and supporters were really miffed. Thirty minutes extra time produced no more goals. A new development by the SFA had the clubs toss for the venue of the second replay and, true to SFA logic, officials from both clubs had to travel to the Royal Hotel, Dundee, to perform the ceremony on Thursday 28 February. Hibs won the toss for the match to go ahead on Monday 4 March but they lost the game 2-3 due to two bad mistakes by goalkeeper Hill and another cup run came to an end.

Goalkeeper Geordie Blyth was quickly recalled then just as quickly transferred to St Johnstone. 'Big Geordie' had been a great favourite of the supporters. Some poor performances ensued as Peter Wilson went to the USA and Canada with the Scottish International Touring Team. Goalkeeper Hill broke two fingers and full-back Duncan Urquhart had to play between the sticks in one game before early season signing James Culley made his debut in goal losing five to Falkirk at Brockville. Hibs finished 11th in the league and in the local cup competitions the Hibees won the East of Scotland Shield with a fine 4-2 victory over Hearts at the Holy Ground.

– 11 –

ENTER THE BOLD MCCARTNEY
1935–1936 TO 1938–1939

Hibernian entered season 1935–1936 with a directors' financial report showing a £294 19s 1d (£294.96) deficit and retiring by rota, director Hartland was re-elected to the Board. A new trainer, Sandy Henderson, who had been 21 years with Falkirk, was brought to Easter Road. Departing the Holy Ground were players such an Peter Flucker, Willie Moffat and Hugh McFarlane.

Chairman Harry Swan and manager Bobby Templeton travelled over to the Emerald Isle and signed Paddy Farrell of Dublin Bohemians, a very classy player but injury prone. Other fine players signed were Tommy Brady from Wishaw Juniors and James Miller from Millwall. In a public practice match at Easter Road at the beginning of August in front of a crowd of 12,000 all the regulars showed up well, as did more newcomers such as Soutar from King's Park, Gorman from Bonnyrigg Rose and Davy Logan. The crowd were treated to a brilliant display from Paddy Farrell but he was taken off with cartilage trouble and, as it turned out, Dr St John Cogan was later to advise an operation was required. A bad blow to the Hibees' plans and it was to be another dramatic struggle against relegation this season.

Hibs opened their league campaign on Saturday 10 August against Queen of the South at Palmerston Park. The Hibees must have taken a big support with them for we are told: 'On the appearance of the Irishmen they were greeted by a tremendous roar from their supporters complete with green scarves and hats and mascots carrying harps and horse shoes.' Willie Black scored for the Hibs in a 1-1 draw. The team was: Hill, Hector Wilkinson, Duncan Urquhart, Peter Wilson, 'Ginger' Watson, Tommy Egan, Rab Walls, Tommy Brady, Willie Black, James Miller and Alfie Anderson.

Seven days later at Easter Road, in front of a crowd of 10,000, Hibs picked up another point in another 1-1 draw, this time against Clyde. Three straight league defeats followed, two of them being at Easter Road, causing a Hibs supporter to write to the press, 'I have never viewed Hibs prospects with more foreboding.' His and all the other supporters' foreboding deepened when that

Saturday, 7 September, Hibs dropped another two points and six goals against Queen's Park at Hampden. The Hibees were at the bottom of the league.

The following week 'mighty Rangers' were visitors to the Holy Ground in front of a crowd of 18,000 and 'the Irishmen were transformed'. We are told: 'the Hibs side improved beyond belief and had Rangers fighting for their lives. The Irishmen had no respect for Rangers footballing greatness and gave their opponents a sore buffeting in a 1-1 draw.' The Green Jerseys who 'got their horns out' that day were: James Culley, Hector Wilkinson, Soutar, Davy Logan, 'Ginger' Watson, Tommy Egan, Rab Walls, Tommy Brady, Willie Black, 'J.J.' Smith and Alfie Anderson.

What was thought to be a Hibs revival came to an abrupt end only four days later when at Easter Road the Hibees went down 2-3 to Airdrie. Worse, much worse, was to follow that Saturday 21 September at Tynecastle, in a league match that produced 11 goals – unfortunately Hibs only scored three of them. Enough said, at least about the score. During the match, 'Ginger' Watson was seen throwing up at goalpost and Duncan Urquhart also did this several times and left the field with what he said was a blow he had received on the body. It was suspected they had been 'on the bevvy' as a reaction to 'Ginger' Watson being barracked this season by the Hibs supporters and Duncan Urquhart having lost the captaincy. Manager Bobby Templeton immediately gave them free transfers so disgusted was he at those two good servants letting the club down so badly, and at Tynecastle of all places. Considering the unsavoury circumstances under which the two players were kicked out of Easter Road, they were lucky to be signed up by Ayr United and Aberdeen respectively.

At last, at their tenth attempt, Hibs actually won a league game on Saturday 28 September, defeating Kilmarnock 3-1 at the Holy Ground and they followed this up with two other victories. It was, however, back to their old ways very soon in their next six league matches from which they picked up only one point. Action was required and it was back to the Emerald Isle for Harry Swan and Bobby Templeton, this time to Belfast to sign, on Wednesday 4 December, two of Linfield's Irish internationalists. Hibs paid a club record – £7,000 – for centre-half James 'Soldier' Jones and £500 for inside-right Willie Gowdy. We are told that 'Soldier' Jones was an attacking centre-half, which was unfashionable in the day of the 'stopper' and he also suffered from indifferent health during his stay at Easter Road and never struck true form. Overall, Harry Swan and Bobby Templeton could have spent Hibs' record fee better.

Two more defeats and a victory followed, then came Hibs' last game of 1935 on Saturday 28 December at Shawfield against Clyde, who were bottom equal with the Hibees; it was a vital clash. For the second time this season Hibs were involved in an 11-goal match: Hibs scored four of them. To be fair,

ENTER THE BOLD MCCARTNEY

the Hibees' collapse came about when goalkeeper James Culley received a terrible blow to the head and he had to be taken from the field by Dr St John Cogan and for the last 20 minutes of the game 'Soldier' Jones played in goal and lost four.

The New Year's Day derby match at Easter Road, on Wednesday 1 January 1936, was viewed with great trepidation after the heavy defeat the Hearts had inflicted back in September. Torrential rain kept the crowd down to 16,000 and on a very muddy pitch Hearts had a one-goal lead at half-time. The Hibees, shooting down the slope in the second half and roared on by the 'most faithful support in Scotland', outplayed the highly-fancied Hearts but a goal would not come until wee Tommy Brady, with only three minutes to go, hooked home a beautiful equaliser 'sending the Holy Ground into fits of delirium'. There was almost a winner for Hibs in the last minute but Alfie Anderson was just foiled. The Hibees who 'gained prestige substantially' were: Hill, Hector Wilkinson, Soutar, Peter Wilson, 'Soldier' Jones, Tommy Egan, Tommy Brady, Willie Gowdy, Willie Black, 'J.J.' Smith and Rab Walls.

Hibs were, however, in big trouble at the bottom of the league, with relegation now looking a distinct possibility and only one point was collected before the weather and the Scottish Cup intervened. In the first round of the cup on Saturday 1 February, Hibernian travelled to Millburn Park, Alexandria, and defeated Vale Ocoba 1-3, but in the second round, a week later at Shawfield, they went down to Clyde.

Three days later on Tuesday 11 February, manager Bobby Templeton resigned 'to benefit everyone and I part with the club and directors on the best of terms.' Bobby Templeton had been with Hibs as a player and manager for 25 years and had played in the 1914 Scottish Cup final. The following day, Harry Swan asked old war-horse Johnny Halligan, who was now a Hibs scout, if he would take the manager's job, which 'Hally' accepted as he was anxious to help Hibs out of their plight, but he made it clear it would only be short term as he did not see himself as a manager. Johnny Halligan had been a member of the 1920s celebrated team and had now been with Hibernian for 15 years. It looked liked 'Hally' had put himself in an impossible position, with Hibs at the bottom of the league and the players' confidence at its lowest ebb, but he was to do a magnificent life-saving job.

Full points were immediately collected in Hibs' next two league games as 'Soldier' Jones and Willie Gowdy were selected to play for Ireland against Wales at Celtic Park, Belfast. More points were dropped and games were running out as the Hibees position became dangerous and it was fortunate that other clubs such as Clyde, Airdrie, Ayr United and Albion Rovers were doing just about as badly.

Johnny Halligan did a fine piece of business in negotiating the loan of Hearts reserve goalkeeper Willie Waugh and on Wednesday 4 April at Rugby Park, in a vital clash with Kilmarnock, he really showed his worth in a match of three penalties. Penalty number one fell to Hibs in the eighth minute, which Tommy Brady coolly converted. Kilmarnock were then awarded two penalties in the 33rd and 39th minutes, and Willie Waugh heroically saved both of them and altogether had a great match which allowed Hibs to collect both points. The Hibees that day were: Willie Waugh, Hector Wilkinson, Munro, Peter Wilson, 'Soldier' Jones, James Miller, Ferguson, Tommy Brady, James Clark, Tommy Egan and Tommy Dunsmore.

Hibs were hanging on by their fingertips, picked up three points from their next two games but needed both points from their last game to be sure of avoiding relegation. They did it in front of a massive Hibs support at East End Park, defeating Dunfermline by the only goal of the game. The Hibees ended up 17th in a league of 20.

Johnny Halligan had done a great job in only two months, bringing in new players to the line-up and putting spirit back into the team but he was greatly relieved when, late in the evening of Monday 21 April at the North British Hotel, the Hibs Board unanimously appointed Willie McCartney manager.

Willie McCartney had been a long-serving manager of Hearts but they had parted company over a policy dispute a year previously. Part of that policy dispute had been over the controversial sale of the Protestant Action Society newspaper at Tynecastle. He had been Hearts' manager since 1919 in succession to his father, so there was a strong Tynecastle connection but Hibs really needed a team builder and the 'Bold' McCartney fitted the bill perfectly. Dapper bowler-hatted McCartney, who always sported a rose in his buttonhole, 'I'll wear a green one when it's invented', accepted the managership of Hibernian without hesitation. He was to be a great boss, laying the foundations of the Famous Five championship era and if it hadn't been for the intervention of World War Two and his untimely death shortly after, who knows what he could have achieved.

The following season, Hibernian issued their annual financial report which showed a loss of £6192 17s 7d (£6192.85), caused largely by the signing of 'Soldier' Jones and Willie Gowdy. The one bright spot in the report showed the steadfastness of the Hibs support, 'the Hibernian have thus ended a harrowing season in a sore plight financially though our income from league matches show an increase.' The report showed chairman Harry Swan two things: just how difficult it had been for the 'ould Irish' for well over 50 years in keeping Hibernian 'safe' and just how much it was the Hibernian support that were the very club itself, not him. In only two short years, Harry Swan had run Hibs into their deepest debt ever, he was, however, with the aid of Willie McCartney to go on and do a great job for the Hibees.

Hibernian's Annual General meeting at the beginning of July featured this dismal financial report but we are told: the 'Irish' shareholders 'were not in a critical mood, they naturally expressed their disappointment with the season's results but sympathised with the Board of Directors on the difficulties they had to face.' It was a short, harmonious AGM and Harry Swan was unanimously re-appointed chairman and Edward Lester, the retiring director by rota, was re-elected to the board for the next four years. New manager Willie McCartney was accorded a very warm welcome by the 'Irish' and he told them, 'it will have to be deeds, not words next season'.

Team building, of course, takes time and season 1936–1937 was not to see any improvement in Hibs' league position. There were, however, improvements in the Holy Ground with the terracing being extended, the boundary wall round the pitch being painted brilliant white and the directors' box being brought more up-to-date.

Eight-year servant, Hector Wilkinson, was given a free transfer and players such an 'J.J.' Smith, Willie Gowdy, Rab Walls, Harry Borland and Hill were all to leave Easter Road. New signings included goalkeeper Alex Gourlay of Partick Thistle and Johnny McKay of Blackburn Rovers who was described as the 'Peter Pan of football'. He had started his career with junior club St Anthony in the early 1920s and had played for many senior clubs since then. Others included Alex Prior, Alex Gardiner, Alex Ritchie, James McLean, Frankie Farrell, Mick Devine, David Anderson, Bryson and Kelso. A public practice match at the beginning of August, played in front of a 12,000 Easter Road crowd, however, showed 'Hibs still have problems to solve'.

Considering Hibernian had struggled for several years now and had narrowly avoided relegation again last season, an incredible crowd of 25,000 were in the Holy Ground for the first league match of the season but were let down with a 1-3 defeat from Aberdeen. The following week the Hibees lost 4-0 against Albion Rovers at Cliftonhill; it was going to be another struggle for survival,

The novelty of Austria FC with a player named Jerusalem in their team, visiting Easter Road for a friendly, did little to lift the gloom as Hibs went down 2-3 to a very clever outfit. That evening, Monday 17 August, the Green Jerseys were: Alex Gourlay, Alex Prior, Bryson, Davy Logan, 'Soldier' Jones, Tommy Egan, Tommy Brady, James McLean, Willie Black, Peter Wilson and Davy Anderson. The Austrians were treated to dinner at the Grosvenor Hotel where they presented Hibernian with a handsome commemorative banner. It is of interest to note that we are told that it was from the example of the

Austrian's strip that the seeds of an idea were first sown to enhance the green jerseys with the addition of white sleeves, although it was to take three years and the impetus of Arsenal before Hibs did this.

Hibs had only one point from their five league matches when, at the Holy Ground on Saturday 5 September, they recorded their first victory, 5-4 over Hamilton Accies. It was a real struggle as the Hibs had to come from behind three times for the win which featured a Willie Black hat-trick. Four days later Alex Prior got married but he still turned out for Hibs at Easter Road for the quick return league match with Albion Rovers which ended in a 1-1 draw.

A 'missionary' friendly by a Hibs eleven down to the Borders on Thursday 17 September is worth a mention. The opposition was Chirnside United who went down heavily 0-7 with their ex-Hibs goalkeeper Dudgeon having a miserable time. Hibs' goalkeeper was a 15-year-old trialist Jimmy Kerr who was to go on to be a great club servant. Jimmy Kerr being spotted by the Hibees was rather fortuitous, for the Hibees had been watching another goalkeeper at a schoolboys' match at Easter Road but it was Jimmy that caught the eye and he was quickly snapped up. After his playing days, he later became a director and today, in his late 70s, Jimmy Kerr, along with Lawrie Reilly, Joe Baker and Pat Stanton can be found entertaining guests in our new North Stand.

A crowd of 25,000 at Easter Road on Saturday 19 September for the league meeting of Hibs and Hearts in a see-saw match which saw Hearts leading 2-3 with only three minutes to go. It looked like another defeat until, after great play by Tommy Brady, he put over an inch-perfect cross for Willie Black to equalise, much to the delight and relief of a big noisy Hibs support, for the Hibees were second bottom of the league.

In their next four league matches, Hibs picked up only four points but a heavy 5-1 defeat at Parkhead against Celtic on Saturday 24 October showed up more weaknesses in the Hibees' defence which handed out very soft goals. It was a pity, for the forwards had been knitting well and Hibs Irish Free Star (later the Republic of Ireland) internationalist Paddy Farrell had returned from injury and was back to his best, scoring a peach of a goal that day with his head. The following week 'Soldier' Jones was playing for Ireland against Scotland in Belfast and the Hibees missed him, going down 0-1 against Third Lanark at Easter Road. Hibs' head trainer Alex Henderson had a disagreement with the Board about training methods and he resigned, with his assistant Hugh Shaw taking over. It was also at this time that Johnny Halligan was appointed Sunderland's chief scout in Scotland.

Two away league matches in successive weeks saw Hibs surprisingly pick up full points and in their next home game they again got two points. The Hibs programme on Saturday 28 November for the Easter Road match against

ENTER THE BOLD MCCARTNEY

Falkirk was full of praise for captain Peter Wilson for the Hibees' recent revival, but in this 2-2 drawn match poor Peter got sent off for punching an opponent. Meantime 'Soldier' Jones was again on duty for Ireland, this time against England at Stoke. Paddy Farrell, however, turned down his chance to play for the Irish Free State against Hungary in Dublin saying, 'The Hibees need me more at this time'. Good for him, putting club before country.

On Boxing Day, Saturday 26 December, Rangers were the visitors to Easter Road and we are told not surprisingly, 'Rangers had most of the luck including two penalties' as Hibs went down 1-4. We are further told: 'The 25,000 crowd rather than becoming angry were very amused the way Rangers claimed for a penalty every time they were in the Hibs box and sometimes outside it.' Having said that, these two Rangers penalties brought to a total of 11 the number of penalties Hibs had awarded against them so far this season, only six of which had been converted.

Another penalty was awarded against the Irishmen in their next match against Hearts at Tynecastle on New Year's Day, 1 January 1937, but Hibs goalkeeper Alex Gourlay saved the great Tommy Walker's effort as rival supporters behind the goal engaged in a pitched battle. The match had started very promisingly for Hibs with a piece of Paddy Farrell magic laying on the opener for James McLean after only ten seconds. Hibs were, however, badly weakened by the absence of Alex Prior and Willie Black and eventually lost 3-2. It was a nasty match with Hearts being physical and their team and supporters became infuriated with the referee. The Green Jerseys were: Alex Gourlay, Bryson, Tommy Dunsmore, Peter Wilson, 'Soldier' Jones, Tommy Egan, Alex Ritchie, James McClean, Harrison, Paddy Farrell and Tommy Brady.

Hibs picked up only two points from their other January games as left-winger Alfie Anderson was transferred to Bolton Wanderers for £1,500. At the end of the month the Hibees travelled to Recreation Park and defeated Alloa 2-5 in the first round of the Scottish Cup but two weeks later, at Douglas Park, Hamilton Accies put them out of the competition 2-1.

In their next five league games, Hibs picked up five much-needed points, which included an excellent 2-2 draw with Celtic at the Holy Ground and featured Alex Gardiner, after a brilliant run, hitting home a 30-yard drive. Also at this time, 'Soldier' Jones was again playing for Ireland against Wales and Willie McCartney signed a lanky centre-half, Charlie Birse, from Broughty ex-Servicemen. Willie McCartney also made another signing, a great signing, on Friday 2 April when a local Hibs supporter, Willie Finnegan, of junior club Bo'ness Cadora, joined his boyhood heroes. Willie Finnegan was a true artist and would later strike up an uncanny understanding with another great Willie McCartney signing, none other than Gordon Smith.

Hibs picked up only one point from their last four league games so it was just as well other clubs in the relegation battle fared just as badly; the Hibees again ended up 17th a league of 20.

The Irishmen had done little in the local cup competitions for several seasons and this season was to be no different. One resurrected and long forgotten trophy, the Edinburgh City Cup, saw Borders team Duns play Hibs in the first round, which ended in a 2-2 draw. Duns goalkeeper was ex-Hibernian James Keenan and he was looking forward to facing his old club again in the replay, which was held over to next season. Tragedy, however, awaited poor James for at the start of the following season in a match between Leith Athletic and Duns at Meadowbank, we are told, 'James Keenan fell awkwardly for a ball and damaged his heart and he died immediately on the field; his ten-year-old son was in the crowd.'

On Wednesday 12 May, the Coronation Day of King George VI was celebrated with a West against East select match at Hampden. Four Hibernians, Paddy Farrell, Peter Wilson, Davy Logan and Tommy Dunsmore were in the East team that lost 2-0.

The very next day Willie McCartney made another outstanding signing in the shape of 'L'il' Arthur Milne who had been released by Dundee United so he could take part in a month's trial with Liverpool. Because of Arthur's lack of inches and an injury he picked up, Liverpool decided not to sign him and Dundee United delayed in re-signing him, so Hibs nipped in smartly to secure the signature of 'L'il' Arthur Milne, 'the tantalising box of tricks'. He was also a very creative player and a real goal-grabber but he would infuriate Hibs supporters by spooning the ball over the bar when only a yard from the goal-line one week but he would delight them the following week by back-heeling a goal from fully 30 yards. We are told: 'Arthur Milne was entertainment value of a high degree but it would take a wee while for him to hit the headlines at Easter Road.'

At the end of the season the Hibernian Annual General Meeting showed the financial loss had been reduced to only £183 which was good news, as was Willie McCartney's team-building plans and Harry Swan's plans for a 70,000 capacity Holy Ground. Both McCartney and Swan came in for a great deal of praise from the 'Irish' shareholders and both were re-elected to their posts, as was retiring by rota director Sean Martin.

At the beginning of August 15,000 turned up at the Holy Ground to see Hibs' public practice match which was a roaring success, crowned by a solo effort from Geordie Young, with a dribbling run half the length of the park before scoring which 'brought the house down'. All the regulars and new faces played well, as did brand-new faces Tommy McIntyre and Willie Rice.

ENTER THE BOLD MCCARTNEY

Another new Willie McCartney signing was Sammy Kean from junior club Kirkintilloch Rob Roy, he was to go on to have an outstanding Hibernian career as a player and later as a trainer.

It was also at this time that Willie McCartney brought back Jimmy McColl of the celebrated 1920s team to join the coaching/training staff, a clever McCartney move, with so many talented young players on the books ready to be moulded into top-class Hibernians. Another clever McCartney move was to sell Irish international centre-half 'Soldier' Jones to Glentoran and immediately replace him with another Irish international centre-half Willie Reid.

Hibs opened their league campaign of season 1937–1938 at Hampden against Queen's Park with a 1-1 draw, the Irishmen's goal coming from Arthur Milne who hit home a Paddy Farrell rebound. A week later, the Hibees picked up another point when 30,000 filled the Holy Ground to see a 0-0 draw with Rangers. Hibs fielded the same team for both these games that featured several of 'McCartney's Babes': Alex Gourley, Davy Logan, Alex Prior, Peter Wilson, Willie Reid, Tommy McIntyre, James McLean, Arthur Milne, Paddy Farrell and Sammy Kean.

A league victory continued to elude Hibs as Willie McCartney made another great young signing in the form of Bobby Nutley from junior club Blantyre Victoria as the boss added to his 'McCartney Babes'. Meantime, another one of his babes, Willie Finnegan, grabbed Hibs' goal to secure another point in a 1-1 draw with Kilmarnock on Saturday 4 September at Easter Road.

Harry Swan maintained Hibs' reputation of looking after their own by arranging a benefit match for old Peter McGinn, the Hibees' centre-half, when they won the Scottish Cup in February 1887. The match came off on Wednesday 8 September at Townhead Park, Cumnock, near to Peter McGinn's home and the opposition was kindly provided by Celtic. A Hibs team of many 'McCartney Babes' beat Celtic 2-3, with goals from Geordie Young, Jimmy Kelso and Willie Finnegan. The famous referee, Tom Dougray, officiated at the special occasion which was a huge success for old Peter. The Hibs team was: James Culley, Paddy Gorman, Tommy Dunsmore, John Rennie, Charlie Birse, Willie Rice, Jimmy Kelso, Geordie Young, Willie Finnegan, James McKie and Sammy Kean. It is of interest to note that Peter McGinn's family in Edinburgh today are the proud possessors of his Scottish Cup winner's medal. It in also of interest that Harry Swan's special guest at Peter's benefit match was the 78-year-old Scottish Cup final team-mate, inside-left Paddy Lafferty.

Also at this time Hibs played two other benefit matches, one in Galashiels for the Borders football club, and another for the opening of the stand of Bonnyrigg Rose.

The Hibees did not record their first league victory until Saturday 18 September when, at Easter Road, they defeated Clyde 6-3 with Arthur Milne and Tommy Egan both scoring hat-tricks. The Green Jerseys were: James Culley, Davy Logan, Alex Prior, Jimmy Tosh, James Miller, Willie Rice, Tommy McIntyre, Tommy Egan, Arthur Milne, James McLean and Bobby Nutley.

Up to the end of the year Hibs had a mixed bag of results and it was during this period that loudspeakers were installed at the Holy Ground and on Christmas Day, Saturday 25 December, when Hibs and Hamilton Accies drew 1-1, the King's Christmas message was broadcast over the loudspeakers at half-time.

Earlier, on Friday 10 December, Hibs captain James Miller had a spooky experience. He always travelled by train and always in the front carriages but that day he felt 'compelled' not to take the train, which was just as well as it crashed at Castlecarry, with everyone in the front carriages tragically killed.

At the New Year's Day derby match, on Saturday 1 January 1938, the crowd in the Holy Ground built up to 38,000, when the police ordered the gates to be shut, leaving more thousands outside. A sensible move because during the game there was a lot of crushing and supporters spilled on to the track causing many injuries. Hearts were second top of the league with high hopes of the championship and fully expected full points from the Hibees who were sixth from the bottom of a league of 20. Hibs had a goal lead at half-time but then Hearts scored two, until the last ten minutes of the game when Davidson headed a glorious equaliser for the Irishmen. The Green Jerseys were: Alex Gourley, Davy Logan, Tommy Dunsmore, Charlie Birse, James Miller, Willie Rice, Tommy McIntyre, James McLean, Arthur Milne, Davidson and Jimmy Kelso.

Hibs picked up another four points from their next three league matches before they played local rivals, second division Edinburgh City, in the first round of the Scottish Cup at Easter Road on Saturday 22 January. It turned out to be a shocker for the Irishmen. With only a few minutes left of the match, Edinburgh City led 2-3 when Arthur Milne was chopped down in the box and a penalty was awarded, presenting the Hibees with the chance of a replay. 'L'il' Arthur took the penalty himself but hit the crossbar and illegally hit home the rebound, which of course had to be disallowed. With seconds to go, Davidson was clean through and shot wildly over the bar, another golden opportunity gone and the Hibees were out of the cup. It was the same team that had played so well against Hearts except that Tommy McIntyre was replaced by Bobby Nutley.

The only consolation for the 'suicidal' Hibs supporters that day was Hearts

ENTER THE BOLD MCCARTNEY

also going out to second division Dundee United at Tannadice. We are told when Hearts supporters hurried off the train returning them from Dundee they were asked 'what's the rush?' and they replied 'to throw ourselves in the canal', only to be advised 'try jumping off the Dean Bridge the canal is full of Hibs supporters'. A few weeks later Hibs signed Edinburgh City's centre-forward Robert Walker.

Hibernian's classy but injury prone inside-left Paddy Farrell who, although he came from the Irish Free State, played for Ireland against Wales in Belfast on Wednesday 16 March, and it was his header that gave the Irish a 1-0 victory.

The Hibees' penultimate league match was at Easter Road on Saturday 16 April against St Mirren and after being a goal down at half-time the Irishmen left it late, with goals from Tommy Egan and Arthur Milne in the last ten minutes to grab both points. The Hibs team was: Alex Gourlay, Davy Logan, Alex Prior, Charlie Birse, James Miller, Willie Rice, Tommy McIntyre, Tommy Egan, Arthur Milne, Paddy Farrell and Bobby Nutley. Hibs eventually ended up 10th in the league with 35 points.

Two days later, again at the Holy Ground, Hibs played Hearts in the final of the East of Scotland Shield and beat them 4-0. Willie Finnegan was on the score sheet with a very clever goal, Tommy McIntyre got two and Bobby Nutley finished the demolition job with a beautiful flying header, Hibernian's four goals being described an 'a scoring riot in the second half.'

The Hibees wore white jerseys that day for the 'immortal green' were already packed for a four-match tour of Ireland and Wales, for which they left immediately after defeating Hearts. First there was a 4-4 draw with Belfast Distillery, the Hibees goals coming from Paddy Farrell, Willie Finnegan and two from Tommy McIntyre. Then the Edinburgh Irishmen headed down south to Cork and defeated a Munster select 1-6 with goals from Paddy Farrell, Willie Finnegan, Bobby Nutley, Tommy McIntyre and two from Arthur Milne. Next they defeated Waterford 2-4 with goals from Davidson, Bobby Nutley, and two from Tommy McIntyre. Harry Swan and Willie McCartney were delighted with the results and 'Hibernians homecoming welcome which they received in the Emerald Isle'. The Hibees then sailed over to Wales and suffered their only defeat 3-2 from Cardiff City at St Ninian's Park. Arthur Milne and Tommy McIntyre were Hibs' scorers that day.

During the tour a Waterford player by the name of Timothy O'Keefe had caught the eye of Willie McCartney, he had also caught Hibs' goalkeeper with a rasping shot and dislocated two of his fingers. Willie McCartney went back to the Emerald Isle a few weeks later and paid Waterford £400 for the signature of Timothy O'Keefe, to add yet another face to his 'McCartney Babes'.

Hibs' financial report in June showed a loss of £1,157 0s 4d (£1157.02 described by the directors as a deficit of 'considerable dimensions,' which was largely due to the early exit from the Scottish Cup. The directors were, however, confident that Willie McCartney's team-building would reap its benefits and this was echoed by the 'Irish' shareholders at Hibs' AGM a few days later: a course and strategy had been set and there was no going back. So there was a vote of full confidence in manager Willie McCartney and the board of Chairman Harry Swan, Thomas Hartland and the three 'Irish' board members Edward Lester, Sean Martin and Owen Brannigan, who was now 76 years 'young' and had already given Hibs 58 years' unbroken service and was working as hard as ever for the 'ould club'. Owen's old friend, Paddy Cannon, at the age of 81 was still performing his duties as assistant groundsman besides doing 101 other jobs around the Holy Ground, having already given Hibernian 43 years service. Owen and Paddy, we are told, 'were greatly loved and respected by everyone at Easter Road not just because of their in-depth knowledge of football and devotion to Hibernian but they were players men, no one was more important then the players and it was they who kept them young'. Dr St John Cogan, while still a general practitioner in Leith, also had a tremendous workload at Hibernian Park and he kept a special eye on the health of Owen and Paddy who 'drove themselves too hard for the Hibees in their old age'. Hugh Shaw and Jimmy McColl, the team-mates from the celebrated 1920s team, were still head trainer and assistant trainer respectively.

The Hibees transferred full-back Tommy Dunmore to Luton Town for £2,000 and Willie McCartney added to his young squad with signings such as Jim Hart from Torquay United, John Boyle of Celtic, John Smith from Parkhead Juniors, Tom Scott from Musselburgh Athletic and Jim Fleming from Forth Wanderers. Two high-scoring practice matches were played at the beginning of August, with well over 20,000 supporters attending them. Alex Gourlay remained first choice goalkeeper but young Jimmy Kerr, who had been farmed out to Ormiston Primrose, was now Hibs reserve goalkeeper and more than ready for first team duty when required.

The Edinburgh Irishmen opened their league campaign of season 1938–1939 against Hamilton Academicals at the Holy Ground on Saturday 13 August 1938, a date which is a landmark in the romance of Hibernian Football Club. Not because the harp and shamrocks at the entrances had been given a bright fresh coat of green paint, as had the stand, and not because the wall round the track and the crush barriers were freshly painted brilliant white. Nor was it because the pitch of Irish turf was in perfect condition as always and the old square goal posts had been replaced with modern oval ones complete with revolutionary green nets. No, what made this a landmark date was that, for the very first time, Hibernian ran out onto the Holy Ground in their now familiar emerald green jerseys with white sleeves. Harry Swan and his fellow directors had kept their promise to the supporters of a 'brighter Easter Road'. We are told: 'The 22,000 Hibs supporters eagerly awaited their team in their bright new strips and a few minutes before they appeared on the field manager Willie McCartney addressed the crowd over the new loudspeakers about the "brighter Easter Road" and he got quite a cheer which reached a crescendo when "McCartney's Babes" appeared.' Hibs' forward line played very well, with Willie Finnegan prominent, as was new face Timothy O'Keefe, but it was another face, Jim Hart, who scored two well-taken goals in the second half. The Hibees then relaxed and Hamilton ended up sharing the points. The 'new Green Jerseys' that historic day were: Alex Gourley, Davy Logan, Alex Prior, Charlie Birse, James Miller, Willie Rice, Bobby Nutley, Willie Finnegan, Arthur Milne, Jim Hart and Timothy O'Keefe. This season the overconfidence of the 'McCartney Babes' in writing off lesser opposition was on occasions to cost them valuable points.

In Hibs' next four league matches they won one and lost three but Willie McCartney stuck to his young players and made another signing, John 'Cubby' Cuthbertson, from junior club Craig-Mer; 'Cubby' would go on to be a very popular Hibernian.

It was a young, talented, if inexperienced squad of players that had a lot to prove and the perfect opportunity to repay the manager's confidence in them came along on Saturday 10 September when 35,000 filled the Holy Ground for the league encounter against Hearts. Young Jimmy Kerr made his league debut that day and we are told 'the youthful Edinburgh Irishmen fulfilled a lot of their promise, probably the occasion made them do so'. It certainly did for a hat-trick from Tommy McIntyre, and one from Aurther Milne, gave Hibernian a resounding 4-0 victory over the 'ould inimy'. We are told: 'It could have been double the score as Hibernian found Hearts weaknesses and hammered upon them.' The McCartney Babes were: Jimmy Kerr, Davy Logan, Alex Prior, Bobby Fraser, James Miller, Willie Rice, Tommy McIntyre, Willie Finnegan, Arthur Milne, James McLean and Bobby Nutley.

Willie McCartney had given Timothy O'Keefe a 'leave of absence' for the young Irishman to rush back to the Emerald Isle when his two sons became seriously ill, but he was back in time two weeks later when Hibs pulled off another surprise by beating Aberdeen 5-0 at the Holy Ground. This time it was Arthur Milne who scored the hat-trick, with one each from Sammy Kean and Tommy McIntyre. Two months later, Willie McCartney allowed a loan of Timothy O'Keefe to struggling Raith Rovers.

Meantime, Willie McCartney added to his 'youth movement' by signing Bobby Gallagher from Broxburn Shamrock, a club Hibs had helped to found in the 1880s and who had supplied Hibs with many fine players over the years. Willie Cummings was also signed from Ormiston Primrose. English clubs West Ham and Leeds United were showing a big interest in Willie Finnegan and Tommy McIntyre respectively but neither player wanted to leave Easter Road and Hibs were certainly not interested in selling them. Next, Manchester United offered £10,000 for Tommy McIntyre and Sammy Kean, but again the Irishmen were not interested. Liverpool were also sent packing when they showed an interest in Jimmy Kerr and Bobby Fraser; Willie McCartney was at Easter Road on a 'team building mission' to restore Hibs' greatness: there was no going back and no selling.

Through October and November the Hibees won five of their eight league games and then, on Saturday 20 November at Easter Road, they defeated St Mirren 6-1 before facing Celtic at Parkhead seven days later. In this 'battle of the Greens' the Edinburgh Irishmen ware trailing 4-2 at half-time and things looked worse when McLean was carried off and did not return to the fray. We are however told: 'The ten young Hibernians had all the traditional fighting Irish spirit of the old Easter Road teams' and two goals from Arthur Milne brought the score level in an 'amazing fightback'. With three minutes left, Celtic scored a blatantly offside goal, the referee hesitated, consulted his linesman and – you've guest it – he gave the goal, amid strong protests. We are told 'even the Celtic supporters found this amusing for they had nothing but loud praise for the Hibernians never-say-die spirit'. We are further told 'these young Hibs players are among the most enthusiastic and entertaining band ever to wear the Irishmen's green jerseys'.

Over the next few weeks, Willie McCartney continued to add to his 'Babes' by signing Gerry Mayes from Sheildmuir Celtic and Sean Gilmartin and Murdo McLeod, both from Johnstone Athletic. He was, however, pipped by Celtic in signing a Dundee Harp player who gloried in the name Kinneard Ouchterlonie.

It was also at this time that a sporting organisation which had an unbroken 50-year connection to Hibernian Football Club celebrated its Golden Jubilee and it is of interest to look at a little of its history.

Hibernian Amateur Swimming Club and Humane Society

In August 1888 in little Ireland, a group of swimming enthusiasts from St Patrick's CMYS got together with some breakaway members of Lorne Swimming Club. They decided to form their own swimming club, with the bold decision taken that it would be non-sectarian and open to everyone, not just members of the CYMS, and that it would be open to women. At an inaugural meeting in a small hall in Niddry Street, off the Cowgate, it was decided to name their swimming club Hibernian after their footballing heroes, so Hibernian Amateur Swimming Club and Humane Society was born. Prominent among the founders were Mick McCourt, the first secretary, John Boyle, Hugh McGinness, Frank Rafferty, James Bennett and Allan McPhee.

Later, several of these men would be on the Hibernian FC committees in the early 1890s which led to the football club being resuscitated on a non-sectarian basis. Also at the inaugural meeting, the swimmers decided to adopt green swim suits and the harp as their crest and pledged to help Hibernian FC financially through their difficulties. Hibernian Swimming Club used Infirmary Street Baths, up from the Cowgate, as their headquarters, and there you will find them to this day.

Hibernian SC closed for the Great War, 1914–18, as the members, men and women, answered the call to serve King and Country. Several members made the supreme sacrifice and those who were parishioners of St Patrick's Church in the Cowgate have their names engraved on the copper plaques in the 1914–1918 war memorial mortuary chapel at the rear of St Patrick's Church.

Harry Swan, the Chairman of Hibernian Football Club, was an Honorary Patron of Hibernian Swimming Club and he attended a special gala at Infirmary Street Baths on Wednesday 14 September 1949, which was then followed by tea in the clubrooms. For this occasion, Hibernian SC had new green swimsuits and beautiful new harp badges for the swimsuits and their blazers, a financial outlay that could be ill-afforded, but they wanted to look their best for Harry Swan. Programmes and tickets were sold out.

Harry Swan was again at a well-advertised Hibernian SC gala on Thursday 12 October 1950 at Infirmary Street Baths, with a large attendance from famous old members and other swimming clubs. Another feature of this gala was Hibernian's continued encouragement of young swimmers, with special invitations to schools such as Abbeyhill, St Anthony's and Holy Cross Academy.

Today Hibernian SC are no longer a power in Scottish swimming, which itself is in decline, but there are still active members who still enjoy their swim on club nights at Infirmary Street Baths. At the time of writing, the baths themselves are closed for refurbishment and the rumour is that city finances may not be able to carry out the work and the baths may never re-open; let us hope not, so that Hibernian SC, who were at one time the most successful club in Scotland, can stay alive. Hibernian Swimming Club are not only part of the folklore and history of Hibernian Football Club, but indeed of the City of Edinburgh.

Back to 1938, and Wednesday 12 December saw the death of a celebrated

Hibs supporter who held an official post at Easter Road. He was a Roman Catholic priest and leading Scottish educationalist, another unsung Hibernian, so it will be of interest to look at a little of his life.

In Memoriam – Monsignor Thomas Miley.

On 15 April 1871, Thomas Miley was born in Little Ireland, the son of Thomas Miley and Mary Wilkie. Always a great Hibernian supporter, he remembered vividly in later years the marvellous teams of the 1880s, Scottish Cup winners and World Champions. The great half-back line-up of McGhee, McGinn, McLaren and the genius of 'Darling' Willie Groves, Sandy McMahon and James Blessington were his household names. He would love to have been a Hibernian player himself, but the vocation of this young man was the priesthood and he studied at the Catholic Blair's College in Aberdeen, where he gained a professorship and he completed his theological and philosophical studies at the Scots College, Valladolid, Spain, where he was ordained priest in 1894. Father Miley returned to Scotland and for the next nine years taught at Blair's College where he developed as a brilliant educationalist.

In 1929, he was further elevated to the title Canon, but he was always popularly known by everyone as Monsignor Miley. Amidst all this mountain of responsibilities, Monsignor Miley was still the humble parish priest of St Ninian's where he became a legend for his work among the unemployed of all denominations. His work for their welfare and dignity was its own reward, for he learned and treasured their wonderful spirit of courage and helpfulness during their difficulties, and he was their champion in the Haig Club for the unemployed.

The only relaxation Monsignor Miley allowed himself was watching his beloved Hibernian. Come what may, he was at every home game for over 30 years. Many Edinburgh and East of Scotland priests were followers of Hibernian and Harry Swan, who became the Club's Chairman in the 1930s, had seats reserved for them in the Centre Stand. The rows of black-suited priests were known as 'The Black Watch'. Monsignor Miley was particularly close to Harry Swan and often Harry sought advice and encouragement from the brilliant priest. Monsignor Miley was particularly good with the young reserve players whom he would help with their personal problems and difficulties, as many were unemployed. Harry Swan appointed Monsignor Miley to the official post of 'Players' Counsellor', the first of its kind. Monsignor Miley attended his last Hibernian game on Saturday 26 November 1938 when St Mirren were defeated by six goals to one.

A few days later, he collapsed in the street. His 68-year-old body was worn out by 44 years' work in the priesthood, 33 of which were spent at St Ninian's in Restalrig. The Nuns of St Raphael's Nursing Home in Edinburgh tended him, but he died on Wednesday 28 December. Monsignor Miley's Requiem Mass was celebrated in St Ninian's on Friday 30 December and the overflow congregation included church dignitaries from every diocese in Scotland. The City of Edinburgh's Civic Officials were there, including Councillor P.H. Allan, Chairman of the Edinburgh Education Committee. Others present were Mr Oswald Barclay OBE, and Colonel W. Robertson VC, representing the Haig Club for the unemployed. An old protestant clergyman friend, ex-bailie, the Reverend Dr Sloan was also there to pay his respects. There was a big contingent from Easter Road. Catholic authorities did not allow floral tributes to be laid on a priest's coffin, but in Monsignor Miley's case, they made a rare exception, but only two wreaths were allowed; one of poppies from The Haig Club for the unemployed, the other of chrysanthemums from The Hibernian Football Club. Monsignor Miley was then buried in Mount Vernon Catholic Cemetery. The following day, Saturday 31 December 1938, Hibernian drew one goal each with Clyde at Easter Road and in the Hibernian Official Programme, Harry Swan wrote this tribute to Monsignor Miley:

> It is with deep regret that we learned of the death of Monsignor Thomas Miley, a good and true Hibernian. He was a most ardent supporter and cheery soul, and an inspiration to all at Easter Road with his kindly encouragement. We mourn the passing of a real friend.

The New Year derby match came off at Tynecastle on Monday 2 January 1939 in front of an 'overflowing 45,000 crowd'. Hearts were all out to avenge their heavy defeat earlier in the season but Willie McCartney pulled off a master-stroke by bringing back 'older head' Irish internationalist Paddy Farrell to the forward line to control his 'eager Babes'. Paddy Farrell and fellow Irish internationalist, centre-half James Miller, another 'older head', had a big say in Hibernian's 0-1 victory. All the 'McCartney Babes' played their usual 'daring, dashing stuff' with Jimmy Kerr 'playing like a veteran, and when Arthur Milne scored the winner with ten minutes to go it was greeted by the huge Hibs support with 'a storm of wild cheering'. The Hibees who did the league double over Hearts were: Jimmy Kerr, Davy Logan, Alex Prior, Bobby Fraser, James Miller, Willie Rice, Tommy McIntyre, Paddy Farrell, Arthur Milne, Sammy Kean and Bobby Nutley.

There was some 'unpleasantness' with the huge crowd swaying and spilling on to the pitch several times and it took mounted police to sort things out. There was also 'a lot of unpleasantness' from a very physical Hearts team. Dr St John Cogan had a very busy game with Willie Rice taking a severe knock,

Arthur Milne having to go off with an injured eye which later had to be stitched, James Miller suffering a suspected fractured jaw and Paddy Farrell having to go off, only to return holding a sponge to his bloody broken nose. Such was the spirit of these players and the expert attention of the doctor that every one of them reported to Easter Road the next day for duty and Willie McCartney let Paddy Farrell and Arthur Milne play in a 2-1 victory over Raith Rovers.

Saturday 14 January was Paddy Cannon's 82nd birthday and the 'McCartney's Babes' made a real fuss of him with lots of presents and jokes before taking a fighting 1-1 draw with Rangers in front of a 34,000 crowd at the Holy Ground. Sammy Kean was the Hibees' scorer in the same team that had defeated Hearts. It was a satisfactory birthday for old Paddy Cannon. It was also a satisfactory day for Hibs Irish centre-half James Miller who played with his fractured jaw. His face was very swollen, he could hardly speak and was in considerable pain. Dr St John Cogan was totally against him playing and James Miller, who lived in Glasgow, had further x-rays there to confirm he had a hairline fracture of his jaw. The persuasive Willie McCartney spoke to him in the Easter Road dressing room,

> You know James, Edinburgh has the best medical institutions in the world and our own Dr St John Cogan is one of the finest doctors and surgeons in Scotland, and you go to quacks in Glasgow. Admittedly you have a slight swelling, a slight suggestion of pain, but to say your jaws broken, well...'.

Turning to a dumbfounded Dr St John Cogan, he told him to give James Miller a gum shield for protection, 'he's OK to play'. Dr St John Cogan knew, of course, he should not play as he had come across this injury many times as Medical Officer of Health for Boxing but if the player had been persuaded to play there was nothing else he could do. This incident well illustrates the persuasive powers of Willie McCartney, the same powers he used to bring so much young talent to Easter Road. It also illustrates the high regard he had for 'old head' James Miller in the centre of his young defence. James was, however, delighted he had been persuaded to play even although he was in considerable pain and heading the ball was agony, 'it was a great result for us to get a draw against Rangers, it was difficult to get any result against them in these days.'

Hibs had a good run in the Scottish Cup, disposing of Forfar Athletic, Kilmarnock and Alloa Athletic. The semi-final came off at neutral Tynecastle on Saturday 25 March against Clyde, in front of 40,000 expectant Hibs supporters, but the unchanged 'McCartney Babes' could not overcome a strong

ENTER THE BOLD MCCARTNEY

experienced Clyde who won by the only goal of the game and went on to lift the cup.

In the league on Saturday 8 April at the Holy Ground the Hibees got sweet revenge on Celtic by beating them 1-0, with the goal coming from Tommy McIntyre. The Edinburgh Irishmen that day were: Jimmy Kerr, Davy Logan, Alex Prior, Charlie Birse, Bobby Fraser, Willie Rice, Tommy McIntyre, Willie Finnegan, Arthur Milne, Sammy Kean and Bobby Nutley. Hibs eventually finished 13th in a league of 20.

A week after the victory in the 'battle of the greens', Hibernian met Hearts at Tynecastle in the final of the East of Scotland Shield and two goals from Arthur Milne and one from Bobby Nutley gave the Irishmen a 1-3 victory with the same team that had defeated Celtic.

Hibernian's reserves had reached the semi-final of the 2nd XI Scottish Cup and they were drawn against Rangers, with the first leg being played at Ibrox and a cracking 4-4 draw was played out. In the second leg at the Holy Ground the 'young Irishmen' disposed of the Ibrox men 2-0, to put the Green Jerseys in the final against Clyde, which was also played on a home and away basis. Hibernian won 4-3 on aggregate to lift the trophy. Hibernian used a 13-player squad to do this: Alex Gourley Davy Shaw (captain), Alex Prior, Davy Logan, Charlie Birse, Bobby Fraser, Murdo McLeod, Sean Gilmartin, George Young, Willie Anderson, Willie Finnegan, Davidson and George Ross.

The captain of the victorious Hibs Reserves, right full-back Davy Shaw whom Willie McCartney had only signed from junior club Grange Rovers in January, was to go on to become a famous Hibernian. There is an interesting photograph taken at the Holy Ground of Davy Shaw showing the 2nd XI Scottish Cup to old director Owen Brannigan, linking 54 years of Hibernian history, for Owen Brannigan was in the Hibs reserves in this competition all these 54 years ago on Saturday 18 April 1885, when they defeated Hearts 3-1 in the final at Easter Road. Hearts had taken the lead but goals from Pat McGrail, Paddy Kirk and Tommy Preston made the young Hibs worthy winners of the national competition for reserve teams. The Hibs reserves that day were: Felix Doherty, Tommy Ryan, Owen Brannigan, Pat McGovern, Frank Higgins, James 'Tailor' Flynn, Tommy Philbin (captain), Geordie 'the Juggler' Smith, Pat McGrail, Paddy Kirk and Tommy Preston. It is of interest to note that in 1885 no trophy had yet been made for this competition and it was known as the 'phantom cup'. It is also of interest to note the tragedy of Tommy Preston who had scored Hibs' third goal in that final, for less than nine months later, he died of lock jaw in Edinburgh Royal Infirmary at the early age of 23.

The Scottish International touring team of the USA and Canada was made up of 17 players and Hibernian's Tommy McIntyre was one of them. Twelve games were played over five weeks in May and June and for this Tommy McIntyre received a £25 'outfit allowance' plus £6 per week and 'out of pocket expenses' – changed days indeed.

Hibernian's financial report for the season showed, at last, a profit of £1,771 6s 3d (£1,771.31½) and director Thomas Hartland, who was retiring by rota, was re-elected.

Hibs ex-trainer Di Christopher, who had had connections with the club for almost 40 years, was now manager of Irish Free State club Waterford, from whom Hibs had signed Timothy O'Keefe and now the young Irishman was transferred back to them. Irishman James Miller had turned down the offer to manage Irish club Coleraine and Hibs sold him to Albion Rovers for £500. Hibernian's other Irish player, Paddy Farrell, was granted a free transfer.

The European political situation was in a crisis in the summer of 1939 and war, once again with Germany, was on the horizon.

– 12 –

HIBERNIAN AND THE WAR YEARS
1939–1940 TO 1944–1945

The young leaves, the green leaves, are falling;
Dark earth with kind fingers shall cull them,
Return them in the dew of the morning
Immortality laden with balm –
Sycamore, willow and palm.

Hibernian youth in its spring-time is falling
In splendour nd light of the morning –
Green leaves for the healing of nations,
Proud pattern of matchless design:
At dawn we shall see them returning,
Mulberry, olive and vine.

Throughout the summer of 1939 Hibs carried out more ground improvements, including making part of the south-east terracing already known an the 'Alps' bigger and with more crush barriers. In winter the supporters occupying this particularly high terracing were known as the 'Polar Bears'. The Holy Ground was well on its way to a 60,000 capacity and spacious car parking facilities were in place. Paddy Cannon's son Tommy was groundsman and Paddy kept an eye on him to ensure he kept the 'the verdant Irish swath of Easter Road in prime condition'.

Injuries to Alex Prior and James McLean had been tended by Dr St John Cogan, they were now fully fit and, along with all the other players, there were 27 'McCartney Babes' at Easter Road, 12 of whom were still teenagers. With the growing political unease at the aggressive military antics of Adolf Hitler's Nazi Germany, we are told young left-winger George Rose was already attending a 'militia camp' and James McLean was awaiting his 'orders'. Mass conscription was on the horizon.

The Hibees played two public practice matches at the Holy Ground in the first week of August, which produced no less than 19 goals and we are told:

'Hibernian have young players of youth and promise, every man of which is imbued with the spirit to see the Edinburgh Irishmen do well.'

Willie McCartney added two more promising 'Babes' to his squad: full-backs Louis Ross and Willie Clark, as Hibernian won their first two home league matches of season 1939–1940. Players on first team duty in August and early September were Jimmy Kerr, Davy Logan (captain), Alex Prior, Davy Shaw, Charlie Birse, Willie Rice, Tommy McIntyre, Willie Finnegan, Arthur Milne, Sammy Kean, Bobby Nutley, Alex Davidson, Sean Gilmartin, Bobby Fraser, James McLean and Willie Anderson.

Two Hibernian players were selected for the Scottish League squad to play the Irish League in Belfast on Wednesday 30 August; Arthur Milne was travelling reserve while Bobby Nutley played on the left-wing in Scotland's 2-3 victory. We are told: 'Bobby Nutley was the major success of the team, he has such surprising confidence in himself'. His son Des Nutley had this to say affectionately of his father: 'He came from the West but he was a right Hibs supporter and a great player for the Hibees, when he pulled on that green jersey he wasn't just confident he was a right arrogant little bastard.' In the coming war, Bobby Nutley was to distinguish himself in battle as an RAF gunner and he was awarded the DFC: a great achievement by a great Hibernian.

That week-end we are told:

> The tension caused by the political crisis was evidenced among the crowds at the soccer matches on Saturday; one noticeable feature was that the attendances were by no means up to the usual standard. It could hardly, of course, be expected otherwise. The games played may be the last for some little time.

On Sunday 3 September, Britain declared war against Germany, as the Nazis had invaded Poland the day before. Unlike the First World War, the battle lines were clearly drawn for the Scots, who were now not being asked to fight just for their homeland but indeed for the survival of civilisation from Adolf Hitler's inhuman Nazi regime, intent on domination of the world.

Football was immediately suspended, as were players' contracts, although their registration remained in effect. Hibs, like all other teams, were basically disbanded and although 'war-time football' would continue in a few weeks, 'McCartney' Babes' by and large lost five of their most promising football years.

To Willie McCartney's great credit, while attracting all this young talent to Easter Road he always advised them to keep their jobs and apprenticeships and the situation now showed how wise he had been.

For instance, Bobby Nutley, Arthur Milne, Sammy Kean and Charlie Birse all took up their trades in the Leith shipyards. Davy Logan, Davy Shaw, and Willie Rice were miners; Jimmy Kerr a plumber; Willie Finnegan a grocer; Bobby Fraser a draughtsman; Tommy McIntyre a press photographer and Sean

Gilmartin was at Jordanhill College of Physical Education. Alex Prior immediately volunteered for service in the RAF before conscription was imposed and many others were to follow him into military service.

The day after war was declared, Willie McCartney put Hibs' appeal to the *Edinburgh Evening News* for a fund for supplying footballs to the forces: 'many thousands of soldiers in the Great War were made happy by the supply of footballs. There in no reason to my mind why such a scheme should not at once be lauded and supported in the keenest way possible.' Harry Swan set the ball rolling by donating £1, while season ticket holder, 'ardent supporter of Hibernian', Willie Murphy of Murphy's Football Pools donated £10.

While the Scottish League and SFA dithered, Hibernian advocated the continuance of football as a morale booster and 'Hibernian's Leith Perseverance' paid off, with friendlies being allowed but only in front of restricted attendances. So Hibernian's first wartime match was a friendly against Hearts at Tynecastle on Saturday 23 September, in front of a 'quiet crowd of less than 6,000', even although the Home Office had allowed a maximum of 8,000. Hearts took the lead but Bobby Nutley made it 1-1 at half-time. In the second half, Hearts again took the lead but the crowd remained 'unnaturally quiet' until 'McCartney's Babes' suddenly turned the game into 'a real old-style derby match' with goals from Sammy Kean, Bobby Nutley and Arthur Milne giving 'the young Irishmen a 2-4 win over Hibernian's arch rivals'. Alex Prior was stationed 'somewhere in England' with the RAF and wasn't released to play, so the Hibees line up was: Jimmy Kerr, Davy Shaw, Davy Logan, Charlie Birse, Bobby Fraser, Willie Rice, Tommy McIntyre, James McLean, Arthur Milne, Sammy Kean and Bobby Nutley. They received payment of £2 per man as laid down by the Scottish football authorities.

Hibs were undefeated in three other friendlies until the Scottish League came up with the idea of two 16-team regional leagues, one East and one West. Not the cleverest idea for war-time football, which was supposed to cut down travelling, as the Hibees still had to journey to the likes of Arbroath and Aberdeen. The new league got underway on Saturday 21 October and the Hibees were able to field Alex Hall in place of full-back Alex Prior. Ex-Dunfermline Athletic Alex Hall was now a Sunderland player doing war-work in Edinburgh and Willie McCartney beat off two other clubs to got Sunderland's permission to attach Alex Hall to Easter Road. Of course, things worked the other way and some of the Hibees war-worker players such as Arthur Milne, Tommy McIntyre, James McLean, Bobby Fraser and Davy Logan were lost to clubs nearest their work-place. Such were the conditions of wartime football and the experience of Willie McCartney was to be invaluable in this situation.

Hibs lost two and drew two of their first four matches in the new Scottish Regional League Eastern Section before Willie McCartney got centre-half Bobby Kane of Leeds United attached to the Hibees. Bobby Kane had started his career with Glasgow junior club St Roch's, before being signed by Celtic, then he moved to Leeds United. On Saturday 18 November Hibernian recorded a 2-7 victory over Kings Park at Forthbank Park, Stirling, their scorers being two each from John 'Cubby' Cuthbertson and Willie Anderson, and one each from Charlie Birse, Sean Gilmartin and Sammy Kean. It is of interest to note that the great Bill Shankley of Preston North End, who was much later to find great fame as manager of Liverpool, played for Kings Park that day.

Matches were producing lots of goals and Bobby Nutley notched a hat-trick in a 6-2 victory over Dundee United at the Holy Ground and a no-scoring draw at Arbroath was an exception. Two goals from Bobby Nutley and one from Willie Finnegan saw Hibs defeat Alloa 3-0 at Easter Road. Young James McLean was now in the Gordon Highlanders and the Hibs team that day was: Jimmy Kerr, Alex Hall, Davy Shaw, Jimmy Fleming, Bobby Kane, Willie Rice, Sean Gilmartin, Gerry Mayes, Willie Finnegan, John 'Cubby' Cuthbertson and Bobby Nutley.

In Memoriam – Richard Power Payne
On Friday 8 December, Richard Payne died aged 75 at his home at 17 Promenade, Portobello. He had been secretary (manager) of Hibernian for two years from July 1889 when the Hibees were run by St Patrick's CYMS. At this time, Hibernian were struggling to survive and he was basically in a no-win situation. Married to Sarah Connor, he remained a regular at Easter Road all his life and his Requiem Mass was celebrated in the RC church of St John the Evangelist, Portobello, before he was buried at Mount Vernon cemetery. Another of the 'ould Irish Hibees' had gone and a short tribute from Easter Road stated:

> Richard Payne was the most genial of souls and in conversation he always liked to recall the beginnings of Hibernian in St Mary's Street Halls and their efforts to stay alive.

High scoring continued at the start of 1940 but severe snow postponed a lot of matches and Rab Walls of Cowdenbeath, a Hibernian favourite of the early 1930s, became re-attached to Easter Road. The Scottish War Emergency Cup was played on the basis of two ties home and away and in the first round, Hibs drew away to Falkirk and the first leg saw the Hibees crash 5-0. The young Irishmen almost saved the tie in the second leg at Easter Road on Saturday 2 March, winning 4-0, but a fifth goal evaded them after a terrific fightback.

HIBERNIAN AND THE WAR YEARS

Willie McCartney's son was now in the Royal Scots and trainers Hugh Shaw and Jimmy McColl were engaged in war-work in the Leith shipyards. On Wednesday 3 April, Hibs recorded a fine 6-0 victory over Dundee at the Holy Ground with a hat-trick from 'Cubby' Cutbertson, two from Bobby Nutley and one from Willie Anderson. Five Hibernians, Alex Hall, Charlie Birse, Willie Finnegan, Bobby Nutley and 'Cubby' Cuthbertson were in a Hibs/Hearts select that defeated a British Army Xl 6-2 on Monday 6 May. Five of the goals came from the Hibernians, with a 'Cubby' hat-trick and one each from Willie Finnegan and Bobby Nutley. The match was played in aid of Red Cross Funds.

A very long season came to an end on Saturday 1 June when, in the final of the Rosebery Charity cup at Tynecastle, the Hibees thrashed Hearts 2-5, the highlight being an Arthur Milne hat-trick and a brace from Willie Finnegan. Another highlight was a brilliant Jimmy Kerr save from a Tommy Walker penalty.

Arthur Milne was now in the army and Bobby Nutley had joined the RAF. From the middle of July the Holy Ground was made available twice a week for the 'Public Keep Fit War Measure'. At the end of July Mrs Skinner, the Easter Road tea lady, a Hibs supporter for over 60 years, sadly died and she was greatly missed by all at Easter Road.

Hibs' financial report showed a loss of £2,195 due to the war conditions and a woefully unpopular league set-up. Edward Lester, the retiring by rota director put himself forward for re-election but later withdraw his name as he went into military service. The Lester family had been connected to Hibernian almost from day one of the founding of the club in 1875. James Drummond Shiels was elected director in Edward Lester's place: another of the 'ould Irish' connections had been broken. Sixteen Hibernian players were now also in the military but the Hibees still had the services of others who were under military age.

A new and more popular Scottish Southern League was set up for season 1940–1941 which meant Hibs could look forward to clashes with Celtic and Rangers again with the gate money they would generate. The Hibees held a public practice match at Easter Road on Saturday 3 August which produced 12 goals, the proceeds from the game going to the Spitfire Fund.

Willie McCartney had been casting about for some available experienced players and three became attached to the Hibees: Ernie Till from Raith Rovers, Tommy Adams of East Fife and ex-East Fife player Eddie McLeod, who was now with Manchester United and they insisted that Hibs insure him for £3,000, which was duly complied with.

Another great capture by Willie McCartney was centre-half Bobby Baxter of Middlesborough and he played in Hibs' fifth league match on Saturday 7 September when, at the Holy Ground, Hibernian defeated Hearts 2-1 with goals from 'Cubby' Cuthbertson and Willie Finnegan. We are told: 'The Hibernians were far too good for the Hearts and the score did not reflect the superiority of the Irishmen.' The Green Jerseys were: Jimmy Kerr, Davy Logan, Alex Hall, Ernie Till, Bobby Baxter, Jimmy Fleming, Tommy Adams, Eddie McLeod, Willie Finnegan, John 'Cubby' Cuthbertson and Sammy Kean.

This league was to produce some high scoring such as Hearts losing ten goals to Clyde. In October Hibs scored four goals in three of their matches, one of them being the 0-4 defeat of Celtic at Parkhead on Saturday 26 October and that was without the services of full-back Ernie Till who was back in the army after some leave. Two weeks later, at the Holy Ground, the Irishmen thumped high-flying Falkirk 7-1, with four of the goals coming from 'Cubby' Cuthbertson. When the Hibees defeated Queen's Park 2-5 at Hampden on Saturday 23 November, 'Cubby' got another four, making him Scotland's leading scorer with 20 league goals.

Hibernian had remained unbeaten in the league at the Holy Ground when, on Saturday 30 November, the big test came from their visitors, table-topping Rangers, but the Green Jerseys rose magnificently to the challenge and beat then 1-0 with a goal from Willie Anderson which ended Rangers' unbeaten run. We are told: 'The under strength reshuffled Irishmen had obstructive tactics in defence and their forwards were full of running.' The Hibs team was: Jimmy Kerr, Davy Logan, Alex Hall, Willie Finnegan, Bobby Baxter, Davy Shaw, Tommy Adams, Sammy Kean, Willie Anderson, 'Cubby' Cuthbertson and Willie Cook.

Hibs then signed young Alex Clark from Ashfield Juniors, as each of the Easter Road players who were away in the armed forces were sent a box of cigarettes for Christmas, something that would be frowned upon in this day and age.

The New Year's Day derby match against Hearts, on Wednesday 1 January 1941, was postponed because Tynecastle was frostbound. The match wouldn't be played for a few months and, as we shall soon see, it would turn out to be of tremendous importance in the history of Hibernian Football Club.

On Saturday 1 February at the Holy Ground, Hibernian did the league double over Celtic by defeating them 2-0. Benny Yorston of Middlesborough was now attached to Easter Road and he scored one of the Hibees' goals; the Green Jerseys were: Jimmy Kerr, Davy Logan, Alex Hall, Sammy Kean, Bobby Baxter, Davy Shaw, Tommy Adams, Willie Finnegan, Benny Yorston, 'Cubby' Cuthertson and Willie Cook.

The Scottish War Emergency Cup was renamed the Scottish Southern

HIBERNIAN AND THE WAR YEARS

League War Cup. Iin the first round, the 16 league clubs were divided into groups of four and played each other on a home and away basis, unfortunately the Hibees failed to qualify for the later stages.

The name Willie Cook had been appearing regularly in Hibs line-ups on the left-wing since the early months of the season and it is worth recording that Willie McCartney had 'coaxed him out of retirement'. He had played for Bolton Wanderers before hanging up his boots and we are told: 'Willie Cook was never quite sure how he succumbed to the blandishments of "the Boss" but when Willie McCartney turned on the charm he could convince a Chinaman that he had Yellow Jaundice.'

This example of the 'Bold McCartney's' irresistible charm and football know-how shows how he attracted talent to Easter Road, especially young talent, and Willie McCartney's next signing was to be a masterstroke, when he captured for Hibernian arguably the greatest player in Scottish football history.

Gordon Smith

> A Gordon fur me, a Gordon fur me,
> If your no a Gordon yir nae use tae me,
> Willie Groves wiz braw,
> Sandy McMahon an' them 'aw,
> But the cocky wee Gordon
> Is the pride o' them 'aw.

Gordon Smith was Edinburgh-born but his family moved to Montrose when he was an infant. Later at Montrose Academy he became a Scottish schoolboy internationalist and he played for an Arbroath juvenile team called Bromford when, at the age of 14, he joined Kirriemuir Harp before moving up to junior grade with Montrose Roselea.

At the age of 16, Gordon was playing centre-forward for the junior club Dundee North End, when he was selected to play for a Scottish Junior Select against a Hibs-Hearts, on Monday 14 April 1941 for the official opening of the new ground of Lochee Harp, a Dundee 'Irish' junior club. Lochee Harp were an off-shoot of the 'Irish' clubs Dundee Harp and Dundee Hibs (later Dundee United) which Edinburgh Hibernian had helped to found in the Jute City many years before. With Hibernian having a long historical connection with 'Irish football' in Dundee, seven Easter Road men, Jimmy Kerr, Alex Hall, Geordie Young, Bobby Baxter, Sammy Kean, Willie Cook and Benny Yorston, played for the capital select which went down 3-2, with a hat-trick from the young Gordon Smith in a dazzling display for the Junior Select.

Present at the match were Hibs manager Willie McCartney and Hearts chairman Mr A. Irvine and the Gorgie man offered Gordon a trial; Willie McCartney didn't need to give Gordon a trial – he had just witnessed a great footballing talent and that was enough for him. While Hearts dithered and the press were incorrectly tying Gordon to the Hearts, Willie McCartney made his move. Contact was soon made and 'the Boss' arranged to meet Gordon at the Seaforth Hotel in Arbroath on Sunday 27 April. Gordon was very impressed by the 'flamboyant McCartney with the tremendous personality' who invited 16-year-old Gordon and his father down to Edinburgh's North British Hotel the following day for signing and there would be no trial nonsense, Gordon would go immediately into the Hibernian first team. Gordon tells us, 'in my heart I had decided to join Hibs' and this he did at tea-time on Monday 28 April in the North British Hotel, receiving a £10 signing-on fee; 'I felt like a millionaire'.

A couple of hours later, 'the football bargain of all time' lined up in Hibernian's famous green jersey against Hearts in the Scottish Southern League match that had been postponed on New Year's Day. One of Gordon's junior Dundee pals failed to show up with his boots and an embarrassed Gordon got a loan of a spare Hibs pair and went on to score a hat-trick in Hibernian's 3-5 defeat of Hearts. Willie McCartney had pulled a real flanker on Hearts by 'stealing' Gordon Smith and 'the Boss' also fielded two other brand new 'Babes' in the forward line, with the instructions: 'keep the ba' on the deck and well away from that big Hearts puddin' Dykes'. The Hibernian team that day was: Jimmy Kerr, Davy Shaw, Alex Hall, Sammy Kean, Bobby Baxter, Willie Rice, Jock Weir, Bobby Combe, Gordon Smith, Willie Finnegan and Tommy Adams. The hat-trick debut against Hearts was to herald Gordon Smith's glittering 18-year career with the Edinburgh Irishmen.

The two other 'McCartney Babes' who made their debut that day were Jock Weir from Leith Renton and Bobby Combe from Inveresk Athletic: both were to become great Hibernians, particularly Bobby Combe, a born and bred Hibs supporter who was to be part of the great teams of the Famous Five era. Ask any old Hibs supporter and they will tell you it should have been the Famous Six, so outstanding was Bobby Combe. Bobby, who had signed for the Hibees the same day as Gordon Smith, had in fact been given training facilities by Hearts but 'Hibs Daft' Bobby had held back from making them any commitment, hoping Hibs would step in for him and this Willie McCartney did, making it a 'double whammy' over Hearts. There is no doubt that Willie McCartney was one of the best things that ever happened to Hibernian Football Club and he wasn't finished yet, not by a long way.

A Scottish national trophy to be played for at the end of the season during the summer months, was the brain-child of Harry Swan and the Scottish football authorities took up the idea and instituted the Summer Cup, with a handsome trophy to be won. Ties were to be played on a two-game home and away basis until the semi-finals.

Hibs got a fearsome draw in the first round against Celtic, with the first leg played at Parkhead on Saturday 7 June but the 'McCartney Babes' won this Battle of the Greens, beating Celtic 2-5 with a hat-trick from Arthur Milne and a brace from Willie Anderson. The Hibernian team was: Jimmy Kerr, Davy Shaw, Alex Hall, Willie Finnegan, Bobby Baxter, Sammy Kean, Tommy Adams, Bobby Combe, Willie Anderson, Arthur Milne and Bobby Nutley.

Celtic won the second leg 0-1 but the Edinburgh Irishmen were comfortably through to the second round against Clyde with the first leg on Saturday 21 June being played at Easter Road and the Hibees lost 1-2, leaving them a mountain to climb in the second leg at Shawfield.

Matt Busby

It is now that the legendary Matt Busby enters into the history of Hibernian Football Club for the next two years. Scots-born Matt Busby was a 'Paddy Mac' from an 'Irish mining family in the west of Scotland' but it was when he was playing with the Stirlingshire club Denny Hibs that his talent was snapped up by Manchester City. He appeared in two English cup finals in 1933 and 1934 and Matt also captained Manchester City to the league championship in 1937 and he gained Scottish international honours. Matt then moved on to Liverpool but, with the outbreak of the war, he was now a tough army sergeant stationed near Edinburgh and the ever-vigilant Willie McCartney swooped to bring him to Hibernian, which delighted Matt greatly, as he had a long-standing affection for the Edinburgh Irishmen.

So Matt Busby made his Hibernian debut when the Hibees travelled to save the Summer Cup 2nd round 2nd leg tie, at Shawfield against Clyde on Saturday 28 June, and save it they did, after an almighty struggle, winning 3-4 to force a play-off. Hibs were trailing 2-1 at half-time, their goal coming from Willie Finnegan, but eight minutes into the second half Clyde went further ahead from a penalty and all looked lost for the Edinburgh Irishmen. Shrewd tactician Willie McCartney thought otherwise and the dapper bowler-hatted 'Boss' surprised everyone by leaving his seat in the stand and shouting instructions from the track for Gordon Smith and Arthur Milne to switch positions and in less that ten minutes the whole picture completely changed, with a goal from Gordon Smith and two from Willie Finnegan for him to complete a hat-trick, although the press tells us: 'Matt Busby was Hibernian's star man'. Matt was to go on to give the 'McCartney Babes' great 'service' and his influential half-back play 'made' Willie Finnegan and Gordon Smith. Willie, Gordon and Matt in turn went on to combine beautifully together, an 'uncanny understanding' letting them know exactly where each other would be, without looking up to pass the ball. After the war, Matt Busby was appointed manager of Manchester United and when Gordon Smith was later awarded a testimonial match he absolutely insisted that it had to be Matt's Manchester United who provided the opposition. Matt, of course, was delighted to oblige the great players he had had so much influence over. By the way, the Hibees took seven goals off Matt's team that day, but that is another story. Willie McCartney too insisted on Matt's club for his testimonial. Matt Busby's brilliant managerial career with Manchester United was based on the influence of Willie McCartney, with Matt developing his 'Busby Babes' to bring his club to greatness. When a short history of Hibernian Football Club, *One Hundred Years of Hibs*, was published in 1975 to celebrate the Hibees' centenary year it was Sir Matt Busby who wrote the Foreword. He modestly recalled, 'I had the luck to play behind a boy who would become a legend in Scottish football, Gordon Smith.' He also recalls the other great Hibernians he played with and the influence of Willie McCartney and Harry Swan and how the Hibs result was the first one he always looked for every Saturday of the season. Sir Matt Busby concluded his Foreword, 'I regard it as an honour and a privilege to write these words on such an occasion as the centenary of Hibernian with its splendid traditions.'

The play-off against Clyde, on Wednesday 2 July, was at neutral Ibrox and after 15 minutes Hibs were a goal down and 'nobody gave a penny for their chances'. We are then further told:

> after half an hour Hibs equalised. Busby brilliantly eluded three defenders and when everybody thought he was going to shoot he slipped the ball to Arthur Milne whose effort was blocked, the rebound going to Willie Anderson who drove it into the net.

At half-time Willie McCartney again switched his forwards around, moving Gordon Smith to the left-wing and Arthur Milne to the right and it worked perfectly when, after only four minutes, 'L'il' Arthur crossed to Gordon who crashed home an unsavable drive to give Hibs a 1-2 victory. A sports commentator, whom one assumes was on magic mushrooms, reported, 'Gordon Smith will never make a winger.' Just how wrong can you be? Another obviously clear-headed reporter earmarked Matt Busby's worth: 'Hibs transformation was thanks mainly to the brilliant play of Matt Busby. No praise is too great to be lavished on Busby for his efforts in getting the Hibernians so far in the Summer Cup competition.' The Green Jerseys were: Jimmy Kerr,

Davy Shaw, Alex Hall, Matt Busby, Bobby Baxter, Sammy Kean, Gordon Smith, Willie Finnegan, Willie Anderson, Arthur Milne and Bobby Combe.

The following day, the happy atmosphere at Easter Road changed with the tragic news that the great Harry Ritchie of Hibs' celebrated 1920s team had died at the early age of 41, following a stomach operation in a Nottingham hospital.

The semi-finals of the Summer Cup were between Hearts and Rangers and Hibs and Dumbarton, with the Hibees' tie being played at neutral Tynecastle on Saturday 5 July. Arthur Milne was still available from the RAF to play and Bobby Baxter had some leave from the 'Brylcreme Boys', so Willie McCartney put Bobby in place of Willie Anderson; otherwise it was an unchanged Hibernian. There was no scoring in the first half although Kean, Combe and Nutley had good tries and 'Willie Finnegan lashed the ball against the post, a grand shot under difficult circumstances.' Matt Busby was off the field for a while, being attended by Dr St John Cogan, but Dumbarton could not take advantage of his absence. Arthur Milne had been holding the ball too much but ten minutes into the second half he beat two defenders in a 20-yard run and 'scored with a neat shot' to put Hibs into the final of the Summer Cup. Their opponents would be the 'unbeatable Rangers' who had easily disposed of Hearts in the other semi.

Willie McCartney had belatedly attached another great player to Hibs, Jimmy Caskie, the Scottish international and Everton left-winger, and the Irishmen had to insure him for a large undisclosed amount. Jimmy Caskie was selected to play in the final in place of the inexperienced and very disappointed 17-year-old Gordon Smith. The equally young and inexperienced Bobby Combe, however, kept his place in the final team. The day before the final Sammy Kean was married, arrangements having been made months earlier and a lot of 'McCartney's charm' and 'players barracking' had to be used to ensure he played as Sammy's new wife was not at all happy about him doing so. We are told: 'The needs of Hibernian Football Club almost had Sammy Kean divorced before he was married'. Bobby Nutley got a 48-hour pass from the RAF and travelled overnight by train from Reading where he was stationed and he had a sleepless journey standing in the corridor. When he reached his home in Blantyre he didn't dare try to catch forty winks, for he knew he would be out cold. We are told: 'Bobby Nutley had reached the stage of over-tiredness and seemed to be standing outside his own body when he ran out on to the Hampden pitch with his Hibernian team-mates on Saturday 12 July.' We are further told: 'Even allowing for Scotland being engaged in a world war for its survival the Hibernian team that had quite a few catholics in it were spat on and jeered with the usual anti-catholic blasphemy by the Rangers supporters'.

There were, however, 15,000 Hibs supporters in the 40,000 war-time crowd and we are told, 'they greeted the Green Jerseys with one almighty roar'.

Hibs were written off before a ball was kicked and this was not surprising as they were up against a truly great Rangers team which had swept everything before them for several years now. Hibs' big centre-half and captain Bobby Baxter won the toss and booked a slight breeze but after only two minutes Rangers were a goal up and another was conceded after 20 minutes to 'the domineering all-conquering Rangers machine which was at the height of its power'. Having said that, the Hibees were playing well and 'never panicked' nor did Willie McCartney, who was back down on the track with another tactical switch with Bobby Nutley and Jimmy Caskie swapping wings. Most teams would have thrown in the towel but not Hibs, instead they grew in confidence and when Arthur Milne was clean through, with the Rangers goal at his mercy, he was crudely chopped down from behind and a penalty was awarded which Willie Finnegan 'without a nerve in his body coolly hit home' to keep Hibernian well in the hunt. Could it be another famous fight-back by the Hibees?

Early in the second half Hibs were denied another stonewall penalty when Arthur Milne was again chopped down from behind but the Green Jerseys kept their composure and, although Jimmy Kerr had to be on his toes, 'Rangers were running out of steam against the sprightly young Irish brigade from Easter Road.' After great play from Matt Busby, the ball went to Sammy Kean who slipped it to the on-rushing Willie Finnegan and he lashed the ball home for his second and Hibs' equaliser; the fat was really in the fire now. Matt Busby's influence continued to be immense in urging Hibs forward and delicately switching play, having Rangers falling over themselves. With only two minutes of the match remaining, Jimmy Caskie took a clever corner to Bobby Nutley who, equally cleverly, returned it to the head of Bobby Baxter who bulleted the ball into the back of the Rangers' net for Hibs to lift the Summer Cup by 2-3 after being two goals down against the 'mighty Rangers'. We are told: 'It was magnificent fight-back and brilliant victory by a young Hibernian team that was all so reminiscent of the old Irish squadrons of Easter Road.' We are further told:

> The victory by the Hibernians, unexpected in most quarters, was all the more noteworthy because of the fact that they were two goals down after 20 minutes play, and to wipe out such a deficit against Rangers was in fact almost unbelievable. But the fact was that the young Hibernians fought Rangers to a standstill. They had youth and stamina on their side, and that told in a gruelling struggle. Rangers reckoned without the Hibernian fighting spirit and the young Green Jerseys literally ran Rangers off their feet. It was a very tired and dispirited Ibrox team at the finish.

And the Hibees did that even without Gordon Smith. The Hibernian team was: Jimmy Kerr, Davy Shaw, Alex Hall, Matt Busby, Sammy Kean, Bobby Nutley, Willie Finnegan, Arthur Milne, Bobby Combe and Jimmy Caskie.

This was Hibs' first national trophy win since 1902 and the Scottish football authorities allowed the Hibs to keep the cup outright; a new cup would be produced for the competition next season. The 'ould Irish shareholders' in turn made a gift of it to Harry Swan. Perhaps it would have been more fitting if it had sat on Willie McCartney's mantelpiece as it was all his astute signings and tactics that masterminded the Hibernian victory, a victory which 'the Boss' emotionally described as 'my proudest moment in a lifetime of football'.

Six days later, on Friday 18 July, Hibs forward Jimmy McIntyre, who was in the forces serving in Egypt, was on a BBC Radio program, *Greetings from Cairo* and before he even asked after his family he jubilantly congratulated Hibernian on their Summer Cup victory over Rangers.

In Memoriam – James McGhee

James McGhee's service to Hibernian Football Club has been recorded in Book 1 and need not be repeated, enough to say that the 'iron-willed captain' of Hibernian and Scottish internationalist of the 1860s holds a special place in Hibernian's Hall of Fame. He was part of the famous half-back line of McPhee, McGinn and McLaren that won the Scottish Cup in February 1887 and World Championship in August 1887. James McGhee emigrated to America about 1910 and now, on Wednesday 30 July 1941, he died in Philadelphia after a two-month illness, the news being intimated to Easter Road by his sister. The passing of this great Hibernian brought to mind the saying of the 'ould Irish' Hibs supporters when the Hibees were struggling for survival in the early 1890s, 'as long as there is James McGhee and ten others there will always be a Hibernian Football Club'.

Matt Busby, who was at an army camp in Kelso, was promoted to sergeant-major instructor and posted to 'somewhere in England' but with leave and 48-hour passes he was still available to play for Hibs many times in the new season, which caused him a lot of inconvenient travelling. Bob Hardisthy, the famous English amateur of Bishop Auckland, Middlesborough and Wolverhampton Wanderers was a signalman in the army stationed near Edinburgh and Willie McCartney snapped him up as cover for Matt. Bobby Nutley's duties with the RAF meant he would only be available now and again but, by and large, the Hibees could depend on most of their squad so no practice matches were played for start of season 1941–1942.

As the season proceeded goalkeeper Jimmy Kerr was badly injured in the ribs and knee so 'the Boss' secured the services of the very able Brentford goalkeeper Joe Crozier who was to keep young Jimmy Kerr out of the team for the season. Jimmy missed his first game in three years when, on Saturday 23 August, Hibs travelled to Coatbridge for their Scottish Southern League match, defeating Albion Rovers 3-8. At one time in the game Hibs actually trailed by two goals but four goals by Bobby Combe helped the Hibees swamp the Rovers.

The annual meeting of the Hibs shareholders 'was as happy as could be and a profit of £480 from last season was considered quite good under the circumstances of war-time conditions.' Retiring by rota, director Sean Martin was unanimously re-elected to the board, as was Harry Swan as chairman, so things remained unchanged with Owen Brannigan, Thomas Hartland and James Drummond Shiels all still in the boardroom.

Matt Busby was available to play in Hibs' fourth league match, on Saturday 30 August, when Hamilton were defeated 4-0 at the Holy Ground but he and Sammy Kean were absent when the Irishmen played their league match against Hearts at Tynecastle a week later. The Hibees still won convincingly 2-4, with a brace from Bobby Baxter and one each from Gordon Smith and Bobby Combe. The Green Jerseys were: Joe Crosier, Davy Shaw, Alex Hall, Bob Hardisty, Bobby Baxter, Willie Rice, Gordon Smith, Willie Finnegan, Willie Anderson, Bobby Combe and Jimmy Caskie.

The Edinburgh Irishmen had accumulated five straight league wins in a row when they came up against Rangers on Saturday 27 September at the Holy Ground. We are told:

> All conquering Rangers are unbeaten this season and hold a four-point lead in the league over Hibernian. The Ibrox men are hell-bent on revenge for that Summer Cup final defeat but if anyone is capable of beating Rangers it is the Edinburgh Irishmen. It is not the first time they have taken Rangers off their pedestal.

Hibernian were to do just that with a truly earth-shattering performance that was to leave Rangers and Scottish football gasping.

Hibernian 8 Rangers 1

The headlines said it all:

> Rangers are humbled.
>
> Hibs record 8-1 victory over Rangers.
>
> Roasting for Rangers – brilliant Hibs – Rangers outclassed.
>
> The Greens smash the Ibrox brigade.'

HIBERNIAN AND THE WAR YEARS

Rangers routed – bewildering combination by Hibernian.

The gates of the Holy Ground were opened at 2pm but were closed before the 3pm kick-off with over 20,000 inside which was 'above the war-time quota.'

We are further told:

Rangers were well aware that in coming to Easter Road they were facing a hard task. What they could not expect – and what they got – was a severe thrashing. To anyone not at the match the natural question would be "How did it happen?" The answer is simple, the Hibernians from start to finish outclassed the Ibrox team.

A brilliant, display of non-stop attacking at Easter Road on Saturday by Hibernians light-weight forwards resulted in a record 8-1 defeat of Rangers who had not suffered a defeat since Hibernians beat them in the Summer Cup. There was no doubting the merit of Hibernians win. The Ibrox men were cut to shreds by bewildering footwork and the score might well have been doubled. Every one of the Hibernians goals was a "picture" effort crowning smart combination.

As to how Rangers came to crumble one can only say that they were outplayed from start to finish. Hibs forwards were masterly in their positioning, tremendously alert and nimbly full of speed and confidence and gifted with unusual hitting power.

It must be said that the Ibrox men did not take their roasting very well, one was booked and another sent off. Let it be said that the trouble was not started by the Hibernians.

The Hibernians support were yelling themselves hoarse as their midget forwards gave the Ibrox defence a tremendous gruelling...The Rangers came a bad cropper. They were out for revenge for the Summer Cup defeat. Instead they got a worse thrashing...Hibernians light-weight forwards were outstanding but every green jersey was a hero and provided a very pleasant memory. It was a performance that will be long remembered in the history of Hibernian Football Club.

The performance was likened to that of the Wembley Wizards. Gordon Smith and Arthur Milne scored two goals each and Bobby Combe scored four. It was a personal triumph for 17-year-old Bobby as no other player had ever scored four goals against Rangers. Two-goal Arthur Milne missed a sitter at the end of the game and Rangers' international goalkeeper Dawson humorously shouted to him 'have you stopped trying Arthur?' Quick as a flash 'L'il' Arthur. replied 'no way but Combe got in your hair today'. That great team of 'McCartney Babes' with its diminutive forward line was: Joe Crosier, Davy Shaw, Bob Hardisty, Bobby Baxter, Sammy Kean, Gordon Smith, Willie Finnegan, Arthur Milne, Bobby Combe and Jimmy Caskie.

Willie McCartney had said after the Summer Cup final defeat of Rangers that it was his 'proudest moment'; he now admitted that this Hibernian performance was his 'new proudest moment'. Chairman Harry Swan said, 'such a Hibernian performance had to come some time, it almost worked against Hearts three weeks ago. Our "bhoys" have been building up their own style for two years now.'

Rangers' only goal had come from a hotly disputed penalty and director Thomas Hartland, who never spoke in public, especially to the press and had 'that same stony expression of all the old Irish directors of Easter Road', suddenly let his mask slip 'it was a pity about that Rangers penalty'.

In October Jimmy Caskie played for Scotland against England at Wembley and a week later, along with Matt Busby and Bobby Baxter, he played for the Scottish League against the English League at Blackpool.

On Saturday 1 November the Hibees had a 4-1 victory over Airdrie at the Holy Ground, with Matt Busby being described as an 'artist' as he provided the ammunition for Willie Finnegan to score a hat-trick. Another hat-trick hero was Bobby Baxter when Hibs put five past Albion Rovers, again at the Holy Ground on Saturday 6 December.

Hibernian travelled to Ibrox on Saturday 27 December and recorded their league double against Rangers with a 0-1 victory in front of a 20,000 wartime crowd. Even although Hibs were without 'flu victim Bobby Baxter and RAF duty-bound Arthur Milne, Rangers could not master the Green Jerseys. Matt Busby, however, was available from the army and he made all the difference with Hibs' half-back line holding the key to this victory. In each half the Hibees were denied a 'stonewall penalty' but it did not upset their poise and combination and they produced all the good football. Fourteen minutes from the end, after good play by Matt Busby, 'Gordon Smith led the way through the Rangers defence and an astute cross to Bobby Combe saw him crash the ball with cool deliberation into the roof of Rangers' net from 20 yards out although he was harassed by two Ibrox defenders.' Matt Busby and Jimmy Caskie almost added to the score while Rangers got a man booked as:

> once again Hibernian mastered the mighty Rangers who suffered their first home defeat of the season and for the first time failed to score. Rangers as always did not take their reverse well, and it was not surprising to see a few Easter Road men suffering from injuries.

The 'McCartney Babes' that day were: Joe Crosier, Davy Shaw, Alex Hall, Matt Busby, Sammy Kean, Bob Hardisty, Gordon Smith, Willie Finnegan, Willie Anderson, Bobby Combe and Jimmy Caskie.

Five days later, on Thursday 1 January 1942, an unchanged Hibernian faced Hearts at Easter Road in the New Year's Day match. Hearts took the lead but Matt Busby equalised with a header. Hearts had a 2-1 half-time lead but in the second half Gordon Smith this time scored the equaliser to finish the scoring. On Saturday 17 January Matt Busby captained Scotland at Wembley and fellow Hibernian Jimmy Caskie also played.

In the Scottish Southern League Cup Hibs failed to qualify in their four-club section with some disappointing displays, during which goalkeeper Joe Crozier had his nose fractured in two places. Hibs were runners-up in the league with 40 points and their two youngest players, Gordon Smith and Bobby Combe, each scored 22 goals in the campaign. They had also played in 29 of the 30 league matches, as had Arthur Milne and Davy Shaw. Willie Finnegan had played in all 30 matches, scoring 12 goals.

In the Rosebery Charity Cup final against Hearts at Tynecastle on Saturday 23 May it was a 1-1 draw with Hibs having no less than six 'guest players' in their team. The destination of the cup was decided on the toss of a coin which Hearts won. It was to prove to be a bad omen for the Hibees.

Hibs' defence of the Summer Cup got underway in early June and in the two legs of the first round against Clyde the Hibees scored four goals and in the two legs of the second round they scored 13 against Third Lanark. In the semi-final at neutral Tynecastle, a 1-3 victory was recorded over Motherwell, taking the Hibees to the final with the opposition again being Rangers.

The Hampden final of the Summer Cup came off on Saturday 4 July in front of a war-time crowd in excess of 40,000 and we are told: 'Hibernian got the bigger cheer when they ran out.' We are further told: 'Rangers had not come to play football, they went into things like a bunch of commandos; all they lacked was Sten Guns.' This observation summed up Rangers' disgraceful unsporting attitude that day; in only four minutes Arthur Milne was carried off in agony to be tended by Dr St John Cogan. Eventually 'L'il' Arthur limped back on to the right-wing but it was really just to make up the numbers; in reality Hibs were down to ten men. Later in the first half he had to leave the field again but such was the spirit of this 'McCartney Babe' he reappeared to help as best he could. Amid all this 'Hibernian were producing all the football and Rangers ruthless defence were lucky to survive the first half.' We are further told: 'The Edinburgh Irishmen should have had two blatant penalties, one a handling offence but they were ignored by the referee.' In the second half Rangers became 'wilder' with Joe Crozier, Sammy Kean and Jimmy Caskie all picking up nasty injuries. Hibs, however, stood strong and Matt Busby marshalled his defence like a 'green general' and still produced great service to 'Hibs clever forwards'. As the 90 minutes drew to a close we are told:

> Entering the closing stages it was still a dour battle, with Hibs hitting back...Rangers had the benefit of some very debatable decisions. It seemed to help the Ibrox men no end when they claimed for everything and anything. How the

referee put up with Rangers cantrips was amazing. He was chased about by nearly every Ibrox player at one time or another...Davy Shaw shot against the crossbar and both he and Matt Busby were injured as 90 minutes play came to an end with no scoring.

Thirty minutes extra time had to be played and now corners were to count and Rangers had two after the 15-minute period. In the second 'never-say-die Hibs rallied again and again', drawing level on corners and it was all even when the final whistle blew. The destination of the Summer Cup was then decided on the toss of a coin and 'justice was not done', with Hibs losing. We are told: 'It had been a very gallant fight by the Edinburgh Irishmen. Rangers jubilation at winning the toss seemed a bit misplaced after their display of spoiling football marred by too many protests.' Other observations were less polite: 'Rangers brutal play had nothing to do with football, they were a total disgrace as was a very weak referee who literally let them away with murder without one word of censure.' The Hibernian team that 'scored a moral victory in keeping Scottish football's head high' was: Joe Crozier, Davy Shaw, Alex Hall, Matt Busby, Bobby Baxter, Sammy Kean, Gordon Smith, Willie Finnegan, Arthur Milne, Bobby Combe and Jimmy Caskie.

Rangers had won everything this season but when the UK military authorities were invited to choose a Scottish club to play against their international studded United Military Services XI in a prestigious War Charities match it was not Rangers but Hibernian Football Club they turned to as 'the Edinburgh Irishmen are the best team in Scotland and have a great reputation for clean, clever, fast football.' We are further told: 'The Hibernians have been paid a high honour in being asked to provide the opposition to an all-star Services team and it is an honour the Easter Road side will undoubtedly uphold.' The military side, which included greats such an Bill Shankly, Frank Swift and Stanley Matthews, to mention but three household names, not surprisingly won a tight match 3-2 in front of a 30,000 Hampden crowd on Saturday 18 July. Hibs lost Jimmy Caskie in the first half with a broken arm but 'Hibernian all the time were playing football of the most pleasing type.' The two main highlights of the game came from Hibernian with 'Alex Hall hardly giving Stanley Matthews a kick of the ball' and 'the uncanny understanding between Willie Finnegan and Gordon Smith which eventually resulted in young Gordon scoring with a glorious 25-yard drive...Hibernian upheld the prestige of Scottish football but then nothing less was expected from the Irishmen.'

It was also in July that news reached Easter Road of the death of Willie Thomson, a goalkeeper Hibs had signed from Kilsyth St Patrick's during the First World War. Now the Second World War had reached truly global proportions with the Germans having invaded Russia the previous year and Japan bombing America's Pearl Harbour. Tens of thousands of Hibs supporters were serving in this world conflict and certainly, as in the First World War, 'Little Ireland was devoid of young men.' Old Hibs supporters from Little Ireland remembered:

> Us teenagers that were under military age volunteered en masse for service in the Home Guard Cadets attached to the Royal Scots after church parades and services in St Patrick's we would be led by the band of the Royal Scots through Little Ireland, real proud we were, and the parades would finish at St Mary's Street Halls for military training and classes.

We are also told: 'thoere were 30 Hibs players in the armed forces as were the sons of manager Willie McCartney and ex-director Edward Lester.'

Season 1942–1943 opened at the Holy Ground on Saturday 1 August with another military benefit match, this time in aid of the RAF Benevolent Fund and Edinburgh War Charities. Again, Hibernian were first choice to represent Scotland and their opponents were the RAF All International XI, many of whom had played against the Hibees in the big Hampden benefit match, and they won 1-3. Willie Harper and Johnny Halligan of the celebrated Hibs team of the 1920s were in the stand for this 'Easter Road Gala', which included an hour's cabaret before the kick-off. We are told: 'Everyone at Easter Road put in an enormous amount of work for this well-organised occasion and even 85-year-old Paddy Cannon had his sleeves rolled up.' Sammy Kean scored Hibs' counter and the team, which was without the injured Jimmy Caskie was: Joe Crozier, Davy Shaw, Alex Hall, Matt Busby, Bobby Baxter, Sammy Kean, Gordon Smith, Willie Finnegan, Arthur Milne, Bobby Combe and Geordie Young. We are told: 'Hibernian and their 18,000 faithful supporters raised a whopping £1,500 for the military charities.'

Hibernian financial report for last season showed a profit of £972 which did not include revenue from the Summer Cup competition, so it was very satisfactory and:

> thanks are due to the players who are responsible for much of the club's success. The splendid team spirit and enthusiasm shown on and off the field has been most favourably commented upon by the SFA, officials of other clubs and the military authorities.

The 'ould Irish' director Sean Martin had died recently and many tributes were paid to this 'longstanding and enthusiastic supporter of Hibernian who had worked on the Board of Directors with unremitting zeal'. It was decided at a meeting of the 'Irish' shareholders not to appoint anyone in his place because of the war-time conditions, leaving Hibs with its chairman Harry Swan and three directors, which included 80-year-old Owen Brannigan the last of the 'ould Irish directors'.

Although we are told 'Hibernians officials, shareholders and manager are one big happy family' some supporters unrealistically thought the club was sliding back to being 'like the closed Irish concern in years gone by'. We are further told, however:

> The Hibs much to the disgust no doubt of a section of their following are almost a closed corporation more so than ever now Easter Road's destiny seems to be falling more completely than ever into the same hands. That at the moment however should cause no qualms. The men who brought Hibs from just another team to the most attractive side in the country are the men still with the power.

For the new season, Willie McCartney attached Stan Williams, the Aberdeen left-winger to Easter Road and John 'Cubby' Cuthbertson, who was a sergeant-pilot in the RAF, was able to return to play many times but overall, military duties of the Hibs players and injuries meant constant reshuffling of teams.

Hibs, however, in their first 13 Scottish Southern League matches remained unbeaten with 10 wins and 3 draws, one of their victories being 0-3 against Celtic at Parkhead in front of a crowd of 30,000. During this unbeaten run, Matt Busby again captained Scotland at Wembley, Willie McCartney signed Sean Tobin from Coatbridge St Patrick's and Bobby Combe and Joe Crozier joined the armed forces.

As the weeks passed we are, however, told: 'Hibs feel the strain due to serious losses in personnel which so far has made their success all the more notable.' When the inevitable defeat came, on Saturday 14 October against Clyde at Shawfield, it came big with a 7-2 reverse and that was after Hibs leading 1-2 at half time. The following week Hibs were back to their winning ways with a 1-4 victory over Albion Rovers at Coatbridge, with the following team: Jimmy Matthews, Davy Shaw, Alex Hall, Bobby Fraser, Bobby Baxter, 'A.N. Other', Gordon Smith, Stan Williams, Willie Anderson, Jimmy Blyth and Arthur Milne.

On Boxing Day, 26 December, Rangers were the visitors to Easter Road for a top of the table league clash and it was spoiled by 'a fanatic Hibs supporter'. With the score standing at 1-1, the second half had just got underway with Hibs shooting down the slope towards the north end when, from a corner, 'Cubby' Cuthbertson beat Rangers goalkeeper Dawson to the jump to head a beautiful goal which the referee, quite rightly, allowed and he ran to the centre spot, only to be chased after by Dawson and other Rangers players. You've guessed right, the weak referee crumpled under 'Rangers' intimidation' and incredibly changed his mind, disallowed the goal and gave the Ibrox men a free kick. Again, as so many times in years past, the Rangers and the referee 'were a disgrace to Scottish football' but it was no excuse for the incident that immediately followed. Hibs supporter, 25-year-old Hugh Duffy, a shipwright in the Leith shipyards barged his way down the north terracing shouting 'gie me a brick.' A small boy, 'a younger son of the Emerald Isle', was collecting empty beer bottles to get the deposit money on them and he offered one to Duffy which he took, throwing it with great accuracy and force, smashing it against Dawson's head and laying him out cold and bleeding. As Duffy was arrested and a section of the Hibs supporters rioted, Rangers almost refused to play on but they did, with the match ending in a 1-1 draw. The Hibs were: Jock Brown, Davy Shaw, Alex Hall, Willie Finnegan, Bobby Baxter, Sammy Kean, Gordon Smith, Bobby Combe, Arthur Milne, 'Cubby' Cuthbertson and Jimmy Caskie.

That Monday at Edinburgh Burgh Court, Hugh Duffy was full of apologies but it did not save him from 60 days' imprisonment.

On Friday 1 January 1943 the New Year derby match saw Hibernian beat Hearts 1-4 at Tynecastle.

Three other January victories saw Hibs at the Holy Ground do the league double over Celtic with a 4-0 win. Matt Busby was back for Hibs that day and 'very influential' and Gordon Smith scored one of the goals. In the two other January victories, Gordon scored a hat-trick in the Easter Road 7-1 hammering of Airdrie and in the 1-5 hammering of Partick Thistle at Firhill. This brought Gordon's goal tally for the season so far to 25 – not bad for a teenage right-winger, and he had more still to come.

In Scottish Southern League Cup in March, Hibs again failed to qualify in their four-club group and in the long-forgotten Mitchell Cup in April, Hibs disposed of Hearts, but lost out to Aberdeen in the semi-final. Meantime, Sammy Kean played for Scotland at Hampden and Willie McCartney signed goalkeeper Mitchell Downie from St Anthony, the junior club from which Hibs signed the great Jimmy Dunn. Downie, the 'McCartney Babe', would eventually give great service to Hibernian. In the East of Scotland Shield final against Hearts, after a 1-1 draw, the Hibees won the replay 3-2 at the Holy Ground on Saturday 13 May. The Green Jerseys were: Mitchell Downie, Davy Shaw, Alex Hall, Willie Finnegan, Bobby Baxter, Sammy Kean, Gordon Smith, Charlie McGillivray, Willie Anderson, Bobby Combe and Jimmy Caskie. A week later, in the Rosebery Charity Cup final, Hearts could still not beat Hibs at football but they beat Hibs in the toss of the coin after a 1-1 draw.

June brought the Summer Cup and in the two legs of the first round, the Hibees took a total of 12 goals off Partick Thistle and in the second round, a total of six against Queen's Park but lost 1-3 against Rangers in the semi-final.

It is worth noting that this season a young Hugh Howie played six games for Hibs' first team; he was to go on to be a great club servant. It is also worth noting this season that Gordon Smith scored a total of 33 goals. Hibs wound things up on Wednesday 7 July by winning the Edinburgh Press Charities Committee five-a-side tournament at Tynecastle by disposing of Edinburgh City, Hearts and an Army Select in the final.

In the middle of July Willie McCartney was notified by the army that his son had been wounded in fighting in Sicily.

Hibs' financial report showed a profit of £1,076, due much to the season ticket and gate money 'of our steadfast support', Thomas Hartland, the retiring by rota director, was unanimously re-elected.

Season 1943–1944 started with a public practice match at Easter Road, in which a young Jock Govan showed up well and who in future years would be a great Hibernian. Some other new faces made a few appearances for Hibs this season but most, like Len Butt from Blackburn Rovers and local lads Pat O'Brien and Willie Croft, would soon be away serving in the military. Bobby Nutley was able to got some leave from the RAF to play now and again for the Hibees. Willie Finnegan picked up an early injury which kept him out of action for many weeks but Hibernian remained unbeaten at home in the league up to the end of November.

One of Hibs' several away victories was an early visit to Tynecastle on Saturday 11 September, when Willie Finnegan scored the only goal of the game, although overall we are told the Hibees' play had 'Hearts defence bewildered.' The Green Jerseys were: Jock Brown, Davy Shaw, Alex Hall, Bobby Fraser, Bobby Baxter, Sammy Kean, Gordon Smith, Stan Williams, Willie Finnegan, Bobby Combe and Jimmy Caskie.

After this game, goalkeeper Jock Brown left for service in the Royal Navy, giving young goalkeeper Mitchell Downie his chance to make his league debut, as did Len Butt. In Hibs' 4-3 victory over Dumbarton at Easter Road on Saturday 18 September, Gordon Smith scored a hat-trick. Also that day, Willie McCartney added to his 'Babes' by signing ex-Blantyre Celtic and Renfrew Juniors centre-forward Tommy Bogan, whose destination had been earmarked for Celtic Park before the 'persuasive Mr McCartney' stepped in. Tommy Bogan was to score 25 goals for the Hibees this season. Tommy's goal-scoring feats were to continue next season and, as we shall see, then he would set a strange Scottish international record. Meantime, Tommy Bogan made his debut for Hibernian on Saturday 9 October at Brockville against Falkirk in a 3-5 victory for the Green Jerseys and Tommy celebrated with a hat-trick.

With 30 Hibs players and thousands of Hibs supporters fighting in the military, Hibernian groundsman Tommy Cannon and his famous old father

Paddy, who acted as his assistant, came up with a very novel idea for the Holy Ground. We are told: 'The Hibernians are being very patriotic even in the cutting at Easter Road. The groundsmen arranged the cutting so that from any viewpoint there are a series of the popular "V" sign'.

As the league campaign continued, Gordon Smith and Bobby Baxter were selected for Scotland to play against the RAF International XI at Hampden. Previous to this, Gordon had been a travelling reserve for an international at Manchester. Meantime, Willie McCartney had secured the services of Jimmy Woodburn of Newcastle United. On Christmas Day, Saturday 25 December, goalkeeper Jimmy Kerr was on leave from the army and made a welcome return to the Hibees in a 1-1 draw with Dumbarton at Boghead.

As Hibs ploughed on into 1944 they had already made over 50 positional changes in the team but, surprisingly, continued to do quite well and at the end of January another 'McCartney Babe', Hugh Colvan, from Port Glasgow St John's, came to Easter Road and he scored in his debut at Love Street in Hibs' 1-2 victory over St Mirren and the following week, Saturday 5 February at the Holy Ground, he scored in the 6-0 demolition of Third Lanark.

Another new 'McCartney Babe' was Jimmy Nelson from Wishaw Juniors and he made a scoring debut at the Holy Ground on Saturday 19 February in a 2-0 victory over Partick Thistle, who had the legendary Bill Shankly in their team. A largely unfamiliar Green Jerseys that day were: George Tweedy, Bobby Fraser, Alex Hall, Willie Finnegan, Bobby Baxter, Sammy Kean, 'Cubby' Cuthbertson, Hugh Colvan, Jimmy Nelson, Jimmy Woodburn and George Marshallsay.

Hibernian had never done much in the Scottish Southern League Cup but this season they were to go all the way. The three other teams in Hibs' first-round group in March and early April were Third Lanark, Albion Rovers and Morton. In the six games, Hibs dropped only one point and scored 20 goals which came from Jimmy Nelson (7), Gordon Smith (4), Tommy Bogan (2), Jimmy Caskie (2), and one each from 'Cubby' Cutbertson, Sammy Kean, Hugh Colvan, George Marshallsay and Sean Devlin, who scored in his first team debut after a season in the reserves. It was a month before the Hibees faced semi-final opponents Clyde at neutral Hampden on Saturday 6 May. Clyde opened the scoring in front of a war-time crowd of 35,000 but Hibs' 'skill and strength saw them win 2-5 in fine style with two goals from Jimmy Woodburn and one each from Bobby Combe, Bobby Baxter and Jimmy Nelson.' The Hibernian team was: Mitchell Downie, Bobby Fraser, Alex Hall, Willie Finnegan, Bobby Baxter, Sammy Kean, Gordon Smith, Bobby Combe, Jimmy Nelson, Jimmy Woodburn and Jimmy Caskie.

So Hibs had reached the final of the Scottish Southern League Cup and their opponents were bitter rivals Rangers and we are told: 'Both clubs are keyed up for a supreme effort and Hibernian are capable of rising to the occasion.' Military duties caused doubt about Hibs' line-up and it was a bad blow when Bobby Combe was not available, but Tommy Bogan was and Willie McCartney had no hesitation in giving him his vote of confidence; otherwise the Hibees were unchanged from the semi-finals. Matt Busby, who was away at an army posting in England, sent a letter of encouragement to Harry Swan, saying, 'I feel as excited about the game as if I was a team member myself, I will drink to the health of Hibernian tomorrow night as cup winners.'

The Hampden final, on Saturday 20 May, was played in front of a 'bumper war-time crowd of 50,000' and in the event of goals being even corners would count. After 17 minutes' play Tommy Bogan collided with Rangers' goalkeeper Dawson who was carried off with a broken leg. Ten-man Rangers played with even more determination but again, as usual, the referee was on their side and Hibs were denied a 'stonewall penalty' when Jimmy Caskie was chopped down as he bore in on goal. There was no scoring in the first half but Rangers led by two corners to one. Mitchell Downie had played very well in Hibs' goal and continued to do so but so were the rest of the team, with Willie Finnegan and Sammy Kean 'working like Trojans'. Gordon Smith was 'outstanding' as Hibs mixed their skill with playing a 'hard game'. As the minutes of the second half ticked away, Rangers were leading 5-4 on corners when, with 12 minutes left, Hibs drew level but there was still no scoring. Excitement was high and 'tempers frayed' when, with only three minutes left, Jimmy Caskie won Hibs a corner which 'was greeted by Hibernian an if it were a goal'. So the Hibees won the Scottish Southern League Cup 5-6 on corners. Considering Hibernian won on football ability and not the toss of a coin, a sour Edinburgh press stated: 'The Irishmen won with not a great deal of glory...it was not a game that left a feeling of satisfaction.' They were most certainly wrong, as it gave Hibernian Football Club and their supporters a great deal of satisfaction in dumping the 'mighty Rangers.'

A week later it also gave Hibernian great satisfaction to overcome the 'ould inimy', Hearts, 1-4 in the final of the Rosebery Charity Cup at Tynecastle. Tommy McIntyre was on leave from the army after seeing a lot of fighting abroad and he celebrated his return in a green jersey by scoring.

In the two legs of the first round of the Summer Cup in June Hibs put a total of seven past Airdrie, with five from Tommy Bogan and two from Gordon Smith. Arthur Milne was back from the fighting in North Africa and he made an appearance once again. In the second round, Hibs went out disappointingly to Morton. Hibs' leading scorers this season were Tommy Bogan with 25 and Gordon Smith with 21.

HIBERNIAN AND THE WAR YEARS

The last season of the Second World War started for the Hibees on Saturday 5 August, with the introduction of the Allison Challenge Cup charity affair between an Edinburgh select and Aston Villa. This fixture against top English opposition was to continue for many years. Five Hibs players – Davy Shaw, Sammy Kean, Gordon Smith, Jimmy Caskie and Bobby Baxter, who was captain – took part in the Tynecastle match, with Aston Villa winning 3-4 in front of a crowd of 30,000.

Two days later, Hibs' Public Practice Match at Easter Road featured many new 'McCartney Babes' but none were quite ready for the big breakthrough. Hibs' financial report showed a loss of £603, but this did not include revenue from the Scottish Southern League Cup or the Summer Cup. Director James Drummond Shiels was retiring by rota and was re-elected to the Board. Harry Swan, who was now a Justice of the Peace, was re-elected chairman and, with Owen Brannigan and Thomas Hartland still on the Board, it was no change at Easter Road as the 'Irish' shareholders were delighted with Hibernian's progress and manager Willie McCartney came in for special praise.

Hibs lost their first two league matches but in their next 12 they won 11 and drew one. Among these was a good 3-1 triumph at the Holy Ground over Hearts on Saturday 9 September, with goals from Sean Devlin, Bobby Nutley and Gordon Smith. The Green Jerseys were: Jimmy Kerr, Davy Shaw, Alex Hall, Willie Finnegan, Bobby Baxter, Sammy Kean, Gordon Smith, Sean Devlin, Arthur Milne, Bobby Nutley and Jimmy Caskie. Taking a break from the league on Monday 18 September, Hibernian went to Tynecastle for the final of the Wilson Cup and thrashed Hearts 2-6 with a Willie Peat hat-trick, two from Tommy Bogan and one from Sean Devlin. It was a Hibs team with a few changes in it because of the war-time conditions: Mitchell Downie, Jock Govan, Alex Hall, Hugh Howie, Bobby Baxter, Sammy Kean, Gordon Smith, Willie Finnegan, Tommy Bogan, Sean Devlin and Willie Peat.

Another excellent league victory was against unbeaten Rangers whom Hibernian defeated 4-1 at the Holy Ground on Saturday 23 September, in front of a 30,000 crowd, with two goals from Arthur Milne and one each from Jimmy Caskie and Gordon Smith. One of 'L'il' Arthur's goals was a cheeky back heeler from all of 20 yards. Rangers' overall attitude had still not changed and they were described as 'the worst sportsmen in Scottish football with their constant fouling and talking back.' The Hibernian team who 'showed up Rangers and taught them how to play football' was: Mitchell Downie, Davy Shaw, Alex Hall, Willie Finnegan, Bobby Baxter, Sammy Kean, Gordon Smith, Tommy Bogan, Arthur Milne, Sean Devlin and Jimmy Caskie.

Hibernian also ran up some other big league victories, including five against Albion Rovers, six against St Mirren and eight against Partick Thistle, and

Gordon Smith scored a hat-trick in the 3-2 defeat of Airdrie at the Holy Ground on Saturday 11 November.

On Saturday 1 October, four Hibs players – Gordon Smith, Arthur Milne, Jimmy Caskie and Bobby Baxter – played for Scotland against England at Wembley in front of a crowd of 90,000. Even Scotland's trainer was Hibernian's Hugh Shaw. A fine achievement for Hibernian Football Club and Arthur Milne scored after only three minutes. On the morning of the match there was, however, a dark cloud for Bobby Baxter when he was notified of the death of his mother. It was a bitter blow for the big centre-half and the Scottish team presented him with a wreath and their condolences. With four players on international duty, Hibernian tried unsuccessfully to have their league match with Celtic postponed but the Hibees still took a creditable 1-1 draw at Parkhead.

In December Hibernian's eight-year servant, left-winger Bobby Nutley, who was a flight engineer in the RAF attached to No. 433 (RCAF) squadron, was awarded the Distinguished Flying Medal for outstanding gallantry in 35 missions over enemy territory. 'Hibs Daft' Bobby was a shipyard platelayer to trade and came from a 'big Irish family', with five sisters and a brother, John, who was serving in the Royal Navy. Modest Bobby, who was 'surprised' at the honour, received a letter of congratulations from the SFA. Bobby Nutley was one of the early 'McCartney Babes' and everyone at Easter Road was very proud of him.

The first two months of 1945 saw mixed results for Hibs as Willie McCartney added to his 'Babes'. Pat Murphy (Wishaw Juniors), Joe Henderson (Larkhall Thistle), Bobby Docherty (Paisley Mossvale) and Frank O'Hagen and Jimmy Clarkson, both from West Calder juveniles were signed. Several others were signed later.

Bobby Nutley was in the Hibs team when Gordon Smith scored his second hat-trick of the season in the 3-0 defeat of Falkirk, on Saturday 13 January at the Holy Ground. The war-reshuffled Green Jerseys were: Joe Henderson, Jock Govan, Willie Callan, Hugh Howie, Bobby Baxter, Tommy McCabe, Jock Weir, George Marshallsay, Gordon Smith, Willie Peat and Bobby Nutley.

In the Scottish Southern League Cup in March, Hibs failed to qualify from their four-club first round section, even although they lost only one game and had taken eight off Albion Rovers.

On Saturday 14 April, a proud Hibernian saw an equally proud 'young Irish McCartney Babe', Tommy Bogan, make his Scottish international debut at Hampden against England. It was a great thrill for young Tommy, as was the fact that he would be playing with the Scottish captain Matt Busby who was now bcak with his club, Liverpool. What should have been a highlight of

Tommy's career lasted only 50 seconds before he was carried off with torn ligaments in his left leg. It was an unfortunate Scottish record Tommy set that day and another record was set that day with, for the first time in an international, a substitute being allowed.

On Saturday 5 May, Hibernian were again the club invited to play a prestigious military charity match in Aid of Sailors, Soldiers and Airmens Families Association and Services Charities. The Hibees drew 2-2 with the Scottish Services XI which contained Matt Busby and the 20,000 Hibs supporters gave him a rapturous welcome back to the Holy Ground.

The Hibees again made the final of the Summer Cup, disposing of St Mirren and Falkirk and with a semi-final victory 0-2 against Celtic at neutral Tynecastle. In the Hampden final, however, the Hibs lost 2-0 against Partick Thistle in a disappointing display, although the legendary Bill Shankly had a big say in the Jags' win. The Hibees also hit the post twice from Willie Finnegan and Hugh Howie.

Tuesday 8 May was VE Day, Victory in Europe Day – the surrender of Germany ended the war in Europe, although conflict in the Far East still continued. Bobby Combe had been reported missing by the army and it was not known if the young man was dead or alive. For a couple of months now Bobby had, in fact, been a prisoner of war in the notorious German Sandbostel camp near Bremen. He had been recently rescued and the first thing he did, within 24 hours of arriving home, was to present himself at the Holy Ground. Willie McCartney immediately included him in the team as captain for the Rosebery Charity Cup final against Hearts at Easter Road, on Wednesday 9 May. In this 'VE celebration game' corners counted and after 90 minutes, with the score at 2-2 and Hibs leading 7-6 on corners; they lifted the cup. The Hibernian team was: Mitchell Downie, Jock Govan, Alex Hall, Willie Finnegan, Bobby Baxter, Sammy Kean, Gordon Smith, Bobby Combe, Jock Weir, Willie Peat and Jimmy Caskie.

A couple of weeks earlier, Hibernian had defeated Hearts 3-1 at the Holy Ground in the final of the East of Scotland Shield and, with the defeat of Hearts in the Wilson Cup at the beginning of the season, the Irishmen had beaten the 'ould inimy' in all three local cup competitions.

A few months later Japan surrendered and the Second World War was over as we entered the atomic age.

So Hibernian Football Club had survived another world war and the parallels between Dan McMichael's efforts in the first conflict and Willie McCartney's in the second conflict were clear to see, with both their inspired signings laying the foundations for the future. It is of interest to note that the latest 'McCartney Babe' was a certain Lawrie Reilly, of the Famous Five, and the most capped player in Hibernian's history. Having already signed Gordon Smith, Willie McCartney was soon to sign Willie Ormond, Eddie Turnbull and Bobby Johnstone to complete his Famous Five. With those and all his other great signings, the tragedy was that 'the Boss' would not live to see the efforts of his expert labours come to fruition on the Holy Ground.

> Willie McCartney and Hibernian,
> A striking pair
> Beyond compare:
> His nibs
> And Hibs.

Yet it is not the death of Willie McCartney that brings to a conclusion *The Making of Hibernian* as recorded in this and my other two books; it is, in fact, the deaths of the last two of the 'ould Irish' Hibernians, director Owen Brannigan and groundsman Paddy Cannon that are the final chapter in *The Making of Hibernian.*

– 13 –

IN MEMORIAM –
OWEN BRANNIGAN AND PADDY CANNON
1946

When you walk into Easter Road stadium, our Holy Ground,
Hibernian ghosts are present
With angels all around,
To comfort in your hour of sorrow
And bring you hope for tomorrow.

The green flag with its harp is your heritage,
So reach out and claim it
With its memories that abound,
For Hibernian Ghosts watch over you
Here at the Holy Ground.

The Making of Hibernian had taken fully 70 years since the club's founding in 1875 'for the recreation of young catholic men from the slums of Little Ireland'. Now, in 1946, Hibernian's longest-serving director, Owen Brannigan, who had been present at their founding in the Catholic Institute (St Mary's Street Halls), had died.

Owen Brannigan had lived through all these 70 years and his official connection with Hibernian had spanned an unbroken 65 years since first signing as a player in 1880. His career, mentioned in all three of my books, need not be repeated. Suffice it to say that he was a player, administrator, director and chairman and he was both an SFA and an East of Scotland FA representative for over 30 years. Owen Brannigan tirelessly pursued Hibernian's charitable birthright all his years at Easter Road and, as a director, he never took payment for his seven days a week work for as he once said: 'It is an honour and a privilege to be a Hibernian, that's something money can't buy.'

Owen Brannigan was an Ulster catholic, born in the Emerald Isle in 1862. As an infant he was brought to the Edinburgh-Irish slum ghetto and grew up to be a brass-finisher to trade, married Mary McIvor and lived at 13 Jeffrey

Street, off the Nether Bow, which was, at least geographically, up in the world from the Cowgate. 'Hibs Daft' Owen had been in failing health for some time but we are told he attended Hibernian matches until just a few weeks before his death, when he was confined to his bed – otherwise you could not keep Owen away from Easter Road, where Gordon Smith was a big favourite of his.

Owen Brannigan, aged 84, died at his home on the morning of Tuesday 15 January 1946 fortified by the Rites of Holy Mother Church. Three days later, his Requiem Mass was celebrated in St Patrick's, attended by an overflow congregation of Hibernians old and new. Harry Swan carried the Hibernian wreath in the form of the traditional broken harp.

A tribute of the time remembered him thus:

> Owen Brannigan was one of the long line of stony-faced Irish directors at Easter Road that disguised a rare sense of humour and a burning passion for Hibernian. He was always great with the players and in later years was popular with the young 'McCartney Babes'. He also had a great affinity with the supporters for director or not he always saw himself simply as a supporter. He was rarely photographed and never gave interviews, Owen kept his own council when it came to Hibernians affairs. It was the same with his Hibernian charity work, no one will probably ever know just how much he achieved but that's the way Owen would want it for that work was its own reward. Owen Brannigan was a very private and Christian man.

Seven mouths, later Paddy Cannon died – the last of the 'ould Irish'. Paddy was in fact Scots, born in Raploch, Stirling, in 1857 of Irish immigrant parents. Paddy's 50 unbroken years' work for Hibernian has already been refered to and again need not be repeated.

It is enough to say that Paddy Cannon had been an outstanding professional runner and in the 1860s had set world records which, incredibly, still stood when he died. He was invited to the post of trainer/groundsman at Easter Road in 1896 which 'Hibs Daft' Paddy readily accepted.

So started Paddy's 50-year 'labour of love' at Easter Road, where he was a superb trainer with very modern methods, transforming 'even ordinary players of indifferent ability into wonderfully fit athletes'. Paddy had a great rapport with the players, one remembering:

> Paddy never had to ask us twice to get through our paces even during his most gruelling sessions, but he was never a hard task-master for the sake of it except when there was any misbehaviour always reminding us to keep away from pubs and bad company, 'you must always be a credit to yourselves and Hibernian in body and mind.

Just after the First World War, in which his sons served, Paddy, at the age of 62, won the Powderhall Ten Mile Marathon.

IN MEMORIAM – OWEN BRANNIGAN AND PADDY CANNON

As the Hibernian groundsman, 'Paddy Cannon had no equal in Scotland, the green swath of Irish turf at Easter Road is always in perfect condition no matter the weather.' As the years caught up with Paddy, his son Tommy, who was also a top-class athlete, became a trainer/groundsman at Easter Road but 'faither was never far away and continued to do a hundred and one things around the Holy Ground.'

At the age of 90, Paddy Cannon died at his Ferry Road home on Friday 23 August 1946, after a short illness. His Requiem Mass was celebrated in St Mary Star of the Sea church, Constitutuion Street, Leith. This church, like St Patrick's, had very close associations with Hibernian. Again, there was an overflow congregation of Hibernians old and new and Leithers of all denominations. Also, Harry Swan again carried Hibernian's wreath of the traditional broken harp.

Paddy's wife Annie just seemed to lose the will to live and only three weeks later she too died.

Of Paddy Cannon, his parish priest had this to say in a short tribute:

> He was a giant of the running track and a giant of Hibernian Football Club. Paddy was also an outstanding catholic and even in the illness of his 90th year he was seen at Holy Mass every Sunday, an example for all to emulate.

Another tribute tells us:

> As the years passed old Paddy was asked by Harry Swan to take it easy but the word retirement was not in Paddy's vocabulary and he would be found every day at his beloved Easter Road. On match days even within a couple of weeks of death he would be seen walking out on to the Holy Ground with his step ladder to put up the nets then inspect the pitch to see it was in proper order and the lines clearly marked. He also took responsibility for the players' kit and laid it out. Gordon Smith was his favourite, and he stoked the boilers for the players' bath water. This was taken as quite normal by everyone at Easter Road even although he was in his ninetieth year.

So the last two of the 'ould Irish' had gone to their 'well earned reward', joining all the others who had been instrumental in *The Making of Hibernian* but Owen and Paddy, who epitomised all the bravery and goodness of Hibernian, were always the first to tell you 'it's the Hibs supporters that make the club the proudest in Scotland.' They would also tell you with straight faces that Irish-born 66-year-old Dr St John Cogan did not qualify as one of the honoured 'ould Irish' as he had given Hibernian only about a quarter of a century of service.

So the 70 years that went into *The Making of Hibernian* were now over and part of a tribute to Owen Brannigan tells us:

At present a new era of prosperity appears to be opening for Hibernian Football Club. Owen Brannigan's death removes a personality who would have been invaluable to a historian of the Hibernian club.

I wish it had been Owen Brannigan who had written these three books on *The Making of Hibernian*, rather than a poor amateur like myself, for he knew more intimately than anyone else all the struggles and romance of these 70 years. We Hibs supporters today still live through struggle and romance but that's all part of the never-ending love affair that makes us proud to be known as 'Hibs Daft'.

– EPILOGUE –

'Aye ony o' us ever wantit wiz a hoose in Jeffrey Street.'
Old lady reminiscing on her life in the Cowgate.
An' history for me
Bides in nae dark entry, but maun forever
Dree it's kenless weird in the bonnier slums
Of Burdieshouse, Gilmerton or even
A heich top-flat in the Dumbiedykes.
For hardly a soul of us ever won to Jeffrey Street.

I hope that this and my other two books on *The Making of Hibernian* are not viewed as dead history, for they do have a potency of life in them. But our Hibernian birthright is far too precious to be buried in books; it should be held up every day by every one of us, and cherished so that our brave Hibernian shall safeguard its unconquered soul and never become just another nonentity. I know we shall never lose our soul because Hibernian Football Club is a living social history of the City of Edinburgh and the Port of Leith.

The Making of Hibernian is all about heroes; and heroes will never be forgotten for they have left their footprints on the sands of time, and we Hibs supporters of unerring faithfulness still supply blood to their ghosts that give us an oasis of comfort for the present and signposts for the future. *The Making of Hibernian* and its echoes from the past are a splendid model for that brave future.

All the goodly company of Hibernian ghosts;
Jesus have mercy.
All who breathed the scents of Edinburgh
And the salt of Leith.

And what happened to the 'ould Irish', the 'Paddy Macs' and the 'Scots-Irish socialists' who supported Hibernian? Many had lived right through the romance, struggle, much hostility and two world wars that went into *The Making of Hibernian*. After they had again made tremendous sacrifices in the Second World War much of the hostility against them and Hibernian came to an end; but this Hibs under-class support was now faced with a huge social upheaval.

In central Leith the city planners swept away the slum ghetto of the Irish Barracks and many other slum areas in the port and consigned these Leithers to the 'bonnier slums' – the 'concrete filing cabinets in the sky'. Others even had to suffer the indignity of being 'exiled' to some new 'heich top-flat' in Edinburgh. St Mary Star of the Sea church, so central to Hibernian's history, still remained a vibrant parish, where the ghosts of Fr O'Carroll OMI, John and Philip Farmer, Dan McMichael, Barney Lester, Paddy Cannon and all the other 'goodly company' of Hibs 'ould Irish Leithers' still haunt the church. The Stella Maris Catholic Young Men's Society attached to the church is still as active as ever for Hibernian.

Up in Edinburgh's Old Town, the devastation of the slum ghetto of Little Ireland was almost complete after the Second World War. This 'Irish slum community unique in the whole of Scotland' was all but destroyed as the city planners scattered them to the four corners of Edinburgh, to the 'new impersonal housing estates'.

A first-hand example were my own parents. When my father returned to Little Ireland from the jungles of Burma after fighting the Japanese, where he and others of the 'Forgotten Army' were awarded the Burma Star, he and mum never 'won to Jeffrey Street'. They, with my elder brother, ended up in a Pennywell prefab, surrounded, at that time, with nothing but fields as far as the eye could see. There were no amenities, not even a church. It is true that any change is a psychological loss, but there was a plus for these 'townies fae the Soothside'. The prefab had an inside toilet, a bath, two bedrooms – and there was even a fridge in the kitchen: luxury, sheer luxury. But how they missed the 'Soothside', and returned every weekend.

Into the 'dreary, soulless housing schemes with no amenities' the community of Little Ireland were forced to go, carrying with them their nostalgia, and, as we Hibs supporters know, nostalgia is a wine that improves with age, which makes us such nostalgia-holics. The nostalgia for the Irish ghetto was a true romance, for it had seen some of Edinburgh's, and indeed of Scotland's, most celebrated and diverse characters. Burke and Hare, William McGonagall, Robert Louis Stevenson, Sir Arthur Conan Doyle, James Connolly and Margaret Sinclair. There were also, of course, Canon Hannan and Michael Whelahan, who co-founded Hibernian Football Club. Michael Whelahan's words in declaring the birth of Hibernian were still in the stones of St Mary's Street Halls, and Canon Hannan's sermons were still in the stones of St Patrick's church in the Cowgate, which is still the spiritual home of Hibernian.

Many of the Little Ireland slums were swept away or left derelict; schools

EPILOGUE

were no longer thronged with children, shops and pubs disappeared, and today Infirmary Street Baths remain closed. Even the favourite 'watering hole' of the 'ould Hibs supporters', the Hibernian Bar in the Cowgate, eventually disappeared. It was there they would relax, remembering in the silent regions of their souls their family and friends, their lives and their loves, and the 'guid ould days' of *The Making of Hibernian*.

> They sit without speaking, looking straight ahead.
> They've said it all before, they've seen it all before.
> They're content.
> They sit without moving; ozymandias and sphinx.
> He says something, and she answers smiling.
> And taps him flirtatiously on the arm,
> Daphnes and Chloe, with Edinburgh accents.

At the time of Owen Brannigan's and Paddy Cannon's deaths an 'ould Irish' Hibs supporter who was known as 'The Mystic', because he was reputedly the seventh son of a seventh son, would hang about the Hibernian Bar imparting his 'inner sight' to anyone who would buy him a nip of whisky. For us Hibs supporters today we are left with one of his 'strange classic gems' to reflect upon:

> Hibernian Fitba' Club is an enigma wrapped in a riddle, an' it goat mair complex when the ould yins died. Their passing wiz an awfi tragedy bit death's real sting wiz that it makes prisoners o' the living.

Date	Fixture	Teams and Score		Venue	Notes

Season 1914–15

Date	Fixture	Teams and Score		Venue	Notes
15/8/1914	Scottish League	Clyde Hibernian	1 0	Shawfield	Tuesday 4 August war declared
19/8/1914	Dunedin Cup Semi Final	Hibernian Raith Rovers	3 0	Easter Road	
22/8/1914	Scottish League	Hibernian Falkirk	1 1	Easter Road	
26/8/1914	Dunedin Cup Final	Hearts Hibernian	6 0	Tynecastle	
29/8/1914	Scottish League	Motherwell Hibernian	3 0	Fir Park	
5/9/1914	Scottish League	Hibernian Airdrie	1 0	Easter Road	
9/9/1914	Benefit in Aid of Broxburn Shamrock	Broxburn Shamrock Hibernian	1 1	Shamrock Park Broxburn	
12/9/1914	Scottish League	Raith Rovers Hibernian	1 1	Starks Park	
19/9/1914	Scottish League	Hibernian Celtic	1 1	Easter Road	
21/9/1914	Scottish League	Hibernian Clyde	3 1	Easter Road	
26/9/1914	Scottish League	Morton Hibernian	0 0	Cappielow	
28/9/1914	Scottish League	Rangers Hibernian	4 2	Ibrox	
3/10/1914	Scottish League	Hibernian Ayr United	0 4	Easter Road	
10/10/1914	Scottish League	St Mirren Hibernian	4 2	Love Street	
17/10/1914	Scottish League	Hibernian Hamilton Accies	0 2	Easter Road	
24/10/1914	Scottish League	Kilmarnock Hibernian	5 1	Rugby Park	
31/10/1914	Scottish League	Hibernian Aberdeen	1 2	Easter Road	
7/11/1914	Scottish League	Hibernian Dumbarton	2 2	Easter Road	
14/11/1914	Scottish League	Queen's Park Hibernian	0 2	Hampden	
21/11/1914	Scottish League	Hibernian Dundee	2 0	Easter Road	

HIBERNIAN RESULTS 1914–1946

Date	Fixture	Teams and Score		Venue	Notes
28/11/1914	Scottish League	Hibernian Partick Thistle	4 1	Easter Road	
5/12/1914	Scottish League	Hearts Hibernian	3 1	Tynecastle	
12/12/1914	Scottish League	Third Lanark Hibernian	2 2	Cathkin	
19/12/1914	Scottish League	Hibernian St Mirren	3 2	Easter Road	
26/12/1914	Scottish League	Dundee Hibernian	2 4	Dens Park	
1/1/1915	Wilson Cup Final	Hibernian Hearts	1 2	Easter Road	
2/1/1915	Scottish League	Hibernian Kilmarnock	3 1	Easter Road	
4/1/1915	Scottish League	Ayr United Hibernian	2 1	Somerset Park	
9/1/1915	Scottish League	Airdrie Hibernian	1 3	Broomfield	
16/1/1915	Scottish League	Partick Thistle Hibernian	3 1	Firhill	
23/1/1915	Scottish League	Hibernian Motherwell	1 2	Easter Road	
30/1/1915	Scottish League	Hibernian Rangers	1 2	Easter Road	
6/2/1915	Scottish League	Hamilton Accies Hibernian 2	2	Douglas Park	
13/2/1915	Scottish League	Hibernian Raith Rovers	2 1	Easter Road	
20/2/1915	Scottish League	Aberdeen Hibernian	0 0	Pittodrie	
27/2/1915	Scottish League	Hibernian Hearts	2 2	Easter Road	
6/3/1915	Scottish League	Celtic Hibernian	5 1	Parkhead	
13/3/1915	Scottish League	Hibernian Morton	1 1	Easter Road	
20/3/1915	Scottish League	Dumbarton Hibernian	1 0	Boghead	
27/3/1915	Scottish League	Falkirk Hibernian	0 0	Brockville	
3/4/1915	Scottish League	Hibernian Third Lanark	4 2	Easter Road	
10/4/1915	Scottish League	Hibernian Queen's Park	4 0	Easter Road	

THE MAKING OF HIBERNIAN 3

Date	Fixture	Teams and Score		Venue	Notes
14/4/1915	Benefit in aid of Belgian Relief War Fund	Edinburgh Select International Select	0 2	Tynecastle	Four Hibernian players in the Edinburgh Select Team
19/4/1915	Friendly	Hibernian Bradford City	5 3	Easter Road	
21/4/1915	East of Scotland Shield Semi Final	St Bernard's Hibernian	0 2	Royal Gymnasium Park	
24/4/1915	East of Scotland Shield Final	Hearts Hibernian	1 0	Tynecastle	
1/5/1915	Rosebery Charity Cup Semi Final	Hibernian Leith Athletic	4 0	Easter Road	
8/5/1915	Rosebery Charity Cup Final	St Bernard's Hibernian	4 3	Tynecastle	Match played on neutral ground

Season 1915–16

Date	Fixture	Teams and Score		Venue
21/8/1915	Scottish League	Hibernian Queen's Park	3 0	Easter Road
28/8/1915	Scottish League	Ayr United Hibernian	2 3	Somerset Park
4/9/1915	Scottish League	Hibernian Clyde	0 1	Easter Road
11/9/1915	Scottish League	Falkirk Hibernian	1 1	Brockville
18/9/1915	Scottish League	Hibernian Morton	0 2	Easter Road
20/9/1915	Scottish League	Hibernian Hearts	1 2	Easter Road
25/9/1915	Scottish League	Raith Rovers Hibernian	1 1	Starks Park
2/10/1915	Scottish League	Hibernian Celtic	0 4	Easter Road
9/10/1915	Scottish League	Kilmarnock Hibernian	0 0	Rugby Park
16/10/1915	Scottish League	Hibernian Partick Thistle	0 4	Easter Road
23/10/1915	Scottish League	Aberdeen Hibernian	1 1	Pittodrie
30/10/1915	Scottish League	Hibernian Dumbarton	1 1	Easter Road
6/11/1915	Scottish League	Hibernian Motherwell	1 2	Easter Road

HIBERNIAN RESULTS 1914–1946

Date	Fixture	Teams and Score		Venue	Notes
13/11/1915	Scottish League	Third Lanark Hibernian	3 0	Cathkin	
20/11/1915	Scottish League	Hibernian St Mirren	2 1	Easter Road	
27/11/1915	Scottish League	Rangers Hibernian	4 2	Ibrox	
4/12/1915	Scottish League	Hamilton Accies Hibernian	3 2	Douglas Park	
11/12/1915	Scottish League	Hibernian Third Lanark	0 1	Easter Road	
18/12/1915	Scottish League	Airdrie Hibernian	1 0	Broomfield	
25/12/1915	Scottish League	Hibernian Dundee	0 2	Easter Road	
1/1/1916	Wilson Cup Final	Hearts Hibernian	0 2	Tynecastle	
3/1/1916	Scottish League	Queen's Park Hibernian	4 2	Hampden	
4/1/1916	Friendly	Clydebank Hibernian	2 1	Clydebank	
8/1/1916	Scottish League	Hibernian Raith Rovers	1 0	Easter Road	
15/1/1916	Scottish League	Celtic Hibernian	3 1	Parkhead	
22/1/1916	Scottish League	Hibernian Airdrie	3 0	Easter Road	
29/1/1916	Scottish League	Morton Hibernian	5 1	Cappielow	
5/2/1916	Scottish League	Hibernian Falkirk	2 1	Easter Road	
12/2/1916	Scottish League	Dundee Hibernian	2 1	Dens Park	
19/2/1916	Scottish League	Clyde Hibernian	2 1	Shawfield	
26/2/1916	Scottish League	Hibernian Kilmarnock	1 0	Easter Road	
4/3/1916	Scottish League	Motherwell Hibernian	1 1	Fir Park	
11/3/1916	Scottish League	Hibernian Rangers	2 3	Easter Road	
18/3/1916	Scottish League	Partick Thistle Hibernian	4 1	Firhill	
1/4/1916	Scottish League	St Mirren Hibernian	3 1	Love Street	

Date	Fixture	Teams and Score		Venue	Notes
8/4/1916	Scottish League	Dumbarton Hibernian	2 1	Boghead	
15/4/1916	Scottish League	Hibernian Aberdeen	0 0	Easter Road	
17/4/1916	Scottish League	Hearts Hibernian	1 3	Tynecastle	
22/4/1916	Scottish League	Hibernian Ayr United	3 1	Easter Road	
26/4/1916	Scottish League	Hibernian Hamilton Accies	1 3	Parkhead	Match was a home fixture for the Hibernian and should have been played at Easter Road but as most Hibernian players live and work in the west and could not travel to Edinburgh in time for kick-off the venue was changed to Parkhead
29/4/1916	Friendly	Hibernian Parkhead Jnrs	3 1	Easter Road	
6/5/1916	Rosebery Charity Cup Semi Final	Hibernian St Bernard's	6 0	Easter Road	
13/5/1916	Rosebery Charity Cup Final	Hearts Hibernian	4 0	Tynecastle	

Season 1916–1917

Date	Fixture	Teams and Score		Venue	Notes
19/8/1916	Scottish League	Hibernian Airdrie	1 1	Easter Road	
26/8/1916	Scottish League	Celtic Hibernian	3 1	Parkhead	
2/9/1916	Scottish League	Hibernian Hamilton Accies	4 3	Easter Road	
9/9/1916	Scottish League	Dumbarton Hibernian	2 1	Boghead	
16/9/1916	Scottish League	Hibernian Dundee	1 2	Easter Road	
18/9/1916	Scottish League	Hearts Hibernian	2 1	Tynecastle	
23/9/1916	Scottish League	Kilmarnock Hibernian	1 3	Rugby Park	
30/9/1916	Scottish League	Hibernian Third Lanark	1 1	Easter Road	

HIBERNIAN RESULTS 1914–1946

Date	Fixture	Teams and Score		Venue	Notes
7/10/1916	Scottish League	St Mirren Hibernian	1 1	Love Street	
14/10/1916	Scottish League	Hibernian Ayr United	1 4	Easter Road	
21/10/1916	Scottish League	Falkirk Hibernian	0 1	Brockville	
28/10/1916	Scottish League	Hibernian Clyde	1 1	Easter Road	
4/11/1916	Scottish League	Motherwell Hibernian	1 1	Fir Park	
11/11/1916	Scottish League	Hibernian Rangers	0 0	Easter Road	
18/11/1916	Scottish League	Hibernian Raith Rovers	3 3	Easter Road	
25/11/1916	Scottish League	Ayr United Hibernian	2 1	Somerset Park	
2/12/1916	Scottish League	Morton Hibernian	1 1	Cappielow	
9/12/1916	Scottish League	Hibernian Aberdeen	3 3	Easter Road	
16/12/1916	Scottish League	Rangers Hibernian	5 1	Ibrox	
23/12/1916	Scottish League	Queen's Park Hibernian	4 1	Hampden	
30/12/1916	Scottish League	Hibernian Morton	2 4	Easter Road	
1/1/1917	Wilson Cup Final	Hibernian Hearts	3 0	Easter Road	
2/1/1917	Scottish League	Dundee Hibernian	3 1	Dens Park	
6/1/1917	Scottish League	Hibernian St Mirren	2 1	Easter Road	
13/1/1917	Scottish League	Raith Rovers Hibernian	2 1	Starks Park	
20/1/1917	Scottish League	Hibernian Kilmarnock	2 1	Easter Road	
27/1/1917	Scottish League	Hibernian Dumbarton	3 1	Easter Road	
3/2/1917	Scottish League	Hibernian Falkirk	1 2	Easter Road	
10/2/1917	Scottish League	Clyde Hibernian	1 2	Shawfield	
17/2/1917	Scottish League	Hibernian Motherwell	2 3	Easter Road	

Date	Fixture	Teams and Score		Venue	Notes
24/2/1917	Scottish League	Hamilton Accies Hibernian	4 1	Douglas Park	
3/3/1917	Scottish League	Third Lanark Hibernian	1 1	Cathkin	
10/3/1917	Scottish League	Partick Thistle Hibernian	0 3	Firhill	
17/3/1917	Scottish League	Hibernian Queen's Park	5 1	Easter Road	
24/3/1917	Scottish League	Hibernian Partick Thistle	1 0	Easter Road	
31/3/1917	Scottish League	Airdrie Hibernian	3 1	Broomfield	
14/4/1917	Scottish League	Hibernian Celtic	0 1	Easter Road	
16/4/1917	Scottish League	Hibernian Hearts	0 2	Easter Road	
21/4/1917	Scottish League	Aberdeen Hibernian	2 1	Pittodrie	
28/4/1917	Friendly	Hibernian St Bernard's	2 0	Easter Road	
5/5/1917	Rosebery Charity Cup Semi Final	Hearts Hibernian	3 0	Tynecastle	

Season 1917–18

Date	Fixture	Teams and Score		Venue	Notes
18/8/1917	Scottish League	Hamilton Accies Hibernian	1 0	Douglas Park	
25/8/1917	Scottish League	Hibernian Kilmarnock	0 3	Easter Road	
1/9/1917	Scottish League	Hearts Hibernian	1 0	Tynecastle	
8/9/1917	Scottish League	Hibernian Clydebank	0 1	Easter Road	
15/9/1917	Scottish League	Rangers Hibernian	3 0	Ibrox	
17/9/1917	East of Scotland Shield Final (1916–1917)	Hibernian Hearts	4 0	Easter Road	Final carried forward from season 1916–1917
22/9/1917	Scottish League	Hibernian Airdrie	3 1	Easter Road	
29/9/1917	Scottish League	Partick Thistle Hibernian	2 2	Firhill	
6/10/1917	Scottish League	Hibernian Dumbarton	0 3	Easter Road	

HIBERNIAN RESULTS 1914–1946

Date	Fixture	Teams and Score		Venue	Notes
13/10/1917	Scottish League	Hibernian Queen's Park	4 2	Easter Road	
20/10/1917	Scottish League	Clyde Hibernian	2 5	Shawfield	
27/10/1917	Scottish League	Ayr United Hibernian	2 2	Somerset Park	
3/11/1917	Scottish League	Hibernian Motherwell	2 2	Easter Road	
10/11/1917	Scottish League	Third Lanark Hibernian	1 0	Cathkin	
17/11/1917	Scottish League	Hibernian Morton	2 2	Easter Road	
24/11/1917	Scottish League	Celtic Hibernian	2 0	Parkhead	
1/12/1917	Scottish League	Hibernian St Mirren	3 1	Easter Road	
8/12/1917	Scottish League	Dumbarton Hibernian	1 0	Boghead	
15/12/1917	Scottish League	Hibernian Hamilton Accies	1 1	Easter Road	
22/12/1917	Scottish League	Falkirk Hibernian	2 2	Brockville	
29/12/1917	Scottish League	Hibernian Partick Thistle	2 1	Easter Road	
1/1/1918	Wilson Cup Final	Hearts Hibernian	1 3	Tynecastle	
5/1/1918	Scottish League	Kilmarnock Hibernian	3 1	Rugby Park	
12/1/1918	Scottish League	Hibernian Clyde	2 0	Easter Road	
26/1/1918	Scottish League	Morton Hibernian	1 1	Cappielow	
2/2/1918	Scottish League	Hibernian Hearts	1 3	Easter Road	
9/2/1918	Scottish League	Hibernian Rangers	0 1	Easter Road	
16/2/1918	Scottish League	Airdrie Hibernian	3 0	Broomfield	
23/2/1918	Scottish League	Queen's Park Hibernian	2 0	Hampden	
2/3/1918	Dunedin Cup Semi Final	Hibernian Raith Rovers	1 0	Easter Road	
9/3/1918	Scottish League	Hibernian Third Lanark	4 1	Easter Road	

THE MAKING OF HIBERNIAN 3

Date	Fixture	Teams and Score		Venue	Notes
16/3/1918	Scottish League	Clydebank Hibernian	2 0	Clydeholm Park	
23/3/1918	Scottish League	Hibernian Falkirk	2 1	Easter Road	
30/3/1918	Scottish League	Motherwell Hibernian	2 1	Fir Park	
6/4/1918	Scottish League	Hibernian Celtic	0 2	Easter Road	
13/4/1918	Scottish League	St Mirren Hibernian	1 1	Love Street	
15/4/1918	East of Scotland Shield Final (1917–18)	Hearts Hibernian	1 1	Tynecastle	
20/4/1918	Scottish League	Hibernian Ayr United	1 1	Easter Road	
27/4/1918	Dunedin Cup Final	Falkirk Hibernian	5 3	Tynecastle	Match played on neutral ground
11/5/1918	Army and Navy Scottish League Benevolent Fund benefit match	East of Scotland Select West of Scotland Select	1 2	Tynecastle	Four Hibernian players in the East team
18/5/1918	Rosebery Charity Cup Final	Hearts Hibernian	0 2	Tynecastle	

Season 1918–1919

Date	Fixture	Teams and Score		Venue	Notes
17/8/1918	Scottish League	Hibernian Celtic	0 3	Easter Road	
24/8/1918	Scottish League	Hamilton Accies Hibernian	1 1	Douglas Park	
31/8/1918	Scottish League	Hibernian Third Lanark	1 5	Easter Road	
7/9/1918	Scottish League	Kilmarnock Hibernian	7 1	Rugby Park	
14/9/1918	Scottish League	Motherwell Hibernian	0 0	Fir Park	
16/9/1918	East of Scotland Shield Final	Hearts Hibernian	2 1	Tynecastle	1st Leg
21/9/1918	Scottish League	Hibernian Clydebank	1 2	Easter Road	
28/9/1918	Scottish League	Queen's Park Hibernian	3 0	Hampden	
5/10/1918	Scottish League	Hibernian Morton	0 3	Easter Road	
12/10/1918	Scottish League	Clyde Hibernian	2 1	Shawfield	

HIBERNIAN RESULTS 1914–1946

Date	Fixture	Teams and Score		Venue	Notes
19/10/1918	Scottish League	Hibernian Hearts	1 3	Easter Road	
26/10/1918	Scottish League	Hibernian Airdrie	2 1	Easter Road	
2/11/1918	Scottish League	Ayr United Hibernian	5 0	Somerset Park	
9/11/1918	Scottish League	Hibernian St Mirren	1 2	Easter Road	
23/11/1918	Scottish League	Dumbarton Hibernian	4 0	Boghead	
30/11/1918	Scottish League	Hibernian Clyde	3 1	Easter Road	
7/12/1918	Scottish League	Rangers Hibernian	5 1	Ibrox	
14/12/1918	Scottish League	Hibernian Falkirk	2 1	Easter Road	
21/12/1918	Scottish League	Hibernian Motherwell	0 3	Easter Road	
28/12/1918	Scottish League	Celtic Hibernian	2 0	Parkhead	
1/1/1919	Wilson Cup Final	Hibernian Hearts	2 2	Easter Road	
4/1/1919	Scottish League	Hibernian Kilmarnock	1 4	Easter Road	
11/1/1919	Scottish League	Hearts Hibernian	3 1	Tynecastle	
18/1/1919	Scottish League	Hibernian Partick Thistle	0 2	Easter Road	
25/1/1919	Scottish League	Hibernian Rangers	1 2	Easter Road	
1/2/1919	Scottish League	Falkirk Hibernian	1 1	Brockville	
8/2/1919	Scottish League	Hibernian Dumbarton	1 0	Easter Road	
15/2/1919	Scottish League	Morton Hibernian	9 2	Cappielow	
22/2/1919	Scottish League	Hibernian Hamilton Accies	1 2	Easter Road	
1/3/1919	Friendly	Hibernian Dundee Hibs	6 2	Easter Road	
8/3/1919	Scottish League	Hibernian Ayr United	0 1	Easter Road	
15/3/1919	Victory Cup 2nd Round	Hibernian Ayr United	1 0	Easter Road	Hibernian had a bye in the 1st round

Date	Fixture	Teams and Score		Venue	Notes
22/3/1919	Scottish League	Third Lanark	4	Cathkin	
		Hibernian	2		
29/3/1919	Victory Cup 3rd Round	Hibernian	2	Easter Road	
		Motherwell	0		
5/4/1919	Scottish League	Clydebank	2	Clydeholm Park	
		Hibernian	1		
12/4/1919	Victory Cup Semi Final	Hibernian	1	Easter Road	Half hour extra time played
		St Mirren	3		
14/4/1919	Friendly	Dundee Hibs	0	Tannadice	
		Hibernian	3		
19/4/1919	Friendly	Cowdenbeath	0	Cowdenbeath	
		Hibernian	0		
21/4/1919	Scottish League	Partick Thistle	2	Firhill	
		Hibernian	0		
26/4/1919	Scottish League	Hibernian	1	Easter Road	
		Queen's Park	0		
28/4/1919	Friendly	Hibernian	3	Easter Road	
		Hull City	3		
3/5/1919	Scottish League	St Mirren	3	Love Street	
		Hibernian	1		
7/5/1919	Wilson Cup Final replay and East of Scotland Shield Final 2nd Leg	Hearts	1	Tynecastle	
		Hibernian	0		
10/5/1919	Scottish League	Airdrie	3	Broomfield	
		Hibernian	3		
12/5/1919	Benefit in aid of Musselburgh Brunstonians FC	Musselburgh Select		Olive Park Musselburgh	
		Hibernian	1 0		
17/5/1919	Rosebery Charity Cup Final	Hearts	2	Tynecastle	
		Hibernian	1		

Season 1919–1920

Date	Fixture	Teams and Score		Venue	Notes
2/8/1919	Practice Match	Hibernian 'A'	1	Easter Road	
		Hibernian 'B'	1		
16/8/1919	Scottish League	Third Lanark	2	Cathkin	
		Hibernian	0		
20/8/1919	Scottish League	Hibernian	3	Easter Road	
		Hamilton Accies	0		
23/8/1919	Scottish League	Hibernian	2	Easter Road	
		St Mirren	1		
30/8/1919	Scottish League	Motherwell	3	Fir Park	
		Hibernian	2		

HIBERNIAN RESULTS 1914–1946

Date	Fixture	Teams and Score		Venue	Notes
6/9/1919	Scottish League	Hibernian Aberdeen	2 1	Easter Road	
13/9/1919	Scottish League	Airdrie Hibernian	2 0	Broomfield	
15/9/1919	Scottish League	Hibernian Hearts	2 4	Easter Road	
20/9/1919	Scottish League	Hibernian Falkirk	2 2	Easter Road	
22/9/1919	Scottish League	St Mirren Hibernian	2 1	Love Street	
27/9/1919	Friendly	Cowdenbeath Hibernian		Central Park Score unknown	
29/9/1919	Scottish League	Albion Rovers Hibernian	1 2	Cliftonhill	
4/10/1919	Scottish League	Hibernian Dumbarton	3 3	Easter Road	
11/10/1919	Scottish League	Celtic Hibernian	7 3	Parkhead	
18/19/1919	Scottish League	Hibernian Partick Thistle	6 2	Easter Road	
25/10/1919	Scottish League	Ayr United Hibernian	1 0	Somerset Park	
1/11/1919	Scottish League	Queen's Park Hibernian	2 2	Hampden	
8/11/1919	Scottish League	Hibernian Raith Rovers	2 0	Easter Road	
22/11/1919	Scottish League	Hibernian Clyde	1 0	Easter Road	
29/11/1919	Scottish League	Hibernian Morton	1 0	Easter Road	
6/12/1919	Scottish League	Rangers Hibernian	7 0	Ibrox	
13/12/1919	Scottish League	Hibernian Kilmarnock	4 1	Easter Road	
20/12/1919	Scottish League	Aberdeen Hibernian	1 1	Pittodrie	
27/12/1919	Scottish League	Dundee Hibernian	3 1	Dens Park	
1/1/1920	Scottish League	Hearts Hibernian	1 3	Tynecastle	
3/1/1920	Scottish League	Hibernian Clydebank	2 0	Easter Road	
6/1/1920	Benefit in aid of Peter Kerr of Hibernian	Hibernian J. McDonald XI	3 2	Easter Road	

THE MAKING OF HIBERNIAN 3

Date	Fixture	Teams and Score		Venue	Notes
10/1/1920	Scottish League	Falkirk Hibernian	3 0	Brockville	
17/1/1920	Scottish League	Hibernian Ayr United	1 2	Easter Road	
24/1/1920	Scottish Cup 1st Round	Galston Hibernian	0 0	Riverside Park	
31/1/1920	Scottish Cup 2nd Round Replay	Hibernian Galston	2 1	Easter Road	
7/2/1920	Scottish Cup 2nd Round	Armadale Hibernian	1 0	Volunteer Park	
14/2/1920	Scottish League	Dumbarton Hibernian	2 0	Boghead	
17/2/1920	Scottish League	Clyde Hibernian	2 0	Shawfield	Match brought forward from 21 Feb to avoid clash with Scottish Cup tie being played in Glasgow
21/2/1920	Scottish League	Hamilton Accies Hibernian	3 2	Douglas Park	
28/2/1920	Scottish League	Kilmarnock Hibernian	4 1	Rugby Park	
6/3/1920	Scottish League	Hibernian Motherwell	0 1	Easter Road	
13/3/1920	Scottish League	Hibernian Albion Rovers	0 1	Easter Road	
20/3/1920	Scottish League	Clydebank Hibernian	3 3	Clydeholm	
27/3/1920	Scottish League	Hibernian Airdrie	1 4	Easter Road	
31/3/1920	Benefit in aid of Bobby Templeton of Hibernian	Hibernian and East of Scotland Select Celtic	2 5	Easter Road	
3/4/1920	Scottish League	Hibernian Third Lanark	1 2	Easter Road	
5/4/1920	Friendly	Hull City Hibernian	2 0	Hull England	
10/4/1920	Scottish League	Morton Hibernian	1 1	Cappielow	
12/4/1920	East of Scotland Shield Semi Final	Hibernian St Bernard's	1 0	Easter Road	
14/4/1920	Scottish League	Partick Thistle Hibernian	1 0	Firhill	
17/4/1920	Scottish League	Raith Rovers Hibernian	1 0	Starks Park	

HIBERNIAN RESULTS 1914-1946

Date	Fixture	Teams and Score		Venue	Notes
19/4/1920	Scottish League	Hibernian Celtic	1 2	Easter Road	
21/4/1920	Scottish League	Hibernian Rangers	1 1	Easter Road	
24/4/1920	Scottish League	Hibernian Queen's Park	3 2	Easter Road	
26/4/1920	Benefit in aid of Bobby Grossert of Hibernian	Hibernian and East of Scotland Select Scottish League International XI	1 3	Easter Road	
1/5/1920	Scottish League	Hibernian Dundee	0 0	Easter Road	
3/5/1920	East of Scotland Shield Final	Hearts Hibernian	1 1	Tynecastle	
5/5/1920	Wilson Cup Final and East of Scotland Shield Final Replay	Hearts Hibernian	3 1	Tynecastle	
8/5/1920	Rosebery Charity Cup Semi Final	Hibernian Armadale	3 2	Easter Road	Half-hour extra time played
15/5/1920	Rosebery Charity Cup Final	Hearts Hibernian	2 0	Tynecastle	

Season 1920-21

Date	Fixture	Teams and Score		Venue	Notes
16/8/1920	Scottish League	Motherwell Hibernian	4 2	Fir Park	
19/8/1920	Friendly	Berwick Rangers Hibernian		Berwick	Score unknown
21/8/1920	Scottish League	Hibernian St Mirren	1 0	Easter Road	
25/8/1920	Scottish League	Hibernian Falkirk	0 0	Easter Road	
28/8/1920	Scottish League	Hearts Hibernian	5 1	Tynecastle	
1/9/1920	Scottish League	Hibernian Airdrie	0 2	Easter Road	
4/9/1920	Scottish League	Hibernian Kilmarnock	0 0	Easter Road	
8/9/1920	Benefit in aid of James Watson of Bo'ness Utd	Bo'ness United Hibernian	1 2	Newton Park	
11/9/1920	Scottish League	Falkirk Hibernian	0 3	Brockville	

THE MAKING OF HIBERNIAN 3

Date	Fixture	Teams and Score		Venue	Notes
18/9/1920	Scottish League	Hibernian Dumbarton	2 0	Easter Road	
20/9/1920	Scottish League	Hibernian Celtic	0 3	Easter Road	
25/9/1920	Scottish League	Airdrie Hibernian	5 1	Broomfield	
27/9/1920	Scottish League	Rangers Hibernian	1 0	Ibrox	
2/10/1920	Scottish League	Hibernian Third Lanark	2 1	Easter Road	
9/10/1920	Scottish League	Aberdeen Hibernian	0 1	Pittodrie	
16/10/1920	Scottish League	Hibernian Motherwell	2 3	Easter Road	
23/10/1920	Scottish League	Partick Thistle Hibernian	3 2	Firhill	
30/10/1920	Scottish League	Raith Rovers Hibernian	2 0	Starks Park	
6/11/1920	Scottish League	Hibernian Albion Rovers	5 2	Easter Road	
13/11/1920	Scottish League	Ayr United Hibernian	2 1	Somerset Park	
20/11/1920	Scottish League	Hibernian Dundee	2 0	Easter Road	
27/11/1920	Scottish League	Morton Hibernian	1 1	Cappielow	
4/12/1920	Scottish League	Hibernian Clydebank	1 1	Easter Road	
11/12/1920	Scottish League	Hibernian Queen's Park	0 2	Easter Road	
18/12/1920	Scottish League	Hamilton Accies Hibernian	1 1	Douglas Park	
25/12/1920	Scottish League	Clydebank Hibernian	2 2	Clydeholm	
1/1/1921	Scottish League	Hibernian Hearts	3 0	Easter Road	
3/1/1921	Scottish League	Dundee Hibernian	1 1	Dens Park	
4/1/1921	Benefit in aid of Willie Wilson of Hearts	Hearts Hibernian and East of Scotland Select	2 0	Tynecastle	
8/1/1921	Scottish League	Clyde Hibernian	2 0	Shawfield	

HIBERNIAN RESULTS 1914–1946

Date	Fixture	Teams and Score		Venue	Notes
15/1/1921	Scottish League	Hibernian Ayr United	3 2	Easter Road	
22/1/1921	Scottish Cup 1st Round	Third Lanark Hibernian	1 1	Cathkin	
26/1/1921	Scottish Cup 1st Round Replay	Hibernian Third Lanark	1 1	Easter Road	
29/1/1921	Scottish League	Queen's Park Hibernian	0 2	Hampden	
1/2/1921	Scottish Cup 1st Round 2nd replay	Third Lanark Hibernian	0 1	Ibrox	Match played on neutral ground
5/2/1921	Scottish Cup 2nd Round	Hibernian Partick Thistle	0 0	Easter Road	
8/2/1921	Scottish Cup 2nd	Partick Thistle Hibernian	0 0	Firhill	
12/2/1921	Scottish League	Albion Rovers Hibernian	0 2	Cliftonhill	
15/2/1921	Scottish Cup 2nd Round 2nd replay	Partick Thistle Hibernian	1 0	Parkhead	Match played on neutral ground
19/2/1921	Scottish League	Third Lanark Hibernian	0 2	Cathkin	
23/2/1921	Scottish League	Hibernian Hamilton Accies	0 1	Easter Road	
26/2/1921	Scottish League	St Mirren Hibernian	0 2	Love Street	
5/3/1921	Scottish League	Hibernian Aberdeen	2 3	Easter Road	
12/3/1921	Scottish League	Dumbarton Hibernian	1 0	Boghead	
19/3/1921	Scottish League	Hibernian Clyde	0 1	Easter Road	
26/3/1921	Scottish League	Hibernian Morton	4 0	Easter Road	
2/4/1921	Scottish League	Kilmarnock Hibernian	0 3	Rugby Park	
9/4/1921	Scottish League	Hibernian Rangers	1 1	Easter Road	
11/4/1921	Benefit in aid of St Cuthberts RC Church and School	Hibernian Hearts	3 1	Easter Road	
13/4/1921	Dunedin Cup Semi Final	Hibernian Falkirk	1 0	Easter Road	

THE MAKING OF HIBERNIAN 3

Date	Fixture	Teams and Score		Venue	Notes
16/4/1921	Scottish League	Hibernian Raith Rovers	1 1	Easter Road	
18/4/1921	Benefit in aid of Matthew Paterson of Hibernian	Hibernian Celtic	0 1	Easter Road	
20/4/1921	Dunedin Cup Final	Hearts Hibernian	2 0	Tynecastle	
23/4/1921	Scottish League	Celtic Hibernian	3 0	Parkhead	
27/4/1921	Scottish League	Hibernian Partick Thistle	2 0	Easter Road	
30/4/1921	East of Scotland Shield Semi Final	Hibernian St Bernard's	4 2	Easter Road	
3/5/1921	Wilson Cup Final	Hibernian Hearts	1 0	Easter Road	
6/5/1921	East of Scotland Shield Final	Hearts Hibernian	0 1	Tynecastle	
7/5/1921	Rosebery Charity Cup Semi Final	Hibernian St Bernard's	1 3	Easter Road	
16/5/1921	Tour of Denmark Friendly	Copenhagen Select Hibernian	2 3	Copenhagen Denmark	
19/5/1921	Tour of Denmark Friendly	Copenhagen Select Hibernian	1 0	Copenhagen Denmark	
16/5/1921	Tour of Denmark Friendly	Aarhus Select Hibernian	1 1	Aarhus Denmark	

Season 1921–22

Date	Fixture	Teams and Score		Venue	Notes
17/8/1921	Benefit in aid of Portobello Thistle FC funds	Portobello Thistle Hibernian	1 1	Wood Park	
20/8/1921	Scottish League	Celtic Hibernian	3 1	Parkhead	
22/8/1921	Benefit in aid of Edinburgh Emmet FC for the signing of Willie Harper by Hibernian	Edinburgh Emmet Hibernian	0 2	Bathgate Park Canongate Edinburgh	
27/8/1921	Scottish League	Hibernian St Mirren	1 1	Easter Road	
31/8/1921	Scottish League	Falkirk Hibernian	3 1	Brockville	
3/9/1921	Scottish League	Airdrie Hibernian	2 1	Broomfield	

HIBERNIAN RESULTS 1914–1946

Date	Fixture	Teams and Score		Venue	Notes
7/9/1921	Scottish League	Hibernian Queen's Park	3 0	Easter Road	
10/9/1921	Scottish League	Hibernian Hearts	2 1	Easter Road	
12/9/1921	Benefit in aid of Belfast Catholic Workmen's Relief Fund	Hibernian Midlothian Junior Select		Easter Road Score unknown	
13/9/1921	Scottish League	St Mirren Hibernian	1 1	Love Street	
17/9/1921	Scottish League	Motherwell Hibernian	4 1	Fir Park	
19/9/1921	Scottish League	Hibernian Celtic	2 1	Easter Road	
21/9/1921	Benefit in aid of Hearts war memorial fund	Hearts/Hibernian Select Glasgow Select	1 2	Tynecastle	
24/9/1921	Scottish League	Hibernian Falkirk	1 1	Easter Road	
1/10/1921	Scottish League	Aberdeen Hibernian	1 2	Pittodrie	
8/10/1921	Scottish League	Hibernian Morton	2 1	Easter Road	
15/10/1921	Scottish League	Clydebank Hibernian	0 2	Clydeholm	
22/10/1921	Scottish League	Hibernian Partick Thistle	2 0	Easter Road	
29/10/1921	Scottish League	Kilmarnock Hibernian	1 1	Rugby Park	
5/11/1921	Scottish League	Hibernian Clyde	2 1	Easter Road	
12/11/1921	Scottish League	Hibernian Dundee	1 1	Easter Road	
19/11/1921	Scottish League	Hamilton Accies Hibernian	1 2	Douglas Park	
26/11/1921	Scottish League	Hibernian Dumbarton	0 0	Easter Road	
3/12/1921	Scottish League	Third Lanark Hibernian	2 1	Cathkin	
10/12/1921	Scottish League	Hibernian Albion Rovers	0 1	Easter Road	
14/12/1921	Benefit Tournament in aid of the Lord Provost's Unemployed Rent Relief Fund semi final	Hibernian Leith Athletic	7 0	Easter Road	

Date	Fixture	Teams and Score		Venue	Notes
17/12/1921	Scottish League	Queen's Park Hibernian	1 3	Hampden	
24/12/1921	Scottish League	Hibernian Rangers	1 1	Easter Road	
31/12/1921	Scottish League	Hibernian Ayr United	1 1	Easter Road	
2/1/1922	Scottish League	Hearts Hibernian	0 2	Tynecastle	
3/2/1922	Scottish League	Dundee Hibernian	0 0	Dens Park	
7/1/1922	Scottish League	Hibernian Motherwell	2 0	Easter Road	
14/1/1922	Scottish League	Clyde Hibernian	2 0	Shawfield	
21/1/1922	Scottish League	Raith Rovers Hibernian	0 0	Starks Park	
28/1/1922	Scottish Cup 1st Round	Hibernian Armadale	3 0	Easter Road	
4/2/1922	Scottish League	Hibernian Kilmarnock	3 0	Easter Road	
11/2/1922	Scottish Cup 2nd Round	Motherwell Hibernian	3 2	Fir Park	
18/2/1922	Scottish League	Hibernian Raith Rovers	2 1	Easter Road	
22/2/1922	Scottish League	Albion Rovers Hibernian	2 1	Cliftonhill	
1/3/1922	Scottish League	Hibernian Third Lanark	0 1	Easter Road	
4/3/1922	Scottish League	Dumbarton Hibernian	1 1	Boghead	
11/3/1922	Friendly	Raith Rovers Hibernian	2 1	Starks Park	
15/3/1922	Scottish League	Partick Thistle Hibernian	2 0	Firhill	
18/3/1922	Scottish League	Hibernian Hamilton Accies	1 1	Easter Road	
25/3/1922	Friendly	Falkirk Hibernian	1 4	Brockville	
28/3/1922	Scottish League	Rangers Hibernian	2 0	Ibrox	
5/4/1922	Scottish League	Morton Hibernian	2 2	Cappielow	
8/4/1922	Scottish League	Ayr United Hibernian	2 2	Somerset Park	

HIBERNIAN RESULTS 1914–1946

Date	Fixture	Teams and Score		Venue	Notes
10/4/1922	Dunedin Cup Semi Final	Hibernian Raith Rovers	0 0	Easter Road	Hibernian won the tie by 14 corners to 2 corners
12/4/1922	Dunedin Cup Final	Falkirk Hibernian	0 1	Tynecastle	Match played at neutral ground
15/4/1922	Scottish League	Hibernian Airdrie	0 0	Easter Road	
18/4/1922	Friendly	Gala Fairydean Hibernian	2 1	Eastlands Park	Hibernian team made up mostly of reserve players
19/4/1922	East of Scotland Shield Semi Final	Hibernian Hearts	2 0	Easter Road	
22/4/1922	Scottish League	Hibernian Aberdeen	0 1	Easter Road	
24/4/1922	East of Scotland Shield Final	Hibernian St Bernard's	3 2	Easter Road	
26/4/1922	Wilson Cup Final	Hearts Hibernian	2 4	Tynecastle	
29/4/1922	Scottish League	Hibernian Clydebank	6 0	Easter Road	
5/5/1922	Friendly	Musselburgh Brunstonians Select Hibernian		Olive Park	Score unknown
6/5/1922	Rosebery Charity Cup Semi Final	Hearts Hibernian	0 1	Tynecastle	
10/5/1922	Benefit Tournament in aid of the Lord Provost's umemployed rent relief fund final	Hearts Hibernian	0 1	Tynecastle	
13/5/1922	Rosebery Charity Cup Final	Leith Athletic Hibernian	0 3	Tynecastle	Match played at neutral ground
29/7/1922	Bailie Bathgate Charity Cup in aid of the Old Hibernian Assoc	Hibernian Hearts	1 2	Easter Road	Both teams made up of old players

Season 1922–23

Date	Fixture	Teams and Score		Venue	Notes
16/8/1922	Scottish League	Hibernian Falkirk	1 0	Easter Road	
19/8/1922	Scottish League	Hibernian Partick Thistle	1 0	Easter Road	
23/8/1922	East of Scotland Shield Semi Final	Hibernian Leith Athletic	4 0	Easter Road	

Date	Fixture	Teams and Score		Venue	Notes
26/8/1922	Scottish League	Third Lanark Hibernian	0 1	Cathkin	
30/8/1922	East of Scotland	Hibernian Hearts	1 1	Easter Road	
2/9/1922	Scottish League	Hibernian Motherwell	2 1	Easters Road	
6/9/1922	Friendly	Edinburgh Emmet Hibernian	 0 1	Bathgate Park	
9/9/1922	Scottish League	Aberdeen Hibernian	2 0	Pittodrie	
16/9/1922	Scottish League	Hibernian St Mirren	0 3	Easter Road	
18/9/1922	Scottish League	Hibernian Celtic	1 0	Easter Road	
23/9/1922	Scottish League	Hearts Hibernian	2 2	Tynecastle	
30/9/1922	Scottish League	Hibernian Kilmarnock	1 1	Easter Road	
7/10/1922	Scottish League	Rangers Hibernian	2 0	Ibrox	
14/10/1922	Scottish League	Hibernian Airdrie	1 0	Easter Road	
21/10/1922	Scottish League	Hibernian Raith Rovers	2 0	Easter Road	
28/10/1922	Scottish League	Alloa Athletic Hibernian	2 1	Recreation Park	
4/11/1922	Scottish League	Falkirk Hibernian	5 0	Brockville	
11/11/1922	Scottish League	Hibernian Dundee	3 3	Easter Road	
18/11/1922	Scottish League	Clyde Hibernian	0 0	Shawfield	
21/11/1922	Benefit in aid of the Highland Institute	Glasgow Select Hibernian/East of Scotland Select	0 0	Firhill	
25/11/1922	Scottish League	Hibernian Albion Rovers	3 0	Easter Road	
29/11/1922	Benefit in aid of John Williamson Testimonial Fund	Hearts/Hibernian East of Scotland Select Glasgow Select	 0 1	Tynecastle	
2/12/1922	Scottish League	Ayr United Hibernian	1 1	Somerset Park	

HIBERNIAN RESULTS 1914–1946

Date	Fixture	Teams and Score		Venue	Notes
9/12/1922	Scottish League	Hibernian Hamilton Accies	2 0	Easter Road	
16/12/1922	Scottish League	Motherwell Hibernian	0 2	Fir Park	
23/12/1922	Scottish League	Hibernian Morton	0 1	Easter Road	
20/12/1922	Scottish League	Kilmarnock Hibernian	1 0	Rugby Park	
1/1/1923	Scottish League	Hibernian Hearts	2 1	Easter Road	
2/1/1923	Scottish League	Dundee Hibernian	1 0	Dens Park	
3/1/1923	Friendly	Hibernian Glasgow Juniors Select	3 3	Easter Road	
3/1/1923	Bailie Bathgate Charity Cup in aid of the Old Hibs Assoc	Hearts Hibernian	6 2	Tynecastle	Both teams made of old players
6/1/1923	Scottish League	St Mirren Hibernian	2 1	Love Street	
13/1/1923	Scottish Cup	Hibernian Clackmannan	4 0	Easter Road	Venue originally Clackmannan but Hibernian made financial arrangement to have match played at Easter Road
17/1/1923	Benefit in aid of Lord Provost of Glasgow Rent Relief Fund	Glasgow Select Hibernian/East of Scotland Select	1 1	Ibrox	
20/1/1923	Scottish League	Hibernian Ayr United	3 0	Easter Road	
27/1/1923	Scottish Cup 2nd Round	Hibernian Peebles Rovers	0 0	Easter Road	
30/1/1923	Scottish Cup 2nd Round Replay	Hibernian Peebles Rovers	3 0	Easter Road	Peebles Rovers agreed to play the match at Easter Road
31/1/1923	Scottish League	Celtic Hibernian	0 0	Parkhead	
3/2/1923	Scottish League	Hibernian Third Lanark	2 0	Easter Road	
10/2/1923	Scottish Cup 3rd Round	Hibernian Queen's Park	2 0	Easter Road	
14/2/1923	Scottish League	Morton Hibernian	1 0	Cappielow	

Date	Fixture	Teams and Score		Venue	Notes
17/2/1923	Scottish League	Hibernian Alloa	2 1	Easter Road	
24/2/1923	Scottish Cup Quarter Final	Hibernian Aberdeen	2 0	Easter Road	
28/2/1923	Scottish League	Hamilton Accies Hibernian	2 1	Douglas Park	
3/3/1923	Scottish League	Hibernian Aberdeen	2 0	Easter Road	
10/3/1923	Scottish Cup Semi Final	Third Lanark Hibernian	0 1	Tynecastle	Match played at neutral ground
14/3/1923	Scottish League	Albion Rovers Hibernian	1 2	Cliftonhill	
17/3/1923	Scottish League	Hibernian Clyde	1 2	Easter Road	
24/3/1923	Scottish League	Airdrie Hibernian	2 1	Broomfield	
31/3/1923	Scottish Cup Final	Celtic Hibernian	1 0	Hampden	Match played at neutral ground
2/4/1923	Scottish League	Raith Rovers Hibernian	2 2	Starks Park	
7/4/1923	Scottish League	Hibernian Rangers	2 0	Easter Road	
16/3/1923	Dunedin Cup Semi Final	Hibernian Raith Rovers	0 2	Easter Road	
21/4/1923	Scottish League	Partick Thistle Hibernian	1 0	Firhill	
23/4/1923	Friendly	Peebles Rovers Hibernian	1 0	Whitestone Park	Hibernian team mostly reserves
25/4/1923	Wilson Cup Final	Hibernian Hearts	0 0	Easter Road	Both teams also had three corners each
27/4/1923	Wilson Cup Final Replay	Hearts Hibernian	2 1	Tynecastle	
28/4/1923	Friendly	Hibernian Dundee	3 3	Easter Road	
30/4/1923	East of Scotland Shield Final Replay	Hearts Hibernian	1 2	Tynecastle	
9/5/1923	Rosebery Charity Cup Semi Final	Hibernian Leith Athletic	6 1	Easter Road	
12/5/1923	Rosebery Charity Cup Final	Hearts Hibernian	2 1	Tynecastle	
15/5/1923	Benefit in aid of the Lord Provost's Rent Relief Fund	Hearts Hibernian	2 1	Tynecastle	

HIBERNIAN RESULTS 1914–1946

Date	Fixture	Teams and Score		Venue	Notes
		Season 1923–24			
15/8/1923	East of Scotland Shield Semi Final	St Bernard's Hibernian	2 2	Logie Green	
18/8/1923	Scottish League	Third Lanark Hibernian	0 3	Cathkin	
21/8/1923	Benefit in aid of St Ninians RC building extension fund	Hibernian Celtic	1 0	Easter Road	
22/8/1923	Benefit in aid of Winchburgh Thistle FC funds	Winchburgh Th Hibernian		Winchburgh Score unknown	
25/8/1923	Scottish League	Hibernian Aberdeen	0 1	Easter Road	
30/8/1923	East of Scotland Shield Semi Final Replay	Hibernian St Bernard's	5 1	Easter Road	
1/9/1923	Scottish League	Kilmarnock Hibernian	2 1	Rugby Park	
5/9/1923	East of Scotland Shield Final	Hearts Hibernian	1 1	Tynecastle	
8/9/1923	Scottish League	Hibernian Hearts	1 1	Easter Road	
15/9/1923	Scottish League	Airdrie Hibernian	1 1	Broomfield	
17/9/1923	Scottish League	Hibernian Celtic	0 0	Easter Road	
22/9/1923	Scottish League	Hibernian Motherwell	2 4	Easter Road	
29/9/1923	Scottish League	Queen's Park Hibernian	1 1	Hampden	
6/10/1923	Scottish League	Hibernian Raith Rovers	4 0	Easter Road	
13/10/1923	Scottish League	St Mirren Hibernian	1 1	Love Street	
20/10/1923	Scottish League	Hibernian Rangers	1 3	Easter Road	
23/10/1923	International Trial	Glasgow Select Hibernian/Hearts Select	2 4	Ibrox	
27/10/1923	Scottish League	Dundee Hibernian	7 2	Dens Park	
3/11/1923	Scottish League	Hibernian Hamilton Accies	1 3	Easter Road	

Date	Fixture	Teams and Score		Venue	Notes
7/11/1923	Benefit in aid of the Edinburgh Poor Fund	Hearts/Hibernian Select Glasgow Select	2 4	Tynecastle	
10/11/1923	Scottish League	Ayr United Hibernian	2 2	Somerset Park	
17/11/1923	Scottish League	Hibernian Clyde	3 1	Easter Road	
24/11/1923	Scottish League	Hibernian Morton	2 1	Easter Road	
1/12/1923	Scottish League	Partick Thistle Hibernian	1 0	Firhill	
8/12/1923	Scottish League	Falkirk Hibernian	1 1	Brockville	
15/12/1923	Scottish League	Hibernian Clydebank	3 2	Easter Road	
22/12/1923	Scottish League	Hibernian Queen's Park	4 0	Easter Road	
29/12/1923	Scottish League	Morton Hibernian	1 0	Cappielow	
1/1/1924	Scottish League	Hearts Hibernian	1 1	Tynecastle	
2/1/1924	Scottish League	Aberdeen Hibernian	1 1	Pittodrie	
5/12/1924	Scottish League	Hibernian Falkirk	1 0	Easter Road	
12/1/1924	Scottish League	Raith Rovers Hibernian	0 2	Starks Park	
19/1/1924	Scottish League	Hibernian Third Lanark	5 2	Easter Road	
26/1/1924	Scottish Cup 1st Round	Hibernian Dundee United	1 0	Easter Road	Dundee United formerly called Dundee Hibs had changed their name
2/2/1924	Scottish League	Hibernian Ayr United	3 0	Easter Road	
9/2/1924	Scottish Cup 2nd Round	Hibernian Alloa Athletic	1 1	Easter Road	
12/2/1924	Scottish Cup 2nd Round Replay	Alloa Athletic Hibernian	0 5	Recreation Park	
16/2/1924	Scottish League	Hibernian Dundee	2 0	Easter Road	
20/2/1924	Scottish League	Clydebank Hibernian	2 4	Clydeholm	

HIBERNIAN RESULTS 1914–1946

Date	Fixture	Teams and Score		Venue	Notes
23/2/1924	Scottish Cup 3rd Round	Rangers Hibernian	1 2	Ibrox	
27/2/1924	Scottish League	Hibernian Kilmarnock	3 1	Easter Road	
1/3/1924	Scottish League	Clyde Hibernian	2 0	Shawfield	
8/3/1924	Scottish Cup Quarter Final	Hibernian Partick Thistle	2 2	Easter Road	
12/3/1924	Scottish Cup Quarter Final Replay	Partick Thistle Hibernian	1 1	Firhill	Half-hour extra time played
15/3/1924	Scottish League	Motherwell Hibernian	2 1	Fir Park	
18/3/1924	Scottish Cup Quarter Final 2nd Replay	Partick Thistle Hibernian	1 2	Parkhead	Match played at neutral ground
22/3/1924	Scottish Cup Semi Final	Aberdeen Hibernian	0 0	Dens Park	Match played at neutral ground
26/3/1924	Scottish Cup Semi Final Replay	Aberdeen Hibernian	0 0	Dens Park	Match played at neutral ground Half-hour extra time played
29/3/1924	Friendly	Dublin Bohemians Hibernian	1 2	Dalymount Park Dublin Eire	
2/4/1924	Scottish League	Hibernian St Mirren	1 1	Easter Road	
5/4/1924	Scottish League	Rangers Hibernian	2 1	Ibrox	
9/4/1924	Scottish Cup Semi Final 2nd Replay	Aberdeen Hibernian	0 1	Dens Park	Match played at neutral ground
12/4/1924	Scottish League	Hibernian Airdrie	2 0	Easter Road	
16/4/1924	Scottish League	Hibernian Partick Thistle	3 1	Easter Road	
19/4/1924	Scottish Cup Final	Airdrie Hibernian	2 0	Ibrox	Match played at neutral ground
22/4/1924	Wilson Cup Final	Hearts Hibernian	4 1	Tynecastle	
23/4/1924	Scottish League	Hamilton Accies Hibernian	2 1	Douglas Park	
26/4/1924	Scottish League	Celtic Hibernian	1 1	Parkhead	

Date	Fixture	Teams and Score		Venue	Notes
28/4/1924	Dunedin Cup Semi Final	Hibernian Falkirk	1 0	Easter Road	
29/4/1924	East of Scotland Shield Final Replay	Hibernian Hearts	2 1	Easter Road	
30/4/1924	Dunedin Cup Final	Raith Rovers Hibernian	1 0	Tynecastle	Match played at neutral ground
3/5/1924	Rosebery Charity Cup Semi Final	St Bernard's Hibernian	1 2	Tynecastle	Match played at Tynecastle as Logie Green was not available St Bernard's were using Logie Green for home fixtures Half-hour extra time played
10/5/1924	Rosebery Charity Cup Final	Hearts Hibernian	0 2	Tynecastle	
3/6/1924	Tour of Austria and Germany Friendly	Vienna Rapid Hibernian	1 3	Vienna Austria	
5/6/1924	Tour of Austria and Germany Friendly	Vienna Select Hibernian		Vienna Austria	Score unknown
7/6/1924	Tour of Austria and Germany Friendly	British Army Select Hibernian		Cologne Germany	Score unknown
9/6/1924	Tour of Austria and Germany Friendly	Munich Select Hibernian		Munich Germany	Score unknown
11/6/1924	Tour of Austria and Germany Friendly	Dresden Select Hibernian		Dresden Germany	Score unknown
13/6/1924	Tour of Austria and Germany Friendly	Dresden Select Hibernian		Dresden Germany	Score unknown
5/7/1924	Bailie Bathgate Charity Trophy in aid of the Old Hibs Assoc	Hearts Hibernian	1 4	Bathgate Park Canongate Edinburgh	Both teams made up of old players

Season 1924–25

Date	Fixture	Teams and Score		Venue	Notes
15/8/1924	Scottish League	Hibernian Partick Thistle	3 2	Tynecastle	Home match for Hibernian but as Easter Road is under construction they have the use of Tynecastle

HIBERNIAN RESULTS 1914–1946

Date	Fixture	Teams and Score		Venue	Notes
18/8/1924	Friendly	Portobello Thistle	0	Woods Park	
		Hibernian	0		
23/8/1924	Scottish League	Kilmarnock	0	Rugby Park	
		Hibernian	1		
27/8/1924	East of Scotland Shield Semi Final	Hearts	0	Tynecastle	
		Hibernian	0		
29/8/1924	Scottish League	Hibernian	1	Tynecastle	Home match for Hibernian see note first match of season
		Motherwell	0		
2/9/1924	Friendly	Vale of Leithan	0	Innerleithen	
		Hibernian	3		
6/9/1924	Scottish League	St Johnstone	2	Recreation Park	
		Hibernian	3		
13/9/1924	Scottish League	Hibernian	2	Easter Road	Hibernian now back at Easter Road after reconstruction
		Queen's Park	0		
15/9/1924	Scottish League	Hibernian	2	Easter Road	
		Celtic	3		
20/9/1924	Scottish League	Raith Rovers	1	Starks Park	
		Hibernian	3		
27/9/1924	Scottish League	Hibernian	2	Easter Road	
		Morton	0		
4/10/1924	Scottish League	St Mirren	2	Love Street	
		Hibernian	2		
11/10/1924	Scottish League	Hibernian	7	Easter Road	
		Ayr United	0		
18/10/1924	Scottish League	Hearts	2	Tynecastle	
		Hibernian	0		
25/10/1924	Scottish League	Hibernian	4	Easter Road	
		Dundee	2		
1/11/1924	Scottish League	Hibernian	1	Easter Road	
		Falkirk	2		
8/11/1924	Scottish League	Hamilton Accies	0	Douglas Park	
		Hibernian	2		
15/11/1924	Scottish League	Rangers	3	Ibrox	
		Hibernian	0		
22/11/1924	Scottish League	Hibernian	4	Easter Road	
		Aberdeen	1		
29/11/1924	Scottish League	Cowdenbeath	1	Central Park	
		Hibernian	1		
6/12/1924	Scottish League	Hibernian	1	Easter Road	
		Airdrie	1		

Date	Fixture	Teams and Score		Venue	Notes
13/12/1924	Scottish League	Third Lanark Hibernian	1 2	Cathkin	
20/12/1924	Scottish League	Hibernian St Johnstone	5 0	Easter Road	
25/12/1924	Benefit in aid of Willie Dornan of Hibernian	Hibernian Rangers	2 4	Easter Road	
27/12/1924	Scottish League	Queen's Park Hibernian	1 0	Hampden	
1/1/1925	Scottish League	Hibernian Hearts	2 1	Easter Road	
3/1/1925	Scottish League	Hibernian Kilmarnock	2 0	Easter Road	
5/1/1925	Scottish League	Aberdeen Hibernian	0 1	Pittodrie	
10/1/1925	Scottish League	Falkirk Hibernian	0 0	Brockville	
17/1/1925	Scottish League	Hibernian Hamilton Accies	2 1	Easter Road	
24/1/1925	Scottish Cup 1st Round	Hibernian Aberdeen	0 2	Easter Road	
31/1/1925	Scottish League	Celtic Hibernian	1 1	Parkhead	
7/2/1925	Scottish League	Hibernian Third Lanark	5 1	Easter Road	Match brought forward from 14 Feb as international match being played in Edinburgh that day
11/2/1925	Scottish League	Motherwell Hibernian	1 1	Fir Park	
21/2/1925	Scottish League	Hibernian Cowdenbeath	4 1	Easter Road	Match brought forward from 11 April
25/2/1925	Scottish League	Hibernian Raith Rovers	3 0	Easter Road	
28/2/1925	Scottish League	Ayr United Hibernian	2 2	Somerset Park	
7/3/1925	Dunedin Cup Semi Final	Hibernian Falkirk	0 1	Easter Road	
11/3/1925	Scottish League	Hibernian Rangers	4 1	Easter Road	
14/3/1925	Scottish League	Partick Thistle Hibernian	3 1	Firhill	
24/3/1925	Scottish League	Hibernian St Mirren	2 0	Easter Road	

HIBERNIAN RESULTS 1914–1946

Date	Fixture	Teams and Score		Venue	Notes
28/3/1925	Scottish League	Morton	2	Cappielow	
		Hibernian	2		
4/4/1925	Scottish League	Dundee	3	Dens Park	
		Hibernian	0		
8/5/1925	Benefit in aid of Willie Grant of Aberdeen	Aberdeen	2	Pittodrie	
		Hibernian	2		
13/4/1925	Friendly	Hibernian	4	Easter Road	
		Glasgow Junior Select	1		
15/4/1925	Wilson Cup Final	Hibernian	1	Easter Road	
		Hearts	0		
18/4/1925	Scottish League	Airdrie	2	Broomfield	
		Hibernian	0		
20/4/1925	Benefit in aid of Willie Miller of Hibernian	Hibernian	1	Easter Road	
		Celtic	1		
22/4/1925	Friendly	Gala Fairydean	1	Eastlands Park	
		Hibernian	5	Galashiels	
25/4/1925	East of Scotland Shield Semi Final Replay	Hibernian	1	Easter Road	
		Hearts	0		
27/4/1925	East of Scotland Shield Final	Hibernian	3	Easter Road	
		Leith Athletic	0		
29/4/1925	Friendly	Hibernian	3	Easter Road	
		Newcastle Utd	1		
2/5/1925	Rosebery Charity Cup Semi Final	Hibernian	4	Easter Road	
		Leith Athletic	0		
16/5/1925	Rosebery Charity Cup Final	Hearts	0	Tynecastle	
		Hibernian	1		
					Eight game tour of Poland cancelled by the organisers
4/7/1925	Bailie Bathgate Charity Trophy in aid of the Old Hibs Assoc	Hearts	1	Bathgate Park Canongate Edinburgh	Both teams made up of old players
		Hibernian	1		

Season 1925–26

15/8/1925	Scottish League	Celtic	5	Parkhead	
		Hibernian	0		
17/8/1925	Benefit in aid of Willie McGinnigle of Hibernian	Hibernian	4	Easter Road	
		Partick Thistle	6		
22/8/1925	Scottish League	Hibernian	8	Easter Road	
		Kilmarnock	0		

253

Date	Fixture	Teams and Score		Venue	Notes
26/8/1925	East of Scotland Shield Semi Final	Hibernian St Bernard's	9 0	Easter Road	
29/8/1925	Scottish League	St Johnstone Hibernian	0 0	Muirton Park	
31/8/1925	Benefit in aid of Portobello Thistle FC funds	Portobello Thistle Hibernian	6 2	Wood Park	Hibernian team mostly reserves
2/9/1925	Benefit in aid of Hugh Shaw of Hibernian	Hibernian Hearts	2 3	Easter Road	
5/9/1925	Scottish League	Hibernian Dundee	2 1	Easter Road	
12/9/1925	Scottish League	Motherwell Hibernian	2 1	Fir Park	
16/9/1925	East of Scotland Shield Final	Hearts Hibernian	1 2	Tynecastle	
19/9/1925	Scottish League	Hibernian Partick Thistle	3 4	Easter Road	
21/9/1925	Scottish League	Hibernian Rangers	0 2	Easter Road	
26/9/1925	Scottish League	Raith Rovers Hibernian	1 0	Starks Park	
3/10/1925	Scottish League	Hibernian St Mirren	0 2	Easter Road	
10/10/1925	Scottish League	Aberdeen Hibernian	5 0	Pittodrie	
17/10/1925	Scottish League	Hibernian Hearts	0 0	Easter Road	
24/10/1925	Scottish League	Queen's Park Hibernian	2 0	Hampden	
31/10/1925	Scottish League	Hibernian Falkirk	3 1	Easter Road	
7/11/1925	Scottish League	Cowdenbeath Hibernian	3 1	Central Park	
14/11/1925	Scottish League	Hamilton Accies Hibernian	1 0	Douglas Park	
21/11/1925	Scottish League	Hibernian Clydebank	5 1	Easter Road	
28/11/1925	Scottish League	Dundee United Hibernian	2 2	Tannadice	Dundee United only recently changed name from Dundee Hibs
2/12/1925	Benefit in aid of Gilfillan of Hearts	Hearts and Hibernian Select Glasgow Select	3 2	Tynecastle	

HIBERNIAN RESULTS 1914–1946

Date	Fixture	Teams and Score		Venue	Notes
5/12/1925	Scottish League	Hibernian Hamilton Accies	8 4	Easter Road	
12/12/1925	Scottish League	Rangers Hibernian	3 1	Ibrox	
26/12/1925	Scottish League	Dundee Hibernian	1 4	Dens Park	
1/1/1926	Scottish League	Hearts Hibernian	1 4	Tynecastle	
2/1/1926	Scottish League	Hibernian Aberdeen	0 0	Easter Road	
4/1/1926	Scottish League	Hibernian St Johnstone	0 3	Easter Road	
9/1/1926	Scottish League	Partick Thistle Hibernian	2 1	Firhill	
13/1/1926	Scottish League	Hibernian Morton	4 1	Easter Road	
16/1/1926	Scottish League	Hibernian Celtic	4 4	Easter Road	
23/1/1926	Scottish Cup 1st Round	Hibernian Broxburn Utd	1 1	Easter Road	
23/1/1926	Scottish Cup 1st Round Replay	Hibernian Broxburn Utd	1 0	Easter Road	Broxburn United agreed to play replay at Easter Road for a financial settlement
30/1/1926	Scottish League	Hibernian Airdrie	1 4	Easter Road	
6/2/1926	Scottish Cup 2nd Round	Hibernian Airdrie	2 3	Easter Road	
10/2/1926	Scottish League	Morton Hibernian	2 5	Cappielow	
13/2/1926	Scottish League	Hibernian Motherwell	3 1	Easter Road	
20/2/1926	Scottish League	Hibernian Queen's Park	1 2	Easter Road	
27/2/1926	Scottish League	St Mirren Hibernian	2 1	Love Street	
6/3/1926	Scottish League	Hibernian Cowdenbeath	1 2	Easter Road	
13/3/1926	Scottish League	Clydebank Hibernian	0 1	Clydeholm	
20/3/1926	Scottish League	Hibernian Raith Rovers	2 0	Easter Road	
27/3/1926	Scottish League	Airdrie Hibernian	5 1	Broomfield	

THE MAKING OF HIBERNIAN 3

Date	Fixture	Teams and Score		Venue	Notes
10/4/1926	Scottish League	Hibernian Dundee United	3 5	Easter Road	
17/4/1926	Scottish League	Falkirk Hibernian	1 1	Brockville	
19/4/1926	Dunedin Cup Semi Final	Hibernian Raith Rovers	4 1	Easter Road	
21/4/1926	Benefit in aid of Peter Kerr of Hibernian	Hibernian Celtic	0 2	Easter Road	
22/4/1926	Dunedin Cup Final	Hearts Hibernian	2 1	Tynecastle	
24/4/1926	Scottish League	Kilmarnock Hibernian	2 1	Rugby Park	
26/4/1926	Friendly	Arsenal Hibernian	5 0	Highbury London	
27/4/1926	Benefit in aid of Dalkeith Thistle FC funds	Dalkeith Thistle Hibernian	1 0	Dalkeith	Hibernian team mostly reserves
28/4/1926	Wilson Cup Final	Hearts Hibernian	2 1	Tynecastle	
1/5/1926	Rosebery Charity Cup Semi Final	Hibernian Leith Athletic	1 4	Easter Road	
10/7/1926	Bailie Bathgate Charity Cup in aid of the Old Hibs Association	Old Hibernian Old Hearts		Easter Road	Both teams made up of old players Score unknown

Season 1926–27

Date	Fixture	Teams and Score		Venue	Notes
14/8/1926	Scottish League	Hibernian St Johnstone	1 5	Easter Road	
16/8/1926	Benefit in aid of Portobello Thistle FC funds	Portobello Thistle Hibernian	 2 2	Woods Park	Hibernian team mostly reserves
21/8/1926	Scottish League	Dundee United Hibernian	0 2	Tannadice	
25/8/1926	East of Scotland Shield Semi Final	Hibernian Leith Athletic	3 1	Easter Road	
28/8/1926	Scottish League	Hibernian Aberdeen	2 3	Easter Road	
4/9/1926	Scottish League	Airdrie Hibernian	3 0	Broomfield	
8/9/1926	Benefit in aid of Harry Ritchie of Hibernian	Hibernian Hearts	0 3	Easter Road	

HIBERNIAN RESULTS 1914–1946

Date	Fixture	Teams and Score		Venue	Notes
11/9/1926	Scottish League	Hibernian St Mirren	2 1	Easter Road	
18/9/1926	Scottish League	Dunfermline Hibernian	4 2	East End Park	
20/9/1926	East of Scotland Shield Final	Hibernian Hearts	1 5	Easter Road	
25/9/1926	Scottish League	Hibernian Celtic	3 2	Easter Road	
27/9/1926	Friendly	Hibernian St Rochs	3 0	Easter Road	Hibernian team mostly reserves
29/9/1926	Benefit in aid of Jimmy Dunn of Hibernian	Hibernian Rangers	2 2	Easter Road	
2/10/1926	Scottish League	Partick Thistle Hibernian	5 1	Firhill	
9/10/1926	Scottish League	Hibernian Motherwell	1 1	Easter Road	
16/10/1926	Scottish League	Hamilton Accies Hibernian	0 1	Douglas Park	
23/10/1926	Scottish League	Hibernian Clyde	3 0	Easter Road	
30/10/1926	Scottish League	Hearts Hibernian	2 2	Tynecastle	
6/11/1926	Scottish League	Dundee Hibernian	3 0	Dens Park	
13/11/1926	Scottish League	Hibernian Rangers	2 2	Easter Road	
20/11/1926	Scottish League	Hibernian Queen's Park	2 0	Easter Road	
27/11/1926	Scottish League	Falkirk Hibernian	2 0	Brockville	
4/12/1926	Scottish League	Hibernian Kilmarnock	5 1	Easter Road	
11/12/1926	Scottish League	Morton Hibernian	3 0	Cappielow	
18/12/1926	Scottish League	Hibernian Cowdenbeath	2 0	Easter Road	
25/12/1926	Scottish League	St Johnstone Hibernian	0 0	Muirton Park	
1/1/1927	Scottish League	Hibernian Hearts	2 2	Easter Road	
3/1/1927	Scottish League	Aberdeen Hibernian	2 5	Pittodrie	
6/1/1927	Friendly	Hibernian Bridgeton Waverley	5 0	Easter Road	Hibernian team mostly reserves

Date	Fixture	Teams and Score		Venue	Notes
8/1/1927	Scottish League	Hibernian Airdrie	2 1	Easter Road	
15/1/1927	Scottish League	St Mirren Hibernian	3 1	Love Street	
22/1/1927	Scottish Cup 1st Round	Cowdenbeath Hibernian	3 0	Central Park	
29/1/1927	Scottish League	Hibernian Dunfermline	2 2	Easter Road	
2/2/1927	Scottish League	Celtic Hibernian	2 3	Parkhead	
12/2/1927	Scottish League	Hibernian Partick Thistle	3 2	Easter Road	
19/2/1927	Scottish League	Motherwell Hibernian	2 1	Fir Park	
26/2/1927	Scottish League	Hibernian Hamilton Accies	3 1	Easter Road	
5/3/1927	Scottish League	Clyde Hibernian	2 0	Shawfield	
12/3/1927	Scottish League	Hibernian Dundee United	3 2	Easter Road	
19/3/1927	Scottish League	Hibernian Dundee	0 1	Easter Road	
29/3/1927	Scottish League	Rangers Hibernian	2 0	Ibrox	
5/4/1927	Scottish League	Queen's Park Hibernian	3 4	Hampden	
9/4/1927	Scottish League	Hibernian Falkirk	1 0	Easter Road	
11/4/1927	Dunedin Cup Semi Final	Hibernian Falkirk	1 1	Easter Road	Falkirk won by 4 corners to 3
20/4/1927	Scottish League	Kilmarnock Hibernian	4 0	Rugby Park	
23/4/1927	Scottish League	Hibernian Morton	1 1	Easter Road	
27/4/1927	Wilson Cup Final	Hibernian Hearts	2 1	Easter Road	
30/4/1927	Scottish League	Cowdenbeath Hibernian	2 0	Central Park	
9/5/1927	Rosebery Charity Cup Semi Final	Hibernian St Bernard's	5 1	Easter Road	
14/5/1926	Rosebery Charity Cup Final	Hearts Hibernian	1 0	Tynecastle	Half-hour extra time played
20/9/1927	Bailie Bathgate Charity Cup in aid of the Old Hibs Assoc	Hearts Hibernian		Tynecastle	Both teams made up of old players Score unknown

HIBERNIAN RESULTS 1914–1946

Date	Fixture	Teams and Score		Venue	Notes

Season 1927–28

Date	Fixture	Teams and Score		Venue	Notes
13/8/1927	Scottish League	Celtic Hibernian	3 0	Parkhead	
20/8/1927	Scottish League	Hibernian Cowdenbeath	3 0	Easter Road	
24/8/1927	East of Scotland Shield Semi Final	Hibernian St Bernard's	7 1	Easter Road	
27/8/1927	Scottish League	Motherwell Hibernian	2 1	Fir Park	
31/8/1927	East of Scotland Shield Final	Hearts Hibernian	2 2	Tynecastle	
3/9/1927	Scottish League	Hibernian Airdrie	2 3	Easter Road	
5/9/1927	Benefit in aid of Johnny Halligan of Hibernian	Hibernian Rangers	2 3	Easter Road	
10/9/1927	Scottish League	Aberdeen Hibernian	4 2	Pittodrie	
13/9/1927	Benefit in aid of Jimmy McColl of Hibernian	Hibernian and Hearts Select West of Scotland Select	2 3	Easter Road	
17/9/1927	Scottish League	Hibernian Bo'ness	3 0	Easter Road	
19/9/1927	East of Scotland Shield Final Replay	Hibernian Hearts	2 1	Easter Road	
22/9/1927	Friendly	East of Scotland Junior Select Hibernian		Meadowbank	Hibernian team mostly reserves Score unknown
24/9/1927	Scottish League	St Mirren Hibernian	3 2	Love Street	
1/10/1927	Scottish League	Hibernian Partick Thistle	4 1	Easter Road	
9/10/1927	Scottish League	St Johnstone Hibernian	2 0	Muirton Park	
15/10/1927	Scottish League	Hibernian Hearts	2 1	Easter Road	
22/10/1927	Scottish League	Clyde Hibernian	0 2	Shawfield	
29/10/1927	Scottish League	Hibernian Hamilton Accies	5 1	Easter Road	
5/11/1927	Scottish League	Hibernian Dundee	4 0	Easter Road	

Date	Fixture	Teams and Score		Venue	Notes
12/11/1927	Scottish League	Rangers Hibernian	4 1	Ibrox	
19/11/1927	Scottish League	Queen's Park Hibernian	6 2	Hampden	
26/11/1927	Scottish League	Hibernian Falkirk	3 1	Easter Road	
3/12/1927	Scottish League	Kilmarnock Hibernian	2 1	Rugby Park	
10/12/1927	Scottish League	Hibernian Raith Rovers	3 2	Easter Road	
17/12/1927	Scottish League	Dunfermline Hibernian	0 2	East End Park	
24/12/1927	Scottish League	Hibernian Celtic	2 2	Easter Road	
31/12/1927	Scottish League	Airdrie Hibernian	2 2	Broomfield	
2/1/1928	Scottish League	Hearts Hibernian	2 2	Tynecastle	
3/1/1928	Scottish League	Hibernian Aberdeen	0 0	Easter Road	
7/1/1928	Scottish League	Hibernian Motherwell	2 2	Easter Road	
14/1/1928	Scottish League	Bo'ness Hibernian	2 1	Bo'ness	
28/1/1928	Scottish League	Hibernian St Johnstone	2 2	Easter Road	
4/2/1928	Scottish Cup 2nd Round	Third Lanark Hibernian	0 2	Cathkin	
8/2/1928	Scottish League	Partick Thistle Hibernian	3 0	Firhill	
11/2/1928	Scottish League	Hibernian St Mirren	1 1	Easter Road	
18/2/1928	Scottish Cup 3rd Round	Hibernian Falkirk	0 0	Easter Road	
18/2/1928	Scottish Cup 3rd Round Replay	Falkirk Hibernian	0 1	Brockville	Half-hour extra time played
25/2/1928	Scottish League	Hibernian Clyde	0 1	Easter Road	
29/1/1928	Scottish League	Hamilton Accies Hibernian	4 1	Douglas Park	
3/3/1928	Scottish Cup Quarter Final	Dunfermline Hibernian	0 4	East End Park	
7/3/1928	Scottish League	Cowdenbeath Hibernian	3 1	Central Park	

HIBERNIAN RESULTS 1914–1946

Date	Fixture	Teams and Score		Venue	Notes
10/3/1928	Scottish League	Dundee Hibernian	4 1	Dens Park	
17/10/1928	Scottish League	Hibernian Rangers	2 1	Easter	
24/3/1928	Scottish Cup Semi Final	Rangers Hibernian	3 0	Tynecastle	Match played at neutral venue
28/3/1928	Scottish League	Hibernian Queen's Park	6 2	Easter Road	
31/3/1928	Scottish League	Falkirk Hibernian	2 2	Brockville	
7/4/1928	Scottish League	Hibernian Kilmarnock	3 1	Easter Road	
14/4/1928	Scottish League	Raith Rovers Hibernian	3 0	Starks Park	
16/4/1928	Dunedin Cup Semi Final	Hibernian Raith Rovers	0 1	Easter Road	
20/4/1928	Benefit in aid of Newtongrange Star FC funds	Newtongrange Star Hibernian	1 2	Newtongrange	Hibernian team mostly reserves
21/4/1928	Scottish League	Hibernian Dunfermline	3 3	Easter Road	
25/4/1928	Wilson Cup Final	Hearts Hibernian	3 0	Tynecastle	
28/4/1928	Benefit in aid of Charlie Orr of Leith Athletic	Hibernian Leith Athletic	2 1	Easter Road	
2/5/1928	Rosebery Charity Cup Semi Final	Hibernian Leith Athletic	1 3	Easter Road	
7/7/1928	Bailie Bathgate in aid of the Old Hibs Assoc	Old Hibernian Old Hearts		Easter Road Score unknown	

Season 1928–29

Date	Fixture	Teams and Score		Venue	Notes
11/8/1928	Scottish League	Hibernian St Johnstone	2 2	Easter Road	
14/8/1928	East of Scotland Shield Semi Final	Leith Athletic Hibernian	0 0	Marine Gardens	
18/8/1928	Scottish League	Kilmarnock Hibernian	1 0	Rugby Park	
14/8/1928	East of Scotland Shield Semi Final Replay	Hibernian Leith Athletic	0 0	Easter Road	
25/8/1928	Scottish League	Hibernian Aberdeen	4 1	Easter Road	

THE MAKING OF HIBERNIAN 3

Date	Fixture	Teams and Score		Venue	Notes
29/8/1928	East of Scotland Shield Semi Final 2nd Replay	Hibernian Leith Athletic	5 0	Easter Road	
1/9/1928	Scottish League	Cowdenbeath Hibernian	2 0	Central Park	
5/9/1928	East of Scotland Shield Final	Hibernian Hearts	3 2	Easter Road	
8/9/1928	Scottish League	Hibernian Falkirk	3 2	Easter Road	
15/9/1928	Scottish League	Clyde Hibernian	0 1	Shawfield	
18/9/1928	Benefit in aid of Geordie Murray of Hibernian	Hibernian Hearts	0 1	Easter Road	
22/9/1928	Scottish League	Hibernian Motherwell	1 1	Easter Road	
29/9/1928	Scottish League	Hibernian Partick Thistle	3 1	Easter Road	
6/10/1928	Scottish League	Airdrie Hibernian	0 2	Broomfield	Match brought forward from 1 Dec
13/10/1928	Scottish League	Queens' Park Hibernian	6 1	Hampden	
20/10/1928	Scottish League	Hearts Hibernian	1 1	Tynecastle	
27/10/1928	Scottish League	Hibernian Third Lanark	6 1	Easter Road	
3/11/1928	Scottish League	Hibernian Rangers	1 2	Easter Road	
10/11/1928	Scottish League	Hamilton Accies Hibernian	2 1	Douglas Park	
17/11/1928	Scottish League	Hibernian Raith Rovers	2 0	Easter Road	
24/11/1928	Scottish League	Hibernian Ayr United	2 2	Easter Road	
8/12/1928	Scottish League	St Mirren Hibernian	1 0	Love Street	
15/12/1928	Scottish League	Hibernian Dundee	2 0	Easter Road	
22/12/1928	Scottish League	Hibernian Kilmarnock	1 1a	Rugby Park	
29/12/1928	Scottish League	St Johnstone Hibernian	4 0	Muirton Park	
1/1/1929	Scottish League	Hibernian Hearts	1 0	Easter Road	

HIBERNIAN RESULTS 1914–1946

Date	Fixture	Teams and Score		Venue	Notes
2/1/1929	Scottish League	Third Lanark Hibernian	2 1	Cathkin	
5/1/1929	Scottish League	Aberdeen Hibernian	0 1	Pittodrie	
12/1/1929	Scottish League	Hibernian Cowdenbeath	1 2	Easter Road	
19/1/1929	Scottish Cup 1st Round	Hibernian St Johnstone	1 2	Easter Road	
26/1/929	Scottish League	Dundee Hibernian	1 0	Dens Park	
2/2/1929	Wilson Cup Final	Hibernian Hearts	1 1	Easter Road	
9/2/1929	Scottish League	Motherwell Hibernian	3 1	Fir Park	
16/2/1929	Scottish League	Partick Thistle Hibernian	3 0	Firhill	
20/2/1929	Scottish League	Hibernian Clyde	3 0	Easter Road	
23/2/1929	Scottish League	Hibernian Celtic	2 1	Easter Road	
2/3/1929	Scottish League	Hibernian Queen's Park	1 2	Easter Road	
9/3/1929	Scottish League	Rangers Hibernian	3 0	Ibrox	
16/3/1929	Scottish League	Hibernian Hamilton Accies	0 1	Easter Road	
23/3/1929	Scottish League	Raith Rovers Hibernian	1 0	Starks Park	
30/3/1929	Scottish League	Ayr United Hibernian	4 1	Somerset Park	
6/4/1929	Scottish League	Hibernian Airdrie	1 1	Easter Road	
13/4/1929	Scottish League	Hibernian Celtic	4 1	Easter Road	Match should have been played at Parkhead but the stand was damaged by fire
15/4/1929	Dunedin Cup Semi Final	Hibernian Falkirk	4 1	Easter Road	
17/4/1929	Dunedin Cup Final	Hearts Hibernian	8 2	Tynecastle	
20/4/1929	Scottish League	Hibernian St Mirren	3 5	Easter road	
27/4/1929	Scottish League	Falkirk Hibernian	2 1	Brockville	

THE MAKING OF HIBERNIAN 3

Date	Fixture	Teams and Score		Venue	Notes
30/4/1929	Wilson Cup Final Replay	Hearts Hibernian	5 1	Tynecastle	
4/5/1929	Rosebery Charity Cup Semi Final	Hibernian St Bernard's	2 1	Easter Road	
11/5/1929	Rosebery Charity Cup Final	Hearts Hibernian	5 1	Tynecastle	

Season 1929–1930

Date	Fixture	Teams and Score		Venue	Notes
2/8/1929	Public Practice Match	Hibernian (Green) Hibernian (Red)	5 1	Easter Road	
5/8/1929	Public Practice Match	Hibernian (Green) Hibernian (Red)	4 4	Easter Road	
10/8/1929	Scottish League	Hibernian Airdrie	3 1	Easter Road	
17/8/1929	Scottish League	Rangers Hibernian	3 0	Ibrox	
21/8/1929	Benefit in aid of Dunfermline and West Fife hospital funds	Hearts Hibernian	3 0	East End Park	35 minutes each way. Hibernian mostly reserves
24/8/1929	Scottish League	Hibernian Hamilton Accies	1 2	Easter Road	
27/8/1929	East of Scotland Shield Semi Final	St Bernard's Hibernian	3 4	Royal Gymnasium Park	
31/8/1929	Scottish League	Ayr United Hibernian	3 2	Somerset Park	
3/9/1929	East of Scotland Shield Final	Hearts Hibernian	4 4	Tynecastle	
7/9/1929	Scottish League	Hibernian Cowdenbeath	1 1	Easter Road	
10/9/1929	Friendly	Vale of Leithen Hibernian	2 1	Innerleithen	Hibernian team mostly reserves
14/9/1929	Scottish League	Queen's Park Hibernian	2 0	Hampden	
16/9/1929	East of Scotland Shield Final Replay	Hibernian Hearts	1 1	Easter Road	Hearts won by 9 corners to 5
21/9/1929	Scottish League	Hibernian Clyde	1 1	Easter Road	
28/9/1929	Scottish League	Morton Hibernian	3 2	Cappielow	
5/10/1929	Scottish League	Motherwell Hibernian	3 0	Fir Park	
12/10/1929	Scottish League	Hibernian Partick Thistle	3 0	Easter Road	

HIBERNIAN RESULTS 1914–1946

Date	Fixture	Teams and Score		Venue	Notes
19/10/1929	Scottish League	Dundee Hibernian	4 0	Dens Park	
26/10/1929	Scottish League	Hibernian Hearts	1 1	Easter Road	
2/11/1929	Scottish League	Celtic Hibernian	4 0	Parkhead	
9/11/1929	Scottish League	Hibernian St Johnstone	3 1	Easter Road	
16/11/1929	Scottish League	Falkirk Hibernian	1 1	Brockville	
23/11/1929	Scottish League	Hibernian St Mirren	2 2	Easter Road	
30/11/1929	Scottish League	Hibernian Kilmarnock	0 0	Easter Road	
7/12/1929	Scottish League	Aberdeen Hibernian	2 0	Pittodrie	
14/12/1929	Scottish League	Hibernian Dundee United	3 0	Easter Road	
21/12/1929	Scottish League	Airdrie Hibernian	3 0	Broomfield	
28/12/1929	Scottish League	Hibernian Rangers	0 2	Easter Road	
1/1/1930	Scottish League	Hearts Hibernian	1 1	Tynecastle	
2/1/1930	Scottish League	Hibernian Dundee	0 1	Easter Road	
4/1/1930	Scottish League	Hamilton Accies Hibernian	3 2	Douglas Park	
11/1/1930	Scottish League	Hibernian Ayr United	1 0	Easter Road	
18/1/1930	Scottish Cup	Hibernian Leith Amateurs	2 0	Easter Road	
25/1/1930	Scottish League	Cowdenbeath Hibernian	0 0	Central Park	
1/2/1930	Scottish Cup 2nd Round	Ayr United Hibernian	1 3	Somerset Park	
8/2/1930	Scottish League	Clyde Hibernian	0 2	Shawfield	
15/2/1930	Scottish Cup 3rd Round	Hibernian Hearts	1 3	Easter Road	
22/2/1930	Scottish League	Hibernian Motherwell	1 1	Easter Road	
1/3/1930	Scottish League	Hibernian Queen's Park	6 3	Easter Road	

Date	Fixture	Teams and Score		Venue	Notes
5/3/1930	Scottish League	Partick Thistle Hibernian	0 0	Firhill	
8/3/1930	Scottish League	Hibernian Celtic	0 2	Easter Road	
15/3/1930	Scottish League	St Johnstone Hibernian	4 3	Muirton Park	
22/3/1930	Scottish League	Hibernian Falkirk	1 0	Easter Road	
29/3/1930	Scottish League	St Mirren Hibernian	1 2	Love Street	
5/4/1930	Scottish League	Kilmarnock Hibernian	3 1	Rugby Park	
12/4/1930	Scottish League	Hibernian Aberdeen	0 1	Easter Road	
14/4/1930	Dunedin Cup Semi Final	Hibernian Raith Rovers	6 0	Easter Road	
16/4/1930	Dunedin Cup Final	Hearts Hibernian	0 0	Tynecastle	Hibernian won by 5 corners to 1
19/4/1930	Scottish League	Dundee United Hibernian	2 2	Tannadice	
23/4/1930	Wilson Cup Final	Hearts Hibernian	0 1	Tynecastle	
26/4/1930	Scottish League	Hibernian Morton	0 1	Easter Road	
3/5/1930	Rosebery Charity Cup Semi Final	Hibernian Leith Athletic	0 2	Easter Road	
12/7/1930	Bailie Bathgate Charity Cup in aid of the Old Hibs Assoc	Old Hibernian Old Hearts	1 0	Easter Road	Both teams made of old players

Season 1930–31

Date	Fixture	Teams and Score		Venue	Notes
2/8/1930	Public Practice Match	Hibernian (Green) Hibernian (Red)	2 3	Easter Road	
5/8/1930	Public Practice Match	Hibernian (Green) Hibernian (Red)	1 1	Easter Road	only half-hour each way player
9/8/1930	Scottish League	St Mirren Hibernian	1 0	Love Street	
16/8/1930	Scottish League	Hibernian Motherwell	2 2	Easter Road	
20/8/1930	East of Scotland Shield Semi Final	Hibernian Leith Athletic	2 2	Easter Road	
23/8/1930	Scottish League	Celtic Hibernian	6 0	Parkhead	

HIBERNIAN RESULTS 1914–1946

Date	Fixture	Teams and Score		Venue	Notes
30/8/1930	Scottish League	Hibernian Leith Athletic	0 1	Easter Road	
3/9/1930	East of Scotland Shield Semi Final Replay	Leith Athletic Hibernian	0 3	Marine Gardens	
6/9/1930	Scottish League	Ayr United Hibernian	1 3	Somerset Park	
13/9/1930	Scottish League	Hibernian Partick Thistle	0 3	Easter Road	
15/9/1930	East of Scotland Shield Final	Hibernian Hearts	4 5	Easter Road	
20/9/1930	Scottish League	Hearts Hibernian	4 1	Tynecastle	
27/9/1930	Scottish League	Hibernian Dundee	2 3	Easter Road	
4/10/1930	Scottish League	Cowdenbeath Hibernian	2 1	Central Park	
11/10/1930	Scottish League	Hibernian Airdrie	2 0	Easter Road	
18/10/1930	Scottish League	Morton Hibernian	5 4	Cappielow	
25/10/1930	Scottish League	Hibernian East Fife	2 1	Easter Road	
1/11/1930	Scottish League	Queen's Park Hibernian	2 2	Hampden	
8/11/1930	Scottish League	Hibernian Clyde	1 2	Easter Road	
15/11/1930	Scottish League	Aberdeen Hibernian	7 0	Pittodrie	
22/11/1930	Scottish League	Hibernian Kilmarnock	3 2	Easter Road	
29/11/1930	Scottish League	Hamilton Accies Hibernian	1 0	Douglas Park	
6/12/1930	Scottish League	Hibernian Rangers	1 2	Easter Road	
13/12/1930	Scottish League	Hibernian Falkirk	5 2	Easter Road	
20/12/1930	Scottish League	Hibernian St Mirren	2 3	Easter Road	
27/12/1930	Scottish League	Motherwell Hibernian	6 0	Fir Park	
1/1/1931	Scottish League	Hibernian Hearts	2 2	Easter Road	
3/1/1931	Scottish League	Hibernian Celtic	0 0	Easter Road	

Date	Fixture	Teams and Score		Venue	Notes
5/1/1931	Scottish League	Dundee	1	Dens Park	
		Hibernian	0		
10/1/1931	Scottish League	Leith Athletic	1	Marine Gardens	
		Hibernian	1		
17/1/1931	Scottish Cup 1st Round	Hibernian	3	Easter Road	
		St Cuthberts Wanderers	1		
24/1/1931	Scottish League	Hibernian	2	Easter Road	
		Ayr United	0		
31/1/1931	Scottish Cup 2nd Round	Hamilton Accies	2	Douglas Park	
		Hibernian	2		
4/2/1931	Scottish Cup 2nd Round Replay	Hibernian	5	Easter Road	
		Hamilton Accies	2		
7/2/1931	Scottish League	Hibernian	1	Easter Road	
		Cowdenbeath	0		
10/2/1931	Scottish League	Partick Thistle	1	Firhill	
		Hibernian	0		
14/2/1931	Scottish Cup 3rd Round	Hibernian	0	Easter Road	
		Motherwell	3		
18/2/1931	Scottish League	Airdrie	4	Broomfield	
		Hibernian	1		
21/2/1931	Scottish League	Hibernian	1	Easter Road	
		Morton	1		
28/2/1931	Scottish League	East Fife	1	Bayview	
		Hibernian	0		
11/3/1931	Scottish League	Hibernian	4	Easter Road	
		Queen's Park	2		
14/3/1931	Scottish League	Clyde	3	Shawfield	
		Hibernian	2		
21/3/1931	Scottish League	Hibernian	1	Easter Road	
		Aberdeen	2		
28/3/1931	Dunedin Cup Semi Final	Hibernian	4	Easter Road	
		Raith Rovers	0		
4/4/1931	Scottish League	Kilmarnock	4	Rugby Park	
		Hibernian	0		
11/4/1931	Scottish League	Hibernian	1	Easter Road	
		Hamilton Accies	0		
18/4/1931	Scottish League	Rangers	1	Ibrox	
		Hibernian	0		
20/4/1931	Dunedin Cup Final	Hearts	3	Tynecastle	
		Hibernian	0		
30/4/1931	Wilson Cup Final	Hibernian	3	Easter Road	
		Hearts	2		
6/5/1931	Rosebery Charity Cup Semi Final	Hibernian	2	Easter Road	
		St Bernard's	3		

HIBERNIAN RESULTS 1914–1946

Date	Fixture	Teams and Score		Venue	Notes

Season 1931–32

Date	Fixture	Teams and Score		Venue	Notes
31/7/1931	Public Practice Match	Hibernian (Green) Hibernian (Red)	5 3	Easter Road	
4/8/1931	Public Practice Match	Hibernian (Green) Hibernian (Red)	4 3	Easter Road	
8/8/1931	Scottish League Division 2	Hibernian Alloa Athletic	1 0	Easter Road	
11/8/1931	East of Scotland Shield Semi Final	St Bernard's Hibernian	3 0	Royal Gymnasium Park	
15/8/1931	Scottish League Division 2	Forfar Athletic Hibernian	1 0	Forfar	
18/8/1931	Scottish League Division 2	Hibernian Arbroath	3 1	Easter Road	
22/8/1931	Scottish League Division 2	Hibernian St Johnstone	6 0	Easter Road	
29/8/1931	Scottish League Division 2	Stenhouemuir Hibernian	2 1	Ochilview Park Larbert	
2/9/1931	Scottish League Division 2	Hibernian Dunfermline	6 2	Easter Road	
5/9/1931	Scottish League Division 2	Hibernian St Bernard's	2 4	Easter Road	
12/9/1931	Scottish League Division 2	Armadale Hibernian	1 1	Volunteer Park	
19/9/1931	Scottish League Division 2	Hibernian Montrose	0 0	Easter Road	
26/9/1931	Scottish League Division 2	Raith Rovers Hibernian	1 2	Starks Park	
3/10/1931	Scottish League Division 2	Hibernian East Stirlingshire	1 1	Easter Road	
10/10/1931	Scottish League Division 2	Edinburgh City Hibernian	2 1	Powderhall	
17/10/1931	Scottish League Division 2	Hibernian East Fife	3 2	Easter Road	
24/10/1931	Scottish League Division 2	Bo'ness Hibernian	2 2	Newtown Park	
31/10/1931	Scottish League Division 2	Hibernian Brechin City	4 0	Easter Road	
7/11/1931	Scottish League Division 2	Dumbarton Hibernian	0 2	Boghead	
14/11/1931	Scottish League Division 2	Hibernian Albion Rovers	4 1	Easter Road	
21/11/1931	Scottish League Division 2	Kings Park Hibernian	1 4	Forthbank Park Stirling	

THE MAKING OF HIBERNIAN 3

Date	Fixture	Teams and Score		Venue	Notes
28/11/1931	Scottish League Division 2	Hibernian Queen of the South	1 4	Easter Road	
5/12/1931	Scottish League Division 2	Arbroath Hibernian	3 3	Gayfield Park	
19/12/1931	Scottish League Division 2	Alloa Athletic Hibernian	1 2	Alloa	
26/12/1931	Scottish League Division 2	Hibernian Forfar Athletic	5 1	Easter Road	
1/1/1932	Scottish League Division 2	St Bernard's Hibernian	1 0	Royal Gymnasium Park	
2/1/1932	Scottish League Division 2	Hibernian Armadale	1 0	Easter Road	
9/1/1932	Scottish League Division 2	St Johnstone Hibernian	2 1	Muirton Park	
16/1/1932	Scottish Cup 1st Round	Hibernian Dundee United	2 3	Easter Road	
23/1/1932	Scottish League Division 2	Hibernian Stenhousemuir	0 2	Easter Road	
30/1/1932	Scottish League Division 2	Montrose Hibernian	0 1	Links Park	
6/2/1932	Scottish League Division 2	Hibernian Raith Rovers	0 1	Easter Road	
13/2/1932	Scottish League Division 2	East Stirlingshire Hibernian	4 1	Firs Park Falkirk	
20/2/1932	Scottish League Division 2	Hibernian Edinburgh City	3 1	Easter Road	
27/2/1932	Scottish League Division 2	East Fife Hibernian	1 1	Bayview	
5/3/1932	Scottish League Division 2	Hibernian Bo'ness	2 1	Easter Road	
12/3/1932	Scottish League Division 2	Brechin City Hibernian	3 3	Glebe Park	
19/3/1932	Scottish League Division 2	Hibernian Dumbarton	0 1	Easter Road	
26/3/1932	Scottish League Division 2	Albion Rovers Hibernian	1 0	Cliftonville	
2/4/1932	Scottish League Division 2	Hibernian Kings Park	2 1	Easter Road	
6/4/1932	Wilson Cup Final	Hearts Hibernian	3 1	Tynecastle	
9/4/1932	Scottish League Division 2	Queen of the South Hibernian	2 3	Palmerston Park	
16/4/1932	Scottish League Division 2	Dunfermline Hibernian	1 1	East End Park	

HIBERNIAN RESULTS 1914–1946

Date	Fixture	Teams and Score		Venue	Notes
20/4/1932	Edinburgh City Cup 1st Round	Hibernian Edinburgh City	3 0	Easter Road	
23/4/1932	Dunedin Cup Semi Final	Hibernian Falkirk	1 1	Easter Road	
27/4/1932	Dunedin Cup Semi Final Replay	Hibernian Falkirk	0 3	Easter Road	
30/4/1932	Edinburgh City Cup Semi Final	St Bernard's Hibernian	3 0	Royal Gymnasium Park	
7/5/1932	Rosebery Charity Cup Semi Final	Hibernian Leith Athletic	3 4	Easter Road	

Season 1932–33

Date	Fixture	Teams and Score		Venue	Notes
29/7/1932	Public Practice Match	Hibernian (Greens) Hibernian (Whites)	4 1	Easter Road	
5/8/1932	Public Practice Match	Hibernian (Greens) Hibernian (Whites)	2 3	Easter Road	
13/8/1932	Scottish League Division 2	Hibernian Dundee United	2 0	Easter Road	
17/8/1932	Scottish League Division 2	Hibernian Leith Athletic	2 1	Easter Road	
20/8/1932	Scottish League Division 2	Albion Rovers Hibernian	2 0	Cliftonville	
24/8/1932	Scottish League Division 2	Hibernian Montrose	4 1	Easter Road	
27/8/1932	Scottish League Division 2	Hibernian East Fife	2 1	Easter Road	
31/8/1932	East of Scotland Shield Final	Hearts Hibernian	4 0	Tynecastle	
3/9/1932	Scottish League Division 2	Dunfermline Ath Hibernian	2 2	East End Park	
10/9/1932	Scottish League Division 2	Hibernian Leith Athletic	3 0	Easter Road	
15/9/1932	Scottish League Division 2	Armadale Hibernian	2 4	Volunteer Park	
17/9/1932	Scottish League Division 2	Brechin City Hibernian	2 4	Glebe Park	
24/9/1932	Scottish League Division 2	Hibernian Kings Park	0 1	Easter Road	
1/10/1932	Scottish League Division 2	Arbroath Hibernian	0 3	Gayfield Park	
8/10/1932	Scottish League Division 2	Hibernian Bo'ness	7 0	Easter Road	

THE MAKING OF HIBERNIAN 3

Date	Fixture	Teams and Score		Venue	Notes
15/10/1932	Scottish League Division 2	Edinburgh City Hibernian	0 4	Powderhall	
22/10/1932	Scottish League Division 2	Alloa Athletic Hibernian	0 3	Recreation Park	
29/10/1932	Scottish League Division 2	Hibernian Raith Rovers	2 1	Easter Road	
5/11/1932	Scottish League Division 2	Montrose Hibernian	1 3	Links Park	
12/11/1932	Scottish League Division 2	Hibernian Armadale	8 2	Easter Road	
19/11/1932	Scottish League Division 2	St Bernard's Hibernian	0 1	Royal Gymnasium Park	
26/11/1932	Scottish League Division 2	Hibernian Stenhousemuir	4 1	Easter Road	
3/12/1932	Scottish League Division 2	Dumbarton Hibernian	3 2	Boghead	
10/12/1932	Scottish League Division 2	Queen of the South Hibernian	0 0	Palmerston	
17/12/1932	Scottish League Division 2	Hibernian Forfar Athletic	2 0	Easter Road	
24/12/1932	Scottish League Division 2	Dundee United Hibernian	0 2	Tannadice	
26/12/1932	Wilson Cup Final	Hibernian Hearts	3 2	Easter Road	
31/12/1932	Scottish League Division 2	Hibernian Albion Rovers	2 1	Easter Road	
2/1/1933	Scottish League Division 2	Leith Athletic Hibernian	0 1	Marine Gardens	
3/1/1933	Scottish League Division 2	Hibernian Brechin City	3 1	Easter Road	
7/1/1933	Scottish League Division 2	East Fife Hibernian	0 5	Bayview	
14/1/1933	Scottish League Division 2	Hibernian Dunfermline	3 1	Easter Road	
21/1/1933	Scottish Cup 1st Round	Hibernian Forfar	2 2	Easter Road	
26/1/1933	Scottish Cup 1st Round Replay	Forfar Hibernian	3 7	Station Park	
28/1/1933	Scottish League Division 2	Kings Park Hibernian	0 0	Forthbank Park Stirling	
4/2/1933	Scottish Cup 2nd Round	Aberdeen Hibernian	1 1	Pittodrie	
8/2/1933	Scottish Cup 2nd Round Replay	Hibernian Aberdeen	1 0	Easter Road	

HIBERNIAN RESULTS 1914–1946

Date	Fixture	Teams and Score		Venue	Notes
11/2/1933	Scottish League Division 2	Hibernian Arbroath	2 0	Easter Road	
18/2/1933	Scottish League Division 2	Hibernian Edinburgh City	7 1	Easter Road	Hibernian would have been playing Scottish Cup 3rd Round tie today but they got a bye. This league match brought forward from 4 March
4/3/1933	Scottish Cup Quarter Final	Hibernian Hearts	0 0	Easter Road	
8/3/1933	Scottish Cup Quarter Final Replay	Hearts Hibernian	2 0	Tynecastle	
11/3/1933	Scottish League Division 2	Hibernian Alloa Athletic	1 0	Easter Road	
18/3/1933	Scottish League Division 2	Raith Rovers Hibernian	1 2	Starks Park	
25/3/1933	Scottish League Division 2	Hibernian St Bernard's	4 1	Easter Road	
1/4/1933	Dunedin Cup Semi Final	Hibernian Raith Rovers	4 2	Easter Road	
8/4/1933	Scottish League Division 2	Stenhousemuir Hibernian	3 2	Ochilview Park Larbert	
15/4/1933	Scottish League Division 2	Hibernian Dumbarton	1 0	Easter Road	
18/4/1933	Edinburgh City Cup 1st Round	Hibernian Edinburgh City	2 1	Easter Road	
19/4/1933	Benefit in aid of Granton Trawler Disaster Fund	Hearts/Hibernian Select Celtic/Rangers Select	2 3	Tynecastle	
22/4/1933	Scottish League Division 2	Hibernian Queen of the South	0 1	Easter Road	
26/3/1933	Dunedin Cup Final	Hearts Hibernian	1 0	Tynecastle	
29/4/1933	Scottish League Division 2	Forfar Athletic Hibernian	3 3	Station Park	
6/5/1933	Rosebery Charity 'Jubilee' Cup Semi Final	Hibernian Motherwell	0 1	Easter Road	50th-year jubilee of the competition Motherwell were allowed to play for the first time

273

Date	Fixture	Teams and Score		Venue	Notes
		Season 1933–34			
1/8/1933	Public Practice Match	Hibernian (Greens) Hibernian (Whites)	1 1	Easter Road	
5/8/1933	Public Practice Match	Hibernian (Greens) Hibernian (Whites)	3 2	Easter Road	Half-hour each way only played
12/8/1933	Scottish League	Queen's Park Hibernian	2 1	Hampden	
15/8/1933	East of Scotland Shield Semi Final	Hibernian Leith Athletic	2 2	Easter Road	
19/8/1933	Scottish League	Hibernian Rangers	0 0	Easter Road	
23/8/1933	Scottish League	Cowdenbeath Hibernian	2 4	Central Park	
25/8/1933	Scottish League	Hamilton Accies Hibernian	4 1	Douglas Park	Match brought forward from 26 Aug to avoid clash with Hamilton Horse Racing Meeting
30/8/1933	East of Scotland Shield Semi Final Replay	Hibernian Leith Athletic	4 1	Easter Road	
2/9/1933	Scottish League	Hibernian Kilmarnock	4 1	Easter Road	
9/9/1933	Scottish League	Hearts Hibernian	0 0	Tynecastle	
13/9/1933	Scottish League	Hibernian Motherwell	0 2	Easter Road	
16/9/1933	Scottish League	Hibernian Clyde	3 0	Easter Road	
23/9/1933	Scottish League	Aberdeen Hibernian	2 1	Pittodrie	
30/9/1933	Scottish League	Hibernian St Johnstone	2 6	Easter Road	
2/10/1933	Friendly	Vale of Leithen Hibernian	5 6	Victoria Park Innerleithen	Hibernian team mostly reserves
7/10/1933	Scottish League	Queen of the South Hibernian	1 0	Palmerston Park	
9/10/1933	Friendly	Selkirk FC Hibernian	0 5	Ettrick Park	Hibernian team mostly reserves
14/10/1933	Scottish League	Hibernian Falkirk	1 3	Easter Road	
21/10/1933	Scottish League	Hibernian St Mirren	2 1	Easter Road	

HIBERNIAN RESULTS 1914–1946

Date	Fixture	Teams and Score		Venue	Notes
28/10/1933	Scottish League	Celtic Hibernian	2 1	Parkhead	
4/11/1933	Scottish League	Hibernian Cowdenbeath	6 1	Easter Road	
11/11/1933	Scottish League	Motherwell Hibernian	2 1	Fir Park	
18/11/1933	Scottish League	Partick Thistle Hibernian	3 2	Firhill	
25/11/1933	Scottish League	Airdrie Hibernian	0 3	Broomfield	
2/12/1933	Scottish League	Hibernian Ayr United	0 0	Easter Road	
9/12/1933	Scottish League	Third Lanark Hibernian	1 0	Cathkin	
16/12/1933	Scottish League	Hibernian Dundee	2 1	Easter Road	
23/12/1933	Scottish League	Hibernian Queen's Park	2 	Easter Road	
30/12/1993	Scottish League	Rangers Hibernian	6 0	Ibrox	
1/1/1934	Scottish League	Hibernian Hearts	1 4	Easter Road	
2/1/1934	Scottish League	St Johnstone Hibernian	0 1	Muirton Park	
6/1/1934	Scottish League	Hibernian Hamilton Accies	1 2	Easter Road	
13/1/1934	Scottish League	Kilmarnock Hibernian	2 0	Rugby Park	
20/1/1934	Scottish Cup 1st Round	Hibernian Clyde	5 4	Easter Road	
27/1/1934	Scottish League	Hibernian Aberdeen	3 2	Easter Road	
3/2/1934	Scottish Cup 2nd Round	Hibernian Alloa Athletic	6 0	Easter Road	Match was to have been played at Alloa but after Hibernian made a financial offer match was switched to Easter Road
10/2/1934	East of Scotland Shield Final	Hearts Hibernian	4 0	Tynecastle	
17/2/1934	Scottish Cup 3rd Round	Hibernian Aberdeen	0 1	Easter Road	
24/2/1934	Scottish League	Hibernian Queen of the South	0 2	Easter Road	

275

Date	Fixture	Teams and Score		Venue	Notes
3/3/1934	Scottish League	Falkirk	3	Brockville	
		Hibernian	1		
10/3/1934	Scottish League	St Mirren	0	Love Street	
		Hibernian	3		
17/3/1934	Scottish League	Hibernian	1	Easter Road	
		Celtic	2		
24/3/1934	Scottish League	Hibernian	0	Easter Road	
		Partick Thistle	2		
31/3/1934	Scottish League	Hibernian	0	Easter Road	
		Airdrie	2		
7/4/1934	Scottish League	Ayr United	4	Somerset Park	
		Hibernian	1		
14/4/1934	Scottish League	Clyde	1	Shawfield	
		Hibernian	0		
21/4/1934	Scottish League	Hibernian	3	Easter Road	
		Third Lanark	1		
23/4/1934	North of Scotland Tour Friendly	Elgin City	0	Elgin	
		Hibernian	4		
24/4/1934	North of Scotland Tour Friendly	Fraserburgh	2	Fraserburgh	
		Hibernian	2		
25/4/1934	North of Scotland Tour Friendly	Inverness Thistle	1	Kingmills Park Inverness	
		Hibernian	2		
26/4/1934	Benefit in aid of East of Scotland League Trophy Fund	East of Scotland League Select	2	Victoria Park Innerleithen	
		Hibernian	3		
28/4/1934	Scottish League	Dundee	1	Dens Park	
		Hibernian	0		
30/4/1934	Wilson Cup Final	Hibernian	0	Easter Road	
		Hearts	2		
2/5/1934	Rosebery Charity Cup 1st Round	Hibernian	1	Easter Road	
		St Bernard's	0		
5/5/1934	Rosebery Charity Cup Semi Final	Hibernian	2	Easter Road	
		St Johnstone	1		
12/5/1934	Rosebery Charity Cup Final	Hearts	2	Tynecastle	
		Hibernian	1		

Season 1934–35

Date	Fixture	Teams and Score		Venue	Notes
4/8/1934	Public Practise Match	Hibernian (Greens)	0	Easter Road	
		Hibernian (Stripes)	2		
11/8/1934	Scottish League	Hibernian	3	Easter Road	
		Hamilton Accies	1		
14/8/1934	East of Scotland Shield Semi Final	Hibernian	3	Easter Road	
		Leith Athletic	0		

HIBERNIAN RESULTS 1914–1946

Date	Fixture	Teams and Score		Venue	Notes
18/8/1934	Scottish League	Kilmarnock Hibernian	0 1	Rugby Park	
22/8/1934	Scottish League	Hibernian St Mirren	0 0	Easter Road	
25/8/1934	Scottish League	Hibernian Aberdeen	2 3	Easter Road	
1/9/1934	Scottish League	St Johnstone Hibernian	2 0	Muirton Park	
8/9/1934	Scottish League	Hibernian Hearts	1 0	Easter Road	
11/9/1934	Scottish League	Celtic Hibernian	4 0	Parkhead	
15/9/1934	Scottish League	Clyde Hibernian	3 2	Shawfield	
17/9/1934	Benefit in aid of J. Kilner of Peebles Rovers	Peebles Rovers Hibernian	1 4	Whitestone Park	
22/9/1934	Scottish League	Hibernian Queen of the South	1 1	Easter Road	
29/9/1934	Scottish League	Rangers Hibernian	4 2	Ibrox	
6/10/1934	Scottish League	Hibernian Queen's Park	5 1	Easter Road	
13/10/1934	Scottish League	Albion Rovers Hibernian	2 0	Cliftonhill	
20/10/1934	Scottish League	Dunfermline Hibernian	2 1	East End Park	
27/10/1934	Scottish League	Hibernian Motherwell	1 1	Easter Road	
3/11/1934	Scottish League	Hibernian Partick Thistle	2 0	Easter Road	
10/11/1934	Scottish League	Hibernian Airdrie	2 2	Easter Road	
17/11/1934	Scottish League	Ayr United Hibernian	1 1	Somerset Park	
24/11/1934	Scottish League	Hibernian Falkirk	2 0	Easter Road	
1/12/1934	Scottish League	Dundee Hibernian	0 2	Dens Park	
8/12/1934	Scottish League	St Mirren Hibernian	1 2	Love Street	
15/12/1934	Scottish League	Hibernian Celtic	3 2	Easter Road	
22/12/1934	Scottish League	Hamilton Accies Hibernian	2 1	Douglas Park	

Date	Fixture	Teams and Score		Venue	Notes
29/12/1934	Scottish League	Hibernian Kilmarnock	1 0	Easter Road	
1/1/1935	Scottish League	Hearts Hibernian	5 2	Tynecastle	
2/1/1935	Scottish League	Hibernian St Johnstone	1 1	Easter Road	
3/1/1935	Friendly	Hibernian Scottish Junior Select	6 2	Easter Road	
5/1/1935	Scottish League	Aberdeen Hibernian	2 0	Pittodrie	
12/1/1935	Scottish League	Hibernian Clyde	4 0	Easter Road	
19/1/1935	Scottish League	Queen of the South Hibernian	0 2	Palmerston	
23/1/1935	Scottish Cup 1st Round	Hibernian Vale of Atholl	5 0	Easter Road	Match should have been played at Pitlochry but Hibernian made a financial offer to switch the match to Easter Road. Also match brought forward from 26 Feb
2/2/1935	Scottish League	Hibernian Rangers	1 2	Easter Road	
9/2/1935	Scottish Cup 2nd Round	Hibernian Clachnacuddin	7 1	Easter Road	
23/2/1935	Scottish Cup 3rd Round	Aberdeen Hibernian	0 0	Pittodrie	
27/2/1935	Scottish Cup 3rd Round Replay	Hibernian Aberdeen	1 1	Easter Road	
2/3/1935	Scottish League	Hibernian Albion Rovers	3 3	Easter Road	
4/3/1935	Scottish Cup 3rd Round 2nd Replay	Hibernian Aberdeen	2 3	Easter Road	
9/3/1935	Scottish League	Hibernian Dunfermline	3 1	Easter Road	
16/3/1935	Scottish League	Motherwell Hibernian	4 1	Fir Park	
23/3/1935	Scottish League	Partick Thistle Hibernian	3 1	Firhill	
29/3/1935	Scottish League	Airdrie Hibernian	7 0	Broomfield	Match brought forward from Sat 30 March to avoid clash with Scottish Cup ties

HIBERNIAN RESULTS 1914–1946

Date	Fixture	Teams and Score		Venue	Notes
13/4/1935	Scottish League	Hibernian Ayr United	1 1	Easter Road	
15/4/1935	Scottish League	Queen's Park Hibernian	3 1	Hampden	
20/4/1935	Scottish League	Falkirk Hibernian	5 2	Brockville	
23/4/1935	East of Scotland Shield Final	Hibernian Hearts	4 2	Easter Road	
27/4/1935	Scottish League	Hibernian Dundee	2 1	Easter Road	
30/4/1935	Wilson Cup Final	Hearts Hibernian	4 0	Tynecastle	
4/5/1935	Rosebery Charity Cup 1st Round	Hibernian Dunfermline Ath	2 3	Easter Road	

Season 1935–36

Date	Fixture	Teams and Score		Venue	Notes
2/8/1935	Public Practise Match	Hibernian (Greens) Hibernian (Stripes)	2 1	Easter Road	
10/8/1935	Scottish League	Queen of the South Hibernian	1 1	Palmerston Park	
12/8/1935	Friendly	Edinburgh City and Queen's Park Select Hibernian/Hearts Select	0 2	City Park East Pilton Edinburgh	
14/8/1935	Wilson Cup Final	Hibernian Hearts	3 4	Easter Road	
17/8/1935	Scottish League	Hibernian Clyde	1 1	Easter Road	
21/8/1935	East of Scotland Shield Semi Final	St Bernard's Hibernian	1 1	Royal Gymnasium Park	
24/8/1935	Scottish League	Aberdeen Hibernian	3 1	Pittodrie	
28/8/1935	Scottish League	Hibernian Arbroath	0 2	Easter Road	
31/8/1935	Scottish League	Hibernian St Johnstone	0 2	Easter Road	
4/9/1935	East of Scotland Shield Semi Final Replay	Hibernian St Bernard's	0 0	Easter Road	
7/9/1935	Scottish League	Queen's Park Hibernian	6 1	Hampden	

THE MAKING OF HIBERNIAN 3

Date	Fixture	Teams and Score		Venue	Notes
14/9/1935	Scottish League	Hibernian Rangers	1 1	Easter Road	
18/9/1935	Scottish League	Hibernian Airdrie	2 3	Easter Road	
21/9/1935	Scottish League	Hearts Hibernian	8 3	Tynecastle	
28/9/1935	Scottish League	Hibernian Kilmarnock	3 1	Easter Road	
5/10/1935	Scottish League	Hamilton Accies Hibernian	2 3	Douglas Park	
12/10/1935	Scottish League	Hibernian Albion Rovers	3 0	Easter Road	
19/10/1935	Scottish League	Hibernian Dundee	2 1	Easter Road	
26/10/1935	Scottish League	Partick Thistle Hibernian	2 1	Firhill	
2/11/1935	Scottish League	Ayr United Hibernian	3 0	Somerset Park	
9/11/1935	Scottish League	Hibernian Celtic	0 5	Easter Road	
16/11/1935	Scottish League	Third Lanark Hibernian	1 1	Cathkin	
23/11/1935	Scottish League	Hibernian Motherwell	2 3	Easter Road	
30/11/1935	Scottish League	Hibernian Dunfermline	2 3	Easter Road	
7/12/1935	Scottish League	Arbroath Hibernian	3 2	Gayfield Park	
14/12/1935	Scottish League	Airdrie Hibernian	3 2	Broomfield	
21/12/1935	Scottish League	Hibernian Queen of the South	3 0	Easter Road	
28/12/1935	Scottish League	Clyde Hibernian	7 4	Shawfield	
1/1/1936	Scottish League	Hibernian Hearts	1 1	Easter Road	
2/1/1936	Scottish League	St Johnstone Hibernian	2 2	Muirton Park	
4/1/1936	Scottish League	Hibernian Aberdeen	1 4	Easter Road	
11/1/1936	Scottish League	Hibernian Queen's Park	0 1	Easter Road	
1/2/1936	Scottish Cup 1st Round	Vale Ocoba Hibernian	1 3	Millburn Park Alexandria	

HIBERNIAN RESULTS 1914–1946

Date	Fixture	Teams and Score		Venue	Notes
8/2/1936	Scottish Cup 2nd Round	Clyde Hibernian	4 1	Shawfield	
15/2/1936	Scottish League	Hibernian Hamilton Accies	3 2	Easter Road	
29/2/1936	Scottish League	Albion Rovers Hibernian	0 1	Cliftonhill	
7/3/1936	Scottish League	Dundee Hibernian	2 1	Dens Park	
14/3/1936	Scottish League	Hibernian Partick Thistle	2 0	Easter Road	
18/3/1936	Scottish League	Rangers Hibernian	3 0	Ibrox	
21/3/1936	Scottish League	Hibernian Ayr United	0 1	Easter Road	
28/3/1936	Scottish League	Celtic Hibernian	4 1	Parkhead	
8/4/1936	Scottish League	Kilmarnock Hibernian	0 1	Rugby Park	
11/4/1936	Scottish League	Hibernian Third Lanark	3 0	Easter Road	
18/4/1936	Scottish League	Motherwell Hibernian	1 1	Fir Park	
25/4/1936	Scottish League	Dunfermline Ath Hibernian	0 1	East End Park	
27/4/1936	East of Scotland Shield Semi Final 2nd replay	St Bernard's Hibernian	3 2	Tynecastle	Match played at neutral ground
6/5/1936	Rosebery Charity Cup Semi Final	Hibernian St Bernard's	2 3	Easter Road	

Season 1936–37

Date	Fixture	Teams and Score		Venue	Notes
1/8/1936	Public Practice Match	Hibernian (Greens) Hibernian (White)	3 0	Easter Road	
8/8/1936	Scottish League	Hibernian Aberdeen	1 3	Easter Road	
12/8/1936	Wilson Cup Final	Hearts Hibernian	3 2	Tynecastle	
15/8/1936	Scottish League	Albion Rovers Hibernian	4 0	Easter Road	
17/8/1936	Friendly	Hibernian Austria FC	2 3	Easter Road	
19/8/1936	Scottish League	Aberdeen Hibernian	1 1	Pittodrie	

Date	Fixture	Teams and Score		Venue	Notes
22/8/1936	Scottish League	Hibernian Queen's Park	2 3	Easter Road	
27/8/1936	Benefit in aid of Portobello Renton FC funds	Portobello Renton Hibernian	1 4	Woods Park	
29/8/1936	Scottish League	Rangers Hibernian	4 0	Ibrox	
1/9/1936	East of Scotland Shield Semi Final	St Bernard's Hibernian	0 1	Royal Gymnasium Park	
5/9/1936	Scottish League	Hibernian Hamilton Accies	5 4	Easter Road	
9/9/1936	Scottish League	Hibernian Albion Rovers	1 1	Easter Road	
12/9/1936	Scottish League	Kilmarnock Hibernian	3 2	Rugby Park	
17/9/1936	Friendly	Chirnside United Hibernian	0 7	Chirnside	
19/9/1936	Scottish League	Hibernian Hearts	3 3	Easter Road	
26/9/1936	Scottish League	Clyde Hibernian	1 3	Shawfield	
3/10/1936	Scottish League	Hibernian Queen of the South	2 2	Easter Road	
10/10/1936	Scottish League	St Johnstone Hibernian	3 1	Muirton Park	
12/10/1936	Benefit in aid of Selkirk FC new pavilion building fund	Selkirk FC Hibernian	1 2	Ettrick Park	
17/10/1936	Scottish League	Hibernian St Mirren	0 0	Easter Road	
24/10/1936	Scottish League	Celtic Hibernian	5 1	Parkhead	
31/10/1936	Scottish League	Hibernian Third Lanark	0 1	Easter Road	
7/11/1936	Scottish League	Motherwell Hibernian	3 4	Fir Park	
14/11/1936	Scottish League	Dunfermline Hibernian	2 3	East End Park	
21/11/1936	Scottish League	Hibernian Arbroath	4 1	Easter Road	
28/11/1936	Scottish League	Hibernian Falkirk	2 2	Easter Road	
5/12/1936	Scottish League	Dundee Hibernian	3 1	Dens Park	

HIBERNIAN RESULTS 1914–1946

Date	Fixture	Teams and Score		Venue	Notes
12/12/1936	Scottish League	Hibernian Partick Thistle	2 2	Easter Road	
19/12/1936	Scottish League	Queen's Park Hibernian	2 0	Hampden	
26/12/1936	Scottish League	Hibernian Rangers	1 4	Easter Road	
1/1/1937	Scottish League	Hearts Hibernian	3 2	Tynecastle	
2/1/1937	Scottish League	Hibernian St Johnstone	3 3	Easter Road	
9/12/1937	Scottish League	Hamilton Accies Hibernian	4 1	Douglas Park	
16/1/1937	Scottish League	Hibernian Kilmarnock	0 0	Easter Road	
23/1/1937	Scottish League	Queen of the South Hibernian	1 0	Palmerston Park	
2/2/1937	Scottish Cup 1st Round	Alloa Athletic Hibernian	2 5	Recreation Park	
6/2/1937	Scottish League	Hibernian Clyde	0 1	Easter Road	
13/2/1937	Scottish Cup 2nd Round	Hamilton Accies Hibernian	2 1	Douglas Park	
20/2/1937	Scottish League	St Mirren Hibernian	1 3	Love Street	
6/3/1937	Scottish League	Hibernian Celtic	2 2	Easter Road	
20/3/1937	Scottish League	Hibernian Motherwell	1 2	Easter Road	
27/3/1937	Scottish League	Hibernian Dunfermline	0 0	Easter Road	
29/3/1937	Scottish League	Third Lanark Hibernian	1 1	Cathkin	
3/4/1937	Scottish League	Arbroath Hibernian	1 0	Gayfield	
10/4/1937	Scottish League	Falkirk Hibernian	4 1	Brockville	
17/4/1937	East of Scotland Shield Final	Hearts Hibernian	6 2	Tynecastle	
19/4/1937	Scottish League	Hibernian Dundee	0 0	Easter Road	
21/4/1937	Scottish League	Partick Thistle Hibernian	3 1	Firhill	Match brought forward from 24 April
22/4/1937	Benefit in aid of East of Scotland Junior league funds	East of Scotland Junior Select Hibernian	0 0	Peebles	

Date	Fixture	Teams and Score		Venue	Notes
26/4/1937	Edinburgh City Cup 1st Round	Hibernian Duns	2 2	Easter Road	
8/5/1937	Rosebery Charity Cup Semi Final	Hibernian Leith Athletic	3 1	Easter Road	
12/5/1937	King George VI Coronation Day Challenge match	Glasgow Select Hibernian and Edinburgh Select	2 0	Hampden	
15/5/1937	Rosebery Charity Cup Final	Hearts Hibernian	2 0	Tynecastle	

Season 1937–38

Date	Fixture	Teams and Score		Venue	Notes
4/8/1937	Public Practice Match	Hibernian (Greens) Hibernian (Whites)	4 2	Easter Road	
7/8/1937	Public Practice Match	Hibernian (Greens) Hibernian (Whites)	1 3	Easter Road	
14/8/1937	Scottish League	Queen's Park Hibernian	1 1	Hampden	
18/8/1937	Wilson Cup Final	Hibernian Hearts	1 4	Easter Road	
21/8/1937	Scottish League	Hibernian Rangers	0 0	Easter Road	
25/8/1937	Scottish League	Hibernian Queen's Park	0 2	Easter Road	
27/8/1937	Scottish League	Hamilton Accies Hibernian	4 0	Douglas Park	Match brought forward from 28 Aug to avoid clash with Hamilton Horse Racing Meeting
4/9/1937	Scottish League	Hibernian Kilmarnock	1 1	Easter Road	
8/9/1937	Borders Charity Cup benefit in aid of the borders football clubs funds	Hearts Hibernian	3 3	Raid Stane Haugh Park Galashiels	
8/9/1937	Benefit in aid of Peter McGinn an old Hibernian player	Celtic Hibernian	2 3	Townhead Park Cumnock	
11/9/1937	Scottish League	Hearts Hibernian	3 2	Tynecastle	

HIBERNIAN RESULTS 1914–1946

Date	Fixture	Teams and Score		Venue	Notes
13/9/1937	Benefit in aid of Bonnyrigg Rose Athletic opening new pavilion	Bonnyrigg Rose Athletic Hibernian	2 1	Bonnyrigg	
15/9/1937	Scottish League	Rangers Hibernian	2 0	Ibrox	
18/9/1937	Scottish League	Hibernian Clyde	6 3	Easter Road	
20/9/1937	East of Scotland Shield Semi Final	Leith Athletic Hibernian	0 2	Meadowbank	
25/9/1937	Scottish League	Queen of the South Hibernian	3 2	Palmerston Park	
2/10/1937	Scottish League	Hibernian Morton	4 2	Easter Road	
9/10/1937	Scottish League	Aberdeen Hibernian	5 0	Pittodrie	
16/10/1937	Scottish League	Hibernian Arbroath	5 0	Easter Road	
23/10/1937	Scottish League	Third Lanark Hibernian	1 0	Cathkin	
30/10/1937	Scottish League	Hibernian Motherwell	1 1	Easter Road	
6/11/1937	Scottish League	Hibernian Ayr United	3 0	Easter Road	
13/11/1937	Scottish League	St Johnstone Hibernian	2 0	Muirton Park	
20/11/1937	Scottish League	Falkirk Hibernian	0 0	Brockville	
27/11/1937	Scottish League	Hibernian Dundee	2 1	Easter Road	
4/12/1937	Scottish League	Partick Thistle Hibernian	4 0	Firhill	
11/12/1937	Scottish League	St Mirren Hibernian	1 0	Love Street	
18/12/1937	Scottish League	Hibernian Celtic	0 3	Easter Road	
25/12/1937	Scottish League	Hibernian Hamilton Accies	1 1	Easter Road	
29/12/1937	Scottish League	Kilmarnock Hibernian	0 3	Rugby Park	
1/1/1938	Scottish League	Hibernian Hearts	2 2	Easter Road	
3/1/1938	Scottish League	Arbroath Hibernian	3 3	Gayfield	

Date	Fixture	Teams and Score		Venue	Notes
8/1/1938	Scottish League	Clyde Hibernian	1 1	Shawfield	
15/1/1938	Scottish League	Hibernian Queen of the South	2 0	Easter Road	
22/1/1938	Scottish Cup 1st Round	Hibernian Edinburgh City	2 3	Easter Road	
29/1/1938	Scottish League	Morton Hibernian	2 4	Cappielow	
5/2/1938	Scottish League	Hibernian Aberdeen	1 1	Easter Road	
19/2/1938	Scottish League	Hibernian Third Lanark	2 2	Easter Road	
26/2/1938	Scottish League	Motherwell Hibernian	1 0	Fir Park	
12/3/1938	Scottish League	Ayr United Hibernian	1 1	Somerset Park	
19/3/1938	Scottish League	Hibernian St Johnstone	2 2	Easter Road	
26/3/1938	Scottish League	Hibernian Falkirk	2 4	Easter Road	
2/4/1938	Scottish League	Dundee Hibernian	1 2	Dens Park	
9/4/1938	Scottish League	Hibernian Partick Thistle	2 1	Easter Road	
16/4/1938	Scottish League	Hibernian St Mirren	2 1	Easter Road	
18/4/1938	East of Scotland Shield Final	Hibernian Hearts	4 0	Easter Road	
20/4/1938	Irish Tour Friendly	Belfast Distillery Hibernian	4 4	Belfast	
24/4/1938	Irish Tour Friendly	Munster Select Hibernian	1 4	Cork	
25/4/1938	Irish Tour Friendly	Waterford Hibernian	2 6	Waterford	
27/4/1938	Friendly	Cardiff City Hibernian	3 2	Ninian Park Cardiff Wales	
30/4/1938	Scottish League	Celtic Hibernian	3 0	Parkhead	
7/5/1938	Rosebery Charity Cup Semi Final	Hibernian St Bernard's	0 1	Easter Road	

HIBERNIAN RESULTS 1914–1946

Date	Fixture	Teams and Score		Venue	Notes

Season 1938–39

Date	Fixture	Teams and Score		Venue	Notes
3/8/1938	Public Practice Match	Hibernian (Greens) Hibernian (Whites)	3 4	Easter Road	
6/8/1938	Public Practice Match	Hibernian (Greens) Hibernian (Whites)	5 4	Easter Road	
13/8/1938	Scottish League	Hibernian Hamilton Accies	2 2	Easter Road	
17/8/1938	Wilson Cup Final	Hearts Hibernian	2 0	Tynecastle	
20/8/1938	Scottish League	Kilmarnock Hibernian	0 1	Rugby Park	
24/8/1938	Scottish League	Hamilton Accies Hibernian	4 1	Douglas Park	
27/8/1938	Scottish League	Hibernian Queen of the South	2 3	Easter Road	
30/8/1938	East of Scotland Shield Semi Final	Hibernian St Bernard's	2 0	Easter Road	
3/9/1938	Scottish League	Clyde Hibernian	3 0	Shawfield	
6/9/1938	Benefit in aid of Borders Football Association funds	Borders XI Hibernian/Hearts Select	0 2	Raid Stane Park Galashiels	
10/9/1938	Scottish League	Hibernian Hearts	4 0	Easter Road	
14/9/1938	Scottish League	Hibernian Kilmarnock	0 1	Easter Road	
17/9/1938	Scottish League	Albion Rovers Hibernian	0 1	Cliftonhill	
24/9/1938	Scottish League	Hibernian Aberdeen	5 0	Easter Road	
1/10/1938	Scottish League	Rangers Hibernian	5 2	Ibrox	
8/10/1938	Scottish League	Hibernian Queen's Park	3 1	Easter Road	
15/10/1938	Scottish League	Raith Rovers Hibernian	1 2	Starks Park	
22/10/1938	Scottish League	Ayr United Hibernian	3 1	Somerset Park	

Date	Fixture	Teams and Score		Venue	Notes
29/10/1938	Scottish League	Hibernian St Johnstone	5 2	Easter Road	
5/11/1938	Scottish League	Hibernian Falkirk	3 0	Easter Road	
12/11/1938	Scottish League	Arbroath Hibernian	2 4	Gayfield Park	
19/11/1938	Scottish League	Hibernian Partick Thistle	1 2	Easter Road	
26/11/1938	Scottish League	Hibernian St Mirren	6 1	Easter Road	
3/12/1938	Scottish League	Celtic Hibernian	5 4	Parkhead	
10/12/1938	Scottish League	Hibernian Third Lanark	1 1	Easter Road	
17/12/1938	Scottish League	Motherwell Hibernian	3 2	Fir Park	
24/12/1938	Scottish League	Queen of the South Hibernian	2 1	Palmerston Park	
31/12/1938	Scottish League	Hibernian Clyde	1 1	Easter Road	
2/1/1939	Scottish League	Hearts Hibernian	0 1	Tynecastle	
3/1/1939	Scottish League	Hibernian Raith Rovers	2 1	Easter Road	
7/1/1939	Scottish League	Aberdeen Hibernian	6 1	Pittodrie	
14/1/1939	Scottish League	Hibernian Rangers	1 1	Easter Road	
21/1/1939	Scottish Cup 1st Round	Forfar Athletic Hibernian	0 3	Station Park	
28/1/1939	Scottish League	Queen's Park Hibernian	2 2	Hampden	
4/2/1939	Scottish Cup 2nd Round	Hibernian Kilmarnock	3 1	Easter Road	
11/2/1939	Scottish League	Hibernian Albion Rovers	1 2	Easter Road	
25/2/1939	Scottish League	Hibernian Ayr United	2 3	Easter Road	
4/3/1939	Scottish Cup Quarter Final	Hibernian Alloa Athletic	3 1	Easter Road	
8/3/1939	Scottish League	St Johnstone Hibernian	2 1	Muirton Park	
11/3/1939	Scottish League	Falkirk Hibernian	1 1	Brockville	

HIBERNIAN RESULTS 1914–1946

Date	Fixture	Teams and Score		Venue	Notes
18/3/1939	Scottish League	Hibernian Arbroath	1 1	Easter Road	
25/3/1939	Scottish Cup Semi Final	Clyde Hibernian	1 0	Tynecastle	
27/3/1939	Scottish League	Partick Thistle Hibernian	4 0	Firhill	
1/4/1939	Scottish League	St Mirren Hibernian	0 0	Love Street	
9/4/1939	Scottish League	Hibernian Celtic	1 0	Easter Road	
10/4/1939	Friendly	Dundee United Hibernian	4 3	Tannadice	
15/4/1939	East of Scotland Shield Final	Hearts Hibernian	1 3	Tynecastle	
21/4/1939	Scottish League	Third Lanark Hibernian	2 0	Cathkin	Match brought forward from 22 April to avoid clash with Scottish Cup final at Hampden
29/4/1939	Scottish League	Hibernian Motherwell	2 1	Easter Road	
6/5/1939	Rosebery Charity Cup Semi Final	Hibernian Leith Athletic	1 2	Easter Road	

Season 1939–40

Date	Fixture	Teams and Score		Venue	Notes
5/8/1939	Public Practice Match	Hibernian (Greens) Hibernian (Whites)	7 2	Easter Road	
7/8/1939	Public Practice Match	Hibernian (Greens) Hibernian (Whites)	8 2	Easter Road	
12/8/1939	Scottish League	Queen of the South Hibernian	2 1	Palmerston Park	
16/8/1939	Wilson Cup Final	Hibernian Hearts	0 2	Easter Road	
19/8/1939	Scottish League	Hibernian Clyde	3 2	Easter Road	
23/8/1939	Scottish League	Hibernian Queen of the South	3 1	Easter Road	
26/8/1939	Scottish League	Aberdeen Hibernian	3 1	Pittodrie	
29/8/1939	East of Scotland Shield Semi Final	St Bernard's Hibernian	0 1	Royal Gymnasium Park	
2/9/1939	Scottish League	Hibernian Albion Rovers	3 5	Easter Road	

THE MAKING OF HIBERNIAN 3

Date	Fixture	Teams and Score		Venue	Notes
23/9/1939	Friendly	Hearts Hibernian	2 4	Tynecastle	
30/9/1939	Friendly	Hibernian St Mirren	5 1	Easter Road	
7/10/1939	Friendly	St Mirren Hibernian	3 3	Love Street	
14/10/1939	Friendly	Hibernian Leith Athletic	3 3	Easter Road	Hibernian team mostly reserves
21/10/1939	Scottish Regional League Eastern Section	Dundee Hibernian	2 1	Dens Park	New league set up due to war two leagues east and west both of 16 teams
26/10/1939	Scottish Regional League Eastern Section	Hibernian St Johnstone	3 3	Easter Road	
4/11/1939	Scottish Regional League Eastern Section	Aberdeen Hibernian	3 3	Pittodrie	
11/11/1939	Scottish Regional League Eastern Section	Hibernian Stenhousemuir	1 2	Easter Road	
18/11/1939	Scottish Regional League Eastern Section	Kings Park Hibernian	2 7	Forthbank Park	
25/11/1939	Scottish Regional League Eastern Section	Hibernian East Fife	2 5	Easter Road	
2/12/1939	Scottish Regional League Eastern Section	Falkirk Hibernian	3 3	Brockville	
9/12/1939	Scottish Regional League Eastern Section	Hibernian Dundee United	6 2	Easter Road	
16/12/1939	Scottish Regional League Eastern Section	Arbroath Hibernian	0 0	Gayfield	
23/12/1939	Scottish Regional League Eastern Section	Hibernian Alloa Athletic	3 0	Easter Road	
30/12/1939	Scottish Regional League Eastern Section	St Bernard's Hibernian	1 6	Royal Gymnasium Park	
1/1/1940	Scottish Regional League Eastern Section	Hibernian Hearts	5 6	Easter Road	

HIBERNIAN RESULTS 1914–1946

Date	Fixture	Teams and Score		Venue	Notes
2/1/1940	Scottish Regional League Eastern Section	Cowdenbeath Hibernian	0 4	Central Park	
6/1/1940	Scottish Regional League Eastern Section	Hibernian Raith Rovers	4 1	Easter Road	
13/1/1940	Scottish Regional League Eastern Section	Dunfermline Hibernian	2 1	East End Park	
17/2/1940	Scottish Regional League Eastern Section	Hibernian Kings Park	2 1	Easter Road	
24/2/1940	Scottish War Emergency Cup 1st Round 1st Leg	Falkirk Hibernian	5 0	Brockville	New Scottish Cup set up due to war
2/3/1940	Scottish War Emergency Cup 1st Round 2nd Leg	Hibernian Falkirk	4 0	Easter Road	
16/3/1940	Scottish Regional League Eastern Section	Hibernian Arbroath	2 4	Easter Road	
23/3/1940	Scottish Regional League Eastern Section	Alloa Athletic Hibernian	2 3	Recreation Park	
27/3/1940	Scottish Regional League Eastern Section	Stenhousemuir Hibernian	2 1	Ochilview Park Larbert	
30/3/1940	Scottish Regional League Eastern Section	Hibernian St Bernard's	3 1	Easter Road	
3/4/1940	Scottish Regional League Eastern Section	Hibernian Dundee	6 0	Easter Road	
6/4/1940	Scottish Regional League Eastern Section	Hearts Hibernian	4 0	Tynecastle	
10/4/1940	Scottish Regional League Eastern Section	St Johnstone Hibernian	4 0	Muirton Park	
13/4/1940	Scottish Regional League Eastern Section	East Fife Hibernian	4 3	Bayview	
20/4/1940	Scottish Regional League Eastern Section	Raith Rovers Hibernian	1 1	Starks Park	

Date	Fixture	Teams and Score		Venue	Notes
27/4/1940	Scottish Regional League Eastern Section	Hibernian Dunfermline	2 3	Easter Road	
4/5/1940	Scottish Regional League Eastern Section	Hibernian Falkirk	5 6	Easter Road	
6/5/1940	Benefit in aid of Red Cross funds	Hibernian/Hearts/ St Bernard's Select British Army XI	6 2	Tynecastle	Five Hibernian players in select team
11/5/1940	Scottish Regional League	Dundee United Hibernian	1 3	Tannadice	
15/5/1940	East of Scotland Shield Final	Hibernian Hearts	2 3	Easter Road	
16/5/1940	Scottish Regional League Eastern Section	Hibernian Aberdeen	2 0	Easter Road	
29/5/1940	Rosebery Charity Cup Semi Final	Hibernian St Bernard's	2 2	Easter Road	Hibernian won by 6 corners to 2
1/6/1940	Rosebery Charity Cup Final	Hearts Hibernian	2 5	Tynecastle	

Season 1940–41

Date	Fixture	Teams and Score		Venue	Notes
3/8/1940	Public Practice Match	Hibernian (Greens) Hibernian (Whites)	9 3	Easter Road	
10/8/1940	Scottish Southern League	Hibernian Queen's Park	3 2	Easter Road	New 16-team war league
14/8/1940	Wilson Cup Final	Hearts Hibernian	3 2	Tynecastle	
17/8/1940	Scottish Southern League	Rangers Hibernian	5 1	Ibrox	
24/8/1940	Scottish Southern League	Hibernian Morton	2 1	Easter Road	
31/8/1940	Scottish Southern League	Clyde Hibernian	2 1	Shawfield	
7/9/1940	Scottish Southern League	Hibernian Hearts	2 1	Easter Road	
14/9/1940	Scottish Southern League	Hamilton Accies Hibernian	2 3	Douglas Park	
21/9/1940	Scottish Southern League	Hibernian Albion Rovers	1 1	Easter Road	
28/9/1940	Scottish Southern League	Dumbarton Hibernian	2 0	Boghead	

HIBERNIAN RESULTS 1914–1946

Date	Fixture	Teams and Score		Venue	Notes
5/10/1940	Scottish Southern League	Hibernian Partick Thistle	4 0	Easter Road	
12/10/1940	Scottish Southern League	St Mirren Hibernian	4 4	Love Street	
19/10/1940	Scottish Southern League	Hibernian Third Lanark	2 2	Easter Road	
26/10/1940	Scottish Southern League	Celtic Hibernian	0 4	Parkhead	
2/11/1940	Scottish Southern League	Hibernian Motherwell	3 3	Easter Road	
9/11/1940	Scottish Southern League	Hibernian Falkirk	7 1	Easter Road	
16/11/1940	Scottish Southern League	Airdrie Hibernian	4 2	Broomfield	
23/11/1940	Scottish Southern League	Queen's Park Hibernian	2 5	Hampden	
30/11/1940	Scottish Southern League	Hibernian Rangers	1 0	Easter Road	
7/12/1940	Scottish Southern League	Morton Hibernian	3 1	Cappielow	
14/12/1940	Scottish Southern League	Hibernian Clyde	2 2	Easter Road	
21/12/1940	Scottish Southern League	Albion Rovers Hibernian	4 3	Cliftonhill	
28/12/1940	Scottish Southern League	Hibernian Hamilton Accies	3 1	Easter Road	
4/1/1941	Scottish Southern League	Partick Thistle Hibernian	1 2	Firhill	
11/1/1941	Scottish Southern League	Hibernian St Mirren	2 4	Easter Road	
25/1/1941	Scottish Southern League	Third Lanark Hibernian	3 2	Cathkin	
1/2/1941	Scottish Southern League	Hibernian Celtic	2 0	Easter Road	
8/2/1941	Scottish Southern League	Motherwell Hibernian	3 0	Fir Park	
15/2/1941	Scottish Southern League	Falkirk Hibernian	2 2	Brockville	
1/3/1941	Scottish Southern League War Cup (Section 4) 1st Round 1st Leg	Clyde Hibernian	2 4	Shawfield	New Scottish Cup competition set up due to war

Date	Fixture	Teams and Score		Venue	Notes
8/3/1941	Scottish Southern League War Cup (Section 4) 1st Round 2nd Leg	Hibernian Hearts	3 2	Easter Road	
15/3/1941	Scottish Southern League War Cup (Section 4) 1st Round 3rd Leg	Queen's Park Hibernian	2 1	Hampden	
22/3/1941	Scottish Southern League War Cup (Section 4) 1st Round 4th Leg	Hibernian Clyde	5 4	Easter Road	
29/3/1941	Scottish Southern League War Cup (Section 4) 1st Round 5th Leg	Hearts Hibernian	5 2	Tynecastle	
5/4/1941	Scottish Southern League War Cup (Section 4) 1st Round 6th Leg	Hibernian Queen's Park	0 0	Easter Road	
12/4/1941	Scottish Southern League	Hibernian Airdrie	2 2	Easter Road	
14/4/1941	Benefit in aid of official opening of Lochie Harps ground	Scottish Junior Select Hibernian and Hearts select	3 2	Beechwood Park	Seven Hibernian players playing
26/4/1941	Scottish Southern League	Hibernian Dumbarton	3 1	Easter Road	
28/4/1941	Scottish Southern League	Hearts Hibernian	3 5	Tynecastle	Match should have been played 1 Jan. Postponed pitch snowbound
31/5/1941	Rosebery Charity Cup Final	Hibernian Hearts	0 2	Easter Road	
7/6/1941	Summer Cup 1st Round 1st Leg	Celtic Hibernian	2 5	Parkhead	
14/6/1941	Summer Cup 1st Round 2nd Leg	Hibernian Celtic	0 1	Easter Road	
21/6/1941	Summer Cup 2nd Round 1st Leg	Hibernian Clyde	1 2	Easter Road	Originally this 1st leg was to be played at Shawfield but SFA reversed the decision
28/6/1941	Summer Cup 2nd Round 2nd Leg	Clyde Hibernian	3 4	Shawfield	

HIBERNIAN RESULTS 1914–1946

Date	Fixture	Teams and Score		Venue	Notes
2/7/1941	Summer Cup 2nd Round 2nd Leg Play-Off	Clyde Hibernian	3 4	Ibrox	Match played at neutral ground
5/7/1941	Summer Cup Semi Final	Dumbarton Hibernian	0 1	Tynecastle	Match played at neutral ground
12/7/1941	Summer Cup Final	Rangers Hibernian	2 3	Hampden	

Season 1941–42

Date	Fixture	Teams and Score		Venue
9/8/1941	Scottish Southern League	Morton Hibernian	2 1	Cappielow
13/8/1941	Wilson Cup Final	Hibernian Hearts	0 1	Easter Road
16/8/1941	Scottish Southern League	Hibernian Clyde	1 4	Easter Road
23/8/1941	Scottish Southern League	Albion Rovers Hibernian	3 8	Cliftonhill
30/8/1941	Scottish Southern League	Hibernian Hamilton Accies	4 0	Easter Road
6/9/1941	Scottish Southern League	Hearts Hibernian	2 4	Tynecastle
13/9/1941	Scottish Southern League	Hibernian Dumbarton	4 0	Easter Road
20/9/1941	Scottish Southern League	Queen's Park Hibernian	1 2	Hampden
27/9/1941	Scottish Southern League	Hibernian Rangers	8 1	Easter Road
4/10/1941	Scottish Southern League	Third Lanark Hibernian	4 2	Cathkin
11/10/1941	Scottish Southern League	Hibernian Celtic	1 3	Easter Road
18/10/1941	Scottish Southern League	Motherwell Hibernian	3 2	Fir Park
25/10/1941	Scottish Southern League	Falkirk Hibernian	1 2	Brockville
1/11/1941	Scottish Southern League	Hibernian Airdrie	4 1	Easter Road
8/11/1941	Scottish Southern League	Partick Thistle Hibernian	3 2	Firhill
15/11/1941	Scottish Southern League	Hibernian St Mirren	5 2	Easter Road
22/11/1941	Scottish Southern League	Hibernian Morton	1 0	Easter Road

Date	Fixture	Teams and Score		Venue	Notes
29/11/1941	Scottish Southern League	Clyde Hibernian	2 3	Shawfield	
6/12/1941	Scottish Southern League	Hibernian Albion Rovers	5 2	Easter Road	
13/12/1941	Scottish Southern League	Hamilton Accies Hibernian	2 2	Douglas Park	
20/12/1941	Scottish Southern League	Hibernian Queen's Park	1	Easter Road	
27/12/1941	Scottish Southern League	Rangers Hibernian	0 1	Ibrox	
1/1/1942	Scottish Southern League	Hibernian Hearts	2 2	Easter Road	
3/1/1942	Scottish Southern League	Dumbarton Hibernian	2 1	Boghead	
10/1/1942	Scottish Southern League	Hibernian Third Lanark	6 0	Easter Road	
17/1/1942	Scottish Southern League	Celtic Hibernian	2 1	Parkhead	
31/1/1942	Scottish Southern League	Hibernian Falkirk	2 0	Easter Road	
14/2/1942	Scottish Southern League	Hibernian Partick Thistle	4 0	Easter Road	
21/2/1942	Scottish Southern League	St Mirren Hibernian	1 1	Love Street	
28/2/1942	Scottish Southern League War Cup (Section 2) 1st Round 1st Leg	Hibernian Hamilton Accies	1 2	Easter Road	
7/3/1942	Scottish Southern League War Cup (Section 2) 1st Round 2nd Leg	Celtic Hibernian	4 2	Parkhead	
14/3/1942	Scottish Southern League War Cup (Section 2) 1st Round 3rd Leg	Hibernian Queen's Park	3 1	Easter Road	
21/3/1942	Scottish Southern League War Cup (Section 2) 1st Round 4th Leg	Hamilton Accies Hibernian	3 1	Douglas Park	
28/3/1942	Scottish Southern League War Cup (Section 2) 1st Round 5th Leg	Hibernian Celtic	1 0	Easter Road	

HIBERNIAN RESULTS 1914–1946

Date	Fixture	Teams and Score		Venue	Notes
4/4/1942	Scottish Southern League War Cup (Section 2) 1st Round 6th Leg	Queen's Park Hibernian	0 1	Hampden	
20/4/1942	East of Scotland Shield Semi Final	Hibernian St Bernard's	7 1	Easter Road	
2/5/1942	Scottish Southern League	Hibernian Motherwell	3 1	Easter Road	
9/5/1942	Scottish Southern League	Airdrie Hibernian	1 2	Broomfield	
16/5/1942	East of Scotland Shield Final	Hearts Hibernian	3 2	Tynecastle	
23/5/1942	Rosebery Charity Cup Final	Hearts Hibernian	1 1	Tynecastle	Hearts won on toss of a coin
30/5/1942	Summer Cup 1st Round 1st Leg	Hibernian Clyde	2 1	Easter Road	
6/5/1942	Summer Cup 1st Round 2nd Leg	Clyde Hibernian	0 2	Shawfield	
13/6/1942	Summer Cup 2nd Round 1st Leg	Hibernian Third Lanark	8 2	Easter Road	
20/6/1942	Summer Cup 2nd Round 2nd Leg	Third Lanark Hibernian	1 5	Cathkin	
27/6/1942	Summer Cup Semi Final	Motherwell Hibernian	1 3	Tynecastle	Match played at neutral ground
4/7/1942	Summer Cup Final	Rangers Hibernian	0 0	Hampden	Half-hour extra extra time played. Corners were to count in extra time and both teams got two. Game decided on toss of a coin, Rangers won.
18/7/1942	Benefit in aid of war charities	United Military Services All-Star XI Hibernian	3 2	Hampden	

Season 1942–43

Date	Fixture	Teams and Score		Venue	Notes
1/8/1942	Benefit in aid of RAF Benevolent Fund and Edinburgh war charities	Hibernian RAF All-International XI	1 3	Easter Road	
8/8/1942	Scottish Southern League	Hibernian Albion Rovers	3 1	Easter Road	

Date	Fixture	Teams and Score		Venue	Notes
15/8/1942	Scottish Southern League	Hamilton Accies Hibernian	1 3	Douglas Park	
22/8/1942	Scottish Southern League	Hibernian Queen's Park	4 0	Easter Road	
29/8/1942	Scottish Southern League	Dumbarton Hibernian	1 4	Boghead	
5/9/1942	Scottish Southern League	Hibernian Hearts	2 2	Easter Road	
12/9/1942	Scottish Southern League	Rangers Hibernian	1 	Ibrox	
19/9/1942	Scottish Southern League	Hibernian Third Lanark	5 1	Easter Road	
26/9/1942	Scottish Southern League	Celtic Hibernian	0 3	Parkhead	
3/10/1942	Scottish Southern League	Hibernian Motherwell	2 1	Easter Road	
10/10/1942	Scottish Southern League	Hibernian Falkirk	4 0	Easter Road	
17/101942	Scottish Southern League	Airdrie Hibernian	0 5	Broomfield	
24/10/1942	Scottish Southern League	Hibernian Partick Thistle	0 0	Easter Road	
31/10/1942	Scottish Southern League	St Mirren Hibernian	1 2	Love Street	
7/11/1942	Scottish Southern League	Hibernian Morton	2 2	Easter Road	
14/11/1942	Scottish Southern League	Clyde Hibernian	7 2	Shawfield	
21/11/1942	Scottish Southern League	Albion Rovers Hibernian	1 4	Cliftonhill	
28/11/1942	Scottish Southern League	Hibernian Hamilton Accies	3 1	Easter Road	
5/12/1942	Scottish Southern League	Queen's Park Hibernian	2 3	Hampden	
12/12/1942	Scottish Southern League	Hibernian Dumbarton	4 1	Easter Road	
19/12/1942	Scottish Southern League	Third Lanark Hibernian	3 2	Cathkin	
26/12/1942	Scottish Southern League	Hibernian Rangers	1 1	Easter Road	
1/1/1943	Scottish Southern League	Hearts Hibernian	1 4	Tynecastle	
2/1/1943	Scottish Southern League	Motherwell Hibernian	2 1	Fir Park	

HIBERNIAN RESULTS 1914–1946

Date	Fixture	Teams and Score		Venue	Notes
9/1/1943	Scottish Southern League	Hibernian Celtic	4 0	Easter Road	
16/1/1943	Scottish Southern League	Falkirk Hibernian	3 1	Brockville	
23/1/1943	Scottish Southern League	Hibernian Airdrie	7 1	Easter Road	
30/1/1943	Scottish Southern League	Partick Thistle Hibernian	1 5	Firhill	
6/2/1943	Scottish Southern League	Hibernian St Mirren	3 1	Easter Road	
13/2/1943	Scottish Southern League	Morton Hibernian	1 0	Cappielow	
20/2/1943	Scottish Southern League	Hibernian Clyde	2 2	Easter Road	
27/2/1943	Scottish Southern League Cup (Section D) 1st Round 1st Leg	Celtic Hibernian	2 1	Parkhead	
6/3/1943	Scottish Southern League Cup (Section D) 1st Round 2nd Leg	Hibernian St Mirren	2 1	Easter Road	
13/3/1943	Scottish Southern League Cup (Section D) 1st Round 3rd Leg	Hibernian Rangers	0 2	Easter Road	
20/3/1943	Scottish Southern League Cup (Section D) 1st Round 4th Leg	Hibernian Celtic	2 1	Easter Road	
27/3/1943	Scottish Southern League Cup (Section D) 1st Round 5th Leg	St Mirren Hibernian	1 3	Love Street	
3/4/1943	Scottish Southern League Cup (Section D) 1st Round 6th Leg	Rangers Hibernian	1 0	Ibrox	Hibernian had to spread their playing resources over these two matches had to
3/4/1943	Mitchel Cup 1st Round 1st Leg	Hibernian Hearts	3 1	Easter Road	be played on the same day
19/3/1943	Mitchel Cup 1st Round 2nd Leg	Hearts Hibernian	1 0	Tynecastle	
24/3/1943	Mitchel Cup Semi Final 1st Leg	Hibernian Aberdeen	1 1	Easter Road	

Date	Fixture	Teams and Score		Venue	Notes
1/5/1943	Mitchel Cup Semi Final 2nd Leg	Aberdeen Hibernian	2 1	Pittodrie	
8/5/1943	East of Scotland Shield Final	Hibernian Hearts	1 1	Easter Road	Match abandoned after 30 minutes as there were only 300 spectators in the ground
15/5/1943	East of Scotland Shield Final Replay	Hibernian Hearts	3 2	Easter Road	Half-hour extra time played
22/5/1943	Rosebery Charity Cup Final	Hibernian Hearts	1 1	Easter Road	Hearts won on the toss of a coin
29/5/1943	Summer Cup 1st Round 1st Leg	Hibernian Partick Thistle	7 0	Easter Road	
5/6/1943	Summer Cup 1st Round 2nd Leg	Partick Thistle Hibernian	2 5	Firhill	
12/6/1943	Summer Cup 2nd Round 1st Leg	Queen's Park Hibernian	1 2	Hampden	
19/6/1943	Summer Cup 2nd Round 2nd Leg	Hibernian Queen's Park	4 0	Easter Road	
26/6/1943	Summer Cup Semi Final	Rangers Hibernian	3 1	Hampden	Match played at neutral ground

Season 1943–44

Date	Fixture	Teams and Score		Venue	Notes
9/8/1943	Public Practice Match	Hibernian (Greens) Hibernian (Whites)	3 0	Easter Road	
14/8/1943	Scottish Southern League	Rangers Hibernian	4 0	Ibrox	
21/8/1943	Scottish Southern League	Hibernian Albion Rovers	3 0	Easter Road	
28/8/1943	Scottish Southern League	Hamilton Accies Hibernian	1 2	Douglas Park	
4/9/1943	Scottish Southern League	Hibernian Queen's Park	2	Easter Road	
11/9/1943	Scottish Southern League	Hearts Hibernian	0 1	Tynecastle	
18/9/1943	Scottish Southern League	Hibernian Dumbarton	4 3	Easter Road	
20/9/1943	Wilson Cup Final	Hearts Hibernian	2 1	Tynecastle	
25/9/1943	Scottish Southern League	Clyde Hibernian	2 1	Shawfield	

HIBERNIAN RESULTS 1914–1946

Date	Fixture	Teams and Score		Venue	Notes
2/10/1943	Scottish Southern League	Hibernian Morton	2 0	Easter Road	
9/10/1943	Scottish Southern League	Falkirk Hibernian	3 5	Brockville	
16/10/1943	Scottish Southern League	Hibernian St Mirren	4 1	Easter Road	
23/10/1943	Scottish Southern League	Third Lanark Hibernian	0 2	Cathkin	
30/10/1943	Scottish Southern League	Hibernian Celtic	2 2	Easter Road	
6/11/1943	Scottish Southern League	Partick Thistle Hibernian	3 1	Firhill	
13/11/1943	Scottish Southern League	Hibernian Motherwell	3 3	Easter Road	
20/11/1943	Scottish Southern League	Airdrie Hibernian	2 5	Broomfield	
27/11/1943	Scottish Southern League	Hibernian Rangers	3 4	Easter Road	
4/12/1943	Scottish Southern League	Albion Rovers Hibernian	2 4	Cliftonhill	
11/12/1943	Scottish Southern League	Hibernian Hamilton Accies	3 5	Easter Road	
18/12/1943	Scottish Southern League	Queen's Park Hibernian	4 2	Hampden	
25/12/1943	Scottish Southern League	Dumbarton Hibernian	1 1	Boghead	
1/1/1944	Scottish Southern League	Hibernian Hearts	0 1	Easter Road	
3/1/1944	Scottish Southern League	Hibernian Airdrie	1 2	Easter Road	
8/1/1944	Scottish Southern League	Hibernian Clyde	3 1	Easter Road	
15/1/1944	Scottish Southern League	Morton Hibernian	3 1	Cappielow	
22/1/1944	Scottish Southern League	Hibernian Falkirk	4 3	Easter Road	
29/1/1944	Scottish Southern League	St Mirren Hibernian	1 2	Love Street	
5/2/1944	Scottish Southern League	Hibernian Third Lanark	6 0	Easter Road	
12/2/1944	Scottish Southern League	Celtic Hibernian	2 2	Parkhead	

Date	Fixture	Teams and Score		Venue	Notes
19/2/1944	Scottish Southern League	Hibernian Partick Thistle	2	Easter Road	
4/3/1944	Scottish Southern League Cup (Section C) 1st Round 1st Leg	Third Lanark Hibernian	0 4	Cathkin	
11/3/1944	Scottish Southern League Cup (Section C) 1st Round 2nd Leg	Hibernian Albion Rovers	2 1	Easter Road	
18/3/1944	Scottish Southern League Cup (Section C) 1st Round 3rd Leg	Morton Hibernian	2 2	Cappielow	
25/3/1944	Scottish Southern League Cup (Section C) 1st Round 4th Leg	Hibernian Third Lanark	4 0	Easter Road	
1/4/1944	Scottish Southern League Cup (Section C) 1st Round 5th Leg	Albion Rovers Hibernian	0 2	Cliftonhill	
8/4/1944	Scottish Southern League Cup (Section C) 1st Round 6th Leg	Hibernian Morton	6 3	Easter Road	
15/4/1944	Scottish Southern League	Motherwell Hibernian	0 1	Fir Park	
29/4/1944	East of Scotland Shield Semi Final	Hibernian Edinburgh City	6 1	Easter Road	
6/5/1944	Scottish Southern League Cup Semi Final	Clyde Hibernian	2 5	Hampden	Match played at neutral ground
13/5/1944	East of Scotland Shield Final	Hearts Hibernian	2 1	Tynecastle	
20/5/1944	Scottish Southern League Cup Final	Rangers Hibernian	0 0	Hampden	Hibernian won by 5 corners to 6 Match played at neutral ground
27/5/1944	Rosebery Charity Cup Final	Hearts Hibernian	1 4	Tynecastle	
3/6/1944	Summer Cup 1st Round 1st Leg	Airdrie Hibernian	2 4	Broomfield	
10/6/1944	Summer Cup 1st Round 2nd Leg	Hibernian Airdrie	3 0	Easter Road	

Date	Fixture	Teams and Score		Venue	Notes
17/6/1944	Summer Cup 2nd Round 1st Leg	Morton Hibernian	1 1	Cappielow	
24/6/1944	Summer Cup 2nd Round 2nd Leg	Hibernian Morton	0 2	Easter Road	

Season 1944–45

Date	Fixture	Teams and Score		Venue	Notes
5/8/1944	War Charities Benefit Match	Hearts/Hibernian Select Aston Villa	3 4	Tynecastle	
7/8/1944	Public Practice Match	Hibernian (Greens) Hibernian (Whites	2 2	Easter Road	
12/8/1944	Scottish Southern League	Hibernian Clyde	0 4	Easter Road	
19/8/1944	Scottish Southern League	Morton Hibernian	3 2	Cappielow	
26/8/1944	Scottish Southern League	Hibernian Hamilton Accies	3 1	Easter Road	
2/9/1944	Scottish Southern League	Dumbarton Hibernian	0 3	Boghead	
9/9/1944	Scottish Southern League	Hibernian Hearts	3 1	Easter Road	
16/9/1944	Scottish Southern League	Queen's Park Hibernian	0 2	Hampden	
18/9/1944	Wilson Cup Final	Hearts Hibernian	2 6	Tynecastle	
23/9/1944	Scottish Southern League	Hibernian Rangers	4 1	Easter Road	
30/9/1944	Scottish Southern League	Albion Rovers Hibernian	0 5	Cliftonhill	
7/10/1944	Scottish Southern League	Falkirk Hibernian	1 3	Brockville	
14/10/1944	Scottish Southern League	Celtic Hibernian	1 1	Parkhead	
21/10/1944	Scottish Southern League	Hibernian Partick Thistle	8 0	Easter Road	
28/10/1944	Scottish Southern League	Third Lanark Hibernian	3 6	Cathkin	
4/11/1944	Scottish Southern League	Hibernian St Mirren	6 2	Easter Road	
11/11/1944	Scottish Southern League	Hibernian Airdrie	3 2	Easter Road	

Date	Fixture	Teams and Score		Venue	Notes
18/11/1944	Scottish Southern League	Hibernian Motherwell	0 1	Easter Road	
25/11/1944	Scottish Southern League	Clyde Hibernian	2 3	Shawfield	
2/12/1944	Scottish Southern League	Hibernian Morton	0 1	Easter Road	
9/12/1944	Scottish Southern League	Hamilton Accies Hibernian	1 1	Douglas Park	
16/12/1944	Scottish Southern League	Hibernian Dumbarton	0 0	Easter Road	
23/12/1944	Scottish Southern League	Rangers Hibernian	5 0	Ibrox	
30/12/1944	Scottish Southern League	Hibernian Queen's Park	2 0	Easter Road	
1/1/1945	Scottish Southern League	Hearts Hibernian	3 0	Tynecastle	
2/1/1945	Scottish Southern League	Motherwell Hibernian	3 0	Fir Park	Match brought forward from 24 Feb
6/1/1945	Scottish Southern League	Hibernian Albion Rovers	4 1	Easter Road	
13/1/1945	Scottish Southern League	Hibernian Falkirk	3 0	Easter Road	
20/1/1945	Scottish Southern League	Hibernian Celtic	2 4	Easter Road	
3/2/1945	Scottish Southern League	Hibernian Third Lanark	2 4	Easter Road	
10/2/1945	Scottish Southern League	St Mirren Hibernian	1 1	Love Street	Hibernian had to split their playing resources
10/2/1945	East of Scotland Shield Semi Final	Hibernian Edinburgh City	5 3	Easter Road	over these two matches
17/2/1945	Scottish Southern League	Airdrie Hibernian	1 1	Broomfield	
24/2/1945	Scottish Southern League Cup (Section A) 1st Round 1st Leg	Third Lanark Hibernian	2 1	Cathkin	
3/3/1945	Scottish Southern League Cup (Section A) 1st Round 2nd Leg	Hibernian Rangers	1 1	Easter Road	

HIBERNIAN RESULTS 1914–1946

Date	Fixture	Teams and Score		Venue	Notes
10/3/1945	Scottish Southern League Cup (Section A) 1st Round 3rd Leg	Hibernian Albion Rovers	1 1	Easter Road	
17/3/1945	Scottish Southern League Cup (Section A) 1st Round 4th Leg	Hibernian Third Lanark	3 1	Easter Road	
24/3/1945	Scottish Southern League Cup (Section A) 1st Round 5th Leg	Rangers Hibernian	2 0	Ibrox	
31/3/1945	Scottish Southern League Cup (Section A) 1st Round 6th Leg	Albion Rovers Hibernian	1 8	Cliftonhill	
16/4/1945	East of Scotland Shield Final	Hibernian Hearts	3 1	Easter Road	
28/4/1945	Scottish Southern League	Partick Thistle Hibernian	5 1	Firhill	
5/5/1945	Charity match in aid of Servicemen's Families Association	Hibernian Scottish Services Select	2 2	Easter Road	
9/5/1945	Rosebery Charity Cup Final	Hibernian Hearts	2 2	Easter Road	Hibernian won by 7 corners to 6
26/5/1945	Summer Cup 1st Round 1st Leg	St Mirren Hibernian	4 2	Love Street	
2/6/1945	Summer Cup 1st Round 2nd Leg	Hibernian St Mirren	7 0	Easter Road	
9/2/1945	Summer Cup 2nd Round 1st Leg	Hibernian Falkirk	3 1	Easter Road	
16/6/1945	Summer Cup 2nd Round 2nd Leg	Falkirk Hibernian	1 0	Brockville	
23/6/1945	Summer Cup Semi Final	Celtic Hibernian	0 2	Tynecastle	Match played at neutral ground
30/6/1945	Summer Cup Final	Partick Thistle Hibernian	2 0	Hampden	Match played at neutral ground